The Jewish Traveler

The Jewish Traveler

Hadassah Magazine's Guide to the
World's Jewish Communities and Sights

Edited by ALAN M. TIGAY

Doubleday

NEW YORK LONDON TORONTO SYDNEY AUCKLAND

Published by Doubleday, a division of
Bantam Doubleday Dell Publishing Group, Inc.,
666 Fifth Avenue, New York, New York 10103

Doubleday and the portrayal of an anchor with a dolphin
are trademarks of Doubleday, a division of
Bantam Doubleday Dell Publishing Group, Inc.

Library of Congress Cataloging-in-Publication Data

The Jewish traveler.

    1. Jews—Social life and customs.   2. Voyages and travels—1951–
—Guide-books. I. Tigay, Alan M. II. Hadassah magazine.
DS143.J46 1987   910'.89924   86–8917
ISBN 0-385-24198-4

For my father,
who gave me his sense of direction

Acknowledgments

I used to read book acknowledgments with disbelief. While every author and editor has help, I thought, surely the litanies of names "without whom this book would not have been written" rivaled Academy Award acceptance speeches for overstatement. I now know better.

Among the many people who were indispensable in the production of *The Jewish Traveler,* preeminence goes to Nancy Kroll Margolis, *Hadassah Magazine*'s former director of advertising. From the beginning she has treated the project as her own. She has been a dedicated partner in putting the magazine's travel columns into book form and the *sine qua non* in persuading Doubleday that the book project was worthwhile. Her efforts are symbolic of a creative and cooperative relationship that is rare in the annals of editorial-advertising rivalry.

My special thanks go also to Rose Goldman, chairman of *Hadassah Magazine,* who believed in the project from the beginning and supported it at every step. Though this is but one of many projects that I have shared with her, it is the one that provides me with the opportunity to say how much of a privilege it is to work with her.

The Jewish Traveler was kept in the air, figuratively and sometimes literally, by Pan American World Airways. With the inauguration of scheduled Pan Am service to Israel in 1985, the airline serves more cities covered in this book than any other. While many at Pan Am have been helpful, I would particularly like to thank Jeffrey Kriendler, Robert A. Drumm, and John Krimsky, Jr.

The list of people who made valuable contributions to this book is as international as the book's contents. Help has come from every city covered, but I'd particularly like to thank Edward Van Vollen in Amsterdam, Daniel Dratwa in Brussels, David Gerschwald in Copenhagen, David P. Bell in Houston, Mark Ejlenberg in Hong Kong, Mario Nudelstejer in Mexico City, Joe King in Montreal, Nancy Crystal in Toronto, and Willy Guggenheim in Zurich. I have also had help from people in New York who are expert in various cities covered in the book; my thanks in this regard go especially to Jonathan Beard and Ethel Blitz. There have been numerous helpful people from the national tourist and information offices represented in New York; two in particular whose assistance cannot go unmentioned are Inge Godenschweger of the German Information Center and Erika Faisst of the Swiss National Tourist Office. I'd also like to express my gratitude to Les Pockell and Karen Johnston of Doubleday, to David Koch of the Joseph Jacobs Organization, and to Mimi Baer of Hilton International.

Throughout the production of *The Jewish Traveler,* in magazine and book form, I have been supported by the best staff an editor could ask for. Roselyn Bell, senior editor of *Hadassah Magazine,* and Zelda Shluker, associate editor, have made indispensable contributions at every level of the project. Each has done some of the more glamorous writing and editing as well as the more mundane reading of galleys, sometimes until bleary-eyed. My two extra right hands throughout the project, particularly in updating and photo editing, have been Pearl Weisinger and Dorothy Silfen. I also had valuable assistance from Batya Spirn and Denise Blanshay.

Finally, I'd like to thank the contributors who covered the world for this book. I would have preferred to write every chapter myself. That other writers made the trips I dreamed of, or dreamed up, is a source of envy. That each one of them did such a good job of turning my dream into his or her own is a source of great respect.

Now that I have made my list of people to thank, I won't be incredulous when reading the acknowledgments in other books. I'll even pay attention to the Academy Award acceptance speeches.

—A.M.T.

Contents

Introduction

Jews have always traveled, not only to escape persecution but also to trade, or simply to see. From the intercontinental travels of Benjamin of Tudela, a century before Marco Polo, to the expression "wandering Jew," the Jewish penchant for movement is enshrined in literature and language. "Our people wandered before they were driven," said Joseph Kalonymos, a character in George Eliot's proto-Zionist novel *Daniel Deronda*. Now that the Jewish homeland has welcomed the driven among us, Jews are wandering still.

And Jews are traveling more Jewishly than ever before, looking for Jewish sights, or Jewish connections to the general sights they see when they travel. It was to meet this growing interest in Jewish travel that *Hadassah Magazine* initiated, in 1983, a monthly column called "The Jewish Traveler." It is the first forty-eight such columns that form this book.

While there are other Jewish guidebooks, this one has some unique features. In some ways, to call *The Jewish Traveler* a travel book at all is an oversimplification. The goal from the beginning has been to present a profile of a city's Jewish community, combined with a description of Jewish sights. In selecting cities to profile, preference has always been given to those places that have a flourishing community today as well as history and sights; this explains the omission of cities in Eastern Europe, for example, that have a lot of history and virtually no Jews.

The most obvious difference between this and other Jewish travel guides is in organization. While others are arranged by country, this book is arranged by city. Of all the world's peoples, Jews have been city dwellers the longest; the city is part of the Jewish identity. Each city has its own ethos, and in each city Jews are affected by, and have an impact on, the surrounding community. One of the most intriguing lessons to be learned in the chapters that follow is the difference between Jewish communities of nearly equal size in the same country —differences that usually parallel the contrasts between the cities themselves. The Jews of Rio de Janeiro, according to a stereotype rooted partly in reality, are secular and recreation-oriented while their fellows in São Paulo are regarded as more hardworking and religious. The community in Antwerp is insular and Orthodox, while that in Brussels is acculturated. Melbourne has a largely East European Jewish community in which Orthodoxy is strong; Sydney is predominantly German and Hungarian with a strong tradition of Liberal Judaism. Montreal Jews have to worry about their political climate, while Toronto Jews do not.

The city arrangement is also prompted by Jewish history itself. Since Jews have lived in cities, most of the sights connected with their story are urban sights. Indeed, with few exceptions, those Jewish sights not located in major cities are within easy traveling distance of a large urban center. Many of the articles in this book include recommended day trips to Jewish sights in the area.

Reading these chapters together can provide unexpected insights into Jewish life and history. One conviction held widely by Jews is that their synagogue architecture suffers badly in comparison to Christian style. The plethora of synagogues worthy of sightseers—from Temple Emanu-El in San Francisco to the Great Synagogue in Copenhagen to Ohel Leah in Hong Kong—should dispel that myth. The world, in fact, is filled with drab, utilitarian synagogues *and* churches. While most American Jews are familiar with their own unprepossessing suburban shuls, the churches with which they are familiar are not the ones around the corner from their synagogue but those that are rightly designated as landmarks or appear on tourist itineraries; hence the misconception.

In addition to information on communities and sights, *The Jewish Traveler* includes added features to make traveling easier and more enjoyable. Listed in every chapter are books that bring the Jewish community to life. Since fiction often illustrates more effectively than fact, there has been an attempt to find at least one novel set in each Jewish community. Where fiction is not available, and often even where it is, memoirs, histories, and sociological studies have been noted. Incidentally, in addition to the books noted with each chapter, there are two sources that were consulted in the preparation of virtually every chapter. The Encyclopaedia Judaica is a particularly rich source of historical information on every Jewish community in the world. The strength of the annual *Jewish Travel Guide* published by London's *Jewish Chronicle* is its comprehensive, worldwide listing of synagogues and Jewish organizations.

Also included in each article is a list of Jewish personalities associated with the place. Since any community is as well known by its human products as by, say, its architecture, this nod to the style of *People* magazine seems entirely appropriate.

A few words of caution are in order for using this book. While synagogues in the United States are quite accessible, security at European synagogues is generally strict. When in Europe, it's best to call a synagogue before visiting. Restaurants come and go with regularity, and kosher restaurants are no exception. While every attempt has been made to be as up to date as possible concerning restaurants listed, it is always best to check ahead. We have tried, wherever possible, to indicate whether restaurants are kosher or mentioned for other reasons but, again, it is always best to check.

One would think that museums are more stable institutions than restaurants, and they are. But one of the things that emerges from these pages is the explosion of Jewish cultural awareness around the world in the form of new Jewish museums. No fewer than six of the forty-eight cities profiled have Jewish museums that were scheduled either to open or to move to larger quarters between 1985 and 1987. Most of the locations and openings were confirmed prior to publication. Otherwise, the information provided is as up to date as possible, from scheduled moving dates (Amsterdam) to addresses of buildings not yet open (Frankfurt). Bear in mind, however, that building and moving schedules are subject to change. A final caveat is in order with regard to telephone numbers.

Some readers may miss cities not included in the book. Since "The Jewish Traveler" is an ongoing column in *Hadassah Magazine,* we will ultimately get to all the important locales, but only in time. One of the advantages of reprinting articles that have appeared in *Hadassah Magazine* has been the ability to restore useful material that had to be cut from the original articles because of lack of space. Another has been the ability to include additions, recommendations, and corrections sent in by readers. Readers of the book, no less than the magazine, are encouraged to send their recommendations for future editions to the magazine's editorial office at 50 West Fifty-eighth Street, New York, New York 10019.

Relieved of the need to wander in search of a homeland, Jews now wander for business, pleasure, and education. The process began when Abraham went forth from Ur. It continues, as does everything else in Jewish tradition, with you. *N'siya tova.*

—ALAN M. TIGAY
New York, August 1986

Amsterdam

Rembrandt House (*Leni Sonnenfeld*)

Talk to Jews in almost any West European community and they'll tell you the same irony of their contemporary existence—they live in an atmosphere of great tolerance but, because of economic or political pressures, their governments are often critical of Israel. The one place where you won't hear this story is Amsterdam, where the government has always held its Jews in esteem and where the esteem extends to the Jewish state, regardless of pressures.

HISTORY: Amsterdam was *makom alef*—the number one place—for the Spanish and Portuguese Marranos who first settled there at the end of the sixteenth century, grateful to have found sanctuary from the horrors of the Inquisition, and delighted that they could once more express themselves in the Hebrew that had been forbidden them. At the time of their arrival, humanist scholars of the new Dutch republic were intent on reviving the classical languages, including Hebrew. And while Dutch is the country's official language, the first Sefardic immigrants left their mark on the local language, with words like *de massel,* Dutch for "good-bye and good luck," (from the Hebrew *mazal),* and *meshoche,* or "crazy" (from the Hebrew *meshuga).*

The Sefardim, delivered from the same Spanish tyranny as the Dutch themselves, were made welcome. As merchants they had the experience, the knowledge of overseas trade routes, and the commercial contacts (with fellow Sefardim all along the Mediterranean from Tunisia to Turkey) that would be such assets to the expanding mercantile economy of the Netherlands and, particularly, of Amsterdam —then, as now, the principal city.

It was not long before Ashkenazim, similarly fleeing oppression, followed the Sefardim—German Jews running from the looting of the Frankfurt ghetto in 1614; Polish Jews escaping from the Bogdan Khmelnitski massacres of 1648; and, much later, German Jews (like the family of Anne Frank) forced to emigrate by the rise of Hitlerism in the 1930s.

Even with the influx of Ashkenazim, Amsterdam remained the intellectual center for Sefardic Jewry throughout the seventeenth century and was nicknamed by them "Dutch Jerusalem." The community produced both scholars and freethinkers, including iconoclast philosophers Uriel Da Costa and Baruch Spinoza, both of whom were excommunicated by the Amsterdam rabbinate. During the excitement aroused by the messianic proclamations of Shabbetai Zevi, a majority of Amsterdam's Jews became followers of the false messiah, and even after his demise, many remained somewhat inclined to Sabbateanism.

Fully accepted into Dutch life, enjoying complete economic and political freedom, Jews could feel comfortable, at last, in a Christian world. As one historian has noted, theirs was a benign situation, "rare in Christian societies," where Jews had "the ability to affect their collective fortunes by their own actions."

The ability was lost—immediately and traumatically—when the Nazis conquered the Netherlands. In 1940 there were 150,000 Jews in the country, about 60 percent of them in Amsterdam. By the end of the war all but thirty thousand had been slaughtered. An organized Jewish community no longer existed.

COMMUNITY: Over the past four decades, another Jewish infrastructure has been laboriously re-created. Amsterdam's fifteen thousand Jews—still a little more than half of the country's Jewish population—now support a variety of institutions whose number and quality would be a credit to a community of far greater size.

Jewish Amsterdam, like Caesar's Gaul, is divided into three parts: the Ashkenazi Orthodox establishment, with nine thousand registered members; the Liberal (Reform) Jews, with two thousand adherents; and the Portuguese Synagogue, whose one thousand congregants cherish the Sefardic ritual of the first Jewish settlers in the city. The remainder of Amsterdam's Jews are not registered with the main congregations.

In addition to common interests, the segments of Amsterdam Jewry —and indeed all the Jews of the Netherlands—are unified by the weekly newspaper *Nieuw Israelietisch Weekblad* (founded in 1875), after London's *Jewish Chronicle* the oldest Jewish publication in the world. Unlike many American Jewish weeklies, which cater to their readers with extensive coverage of weddings and fund-raising dinners, the *Weekblad* uncompromisingly devotes itself to lively and literate reportage of politics and culture, in the best tradition of European journalism.

Book publishing had been a special Dutch Jewish enterprise since the early seventeenth century, when Menasseh ben Israel, a friend of Rembrandt, founded the first Hebrew printing press in Amsterdam.

World War II and the Final Solution destroyed Jewish eminence in publishing, as well as in textile and diamond production; and the first generation that grew to maturity after World War II was geared to "making it" in law or business or medicine, rather than in more intellectual or artistic pursuits.

The recently established Amphora Press, a small firm devoted to the publication of works by Dutch Jews and Israelis, marks the return of the second postwar generation to the intellectual values of the grandparents. Young historians like Joel Cahen, playwrights like Judith Herzberg, and novelists like Minnie Mock are thinking and writing about the Holocaust and its effect on Dutch Jews today.

Anti-Semitism is hardly a problem. The mayor, or *burgemeester*, of Amsterdam, Ed Van Thijn, is a Jew, as were his two immediate predecessors, Wim Polak (the only member of his family to survive the death camps) and Ivo Samkalden.

SIGHTS: As the heart of a vital community, one of the glories of the diaspora for 350 years, the Jewish Quarter no longer exists. Even before World War II, affluent Jews had fled its crowded streets, open-air markets, and neighborhood shuls and yeshivas for the greener lawns of Amsterdam South and the suburbs of Amstelveen and Buitenveldert, which remain the main areas of Jewish settlement. The quarter had been the domain of the Jewish working class, engaged principally in the diamond industry and organized into a powerful trade union by Henri Polak, an uncle of the recent mayor and, for many years, a Socialist member of the Dutch Parliament. That working class was nearly wiped out by the Nazis.

It is not only the people of the quarter who are gone. The very houses in which they lived have also disappeared. A few landmarks remain, but the blocks and blocks of wooden buildings (the city's equivalent of the Lower East Side's Old Law tenements) have all been torn down. The flimsy frame structures were dismantled, plank by plank, during the famine-and-freeze winter of 1944 and used by the desperate people of Amsterdam for firewood; the few remaining were bulldozed after the war to make way for the freeway that runs through the quarter and for the new metro that runs under it.

You should begin your walking tour of Jewish Amsterdam at the Nieuwmarkt metro station. Huge photomurals of the Jewish Quarter at its heyday line the walls. Above, and at the opposite side of a broad cobblestoned plaza, is the Jewish Historical Museum, a starting point for sightseeing. The museum occupies De Waag, or weighhouse, a shabby, multipinnacled, faded brick fifteenth-century building half obscured, and surrounded, by a circle of open-air stalls loaded with fresh loaves of bread, hills of Edam and Gouda cheeses, and arrays of *broodje haring met rauwe uitjes*, the raw-herring-and-onion sandwiches that are the staple street food of the Netherlands.

The museum itself has a permanent display of the artifacts of 350 years of Dutch-Jewish history, as well as special exhibits, such as a recent one on the position of women in Judaism, which ran through 1986.

Across Nieuwmarkt Square is the house, now a museum, which Rembrandt's beloved Saskia bought for the artist. Here, at the head of Jodenbreestraat (Jews' Street), he spent his most productive years. The Jews of the quarter were his neighbors and friends, and he used them as models for his biblical works and for individual portraits which have been preserved in the collection of 250 etchings on display. Notes Simon M. Schama, an art historian at Harvard: "Michelangelo's Moses has horns; Rembrandt's does not. Freed from the demonology of Christ-murderers, well poisoners and child slayers, Jews confront the spectator in Rembrandt's paintings and etchings much as one supposes they wished to be represented: as rabbis, scholars and physicians."

At the end of the short street is the great Portuguese Synagogue, the most important relic of the quarter and one of the city's architectural gems. It was built in 1675 at the then astronomical cost of 186,000 guilders, because the Sefardim who worshipped there wanted it to be the finest in the world—a magnificent sanctuary in which they could pray openly after two centuries as Marranos, forced to practice Judaism in secret. In addition to its splendor, the Portuguese congregation also achieved a place in Jewish history when it excommunicated the Dutch-Jewish philosopher Baruch Spinoza in 1656.

The synagogue has changed little in three hundred years. The municipal authorities saved it from Nazi destruction by declaring it a national monument. Intact are the ark and bimah of carved Brazilian rosewood, the twelve stone columns (representing the tribes of Israel) that support the women's gallery, the sand-covered floors (a reminder of Marrano worship in Spain, to muffle the footsteps of the congregants), the vast sanctuary with room for two thousand, and the brass candelabra that are still used to illuminate the enormous enclosure (there is no electricity) with 613 candles.

Behind the synagogue stands the monumental Dockworker's

Statue, at which the Jews of Amsterdam gather every February 25 to pay tribute to the stevedores of the city. On that day in 1941, the dockworkers staged a general strike to protest the first roundup of 425 young Jewish men for shipment to the concentration camps. Jacob Presser, the Dutch historian of the Holocaust, writes: "The February strike was for many Jews the greatest experience of the whole war. Behind them there now stood openly . . . their fellow citizens, men with whom they had lived at peace for centuries . . . ready to sacrifice life and property for them."

Across the street from the statue is the complex of four Ashkenazic shuls, built earlier than the Portuguese synagogue. Three of the four —the Great Synagogue, the Neie Shul, and the Obbene Shul—were gutted by the Nazis but are now being restored with national and municipal funds. The fourth and smallest of the group, the Dritte (Third) Shul, was until recently used by a small group, barely a minyan, of pious Dutch Jews who had revived the ritual of their remote Polish and Russian forebears. All four—located at Jonas Daniël Meijerplein—are scheduled to become the new home of the Jewish Historical Museum in May 1987.

Around the corner from the synagogue complex is the Hollandse Schouwburg (Dutch Playhouse) at 24 Plantage Middenlaan. Here Jewish actors performed for largely Jewish audiences, until the Germans closed the theater down and used it as the staging area for the people of the quarter, who assembled there only to be marched off to the freight cars to Auschwitz. Today only the façade and side walls of the Schouwburg remain; the interior is now a quiet garden and memorial.

Another place of remembrance, and the ultimate destination of the tour, is the justly famous Anne Frank House, at 263 Prinsengracht. The modest three-story building was office and warehouse for Otto Frank's spice-importing firm. On the top floors of a second building, directly behind, the eight protagonists of Anne's *Diary* lived for the two difficult years before they were discovered and deported. Now a museum, the Anne Frank House is the second most frequented tourist site in Amsterdam, after the Rijksmuseum. Each year more than four hundred thousand visitors squeeze through the tiny rooms, climb the narrow ladderlike stairs, examine the pencil marks on the walls by which the Franks and the van Daans marked the growth of their teenage children, and look tearfully at the magazine cutouts Anne pasted up (a picture of Rudy Vallee was a favorite).

The Anne Frank House is more than a poignant remembrance of

the past. The Jews of Amsterdam, who have contributed so substantially to its support, utilize it for a series of changing exhibits relating to Anne's struggle for a better world. Exhibit themes go beyond Hitlerism to current manifestations of anti-Semitism, to examples of racism in South Africa, of human rights violations around the world, and even of the intolerance directed against Amsterdam's "guest workers" from Turkey, Suriname, and Indonesia.

READING: In addition to *The Diary of Anne Frank,* there is *Memorbook: History of Dutch Jewry from the Renaissance to the Present* by Mozes H. Gans, an encyclopedic storehouse of reminiscences, photographs, and drawings testifying to the richness of Dutch-Jewish life before Hitler. Jacob Presser's *The Destruction of the Dutch Jews* is a definitive, scholarly, and passionate account of the Holocaust in the Netherlands. *A Guide to Jewish Amsterdam,* published by the Jewish Historical Museum, includes both history and walking tours. Judith Belinfante, the museum's director, has also produced an illustrated catalog of the museum collection, rich in comments on the social and economic background from which the silver ornaments, manuscripts, and paintings evolved.

RECOMMENDATIONS: To give yourself an idea of the essential character of the city, you should take at least one boat ride through the network of canals lined with seventeenth-century town houses overlooking something like a thousand bridges and six thousand historical monuments. You can rent a bicycle (there are 550,000 in the city), or you can walk, covering the Jewish Quarter quite easily in two or three hours, as well as the city's center (in which the quarter is located). Everything is pretty much concentrated in this area of winding streets and canals radiating outward from the Centraal Station. From the station, armed with an all-day unlimited ticket (which costs about $2), you can ride everywhere by bus or trolley or the marvelous new metro (clean, quiet, uncrowded, and graffiti-free).

In this age of look-alike international hotels, the Amstel has the charisma and elegance of the mid-Victorian era, when it was established. This grand hotel on the banks of the Amstel River, just off Sarphatistraat (named after a nineteenth-century Jewish social reformer), is a five-minute walk from the heart of the Jewish Quarter.

EATING: Street eating is good in Amsterdam. Even better is a sit-down meal at one of the city's several Jewish restaurants. The only strictly kosher place is Sal Meyer's Sandwichshop, at Scheldestraat 45 in South Amsterdam, where most of the city's Jews now live. It's a friendly and informal delicatessen where everyone knows everyone else, and where the *broodjes* (rolls) are piled high with *pekelvlees* (corned beef). Nearby, at Rijnstraat 75, is Betty's Coffeeshop, a favorite of the young Jews of the neighborhood. Betty herself is up front greeting patrons by their first names. Near the Concertgebouw and the Rijksmuseum, at Willemsparkweg 87, is Restaurant Swart, where traditional Jewish dishes are served with rather more formality.

SHOPPING: Just down the street from Meyer's, at the corner of Scheldestraat and Europaplein, is Joachimsthal's Boekhandel, with certainly one of the most comprehensive selections of books of Jewish interest, in all languages, anywhere in the world. For antiquarians and collectors of rare Judaica and Hebraica there are two major establishments—De Pampiere Wereld, at 428 Keizersgracht, and Spinoza, at Prinsengracht 493. Mozes Gans, author of the *Memorbook,* is the proprietor of Premsela Hamburger, at Rokin 120, a firm of jewelers and silversmiths that has been in the service of the royal family since the nineteenth century. Herman Schipper, at Rokin 11, is one of the few diamond establishments still in Jewish hands.

PRAYING: "Hot lines" for information on synagogue services and other community activities are: Ashkenazi, 460046; Liberal, 423562; and Portuguese, 245351. All Amsterdam Jews, without exception, are fluent in English, so there's never a problem communicating with them.

TRIVIA: Rabbi Hans Rodrigues Pereira, scion of an ancient Portuguese family and educated at Etz Haim, the Sefardic seminary, was until recently the spiritual leader of the Ashkenazic community; Rabbi Barend Drukarch, whose ancestors migrated to Amsterdam from Poland and who was ordained at an Ashkenazic seminary in New York, is spiritual leader of the Portuguese community. Professor Hans Bloemendal, cantor of the Ashkenazic shul, teaches chemistry at the Catholic University of Nijmegen. Tolerance, Dutch style, seems to work in all directions.

—GABRIEL LEVENSON

Antwerp

Diamond Exchange *(Belgian National Tourist Office)*

Carol Channing notwithstanding, diamonds are no longer a girl's best friend. Career, marriage, motherhood, or passage of an equal rights amendment are decidedly more important. But the precious stones continue to play the major role in the lives of the thirteen thousand Jews of Antwerp, Belgium's great port city on the river Schelde.

Indeed, the port and the diamond industry are the very core of Antwerp's economy. The former is the third busiest and the latter is by far the biggest in all the world. Most of the city's adult Jews are involved in the cutting and polishing of diamonds, or in their purchase and sale; and the industry as a whole is still largely in Jewish hands.

HISTORY: History and geography have combined to give Jews preeminence in the field, ever since the Middle Ages, when the diamonds of India first appeared in Europe. The trade routes from West to East passed through the Indian Ocean, Asia Minor, and the Mediterranean by way of the ports and urban centers in which Jews had reestablished themselves after the destruction of the First and Second temples and their own dispersion from ancient Israel.

Diamonds were still so new and rare a commodity in Europe that the medieval guilds had not yet gotten around to barring Jews from dealing in them. Settled in the key shipping points, from Madras to Marseilles, Jewish merchants became entrenched in diamond commerce and diamond processing, about which the established world then knew little and cared less.

When the Sefardim were expelled from Spain and Portugal at the end of the fifteenth century and found refuge in the Protestant Low Countries (modern Holland and Belgium), they carried with them to Amsterdam and Antwerp the skill of generations of traders, cutters, and polishers of diamonds. Admitted to England 150 years later, the Spanish and Portuguese Jews organized the diamond exchange in London as the terminal point for the shipment of raw stones from India, later Brazil, and more recently South Africa. From London the unprocessed items were, and still are, sent on to Amsterdam and Antwerp.

The demanding tasks of classifying, cutting, and polishing remained the monopoly of the Sefardim in these two cities, their numbers increased starting in the 1880s by the poor Ashkenazic immigrants fleeing the pogroms in Eastern Europe, who were first hired as unskilled workers, and many of whom eventually set up their own shops. As more and more refugees poured into Amsterdam and Antwerp, an Ashkenazic majority developed among both bosses and workers in the industry.

By the turn of the century, two unrelated circumstances had joined to bring unexpected prosperity to the Antwerp Jewish community. The city had become a major port of embarkation for the mass Jewish migration to America; at the same time, the discovery of diamonds in South Africa, replenishing the dwindling supply from India, and the spectacular growth of the industry seduced many of the would-be Americans into staying in Antwerp.

It was a boom period. Poor Jews who had eked out a meager living as tailors in the mud alleys of East European shtetls, as well as some who had been diamond merchants in the cities and towns of Poland, could now adapt their craftsmanship to cutting and polishing diamonds in a civilized city. The pay was good and would get better, as powerful diamond workers' unions were formed in both Antwerp and Amsterdam.

Diamond processing and trading became central to the community. The concentration of Jews in the industry and the enterprise they brought to it made Antwerp the diamond capital of Europe. Even the Nazi invasion of Belgium could not permanently topple that eminence. As the German troops were taking over the city, the diamond industry was leaving for London, New York, Cuba, and Palestine. Ten days after Belgium was liberated from German occupation, diamonds were back in Antwerp—factories, exchanges, and shops. Despite the war and the heavy losses the Jewish community had suffered, its dominant position in Antwerp diamonds would remain.

The Antwerp Jews who survived the German occupation did so through the efforts of the National Committee for Jewish Defense. Affiliated with the Belgian resistance movement, this group saved the lives of ten thousand adults and found refuge with Belgian Christian families for three thousand children. Almost all of them were returned to their own families after the liberation. In Belgium there were none of the tragic legal fights, as in France and other occupied countries, where Jewish parents had to sue to regain custody of their own children who had been reared in Christian homes or institutions and had been baptized.

Survival was also based on strong support from the Belgian Government, the Catholic Church, and the general, particularly the French-speaking, population. Unlike the French police, who methodically rounded up the Jews of Paris for shipment to the concentration camps, the Belgian police refused to collaborate. In May 1942, when the Germans demanded that Jews put on the hated yellow badge, they could not find a single Belgian policeman who would help carry out their orders.

That year, Elisabeth, the Queen Mother, actively intervened to save Jews. Joseph Ernest Cardinal van Roey ordered his priests to denounce publicly the yellow badge decrees and alerted the Vatican (to little avail) to the "anti-Christian" implications of such racist measures.

COMMUNITY: Today, on Antwerp's Pelikaanstraat, the main street of the diamond district, Yiddish is the lingua franca. More than 80 percent of the city's Jews work and live in this area. Shop signs are in Yiddish, the bearded men hurrying along the sidewalks wear the wide-brimmed black hats and overcoats of Hasidim, and even the blond, young, conspicuously Aryan policeman walking his beat on a Friday afternoon offers storekeepers a *gut Shabbos* greeting—with a Litvak accent.

There is no longer so concentrated and lively a Jewish presence in all of Europe, except, on a smaller scale, along the Rue des Rosiers in Paris. The Jews of Amsterdam who survived the Hitler years are dispersed on the outskirts of the city. Its diamond industry has never recovered: a few Jews remain as diamond merchants, but there is no longer a Jewish working class, once the spearhead of a powerful trade union movement that successfully struck for minimum wage laws almost a hundred years ago.

The revival on Pelikaanstraat in Antwerp is in marked contrast, despite the Jewish community's massive losses during the four years of German occupation. Before World War II it numbered more than fifty-five thousand persons, 20 percent of the city's population. When Antwerp was liberated in 1944, some eight hundred Jews returned from the hiding places in which they had been supplied with food and other essentials by the Jewish underground.

They were the nucleus of a present-day community that is, for the most part, an Eastern European transplant, composed largely of refugees, or their children, from the displaced persons camps of the years immediately after World War II. They cling to the Orthodoxy of the prewar shtetl or the ultra-Orthodoxy (half the community are Hasidim) in which many Holocaust survivors found spiritual and psychological support. Liberal Judaism, strongly entrenched in neighboring Holland and in nearby Brussels, has few adherents in Antwerp.

David Wachstock, director of the Romi Goldmuntz Center (a miniversion of New York's 92nd Street Y), speaks of the "remarkable cohesion" of this community. It has an economic base in diamonds, where almost all Jews work. Such a base permits a viable, self-contained, and self-imposed ghetto to thrive. There is no need to assimilate into an outside gentile world. Intermarriage is still a rare phenomenon. Even doctors, lawyers, and other professionals who function outside the diamond eruv—and there is one in fact, its boundaries recognized by municipal authorities—look inward to the community as their spiritual and social heart.

There is a tight network of institutions, including the day schools, which enroll 95 percent of the Jewish children in Antwerp (the highest proportion in the world). They start at the nursery school level and continue within the system through high school. The teachers—like the rabbis, cantors, and other religious functionaries—are paid by the state, and at the prevailing wage. Judaism is recognized as one of the four national faiths entitled to state subsidies. Secular subjects taught in Jewish schools are paid for by the government.

Flemish is the language of instruction in the day schools, but pupils are almost equally fluent in French, the country's co-official language, and in Hebrew, since most of the university-bound will do their studies in Israel. They are also likely to speak Yiddish, the mother tongue of their grandparents, and English, increasingly a necessity in the international diamond community, whose members fly between Antwerp, New York, Tel Aviv, and Johannesburg with the greatest of ease and frequency.

SIGHTS: Pelikaanstraat begins at the central railroad station and runs a half-dozen blocks parallel to the train tracks. A few of the more affluent have moved to the other side of the tracks—the "right bank" —but most Antwerp Jews live where they work: on Pelikaanstraat itself or on the narrow side streets leading to it.

On the second floor of No.106 is the office of Louis Davids, editor of the *Belgisch Israelitisch Weekblad,* a weekly newspaper (circulation 8,500) that reaches every Jewish household in the country. Here one can buy the latest edition of the publication's annual travel guide, a detailed fact book on synagogues, kosher restaurants, bookshops, and other institutions in Antwerp, Brussels (the national capital), and other European Jewish communities.

If Pelikaanstraat is a city within a city, then its generally inaccessible diamond center is a city within a city within a city. However, tourists can now visit a reasonable facsimile—the recently opened Diamondland, just around the corner from the central railroad station. Workers there perform the various processing phases, and guides tell visitors everything they ever wanted to know about the "four C's" of diamonds: their color, clarity, cut, and carat (weight). Purchases can be made at a savings of 40 to 50 percent. Entrance is free, but passports must be shown. Diamondland is at Appelmansstraat 33A (telephone, 234-36-12).

One needs special permission to get into the closely guarded diamond exchange at the head of Pelikaanstraat, or to lunch at the kosher dining rooms within that complex of bourses, offices, and workshops. But down the street is a welcoming array of bakeries and restaurants, bookstalls and jewelry stores, where one can breathe, eat, speak, and feel Jewish to the full extent of stomach, eye, heart, and mind.

Nearby is the Goldmuntz Center, at 12 Nerviersstraat (239-39-11), where excellent, moderately priced lunches are served. The modern building hums with activity. This is the place to meet local people—at Israeli folk dancing, a lecture on Kafka, a concert of J. S. Bach or Ernest Bloch, a table of bridge, or a lively game of Scrabble (in Flemish).

Well worth the effort is a visit to one of the two major schools—the Tachkemoni, for example (313 Lang Leemstraat), whose orientation and curriculum might be described as modern, state-of-the-art Orthodoxy. Such a trip can be arranged through Bernard Kahan, a trustee of the school and proprietor of the bookshop at 112 Pelikaanstraat that his father founded eighty years ago and which he has run for the past half century.

Jewish Antwerp is a self-contained entity. Technology, computers, and electronic security systems give its essential core—the diamond center—the content of the 1980s, but the outward look of Pelikaanstraat is of a century earlier.

GENERAL SIGHTS: Antwerp is a bustling, modern, highly mechanized seaport, and a treasure-house of medieval guildhalls, Gothic churches, Flemish building façades, and museums filled with the works of such favorite sons as Rubens, Van Dyck, and Pieter Brueghel, the younger.

Travelers should spend at least a day in leisurely exploration of Pelikaanstraat and at least three more just skimming the cream off Antwerp's cultural riches. One inevitably visits the Rubens House, its elegant rooms decorated with paintings by the master and furnished with the household objects he collected in the course of a brilliant and successful career.

On everyone's sightseeing agenda are the Town Hall, a magnificent Renaissance structure, and the Plantin-Moretus Museum, the definitive exhibit hall of the art of printing. It contains, along with its centuries-old printing presses and fonts of type, a rare Gutenberg Bible and a copy of the Polyglot Bible, a monumental eight-volume work in five languages—Hebrew, Aramaic, Syriac, Greek, and Latin.

Less well known are the zoo, right in the heart of Antwerp, next to the central railroad station, and the open-air museum at Middelheim, on the city's outskirts. Here in a landscaped park are more than three hundred great works by such nineteenth- and twentieth-century sculptors as Rodin, Maillol, Zadkine, and Henry Moore. This permanent display is unguarded. According to the season, snow may drape marble, bronze, or steel surfaces; raindrops may trickle down, or glittering sunlight be reflected. But there is never the mark of a vandal or graffiti doodler.

Behind the Town Hall is the extraordinary low-cost modern housing development built around and in harmony with the sixteenth-century Butchers' Hall (Vleeshuis). The hall, now a museum, was commissioned by the butchers' guild as the one meat market in all Antwerp, and it continued as such until the French Revolution, when the guilds were abolished. Now the Butchers' Hall exhibits the arts and crafts of the city, including a unique collection of locally produced harpsichords. They must be played frequently to keep them in tune; and Japanese tourists, conscientious in these matters, always pause to tickle the keys—a finger exercise of goodwill that drives the unappreciative museum guards quite mad. The high, penetrating, metallic tinkle is one the human ear can endure only at infrequent intervals.

The tall museum building overlooks the docks of the river Schelde, from which thousands of Jewish migrants embarked on the steam vessels of the Red Star Line for the final stage of their long journey from Eastern Europe to America. One recent Jewish refugee from Russian tyranny who lives in Antwerp is Valery Panov, the dancer and choreographer, now the artistic director of the Royal Ballet of Flanders.

ACCOMMODATIONS: Directly opposite the central railroad station is the DeKeyser Hotel, a five-star establishment patronized mainly by knowledgeable visitors and diamond merchants. The other world of Pelikaanstraat is just around the corner.

—GABRIEL LEVENSON

Baltimore

Lloyd Street Synagogue *(Morton/Maryland Jewish Historical Society)*

F. Scott Fitzgerald and the talk show host Larry King might not have much in common, but they agreed on Baltimore. Fitzgerald dubbed it "the beautiful little city on the harbor"; King says it is America's most underrated city. The point both have made is that Baltimore is somehow overlooked, but it was not always so. It was once a bustling port, the second-largest city in the United States. It also attracted weary Jewish immigrants right from the boat.

Today the city is best known for its urban renaissance—a jazzy revival for a restrained, subtly genteel city proud of its distinctive ethnic neighborhoods. Like other groups, Jews have their own enclaves, the most conspicuous euphemistically referred to as the "Rue des Synagogues," otherwise known as Park Heights Avenue, a thoroughfare boasting one synagogue after another. But Baltimore's Jews can be proud of more than temples. They have made a disproportionate contribution to the city's modernization and cultural revitalization.

HISTORY: Maryland was not one of the colonies noted for religious tolerance, and Jews avoided it for nearly a century and a half after its founding in 1634. One Jew who did wander into the colony, Jacob Lumbrozo, was arrested under a law that made denial of Christianity a capital offense; luckily, he was freed in an amnesty.

The atmosphere changed with the oncoming Revolution and the diversification of Maryland's economy. The first Jew arrived in Baltimore in 1773. Unlike many who were to follow from across the ocean, Benjamin Levy, a businessman, did not make a particularly long trip: he came from Philadelphia. Several Jewish families made Baltimore their home shortly thereafter, but some restrictions remained until 1826. That was the year Maryland passed its "Jew bill," enabling Jews to hold public office without taking a Christian oath. Solomon Etting and Jacob Cohen, two leading Baltimore Jews, were joined by the non-Jewish legislator Thomas Kennedy in pushing for the bill's passage.

It was in the 1830s and '40s that Baltimore attracted its first wave of Jewish immigrants, from Germany, settling near the port in East Baltimore. It was there that the Lloyd Street Synagogue, the third-oldest in the United States, was built in 1845 (by a congregation established fifteen years earlier). Subsequent waves of immigrants boosted the Jewish community from a thousand in 1840 to eight thousand in 1860. During this period Baltimore saw battles over Jewish religious ideology. The leaders of the camps were Rabbi David Einhorn, who took over the Reform Har Sinai Congregation in 1855; the Orthodox Rabbi Abraham Rice; and Rabbi Benjamin Szold, who arrived in 1859 and advocated both moderation and tradition.

During the Civil War, Baltimore's Jews were as divided as the rest of Maryland. Rabbi Einhorn led the Jewish antislavery group, while Rabbi Bernard Illowy defended the status quo. Leopold Blumenberg fought with the Union Army and achieved the rank of major general.

The mid-nineteenth century saw the beginnings of a mercantile and business class which persists to this day among Baltimore Jews. Men who started as peddlers took advantage of Baltimore's location as the "Gateway to the South" to amass fortunes in industry and commerce. The first merchants, mostly German, became known as "Uptown Jews," and some of their heirs are still prominent in the community.

East European Jews, particularly from Russia, began arriving in the 1880s, fleeing pogroms and repressive regimes. By the time large-scale immigration was cut off in 1924 they had transformed Baltimore Jewry into a community of sixty-five thousand. The newcomers, who became the "Downtown Jews," moved into the East Baltimore areas from which the wealthier Germans had begun to escape, many going to work in garment sweatshops owned by German Jews.

Though American history is replete with stories about established Jews looking down on more recent arrivals, Baltimore had one particularly prominent exception. Henrietta Szold, daughter of Benjamin Szold, and a local teacher and social worker, could often be seen at Fells Point (now a colorful harbor neighborhood of captains' houses and fine restaurants) meeting the boatloads of often penniless, dazed immigrants. Many learned English at Szold's "Russian Night School," which became the prototype for night schools across the country. Henrietta Szold herself went on to greater prominence as editor of the American Jewish Year Book, the first woman to study at the Jewish Theological Seminary in New York, and ultimately, in 1912, the founder of Hadassah.

Baltimore welcomed a smaller stream of immigrants—refugees from Nazi Germany—in the 1930s and '40s. Today the community is experiencing some growth as Jews, particularly Orthodox, arrive from other parts of the United States.

COMMUNITY: Baltimore's Jewish community of ninety-two thousand is a microcosm of American Judaism. Orthodox Jews carrying tefillin can be seen passing Reform temples on their way to tiny shtiebls. It is the home of both the Orthodox Ner Israel Rabbinical College and Har Sinai, the oldest continuously operating Reform congregation in the country. In this traditional and tightly knit community, it is not unusual to find children, parents, and grandparents living in the same neighborhood throughout their lives.

Most of Baltimore's Jews live in Park Heights and nearby Mount Washington or in Pikesville. Park Heights, closer to the center of town, is an established neighborhood of two- and three-story homes built before World War II. Most of the city's Orthodox community is there, as well as the major synagogues and the main Baltimore Jewish Community Center. Along the streets, including the "Rue des Synagogues," it is not uncommon to hear a sprinkling of German, Yiddish, or Hebrew, or to spot large signs admonishing residents to "Save Soviet Jewry."

Pikesville, outside the city limits, is emerging as the new center of Baltimore Jewry. Built after the war, it is a typical American suburb with ranch-style homes and shopping centers.

The sense of tradition is fueled by Baltimore's rich and varied Jewish educational system. Children from the Washington area— where the Jewish community is considerably larger but much weaker in roots—are bused to Baltimore Jewish day schools. The Baltimore Hebrew College is the only institution in America that awards Ph.D.s in Jewish communal service, in addition to offering the traditional courses of Jewish studies.

PERSONALITIES: Baltimore has long been a Zionist stronghold. Funds were raised there for Palestine as early as 1847, and the only American delegate to the First Zionist Congress in 1897 was from Baltimore. In addition to Henrietta Szold, the city was home to Harry Friedenwald, a founder of the Zionist Organization of America.

The city's Jews have contributed to the general as well as Jewish welfare. Joseph Meyerhoff, a real estate developer, was behind virtually all of the city's major cultural institutions, from the Baltimore Symphony (which plays in the Joseph Meyerhoff Symphony Hall) to the Baltimore Museum of Art, the Walters Art Gallery, the Mechanic Theatre and the Center Stage. He was also the main benefactor be-

hind the University of Maryland's Jewish studies program. Jacob Blau-
stein, who made his fortune in oil, has also contributed much to
Baltimore's cultural institutions.

Other Jewish names that have emerged from Baltimore include
Jerold Hoffberger, onetime owner and still a director of the Baltimore
Orioles; Alan Guttmacher, long-time president of the Planned Parent-
hood Federation; Bernard Sachs, the neurologist who first described
Tay-Sachs disease; and Louis Bamberger, founder of the department
store chain. The city has also produced writer Leon Uris; rock composer Jerry Leiber, who wrote many of Elvis Presley's hits; and
"Mama" Cass Elliot. Of the many Jewish politicians in Maryland history, Isidor Rayner, a U.S. senator from 1905 to 1912, stands out for
his advocacy of civil rights at a time when segregation ruled his state.

SIGHTS: Reminders of a Jewish presence in the city's core are the
Lloyd Street and B'nai Israel synagogues, which, together with the
Jewish Historical Society of Maryland, at 15 Lloyd Street, comprise
the Jewish Heritage Center, in the heart of Baltimore's old Jewish
neighborhood.

The Lloyd Street Synagogue, at the corner of Lloyd and Watson, is a
Greek Revival building with some features intact since 1845 and others faithfully reconstructed. One of the synagogue's two mikvahs
dates from the building's construction and its Torah ark is a replica of
the original. It also has a stained-glass window believed to be the first
in the United States that incorporates a Star of David as a motif.

B'nai Israel, at Lloyd and Lombard, is a Moorish-Gothic building
dating to 1875. One of the synagogue's most striking features is its
hand-carved wooden ark. Unlike the Lloyd Street Synagogue, B'nai
Israel still holds Shabbat services.

The Jewish Historical Society of Maryland collection ranges from
religious objects to art to documents. Included are the complete papers of Benjamin Szold; the paintings and papers of the artist Saul
Bernstein; and ceremonial objects, furniture, papers, and possessions
of prominent founders of the Maryland Jewish community. The society has a library noted for its genealogical resources and also mounts
periodic exhibits, such as a recent one on immigration and early
Jewish life in Baltimore. Call the society at (301) 732-6400 for details
of events and exhibits or for information on its free tours of Jewish
Baltimore.

Lloyd Street, by the way, runs into Lombard Street, whose unofficial, and perhaps equally known, name is "Corned Beef Row." Attman's and Jack's delis are still on Lombard, but they're not kosher.

The Jewish march northwest from the center of town is reflected in the eclectic architecture in buildings put up as synagogues which now, by and large, house churches. The collection includes Greek Revival, American Moorish, Romanesque, and Bauhaus designs. This architectural path leads to Park Heights, where the synagogues are less distinctive, perhaps, but seem to be more permanent. One of the Park Heights synagogues most worth seeing is the Baltimore Hebrew Congregation, at 7401 Park Heights Avenue. Founded in 1830 as Nidchei Yisrael, it is the descendant of the Lloyd Street Synagogue. Initially Orthodox, it joined the Reform movement in the 1890s. In its present home, built in the 1950s, the most striking features are sixteen stained-glass windows tracing the history of the Jewish people from the Bible to the establishment of modern Israel.

At 7310 Park Heights Avenue is Temple Oheb Shalom, another descendant of Baltimore's first Jewish congregation. Before the Baltimore Hebrew Congregation itself joined the Reform movement, some of its younger members became dissatisfied with what they regarded as rigid orthodoxy. They left the congregation in 1853 and founded Oheb Shalom and, five years later, brought Benjamin Szold to Baltimore to be their rabbi. Today the two related synagogues face each other. Oheb Shalom's current home was designed by Walter Gropius and features a vaulted sanctuary and a peaceful landscape punctuated by tall pines.

In addition to its synagogues, Park Heights is the area for Jewish shopping and eating. The Jewish stores—groceries, bakeries, bookstores, etc.—are mostly on or near Reisterstown Road. Kosher restaurants include Tov Pizza (dairy) at 6313 Reisterstown; the Royal Restaurant (meat) at 1630 Reisterstown; and O'Fishel's (meat), located in the Park Heights Jewish Community Center.

CULTURE: The Jewish community's annual showcase is the Jewish Festival, held the Sunday before Labor Day in Hopkins Plaza, downtown. It features continuous entertainment and Jewish artists and craftsmen.

The Jewish Community Center, at 5700 Park Heights Avenue (telephone, 542-4900), is a lively spot for exercise and entertainment. It offers lectures, concerts, theater, and art exhibits, all with a Jewish flavor. During Jewish Book Month, in November, it hosts a book fair with more than twenty thousand books of Jewish interest. (There is another Jewish Center farther out in suburban Owings Mills [at 3506 Gwynbrook Avenue]; call 356-5200 for information on events and activities.)

In addition to being the best place to check for Jewish events, the *Baltimore Jewish Times* is perhaps the best Jewish weekly in America. Founded in 1919 by David Alter, and still independently published by Alter's grandson, the paper is known for its probing, sometimes controversial articles. The editor, Gary Rosenblatt, was nominated for a Pulitzer Prize in 1985, a rare distinction for an ethnic newspaper.

GENERAL SIGHTS: Baltimore's downtown Inner Harbor, which Jews, including Joseph Meyerhoff, were prominent in planning, is a glittering tribute to the city's renewal. Once an eyesore, it is now home to boutiques, restaurants, an aquarium, and a diverse array of street performers.

The city's Bolton Hill section will give the visitor a feel for Baltimore's Victorian era. Often compared to Boston's Beacon Hill, Bolton Hill has been called more a state of mind than a neighborhood. F. Scott Fitzgerald, Alger Hiss, and Gertrude Stein all chose to live in what is still one of the city's most attractive neighborhoods.

Not far to the north of Bolton Hill is Johns Hopkins University. After visiting the pleasant wooded campus which had its beginnings in 1874, take a drive through nearby Roland Park, an area of large stately homes and mansions and the most chic part of town.

DAY TRIPS: Astride Chesapeake Bay, the nation's largest, Baltimore is a convenient base from which to explore the beauty and lush heritage of the area immortalized, most recently, in James Michener's *Chesapeake.* Less than an hour to the south lies Annapolis, chartered in 1708 and named for Princess Anne, later Queen of England. Its eighteenth-century waterfront and adjacent back streets and narrow alleys are exquisite examples of colonial charm. In addition to being the Maryland capital, Annapolis is home to the U.S. Naval Academy, established in 1845. The academy's spacious grounds and imposing architecture provide a tranquil contrast to the bustle of the nearby harbor.

The Jewish community of Annapolis numbers two thousand. The oldest synagogue is the Orthodox Kneseth Israel at Spa Road and Hilltop Lane. Many Jewish midshipmen worship there or in suburban Arnold at Conservative Congregation Kol Ami (517 Mystic Lane) and Reform Temple Beth Sholom (1461 Old Annapolis Road).

For those interested in a longer day trip out of Baltimore along the bay, there are the many old fishing villages of Maryland's Eastern Shore. Two fine examples are Oxford and St. Michaels. Oxford, population eight hundred, was one of Maryland's most important pre-Revolutionary ports and a haven for pirates such as "Blackbeard" Teach. A visit to Oxford must include the Robert Morris Inn, restored home of Robert Morris, whose son, Robert, was a signatory of the Declaration of Independence. Nearby St. Michaels, once a shipbuilding center, is no less picturesque. A visit there should include fresh seafood and beer at one of the town's open air dockside restaurants.

READING: A good place to find the flavor of Baltimore's early Jewish community is in the many biographies of Henrietta Szold. The three best are *Summoned to Jerusalem* by Joan Dash (Harper & Row); *Woman of Valor* by Irving Fineman (Simon & Schuster) and *The Szolds of Lombard Street* by Alexandra Lee Levin (Jewish Publication Society). Other books worth looking at are *The Making of an American Jewish Community* by Isaac M. Fein (Jewish Publication Society) and *The Maryland Bicentennial Jewish Book,* edited by A. D. Glushakow (Jewish Voice Publishing). For a fictional look at Baltimore, try William Manchester's *The City of Anger* (Little, Brown) or Anne Tyler's *The Accidental Tourist* (Random House).

—GINNI WALSH

Basel

Herzl at the Rhine *(Courtesy of Phyllis Ellen Funke)*

In Basel, residents often carry three billfolds, since they may play tennis in West Germany at lunchtime and eat dinner in France before returning to sleep in Switzerland. Indeed, situated where the three countries come together, Basel, Switzerland's second-largest city, has a special multinational flavor.

Not surprisingly, it harbors a Jewish community, small but vigorous, that reflects this crossroads location. But Basel lives in the annals of world Jewry for a more significant reason: it is where Theodor Herzl held the First Zionist Congress, leading to the establishment of the State of Israel.

HISTORY: The First Zionist Congress was not supposed to take place in Basel; it had been scheduled for Munich. Because of rabbinical protests in Germany, Herzl shifted it to a Basel concert hall, the Stadt-Casino. Held on August 29–31, 1897, it concluded with the adoption of the Basel Program, which became the fundamental guideline for the Zionist movement until Israel's founding. On September 3, 1897, Herzl wrote in his diary: "To summarize the Basel Congress in one sentence—which I shall be careful not to pronounce publicly—it is this: I have founded the Jewish state in Basel."

Herzl wanted to make Basel the permanent center of the Zionist movement, with a special congress building there to be called the "House of the Jewish People." This wish was unfulfilled, but Basel did host nine more congresses, including the second, attended by Chaim Weizmann; the sixth, at which Herzl agreed to accept a British plan for settlement in Uganda; the tenth, which was conducted in Hebrew for the first time, and the twenty-second, the last held in the galut, or exile, in December 1946.

Basel has known three Jewish communities. The first was established in the early thirteenth century, when Basel was a German free city and Jews could buy and sell land, as well as lend money, even to Basel's bishops. Protected by the city council, they prospered until the Black Death of 1348, when they were accused of poisoning wells.

At the instigation of the guilds—which they could never join—six hundred Jews were burned at the stake, and in 1349 the community disbanded. A church council edict in 1434, requiring compulsory attendance by Jews at conversionist sermons, helped ensure that there would not be another community in Basel for four centuries.

Thanks to its paper mills and printing presses, Basel became in the sixteenth century a center for humanism and, as such, printed Hebrew texts. Christian printers there published the Psalms, a Hebrew Bible, a censored version of the Talmud, and the works of Hebrew teachers at Basel's university. To have such works properly proofread, they obtained residency permits for Jews.

During the French Revolution, when anti-Semitism was rampant in Alsace, Basel permitted Alsatian Jews in the city temporarily, and by 1805 there were enough to form another community. While they were under severe civil and religious restrictions, and underwent at least two expulsions between then and the emancipation of Swiss Jewry in 1866, contemporary Basel Jews date their community from the start of the nineteenth century.

The Jews of Basel established a small congregation in the 1840s, consecrating their Great Synagogue in 1868, and after the granting of full civil rights in 1872 the community grew rapidly. First, Jews from southern Germany arrived; later, pogroms drove in Jews from Russia and Poland. Though constrained by Swiss immigration laws, Basel also provided a temporary refuge for some Jews escaping Hitler and after World War II became a haven for Jews from Hungary and Czechoslovakia.

COMMUNITY: There are about three thousand Jews in Basel. Except for a handful of Jews of Eastern European origin who have separated themselves into an ultra-Orthodox community, complete with a synagogue at Ahornstrasse 14, most belong to the Great Synagogue at the corner of Eulerstrasse and Leimenstrasse, not far from downtown Basel.

If there is a Jewish neighborhood in Basel, it extends from the Great Synagogue to Ahornstrasse, a distance covered with a half hour's walk. The area, in the southwestern section of the city, is called the Schützenmatt Quarter, after a main street that runs through it. In general, the Jews of Basel consider themselves completely integrated into the life of the city—the government includes a Jew along with representatives of other faiths at all official functions—and they hold positions in academia, the arts, local government, and banking. The Jewish-owned Dreyfuss Bank is one of Basel's most important private banking institutions. Many Jews own shops, including several on the Freiestrasse, Basel's main shopping street.

SIGHTS: Built around a medieval core, Basel blends the present with the past in a manner that blurs the distinction. The city is the home of pharmaceutical giants Sandoz, Ciba-Geigy, and Hoffmann-La Roche and of several major cultural and artistic institutions. But it also harbors its share of quaint little streets, hidden courtyards, and fanciful fountains, among which the sites of Jewish interest are closely intermingled.

Right behind the towering Barfüsser (Barefoot) Church, a fourteenth-century Franciscan structure, between the bustling Steinenberg and Barfüsserplatz stands the Stadt-Casino, site of the First Zionist Congress. A concert hall now as in Herzl's time, it is not officially open for viewing. Yet, to the distress of those rehearsing, visitors always seem to find their way to the auditorium where the 208 original delegates gathered. On the wall to the right of the stage there is a bronze plaque that reads: "On Theodor Herzl's initiative and under his guidance, the first Zionist organization was established leading to the foundation of the State of Israel."

Across the old city—about a fifteen-minute walk past the marketplace in the heart of town, with its shocking-salmon and gilt-colored town hall—is Die Drei Könige Hotel (The Three Kings Hotel) where Herzl stayed during the congress. Founded in 1026 and said to be Switzerland's oldest hostelry, this massive national landmark has been visited by Napoleon, Dickens, Voltaire, Metternich, and a Japanese shogun. The famous photograph of Herzl standing on a balcony looking across the Rhine was taken outside room 122.

From the hotel it is only a few steps into the town's old streets, lined with Gothic, Renaissance, and Baroque houses in shades of bubblegum pink, mint green, and lemon. No. 12 on Spalenberg is a fourteenth-century balcony-rimmed cabaret, the Theater Fauteuil. During the early nineteenth century, it was home to a founder of the Dreyfuss Bank.

Forking off Spalenberg is Heuberg, or Mount of Hay, so called because the butchers who once lived there grew hay on their roofs to feed their livestock. The courtyard of No. 33 is adorned with stone slabs bearing Hebrew inscriptions. And on Unterer Heuberg, which curves away from Heuberg, are the sites of earlier synagogues, at No. 9 and No. 21. To the left of No. 21 is a green door leading to a narrow alley, Güggeliallee, or Chicken Alley. Reputedly, it is so named because some of the chickens killed by the shohet would fly, in spasms, over the wall into the alley.

Nearby, at Kornhausgasse 8, is Basel's small but fine Jewish Museum. The only one in Switzerland, it contains memorabilia, from huppahs to Torah covers, of the Jews of Alsace, Lengnau, and Endingen—the latter two places being the only other Swiss enclaves where Jews previously were allowed to own land. Also on display are sixteenth-century books in Hebrew that were printed in Basel, including a Hebrew grammar from 1524 and a Latin and Hebrew Bible from 1546. A montage presents photographs of delegates to the First Zionist Congress. In addition, there is a first-edition copy of Herzl's *Der Judenstaat* and a number of his letters. The museum's courtyard is adorned with fragments of Jewish tombstones found in and around Basel, dating as early as 1222. The museum is open Mondays and Wednesdays, 3–5 P.M., and Sundays 10–12 A.M. and 3–5 P.M. Admission is free.

The Great Synagogue, at Leimenstrasse 24, is an imposing buff-colored building, topped by two large Byzantine cupolas and decorated with yellow and orange stained-glass windows that cast a golden glow in the sanctuary. Officially, it is Orthodox, but there is a men's choir and its members embrace a broad spectrum of opinion. The structure also encompasses a second, smaller, synagogue and a mikvah (telephone, 23-98-50). Next door to the Great Synagogue is the community center and Hebrew day school, as well as a library and various social facilities.

Mostackerstrasse runs behind the synagogue, and at No. 17 stands Victor Goldschmidt's bookshop of Jewish incunabula, prayer books, and articles for the Jewish home.

Two other synagogues are at Birmannsgasse 7 (telephone, 24-77-16) and Rudolfstrasse 28 (24-28-45).

CULTURE: The community center hosts a wide range of cultural activities, including stage productions and lectures. For information, call 23-17-79 or the Great Synagogue. A booklet, in German, *Wissenswertes . . . Jüdisches Leben in Basel,* lists all organizations, institutions, and activities of interest to Jews, and a guide in English is being published. Basel has three Jewish periodicals, including the weekly *Jüdische Rundschau–Maccabi.*

PERSONALITIES: Jews from Basel who made a mark beyond city limits include Tadeus Reichstein, who won the Nobel Prize for medicine in 1950; art historians Adolf Goldschmidt and Werner Weissbach;

and the antique dealer George Segal, who has been the president of Switzerland's Art and Antiques Fair. The most widely known of Basel's Jewish community are the four "Oscars"—Academy Awards. They belong to movie producer Arthur Cohn, grandson of a chief rabbi of Basel, who won them for *The Garden of the Finzi-Continis,* among others.

GENERAL SIGHTS: Worth a visit is the Kunstmuseum (St.-Alban-Graben 16), established in 1662 and considered the world's first public art gallery; its collection includes *The Rabbi* by Marc Chagall and *The Synagogue* by Konrad Witz. Also worth seeing are Jean Tinguely's fountain of wrought-iron objects and figures that splash, spray, and sprinkle water (in front of the Basel City Theater); and Basel's crowning structure, the red and gray sandstone cathedral, the Münster (at Münsterplatz), in which, on the east side of the transept, there is a Star of David. (An employee in the cathedral, recently asked about the star, explained matter-of-factly that it was a symbol of the House of David, of which Jesus was a descendant.) Behind the Münster is a terrace called the Pfalz, which looks across the Rhine to the Vosges Mountains and the Black Forest.

EATING: The kosher restaurant Topas operates in the Jewish Community Center. Proprietor Albert Dreyfuss creates kosher dishes with a French and Swiss flavor. His menu, while including such Eastern European staples as potato kugel and kreplach, also offers entrecote, with a Café de Paris sauce, and the Swiss dishes rösti and Geschnetzeltes—finely cut veal with mushrooms and onions in a "cream" sauce. The Hilton, Euler, Drei Könige, and International hotels also offer kosher food.

For an unusual snack, visit Marcel Hess, the Kosher Sausage King, at Leimenstrasse 41. Officially, this emporium, its windows covered with paintings of sausages, is one of Basel's two kosher butcher shops, but it is also the headquarters of the "kosher" winner of two gold medals in treife Swiss sausage contests. Hess, who has never tasted a nonkosher sausage, relies on others to tell him if he's gotten the flavor right. Like Herzl's first efforts in Basel, Hess's obviously come to a good end.

—Phyllis Ellen Funke

Bombay

Keneseth Eliyahoo Synagogue *(Alan M. Tigay)*

Bombay is to India what New York is to the United States: a brawny, bustling gateway akin to, but atypical of, the country onto which it opens.

This is India's wealthiest city—its primary port, its commercial hub, even its Hollywood. Indeed, Bombay produces more films annually than the United States; its high-rises command rents that rival New York's. Cars and people clog its streets; it teems and throbs at all hours of the day—and night.

By Indian standards, Bombay is untraditional; change touches it far faster than it does other spots, making it the country's pacesetter. Furthermore, it is cosmopolitan, attracting both foreigners and Indians from every corner of the land. Hundreds pour in each week to a metropolis that offers jobs, if not housing. The newcomers speak ten —maybe twenty—different tongues; they mingle with others of variegated background. Hindus, Muslims, Sikhs, Jains, Christians, and Parsis all participate in the whirl of Bombay. So, too, do Jews.

COMMUNITY: The Jewish community in Bombay today—perhaps five thousand in all—is actually made up of the remnants of three decidedly distinct communities. The oldest—and by far the largest—group in the city are members of B'nai Israel, those Jews who consider themselves indigenous; who speak Marathi, the language of Bombay's state of Maharashtra; and who date their presence in the region back two thousand years. The tiniest segment—if, indeed, a mere handful can be considered that—are Cochinese, whose ancestors arrived in India one thousand years ago. And 150, maybe a few more, remain of those who came to India last, but made the biggest splash—Jews from Iraq called Baghdadis, who settled only in the nineteenth century, but whose numbers included members of the renowned Sassoon dynasty.

Once the Cochin Jews had had a thriving community of their own on India's Malabar Coast, 650 miles south of Bombay. The Baghdadis had been primarily businessmen who spoke Arabic, hobnobbed with the British, and held themselves aloof from the other Jews. Among the many buildings they erected were two synagogues in Bombay and one, a churchlike structure, in Poona (or Pune), a hill city about a

hundred miles from Bombay. The B'nai Israel themselves once numbered thirty-five thousand, had entered many walks of Indian life, and
had eight synagogues in Bombay and fourteen in nearby areas.

What decimated all these groups was the birth of independent India
in 1947 and of Israel in 1948. The Baghdadis, fearing reprisal for their
close association with the British, headed primarily for England, Canada, and the United States, while the Cochinese and the B'nai Israel,
motivated by both economics and idealism, emigrated to Israel.

Thus, even in Bombay, India's Jewish center, the remaining Jews
have more or less banded together. They intermarry, share social,
civic, and philanthropic events, and visit one another's synagogues.
Indeed, the Baghdadis, who once scorned the B'nai Israel way of
practicing the Sefardic rite, now hire B'nai Israel men to make a
minyan. Essentially, then, the Bombay Jewish community of today is a
B'nai Israel one—as it was originally.

HISTORY: The B'nai Israel of Bombay, who have lived far removed from the mainstream of Judaism, tell a story that, both in
length and in content, differs decidedly from most other diaspora
communities. Indeed, a key feature in this history, which, after all, is
not of the Western world, is the total absence of anti-Semitism.

The start of the tale is not certain. It may have begun with Jews
escaping persecution in Israel following the destruction of the First
Temple or, perhaps, the Second Temple. Or these Jews may have
merely been traders sailing the route of King Solomon's ships to the
once flourishing port, just north of Bombay, of Suparika (now Nala-
Soparal)—which some today think was the biblical Ophir.

In any event, B'nai Israel tradition says that, off the Konkan Coast—
which is the mainland just across the creek from the islands that have
formed Bombay—there was a shipwreck, which only seven couples
survived. They settled where they climbed ashore, at Navgaon, down
the coast from Bombay, and became coconut-oil pressers.

Because, in a caste-conscious land, this had a low social rating, some
say the Jews chose it to render their women undesirable to the local
populace. Probably, though, they adopted this occupation initially
because they knew it from their homeland. Later they worked in
agriculture and the military, in the service of nawabs and maharajahs
who appreciated their lack of allegiance to either the Hindu or the
Muslim cause.

Since all had been lost in the shipwreck, the B'nai Israel had no
written guidelines for practicing Judaism. Thus, as the centuries

passed and they spread out along the Konkan Coast, they began adopting some of their neighbors' practices. However, they did keep those rituals they remembered—certain dietary laws, circumcision, the Sabbath (at first they were dubbed *Shanwar telis* or "Saturday oilmen" for not working that day), and the Shema, which became an all-purpose prayer.

Then, in the eighteenth century (although a B'nai Israel legend places it in the eleventh), a Sefardic Jew, David Rahabi, visited the B'nai Israel, decided they were indeed Jewish, and began instructing them in Judaism—which they took to Bombay.

They weren't the first Jews to set foot there, however. In the sixteenth century, when Bombay was still a group of seven fishing islands controlled by Portugal, the Portuguese leased the main one, for his services to the viceroy, to Garcia da Orta, a noted Marrano scientist and physician. A century later, though, in 1661, Portugal gave the islands to England as part of the dowry for Catherine of Braganza when she married Charles II. And shortly afterward one Benjamin Franks jumped a ship under Captain William Kidd's command there and provided the deposition that led to Kidd's London trial for piracy.

The B'nai Israel began crossing the creek to Bombay when the British started turning it into a trading area and a fort. With their military prowess, they assumed they could find government jobs. At least one distinguished himself early on. Samuel Divekar, who joined the East India Company in 1750, ultimately became a commandant and went into battle against the powerful Tipu, Sultan of Mysore. Tipu was a ruthless Muslim who gave his prisoners of war a choice: conversion to Islam or death. According to legend, when Divekar was captured, brought before Tipu, and asked his religion, he stated it. The sultan's mother, who was watching, interrupted, saying that because the Koran spoke well of the Jews Divekar should be spared.

When he returned to Bombay in 1796, in gratitude he built the first B'nai Israel synagogue. Initially it was called the Samuel Street Synagogue, because the street on which it stood had been named for Divekar; it was later renamed Shaar Harahamim, or Gate of Mercy.

At about this time the Baghdadis, driven by persecution in Iraq, began moving East, and David Sassoon, founder of the Sassoon dynasty in India, arrived in 1833. He and his eight sons and their descendants made their mark as the "Rothschilds of the East." Internationally, they developed a great trading empire—a major item was opium—and in Bombay they built hospitals, schools, and libraries, as well as its two Baghdadi synagogues, Magen David, in 1861, and Keneseth Eliyahoo in 1884. Among the Sassoons—and family members—who distinguished themselves individually were Albert Sassoon, who constructed the Sassoon Docks, the port's first major pier; Flora Sassoon, considered Bombay's first businesswoman; and Sir Sassoon J. David, founder and chairman of the Bank of India and a mayor of Bombay.

Since the Baghdadis did little, however, to teach Hebrew to the B'nai Israel, Scottish and American missionaries with thoughts of conversion filled the gap. Though they didn't achieve their goal, Hebrew and Hebrew studies became—150 years ago—a program for a degree at Bombay University.

Meanwhile, B'nai Israel Jews were producing leading military officers—in fact, 50 percent of the Indian officers of the East India Company were B'nai Israel—and later contributed at least two generals, a rear admiral, and a host of colonels to the Indian armed forces.

Bombay also had a B'nai Israel mayor, Elijah Moses; as well as actor David Abraham, popularly known as "David"; the actress Ruby Meyers; and Joseph David Penkar, who wrote the script for India's first talkie. Dr. Jerusha J. Jhirad became the country's first Indian chief medical officer, and Dr. Abraham S. Erulkar was Mahatma Gandhi's personal physician. Another Jewish doctor who made his mark in India, though not born there, was Waldemar Mordecai Haffkine. He created the first effective anticholera and antiplague vaccines and was the initial director in chief of the Haffkine Institute in Bombay, now the center of India's bacteriological research.

Two contemporary Bombay Jews noted on the international scene are Professor Nissim Ezekiel, a poet who heads the English Department of Bombay University; and Abraham Sofaer, the judge who presided over the trial of Ariel Sharon versus *Time* magazine in New York. One non-Jew from Bombay whose link with the Jewish people is profound is Zubin Mehta, director of the New York and Israel Philharmonic orchestras.

Jewish communal activity in Bombay today revolves around philanthropic and social work. Jews now living in the city run the gamut from the real estate speculator who owns nearly three thousand acres of downtown Bombay and lives in a first-class neighborhood on Malabar Hill to the barefoot and indigent who live in the "hutments," or shantytowns. To promote the general welfare and well-being of the entire Indian Jewish community, the Council of Indian Jewry has been formed.

India's apparently anti-Israel position does not seem to disturb its Jews. They see it as a pragmatic outgrowth of the fact that their country is one-ninth Muslim and nonaligned, as well as of the inevitable viewpoint of a country that itself opposed, and still opposes, a British partition plan. Besides, the Israeli flag flies over the Israeli consulate in Bombay and India's Jews travel back and forth freely—via Cairo.

SIGHTS: When on the trail of Indian Judaica in and around Bombay, sightseeing assumes more than the usual dimensions as Westerners are thrust into a world far removed from most hitherto experienced. Indeed, even within the city, many sights are tucked behind unprepossessing, graffiti-covered walls and gates in neighborhoods reminiscent of Kipling. Pushcarts—and pullcarts—still running on wooden wheels rumble up and down winding, twisting, unpaved streets. Naked and near-naked children play in front of peeling, often crumbling, houses and huts. Barefoot vendors hawk nuts and fruits, baubles and old clothes; others, beturbaned, squat atop burlap bags in tiny dark cubbyholes. The crush is claustrophobic; the din is deafening; the air is redolent of spices. And then, at the moment of greatest disorientation, from a hovel steps a man in a dhoti or a woman in a sari who offers the greeting "Shalom."

Indeed, a visit to Bombay's old Jewish neighborhoods—Dongri, Mandvi, and Byculla—means leaving the beaten tourist trail completely. Even if you are armed with addresses, it is virtually essential to travel with a guide, so difficult is it to find the right path or alley, and so regularly do street names change. En route to the Jewish sites are the city's largest train terminal, the Indo-Gothic Victoria Station, and the frenetic Crawford Market. But quickly the scene becomes one of dilapidated, decaying tenements with wash flapping from balcony railings. Jews once lived in these buildings, some still adorned with delicately carved woodwork and traces of turquoise and pink paint; Jews even once owned many of them. But today they are filled primarily with Muslims.

These areas harbor several synagogues and prayer halls—some nearly derelict, others still functioning. And each has its own special flavor and treasure—be it a particularly elaborate Torah covering or an intricately woven Indian carpet on the floor. Yet, there are similarities as well. The synagogues are small, sometimes only storefront size and, in Sefardic tradition, have altars in the center of the room with women's galleries upstairs. Almost all use teak for the Ark. Many are decorated with strings of tiny colored Christmas-tree-type lights. Hanging all around are large, acorn-shaped, glass lamps fueled with coconut oil, which are lit when donations are made. And all synagogues are entered barefoot.

Among those B'nai Israel places of worship worth seeing are: Shaar Harahamim, with its ornate Ark carvings and its ten wood-encased Torahs covered in crimson, royal purple, and blue velvet (254 Samuel Street); Shaare Rason, with its cut-glass lamps, its Ark outlined with red, green, orange, and yellow lights, and its Indian-rug-covered altar (90 Tantanpura Street); Tiferet Israel, with its red and green lights, its green, blue, and decal-covered oil lamps, and its carpeted altar (92 K. K. Marg, Jacob Circle); Magen Hasidim, a well-kept ocher and brown building, with two pillars framing its front entrance, a tiled, outdoor pavilion, and an illuminated Magen David (8 Mohomed Shahid Marg, formerly Moreland Road); Etz Hyeem Prayer Hall, upstairs in a rickety building, and sharing a floor with the office of the Friends of Indian Jews, a charitable organization helping the destitute (19 Umerkhadi, 2nd Cross Lane). Diagonally across the way from the prayer hall building is a white sign with red lettering. In Marathi and Hebrew, it says *"basar kasher,"* one of three kosher butchers in and around Bombay. (The others are in Kurla and Thane, the latter, an outlying suburb with a fair-sized Jewish community these days and an active synagogue.)

Not far from the prayer hall is Mazagaon Road, where the Sir Elly Kadoorie School Compound, with ORT India, is located. The Kadoorie School is one of two Jewish high schools in Bombay (the other is the Jacob Sassoon High School), but it now admits children of all backgrounds, as do both the boys' and girls' schools. In Byculla, at 36 Sussex Road, is Rodef Shalom Synagogue, which appeals to young people because it is Reform.

The first Baghdadi synagogue, Magen David, is located on Sir J. J. Road, sharing grounds with the Jacob Sassoon school; while Keneseth Eliyahoo, an airy, powder-blue synagogue with a marble floor, is conveniently found in the downtown Bombay Fort area, on Dr. V. B. Gandhi Marg.

SIDE TRIP: But to understand truly the circumstances from which the B'nai Israel come, the Konkan Coast itself must be visited. This lush area, so covered with palm and mango trees that often the sunlight cannot get through the leaves, can easily be seen in a day with a car and driver.

Just a half hour beyond the bridge to the mainland is Panvel (or Penwel), a typical Konkan Coast town with dirt streets trod by cows and barefoot people transporting major loads on their heads. This is home to seventeen Jewish families—about eighty persons in all—and the Beth-El Synagogue on Mahatma Gandhi Road.

This synagogue is in a "courtyard" edged by dark shacks which use sheets for walls; on the ground outside these living quarters are spread burlap bags for drying peppers in the sun. Inside the synagogue—the paint peeling from its aqua-colored walls—are several Torahs adorned with gold and silver—and the inevitable hanging lamps.

About a half hour further, there is another synagogue in the town of Pen. But the primary Konkan destination is Alibag, about two hours from Panvel, and its surroundings—since this is the area where the Jews first settled.

The sky-blue synagogue in Alibag is set among the palm trees (as is the turquoise, pink, and yellow one at nearby Rewdanda). It stands off a road of thatched-roof shacks once inhabited by B'nai Israel. This is a town where many women still wash their pots and pans in the streets and draw water from a common well. It is progressive, however, when compared with the villages around, where perhaps a hundred Jews still live, some in grand houses, but others in huts so deep among the palms that a trail of breadcrumbs along the winding dirt paths seems in order.

About a mile and a half from Alibag is Khadala—a special site for the B'nai Israel. They venerate the prophet Elijah, almost as if he were a patron saint, keeping his picture in their homes and holding special celebrations in his honor. On a rock well off the road, overlooking a pond, is a marking that is said to have been made by his chariot and the horse's hooves as it bore the prophet to Heaven.

About ten miles from Khadala is Navgaon, the exact place where the B'nai Israel believe their ancestors landed. There is an ancient cemetery there with plain rock markers allegedly over the graves of the original survivors and those who drowned. A large white monument with a six-pointed star as its base has recently been erected here in their memory.

GENERAL SIGHTS: On Elephanta Island, seven miles by launch from the triumphal arch known as the Gateway of India, are four rock-cut temples with large sculptures and sculptured panels dedicated to the god Shiva, which are thought to have been hewn between 450 and 750 C.E. This is a half-day trip.

Along the Bombay waterfront is Chowpatty Beach, where virtually no one swims but everyone "hangs out," doing their own thing. The annual Ganesh Chaturthi Festival, when clay statues of the elephant-headed god are thrown into the sea, winds through the city and culminates at Chowpatty Beach.

Atop Malabar Hill, an upscale residential area with good views of town, are the Hanging Gardens, with hedges cut into animal shapes. Nearby are the Towers of Silence, where Parsis lay out their dead. The Parsis, incidentally, feel a strong kinship with the Jews and are very much like a Jewish minority—well educated and constituting a largely commercial class. It is probably no accident that Zubin Mehta comes from their ranks.

Among Bombay's museums are the Prince of Wales Museum, with archaeological and natural history exhibits and, within the same compound, the Jehangir Art Gallery, Bombay's leading gallery specializing in modern Indian art.

READING: *The Bene Israel of Bombay* by Schifra Strizower (Schocken) is a good sociological study of Bombay's Jewish community.

RECOMMENDATIONS: The Searock Hotel, though out of the center of Bombay, is an exceptionally friendly hostelry, with a strictly vegetarian restaurant on its premises. For assistance with visiting Jewish sights in and around Bombay, good contacts are Esther Moses of the Indian Government Tourist Office (telephone, 29-31-44) and the Council of Indian Jewry (27-04-61). Such contacts are particularly useful in a city where everything—from phone numbers to street names—changes with regularity. Bombay is a place to expect the unexpected. Fortunately, most of what is unexpected will enrich the journey.

—PHYLLIS ELLEN FUNKE

Boston

The Harvard Yard *(Harvard University News Office)*

Boston is a city on a hill, a city by the sea, and one of America's historical treasures. The history-book stories resonate from childhood studies, so that names such as Adams, Thoreau, Emerson, and Alcott seem like personal as well as public memories. Boston is also very much a city of the 1980s. Rich in world-renowned universities, medical centers, and cultural institutions, it retains its reputation as the "Athens of America," even as it acquires new fame as a high-tech mecca.

"The Hub," as natives like to call it—that's short for hub of the universe—is a walkable city. You can get from the posh shops on Newbury Street, by way of blooming Boston Garden with its famous Swan Boat pond, down to Faneuil Hall Marketplace and the harbor in a short hour's stroll. Tourists come from all over the world to walk the brick sidewalks along the road of Paul Revere's famous horseback journey.

As you walk through Revere's old neighborhood and visit the white spire of the Old North Church, where the signal was "one if by land, two if by sea," you find yourself in the middle of one of Boston's most distinctive ethnic areas—the North End. The cafés and snatches of conversation on the street tell you that you're in an Italian immigrant neighborhood. There is no trace of the vibrant Jewish community that the narrow brick tenements of the North End housed during the nineteenth century.

HISTORY: Boston's Jewish presence is pervasive but subtle—a mixture of circumspection and pride that reflects a past of rejection and success. For its first two hundred years, there was no Jewish community in Boston. Indeed, the history of Jewish Boston during the colonial period is the story of a handful of individuals. The first known Jew who arrived received a very chilly welcome. Solomon Franco sailed into the harbor in 1649 with cargo for one of the colonists. A dispute arose and within twelve days he was warned out of town.

The Puritan settlers were inhospitable to dissenting Christians, like Roger Williams and Anne Hutchinson, who were also shown the door. But there was special irony in their treatment of Jews, since the Puritans liked to think of themselves as a "chosen people," whose migration and search for a "promised land" echoed the story of the ancient Hebrews. Indeed, the Hebrew language was honored as God's own and was a required part of the curriculum at Harvard College. Judah Monis—the only Jew to receive a Harvard degree before 1800—taught Hebrew at Harvard, but only after he consented to convert to Christianity. Even so, history records that Monis insisted on keeping the Sabbath on Saturday.

With a few notable exceptions, Jews steered clear of the Massachusetts Bay Colony and Boston until nearly the middle of the nineteenth century, when New England's need for labor coincided with the immigration of German Jews. By 1845, Boston's first synagogue was founded. In the 1880s, Russian and Eastern European Jews arrived in large numbers. By 1900, there was a community of some two thousand, with four hundred self-help and charitable organizations—from burial societies to baseball teams.

In the early part of this century, Boston boasted seven Yiddish newspapers. Zionism found many strong supporters in the North End community, where some of the nation's first Ivrias—schools for teaching modern Hebrew—were established. In 1921, the first Bureau of Jewish Education was organized. Among its first acts was the opening of the first Hebrew teachers college.

COMMUNITY: In its role as an educational center, Boston's importance to the national Jewish community is out of proportion to its numbers. Although it is only the sixth largest Jewish community in America, countless Jews have spent important parts of their lives at one of the area's fifty-four colleges and universities—as undergraduates, medical students, postdoctoral fellows, or law students. Of the 170,000 Jews in Greater Boston, between 35,000 and 40,000 are college students. Over 75 percent of Boston's Jews have college degrees.

Judah Monis's experience is a very distant footnote today, as Jews are esteemed members of virtually every faculty in the city. Of the thirteen Harvard University Nobel Prize winners since 1967, seven were Jewish, their fields ranging from medicine and chemistry to physics and economics; of six Nobel laureates at the Massachusetts Institute of Technology during the same period, four were Jews.

Brandeis University was founded, in 1948, as a result of nationwide fund-raising and organizing. The youngest university with a comparable reputation for academic excellence, its 250-acre campus in suburban Waltham is a point of pride among Boston Jews, who attend lectures there and support its programs in the arts. In Brookline, Hebrew College, which trains Hebrew teachers, has become a community-wide *lehrhaus,* a place for continuing adult education on topics ranging from hasidic art to Jewish business ethics.

While Brandeis claims the largest Judaic studies program in the nation, specifically Jewish learning isn't limited to Jewish institutions. Novelist Elie Wiesel teaches at Boston University and Rabbi Isadore Twersky is professor of Jewish studies at Harvard, to mention only two. No wonder the American Jewish Studies Conference, which brings together the best and the brightest, meets annually in Boston.

Boston is as religiously diverse as any Jewish community in the world. Nearly 120 congregations serve the greater Boston area. Additionally, there are dozens of independent minyans and havurot, small groups that meet for religious study and observance in people's homes. The Bostoner Rebbe, Grand Rabbi Levi Yitzhak Horowitz, is known around the world for his great hospitality; the hasidic leader invites everyone to share a meal at his tish (table). Another revered teacher who makes Boston his home is Rabbi Joseph Baer Soloveitchik, known as the Rav. A Talmudic scholar and leader of modern Orthodoxy, he founded the Maimonides Hebrew Day School.

Boston is also the home of alternative Judaism. Havurat Shalom, founded in 1968 as a religious community and seminary, helped give rise to what has come to be called the Jewish renewal movement.

Diversity of opinion is also reflected in the variety of Jewish publications in Boston; in addition to the *Jewish Advocate* and *The Boston Jewish Times,* the weekly community newspapers, Boston is also home to *Moment,* an independent national magazine, and *Genesis 2,* a monthly committed to Jewish renewal.

SIGHTS: Boston is known as a city of ethnic neighborhoods and, during their history in the city, Jews have lived in many of them— starting in Boston's South End, moving to the North End, then to the now-destroyed West End. The forties and fifties saw Jews in the tripledeckers and elegant homes of Roxbury, Dorchester, and Mattapan, where the imposing synagogues now serve as churches and county buildings for the area's predominantly black population.

Today Jews live throughout the Boston area, in virtually every suburb, with communities in quaint Yankee ports like Marblehead on the North Shore, western "bedroom" towns like Sudbury, and southern exurbs like Sharon. But the heart of this far-flung community is

Brookline. On Harvard Street, the main commercial thoroughfare, you will still hear Yiddish spoken. People come from all over the region to buy hallah and kosher meat, Judaica and Jewish books. The shop windows are papered with announcements about concerts of Jewish music and lectures on Jewish topics. Here are found two kosher restaurants: Rubin's deli and the vegetarian-dairy Café Shalom.

Boston's oldest synagogue, founded in 1845, is Congregation Ohabei Shalom, now housed in a beautiful Byzantine-Romanesque structure, featuring a large blue-green dome on tree-lined Beacon Street in Brookline. The brick and granite building is reminiscent of early synagogue architecture in the Near East. Its sanctuary, beneath the impressive dome that hangs one hundred feet above street level, contains no columns, making for a spacious and airy worship space.

Temple Israel of Boston (at Longwood and Plymouth) makes a completely different architectural statement. With some seventeen hundred families, it is the largest congregation in New England and is housed in a meeting house of Greek Revival granite, complete with graceful Ionic columns. It is located a few blocks from Beth Israel Hospital, founded in the nineteenth century, which may be the most visible manifestation of the Jewish community to non-Jewish Boston.

The low-lying modern structures of the Brandeis campus nestle among wooded rolling hills in Waltham. The most distinctive building is the Castle, a medieval-looking tower left over from the days when the land was occupied by a small medical school. The Castle now functions as a dormitory and student center.

The handsome new Gosman Jewish Community Center, located on twenty-eight acres in Newton, opened in 1982 and has a membership of ten thousand. The center provides a full range of social, educational, athletic, and cultural activities. A complex of housing for the elderly has also been opened on the site.

Less apparent to the visitor is the wealth of Judaica in Boston's many fine libraries. Harvard University has more than 150,000 volumes in Hebrew, Yiddish, and English; Brandeis over 90,000 books, and Hebrew College some 85,000 volumes. The Boston and Brookline public libraries also have impressive collections. The American Jewish Historical Society, located on the Brandeis University campus, houses an additional 75,000 volumes and nearly seven million manuscripts.

The Historical Society is also a repository for photographs, newspapers, and artifacts of the Jewish experience throughout the Americas. These archives include the papers of organizations like the American Jewish Congress and the Jewish Welfare Board as well as the papers of individuals like Rabbi Stephen S. Wise and actress Molly Picon. The society is open to the public and exhibits from the collection are always on view. A display of wonderful Yiddish theater posters hangs in the main room.

CULTURE: Boston boasts an internationally acclaimed symphony orchestra and one of the finest art museums in the nation. It is also rich in Jewish arts—especially Jewish music of every description. With three albums to its credit, the Klezmer Conservatory Orchestra is one of the leading forces in the popular revival of the Yiddish repertory of Eastern Europe. The Zamir Chorale, a twenty-six-year-old community chorus, performs Israeli folk songs as well as major choral works by Handel and liturgical music from many centuries. Safam has produced many albums of original folk-rock Hebrew and English songs. Performing in Ladino, and using ancient instruments, Voice of the Turtle plays the Sefardic songs of Spain. And Hamakor, a local Israeli folk dance troupe, has created movement for virtually every kind of Jewish music. (For information about performances, check the shop windows along Harvard Street in Brookline, or pick up a copy of the *Jewish Advocate, Genesis 2,* or *The Boston Jewish Times.*

In the visual arts, the Pucker Safrai Gallery on gallery-studded Newbury Street displays some of the world's finest Jewish painters, printmakers, and sculptors, including David Sharir, Shraga Weil, Reuven Rubin, and Marc Chagall. In addition to a collection of prints and paintings with Jewish themes, Kolbo, on Harvard Street in Brookline, is the premiere showcase for original American Judaica on the East Coast, with works in porcelain, wood, paper, fabric, and stone.

READING: Boston plays a large part in three memoirs of different eras. Mary Antin's classic, *The Promised Land: The Autobiography of a Russian Immigrant* (Ayer), chronicles the misery of Jewish Boston in the 1800s. Theodore H. White's book *In Search of History: A Personal Adventure* (Harper & Row) includes memories of his Dorchester childhood. Finally, Burton Bernstein's *Family Matters: Sam, Jenny and the Kids* (Summit) follows one family's movement as Jewish Boston emigrated from Dorchester and Roxbury into suburbs like Newton and Sharon; it also provides fascinating biographical details about the author's brother, composer, and conductor Leonard Bernstein.

PERSONALITIES: Boston Jews of national and international fame include other musicians, as well as authors, jurists, and sports figures. The late Arthur Fiedler, conductor of the Boston Pops, made his home there, and the Boston Celtics wouldn't be the Boston Celtics without Arnold "Red" Auerbach. Justin Kaplan, the Pulitzer Prize–winning biographer, lives in Cambridge with his wife, novelist Anne Bernays. Martin Peretz, publisher of *The New Republic,* and historian Oscar Handlin are Bostonians—as are *New York Times* columnist Anthony Lewis, *Boston Globe* columnist Ellen Goodman, and attorney Alan Dershowitz. It was altogether fitting that America's Jewish-sponsored, nonsectarian university should be named after Bostonian Louis Brandeis, the first Jew appointed to the United States Supreme Court. Barbara Walters and Leonard Nimoy, two Bostonians who have made their mark away from home, round out a highly selective list.

The Jewish presence is especially prominent in the city's impressive medical establishment and in the arts. Some twenty-nine of the Boston Symphony Orchestra's one hundred members—as well as the chairman of its board of trustees—are Jews. Even so, the Jewish community shares some of the sternly private, self-effacing qualities of the Puritans and Yankees who set the city's tone. Although they live only a few hundred miles apart, Boston Jews and New York Jews sometimes seem as different in their habits as Sefardim and Ashkenazim.

GENERAL SIGHTS: Boston has something for everyone. During the summer, large boats sail the harbor at sunset and in the evenings, featuring music, dinner, and dancing. A few blocks from the famous Museum of Fine Arts is the less known but much more Bostonian Isabella Stewart Gardner Museum, at 280 Fenway, whose extensive greenhouses make for beautiful displays in the mansion's courtyard.

For the inveterate shopper, Filene's basement is an absolute must. It just so happens that Filene's was founded by one of the city's most prominent early Jewish families, which started in the dry goods business with one Yiddish Yankee peddler. Today, Filene's is one of New England's largest retailing operations.

Solomon Franco would be amazed by modern Boston. On Yom Haatzmaut, Israel Independence Day, Jews of every affiliation and opinion turn out for a celebration at the Hatch Shell Amphitheater on the Esplanade, part of a city-wide system of parks called the Emerald Necklace. Thousands of people come to enjoy a program of speeches,

Israeli music and dance. With the city's skyline of old brick and new glass reflecting in the Charles River, this celebration has become a perfect expression of how Jews have come to feel at home in Boston.

—ANITA DIAMANT

Brooklyn

Brooklyn Bridge *(Chuck Lewis/Borough of Brooklyn)*

You can take Manhattan—if you want glitz and glitter. But to experience traditional Yiddishkeit in the borough with the largest Jewish community in the United States—go to Brooklyn, my friend.

Once home to tribes of Algonquin Indians, Brooklyn today has nearly 413,000 Jews, a veritable ingathering from Eastern Europe, Asia, and Africa. The Jewish population had peaked in the early 1950s at around a million, before the movement to Queens and Long Island. Jewish Brooklynites have enriched the borough for over 150 years, not only religiously, but culturally, politically, and economically.

HISTORY: Although there was a Jewish presence in "Bruecklen" as far back as 1660, when Asser Levy bought property there, there was no permanent Jewish community until the 1830s; the first settlements were Borough Hall and Williamsburg. An apocryphal story relates that the new settlers had to row across the East River to Manhattan on Friday afternoon for services and return to Brooklyn on Sunday. Public Jewish worship wasn't held until 1851, when the first Jewish congregation, Kahal Kodesh Beth Elohim, was organized in the home of Moses Kessel; its first synagogue was erected in 1876 at 274 Keap Street and continues to function as the "Keap Street Shul."

Many early Jews first visited Brooklyn to attend funerals, after burials were banned in Manhattan. The first Jewish cemetery in Brooklyn, Union Fields in Cypress Hills, opened in 1848. The graves of Supreme Court Justice Benjamin Cardozo, Emma Lazarus, Commodore Uriah P. Levy, and Rabbi Judah L. Magnes are in the old section; in the newer Mount Carmel Cemetery lie Sholom Aleichem and Benjamin Schlesinger, founder of the International Ladies Garment Workers Union.

The first Jewish settlers suffered their share of anti-Semitism. In 1877 in Plymouth Church, the Reverend Henry Ward Beecher—brother of Harriet Beecher Stowe, who wrote *Uncle Tom's Cabin*—defended the Jews, creating a national stir in a sermon that remains a classic of philo-Semitism.

Soon there were Jews living in the shorefront communities of Coney Island, Brighton Beach, Manhattan Beach, and Seagate. A still-functioning landmark on the boardwalk—once the amusement park of the East—is Nathan's Famous where, beginning in 1915, proprietor Nathan Handwerker promoted the nickel hot dog.

In 1881, after Tsarist pogroms, a flood of East European Jews poured into Brooklyn, joining the German-Jewish immigrants. One of the most dynamic communities was Brownsville which, by 1917, rivaled the Lower East Side as an all-Jewish neighborhood. Many of Brooklyn's first Jewish labor, educational, and community institutions were started there. Today none of Brownsville's two hundred synagogues remains open.

With the construction of the Williamsburg and Manhattan bridges early in this century, as well as the elevated and subway lines, Williamsburg became the first stop to suburbia. Prospering Jews moved there from the Lower East Side and then on to Borough Park, Crown Heights, and Bensonhurst. The Manhattan Bridge was designed and built by Leon Solomon Moisseiff, a Russian-born Jew.

COMMUNITY: After World War II, Hasidim, particularly Satmar, moved to Williamsburg, the "Jerusalem of America." Flatbush, however, has become the "Aleppo" of the more than twenty thousand close-knit Syrian, Egyptian, and Lebanese Jews in Brooklyn. Many live along Ocean Parkway, one of the more attractive areas in the borough.

Recently, Brighton Beach has been transformed from the "Miami of the senior set" into a revitalized "Little Odessa," with the influx of over twenty-five thousand Soviet Jews, putting back the neighborhood's bloom with Russian nightclubs, shops, and an enlivened boardwalk. In Williamsburg, Yiddish signs proclaim Lee Avenue as the main shopping area for the hasidic community; most Hasidim live in the Bedford Avenue brownstones. The decrepit exteriors contrast with the safety and vibrancy of this community. While hasidic entrepreneurs work in a variety of fields, many are employed in New York's diamond district on Forty-seventh Street. Because the Satmar do not wish to mingle with "outsiders," they maintain their own bus system. Satmar headquarters is at Congregation Yetev Lev D'Satmar at 152 Rodney Street.

Lubavitcher Hasidim are deeply entrenched in Crown Heights. They have political clout and proprietary rights in a neighborhood once threatened with deterioration and desertion by its Jews.

Canarsie, Flatbush, and Bensonhurst are Jewish strongholds. Congested and drab Borough Park has Yemenite, Israeli, and "modern"

Jews, but primarily it is hasidic territory—with more than twenty hasidic dynasties.

Borough Park, where Orthodoxy predominates, is probably the most thriving and dynamic area of Jewish Brooklyn. Though many residents are professionals or are engaged in a variety of businesses and trades, the hundreds of shuls, yeshivas, and rabbinical seminaries would seem to be the main industry, to judge by their proliferation. There are 40 yeshivas and 250 shuls in a 200-square-block radius in Borough Park.

In Williamsburg, Bensonhurst, and Crown Heights, as well as in Borough Park, shtreimels, sheitels, payes, and tzitzis are alive and well and worn with pride. Neither is Brooklyn Yiddishkeit just a local brew; its influence is worldwide. The Lubavitcher Rebbe, Menachem Mendel Schneerson, directs his hasidic empire from 770 Eastern Parkway in Crown Heights. Indeed, outsiders who come to study and shop in these neighborhoods take home with them more than the seforim, mezuzahs, kosher pizza, and shmura matza they purchase.

You can also find a Jewish Yuppieville in the lovely Park Slope section. Young Jewish professionals are renovating the nineteenth-century brownstones along Carroll, Garfield, and Montgomery streets, near Congregation Beth Elohim—the Garfield Place Temple —Brooklyn's first Reform synagogue.

Brooklyn has its share of organizations. The Borough Park Community Council, in particular, works for the political and social betterment of the Jewish neighborhoods.

PERSONALITIES: One of the most politically prominent Jewish sons of Brooklyn is Abraham D. Beame, who became New York's first Jewish mayor, in 1973. Howard Golden is the most recent in a long line of Jewish borough presidents.

Many major cultural institutions in Brooklyn grew because of Jewish vision and philanthropy. Nathan Jonas played a key role in establishing Brooklyn College, which has graduated several generations of Jewish students. Joe Weinstein, an immigrant who built the Mays department store chain, was called "Mr. Brooklyn" because of his munificent endowments to a variety of organizations. Julius Bloom, once director of the Brooklyn Academy of Music, made it the borough's principal mecca for the arts. A success with several stores in the electronics market in the Metropolitan area—attributable in part to his "insane commercials"—is Crazy Eddie's Eddie Antara, a Sefardi from Brooklyn.

The roll call of prominent Jews—many in the entertainment industry—with roots in Brooklyn is inordinately long. To name a few: film directors and comedians Woody Allen and Mel Brooks; novelists Norman Mailer, Bernard Malamud, Erich Segal, Joseph Heller, and Alfred Kazin; playwright Arthur Miller; science-fiction writer Isaac Asimov; actors Elliot Gould, Zero Mostel, and Alan Arkin; actress Lauren Bacall; columnist Sylvia Porter; opera star Beverly Sills; theatrical impresario Joseph Papp; economist Milton Friedman; Colonel David "Mickey" Marcus, a West Pointer who organized and led the Israeli Army; singer Barbra Streisand; singer-composers Neil Sedaka, Marvin Hamlisch, and Barry Manilow; composers Aaron Copland and George Gershwin; magician Harry Houdini; and Dodgers' pitcher Sandy Koufax.

SIGHTS: The subway is convenient to get to most places—although it is not noteworthy for its esthetics. Given the dispersal of Jewish sights, however, a car can be equally convenient. The best way to start with any of the main Jewish neighborhoods is to walk to its main street—Lee Avenue in Williamsburg, for example, or Brighton Beach Avenue in "Little Odessa."

Be in Williamsburg on Simhat Torah or Purim or for a hasidic wedding—all spill out into the streets. Call Lubavitch, (718) 493-9250, to find out where you can watch the baking of shmura matza before Pesach.

Walk down Forty-eighth Street in Borough Park to watch the people, especially the stylish young mothers pushing their baby carriages; read the signs in store windows to find out about concerts and lectures; enter the bookstores to marvel at the breadth of the collections of Judaica. Visit the new three-million-dollar Bobover shul, at Fifteenth Avenue and Forty-eighth Street, with its Moorish arches, rounded stained-glass windows, and Venetian floral motifs. Its angled ark and podium is modeled after that of the Portuguese Synagogue in Amsterdam. One-way mirrors, designed by architect and travel writer Asher Israelowitz, allow women to see and enjoy the services from the balcony, but prevent the men from viewing the women.

The Sephardic Community Center, 1901 Ocean Parkway, in Flatbush, built in 1982, is a centerpiece of modern architectural beauty—with a Mediterranean flavor—and Sefardic culture. Go when there is a presentation of authentic Middle Eastern traditional music. Telephone, (718) 627-4300.

Magnificent synagogues abound. Congregation Beth-El of Boro Park (Orthodox), 4802 Fifteenth Avenue, has lights in its dome that form the pattern of a Star of David. The Brooklyn Jewish Center (Conservative), 667 Eastern Parkway, in Crown Heights, is the forerunner of the synagogue center and has been a landmark since 1920.

Union Temple (Reform), 17 Eastern Parkway, with twelve stories, may be the world's tallest synagogue. Its frescoed ceiling depicts the temple's history.

Congregation B'nai Yosef, 1616 Ocean Parkway in Flatbush, has eight thousand square feet and two levels that are completely covered with murals. Artist Archie Rand's iconograpy on thirty-seven themes was declared "kosher" for the Orthodox synagogue by Rabbi Moshe Feinstein, the leading halakhic deciser of his time.

The United Munkacser Yeshivos at Forty-seventh Street and Fourteenth Avenue is another huge, impressive edifice.

The borough's cornucopia of yeshivas may be its crowning glory. There are 217 Jewish schools in Brooklyn—165 of them are yeshivas and day schools. Day schools, such as the Yeshiva of Flatbush, at 919 E. Tenth Street, and yeshivas and rabbinical seminaries, such as Torah Vodaath, 425 E. Ninth Street, also in Flatbush, have worldwide reputations.

If you want an insider's look around the borough, contact Brooklyn born-and-bred Lou Singer—he'll share his intimate knowledge of the area's architecture, ethnic neighborhoods, history, and good dining. Call him at (718) 875-9084.

CULTURE: *The Jewish Press* and *The Jewish Week,* both weeklies, are good sources for finding out what's happening culturally in the Jewish community. Walt Whitman Hall at Brooklyn College in Flatbush is where Yoel Sharabi, Mordechai Ben David, Shlomo Carlebach, the Miami Boys Choir, and the Shteeble Hoppers concerts are usually presented. A recent innovation on the Jewish entertainment scene is Ashira, an Orthodox woman singer who performs for all-female audiences.

There once were two Jewish theaters in Brownsville, when that area enjoyed its Yiddish heyday. Today you can drop in at the Shorefront Y in Brighton Beach on a Friday night, from the end of April until the High Holidays, to enjoy folk dancing. Don't be surprised if you see more than three thousand people fill the huge outdoor lot with lively dancing.

The Brooklyn Museum, Eastern Parkway and Washington Avenue, telephone, (718) 638-5000, closed Mondays, has no permanent Judaica collection but does occasionally have special exhibits on Jewish subjects. Of interest, however, is a frieze of Moses, Daniel, Jeremiah, and Isaiah on the exterior of the museum, while inside are busts of Brooklyn-born comedian Alan King and entertainer Danny Kaye.

The Chai Gallery (Chasidic Art Institute), 375 Kingston Avenue in Crown Heights, is unusual in that it showcases the considerable talents of hasidic artists. Telephone, (718) 774-9149. Don't miss it.

You may also want to pay a visit to the Center for Holocaust Studies, 1610 Avenue J in Flatbush. Directed by Yaffa Eliach, a Holocaust survivor and author of *Hasidic Tales of the Holocaust* (Oxford University Press), the center has tapes of interviews, slides, movies, photos, and clothing related to that devastating period. It is open Monday through Thursday. Telephone, (718) 338-6494.

EATING: There is no dearth of kosher pizza and felafel shops, dairy, deli, and meat restaurants. In Borough Park, several are located along Thirteenth Avenue. Sefardic delicacies are found in stores along Kings Highway; other eateries are on Avenue J, all in Flatbush. For kosher Chinese cuisine there is Shang-Chai, 2189 Flatbush Avenue and Yun-Kee, 1424 Elm Avenue, both in Flatbush.

HOTELS: If you are attending a simha in Borough Park and all you need are sleeping accommodations, try the Park House Hotel, 1206 Forty-eighth Street. It has no dining facilities.

READING: *Jewish Landmarks of New York* by Bernard Postal and Lionel Koppman (Fleet Press) blends history and anecdotes of early Brooklyn. The distinctive Sefardic odyssey in America is detailed in *Magic Carpet: Aleppo-in-Flatbush* by Joseph A. D. Sutton (Thayer-Jacoby). *From Suburb to Shtetl, The Jews of Boro Park* (Temple University) by Egon Mayer is a thoughtful sociological study.

In fiction, there is *The Chosen* by Chaim Potok (Fawcett); *To Brooklyn with Love* by Gerald Green (Trident); *The Assistant* by Bernard Malamud (Farrar, Straus & Giroux); *Sophie's Choice* by William Styron (Random House); *Before My Life Began* by Jay Neugeboren (Simon & Schuster)— all of which deal with past generations growing up in Brooklyn. *Damaged Goods* by Thomas Friedman (Permanent Press) presents a more recent look at the Orthodox Brooklyn milieu. *Holy Days: The World of a*

Hasidic Family (Summit) by Lis Harris offers an unusually colorful, yet objective portrait of Eastern Parkway Lubavitch culture.

But don't spend too much time reading. Brooklyn is there to be experienced.

—ZELDA SHLUKER

Brussels

St. Michel Cathedral *(Belgian National Tourist Office)*

Brussels is best known for waffles, chocolate, mussels, french fries, and parks. There may not be Jewish elements in all of these noted items, but two of the city's parks do have Jewish connections. The Botanic Garden, on the Boulevard du Jardin Botanique, was created by Leo Errera, a nineteenth-century Belgian Jewish botanist. The Bois de la Cambre, south of the center of town, in the closest thing Brussels has to Jewish suburbs, is the place where local Jews enjoy the out-of-doors.

HISTORY: The first century of Jewish presence in Brussels was the stuff of which Jewish misery is made. During the Black Death epidemic of 1348–49, Jews were accused of poisoning the wells and were massacred. The community had barely reconstituted itself when, in 1370, Jews were accused of desecrating some Hosts—the consecrated wafers used in communion. Several Jews were burned at the stake and the community was expelled.

Some Marranos arrived from Spain in the sixteenth and seventeenth centuries, but there was no significant Jewish presence in Brussels again until the Treaty of Utrecht in 1713. In the succeeding hundred years, during which Belgium was under Austrian and French rule and united with Holland, Jews from Germany, the Netherlands, and Alsace settled in Brussels. When Belgium achieved independence in 1830, religious freedom was decreed.

Immigration from Poland and Russia fed the community in the late nineteenth and early twentieth century and, after 1933, refugees from Germany arrived. On the eve of World War II, there were thirty thousand Jews in the city. Many of Belgium's Jews, perhaps a majority, fled to France or overseas in advance of the German invasion of 1940, but some were lured back by Nazi efforts to assuage Jewish fears at the beginning of the occupation. Deportations began in July 1942; Jews were sent first to an assembly camp near Mechlin and then to extermination camps in the east. Roughly half of Brussels's prewar Jewish population died in the Holocaust. The Belgian people, including the Catholic Church and the Royal Family, were notable in their defense of Jews during the war. After the war, Queen Elisabeth became the first member of a royal family to visit Israel.

Brussels was an important transit point for postwar Jewish migrants to Israel and the United States; there was a time during the 1950s when the Jewish population approached the prewar level. By the 1960s, however, it had stabilized and today numbers twenty-five thousand.

Jews were prominent in all phases of Belgian life by the beginning of the twentieth century. Four-time Foreign Minister Paul Hymans became president of the League of Nations Assembly. General Louis Bernheim was one of the nation's most decorated soldiers in World War I. Between the wars General Ernest Wiener was commander of Belgium's military academy. Brussels has also produced personalities as diverse as anthropologist Claude Lévi-Strauss, Gerald Frydman, one of the chief animators for Walt Disney Studios, designer Diane Von Furstenberg, and chanteuse-hostess Régine.

COMMUNITY: One can hardly describe the Jewish community of Brussels without distinguishing it from that of Antwerp. No other country has two Jewish centers so nearly equal in size and so different in character. Antwerp, in the Flemish-speaking part of Belgium, has thirteen thousand Jews; the community is close-knit, predominantly Orthodox, Yiddish-speaking, and heavily concentrated in the diamond business. The Jews of Brussels are acculturated, French-speaking, Zionist but secular, and widely distributed professionally. They share more with the Jews of Paris than with the Jews of Antwerp. Intermarriage, comparatively rare in Antwerp, is about 50 percent in Brussels. Like America, however, Brussels is experiencing a rise in non-Jewish spouses becoming involved in Jewish affairs and converting to Judaism. About 20 percent of the city's Jewish children attend Jewish day schools and an additional 70 percent take Jewish-studies classes offered in the public schools.

There is nothing in the way of an old Jewish neighborhood. Jewish stores exist but are not concentrated in one area. The neighborhoods with the largest Jewish presence are Uccle, Ixelles, and Forest (near the Bois de la Cambre) and, closer to the center, St. Gilles, upper Anderlecht, and Schaerbeek.

SIGHTS: While Brussels is not known for Jewish sights and attractions and you may not want to go there for Jewish activities alone, it is nice to know that if the Belgian capital is on your itinerary, there are many places of Jewish interest.

There are no signs left, but the stairway leading up from Rue Ravenstein to the Palais des Beaux-Arts is the approximate site of the entrance to the Jewish ghetto destroyed in the fourteenth century. A few blocks to the north, at the Cathedral of St. Michel (also known as Ste. Gudule), you can see how the fourteenth-century ritual accusation against the Jews has been preserved in memory. A stained-glass window in the beautiful church depicts Jews desecrating the Host. A plaque near the window says that the scene depicted is legend, not fact. The church is undergoing renovation, however, and at any given time several of the stained-glass windows are covered.

Several blocks south of the Ravenstein ghetto site is the Rue de la Régence Synagogue, the most attractive in Brussels. (The entrance is at 2 Rue Dupont.) The stately traditional synagogue, built in 1878, is distinguished by its own stained-glass windows, carved wood bimah, arched white stone and high-backed wooden pews. It also has a priest's pulpit, at the top of a curved stairway, used only on Yom Kippur. The Belgian Jewish Museum is located in the synagogue building, which also houses several Jewish organizations.

The National Monument to the Jewish Martyrs of Belgium is in Anderlecht, at the corner of Rue Émile Carpentier and Rue Goujons. It stands in the middle of a quiet residential neighborhood, a stark square with a menorah made of chains and a wall bearing the names of the 23,838 Jews killed after deportation from Belgium during the German occupation. Behind the main square is a smaller memorial to Jews who fought in the Belgian resistance, with dates that carry a message of their own, such as Helena Ascheim, 1928–42, and Sally Dussman, 1925–44.

CULTURE: Perhaps the best place for Jewish culture is the Centre Communautaire Laic Juifs at 52 Rue Hôtel des Monnaies. The center hosts lectures and seminars that feature leading Jewish figures—who speak French. Lecturers in the past few years have included Shimon Peres, Albert Memmi, Saul Friedländer, Arthur Hertzberg, Bernard Henri Levy, Beate Klarsfeld, and Simone Weil. The center also hosts concerts and art exhibits as well as a Yiddish theater troupe that performs mainly during the winter. It also produces a monthly magazine, *Regards,* which carries news of community affairs and events. Call 537-82-16 for the latest cultural activities. Another good place for lectures is the Martin Buber Institute at 44 Avenue Jeanne (telephone, 648-81-54).

There are two Israeli nightclubs, and several other Israeli-owned shops, on the Rue de la Fourche in the center of the city.

GENERAL SIGHTS: Brussels is, above all, a great city for walking. The center of the city is a maze of narrow old-world streets. The Grand Place, just down the street from the Israeli nightclubs, is one of the most charming squares in Europe. The Royal Museum and the Albert I Library (both of which have Judaica as well as general exhibits) and the Parc de Bruxelles are all within walking distance of the Grand Place.

The David and Alice Museum, 41 Avenue Leo Errera in Uccle, houses the art collection of David van Buuren—a Dutch Jew transplanted to Brussels—and his wife Alice. The building is Art Deco, the collection includes masters as well as modernists, and it is set in a beautiful, labyrinthine garden.

SIDE TRIPS: Knocke and Ostend are beach resorts frequented by Belgian and British Jews. The trip to either from Brussels is little more than an hour, but it's worthwhile to stop for a day along the way in Bruges, a medieval city whose canals have earned it the title "Venice of the North."

RECOMMENDATIONS: There are many fine hotels in Brussels. The best combination of luxury and location is to be found in the Hyatt Regency on Rue Royale, next to the Botanic Garden. It is about a fifteen-minute walk from the Schaerbeek Synagogue at 126 Rue Rogier or the Sefardic Synagogue at 47 Rue du Pavillon and about a half-hour walk from the Rue de la Régence Synagogue.

To find out about kosher food and prayer times at various Brussels synagogues, call the Consistoire Central Israélite de Belgique at 512-21-90. If you want one more Jewish activity before you leave Brussels, remember that the international airport has a synagogue.

—Alan M. Tigay

Buenos Aires

Congregación Israelita de la República Argentina *(Phyllis Ellen Funke)*

Along the streets in the heart of town, crowds stream past, licking ice cream cones and listening to the blare of music from the record shops that never close. In the dimly lit cafes, reminiscent of 1930s Paris, handsome men and stylish women hold muted conversations over cups of coffee and plates of pastry. And in clubs in corners around the city, suave singers croon and lithesome couples bend to the sensuous sway of the tango. This is Buenos Aires today—a city humming with hope.

Once the premier capital of Latin America—11 million people make it the third largest city—Buenos Aires, like the rest of Argentina, has suffered in recent decades from the country's on-again, off-again military regimes. But since the ascension, in December 1983, of Raúl Alfonsín's democratic government, a spirit of revitalization is pervasive.

Among the beneficiaries of the current climate are Buenos Aires's two hundred thousand Jews. About 80 percent of the Jews in Argentina, they constitute the largest Jewish community in Latin America, despite an estimated loss of half their numbers in the last twenty years.

Jewish *porteños*—as natives of Buenos Aires are called—are deeply involved in municipal life. Their textile mills, clothing designers, and shops dress a good portion of the city; their actors and musicians entertain it, and their Hasidim have even been seen strolling on Florida Street, one of Buenos Aires's chic thoroughfares.

Yet despite inclusion in the city's fabric, there is a quality of reserve to Jewish participation, an absence of trumpets. This in all likelihood results from the undercurrents of anti-Semitism that ripple through certain aspects of Argentine life, at times more forcefully than others. Argentina's lack of separation of church and state—indeed, its presidents must be Catholic—legislates against the cultural pluralism that would foster fuller acceptance. Yet Alfonsín is addressing this problem, too.

HISTORY: Not long ago, a *porteño* came before Dr. Richard A. Freund, vice rector of the Seminario Rabínico Latinoamericano, and told him that, although Catholic, she believed she was Jewish. After hearing a lecture on Jewish customs, the woman remembered her grandmother soaking and salting meat and baking with oil instead of butter. What was more, her last name was "Mirrani."

Like other such episodes, this indicates the extent to which the Marranos, escaping the Inquisition, melted into Argentine society. Though only hints of their presence exist, they probably arrived when Buenos Aires was established for the second time in 1580 and continued to come throughout the next century. By the 1700s, however, they were so indistinguishable from their *confrères* that virtually all traces of their existence vanished.

Jews appeared again on the Argentine scene during the great immigrations of the nineteenth and early twentieth centuries. Along with the masses of Spaniards and Italians who were to provide Argentina with its primary population, they came—at first, in small numbers, from Western Europe, later, in large numbers, from Eastern Europe and the Levant. Many established agricultural colonies—Moisesville and Colonia Clara, for example—in the provinces of Buenos Aires, Entre Ríos, La Pampa, and Santa Fe, sponsored by Baron Maurice de Hirsch. Other Jewish immigrants went directly to Buenos Aires.

The first congregation, Congregación Israelita de la República Argentina, formed in 1868 around an English businessman, Henry Joseph. Six years earlier, Joseph, not knowing where to pray on the High Holy Days, went to a Buenos Aires cemetery. Instead of finding himself alone there as he had expected, he encountered enough men with prayerbooks to make the minyan that presaged the congregation, now at Libertad 773.

Until 1917, Argentine Jews faced few external problems. Among themselves, however, they had a major difficulty. Since the overwhelming majority of immigrants were men and there was a shortage of the opposite sex, some enterprising individuals began advertising in Eastern European papers for brides. But when the girls arrived, they were snagged for brothels.

The white slavers were so shunned by the Jewish community that they banded together into their own self-help group called, suggestively, Zvi Migdal (deer's tower), and established their own synagogue and cemetery. Because of the question of the legitimacy of the progeny of the prostitutes during the 1920s, Chief Rabbi Abraham Isaac Kook of the Yishuv in Palestine threatened Argentina's rabbis with excommunication if they performed conversions. This ban has left many Argentines with Jewish blood in spiritual limbo. By the time white slavery was outlawed in 1930, however, some of Buenos Aires's great Jewish fortunes had already been amassed from its conduct.

The Russian Revolution fanned anti-Semitism in Buenos Aires because Jews were equated with Russians who were equated with Bolsheviks, whom the government feared. Antirevolutionary sentiment culminated after a general strike when, during the Semana Trágica (Tragic Week), January 7–13, 1919, a pogrom occurred.

As Argentines grew increasingly nationalistic and xenophobic, anti-Semitism grew stronger. The situation was periodically exacerbated by such events as World War II and the capture by Israel of Adolf Eichmann in Argentina. Nevertheless, Jews continued to arrive and thrive and, during the Perón days, even experienced a lessening of tensions. During the "dirty war" of the 1970s, when suspected subversives were seized without due process by government forces, a disproportionate number of Jews were taken and received worse treatment from the military and the police than others. While outside observers see this as a time of virulent anti-Semitism, many Argentine Jews maintain that the seizures occurred for political reasons only.

COMMUNITY: The Buenos Aires Jewish community's diversity includes divisions and unions cutting across many lines. About 25 percent of the *porteño* Jews are Sefardim; the majority, German and Ashkenazim. The Sefardim tend toward Orthodoxy; the others are generally Conservative or Reform, with large numbers regarding themselves as secular Jews. There are about fifty synagogues in Buenos Aires and a renaissance of interest in matters Jewish is taking place among young people—thanks in part to the work of the Seminario Rabínico, established by the American rabbi Marshall T. Meyer (who returned to the United States in 1984). He also founded a synagogue, Comunidad Bet El (Sucre 3338), which cuts across ethnic lines. Recently, Sefardim have become more active in cultural affairs.

There is a Jewish hospital and Ashkenazi, German, and Sefardic homes for the aged. More than twenty-two thousand youngsters attend seventy-one Jewish primary and secondary schools in greater Buenos Aires and twenty-seven Jewish schools in the provinces. The Argentine parochial school system is considered by some to be the best Jewish educational network in the world. There are also eight yeshivas.

Among the most important umbrella organizations are the Asociación Mutual Israelita Argentina (AMIA), a multidimensional Ashkenazi group that is the largest Jewish organization in the country; the

Entidad Coordinadora Sefardi Argentina, which seeks to centralize Sefardi communal affairs; the Organización Sionista Femenina Argentina, the most important women's organization; and the Delegación de Asociaciones Israelitas Argentinas (DAIA), which represents the Jewish community on political matters before the Argentine Government and deals with the issue of anti-Semitism.

A singular feature of Jewish life in Buenos Aires is its clubs. In their urban manifestations, they resemble the YM-YWHAs of the United States, with ongoing cultural and athletic programs taking place in large and well-apportioned facilities. Often, though, they have related rural operations as well—developments of weekend homes and retreats organized around a variety of outdoor activities. Such clubs serve as the hub of their members' existence. Some leading ones are Sociedad Hebraica (Sarmiento 2233), Maccabi (Tucumán 3135), CASA (Avenida Del Libertador General San Martín 77, Vicente López), and Hakoaj (Estado de Israel 4156), a club which was founded more than half a century ago for Jews who could not join other rowing clubs.

Zionism has a powerful hold on the Buenos Aires community; after Uruguay, Argentine Jews have had the highest per capita aliyah rate in Latin America.

Though Buenos Aires has no Jewish section per se, many Jews are concentrated in the beautiful, tree-lined neighborhood of Belgrano.

CULTURE: Among the various publications read by Buenos Aires Jews are the almost seventy-year-old *Die Presse,* South America's only Yiddish daily; *Judisches Wochenblatt,* a German-Spanish weekly; *La Luz,* a fortnightly Spanish magazine; and *Nueva Presencia,* the weekly Spanish supplement of *Die Presse* and perhaps the best source for cultural information and Jewish listings. Jews can also tune their radios in on Sundays to the "Music and Life of Israel," from 10:30 to 11 A.M. and the "Young Hebrew Hour," from 11 A.M. to 1 P.M. The Sociedad Hebraica has an art gallery.

While Buenos Aires no longer boasts a professional Yiddish theater, performances in Yiddish are held periodically around town. The AMIA has a 350-seat theater that presents almost year-round works of Jewish interest, including semiprofessional Yiddish productions and new Spanish ones, such as *Le Jaim Moisesville,* a musical comedy about the settlement as the young people leave it. AMIA is also trying to develop a Hebrew theater. Zak Jorge of AMIA will provide visitors with information. Call 47-9096 through 9099.

The Fundación Banco Mayo, the philanthropic arm of the Jewish-run Banco Mayo, sponsors a chamber orchestra, Orchestre de Camera, that periodically gives concerts in Buenos Aires's world-class theater, Teatro Colón, and monthly philanthropic concerts in Auditorio Belgrano.

EATING: In this land of superb beef, kosher and kosher-style restaurants come and go. A strictly kosher institution with staying power is Sucat David, an unadorned storefront, currently at 583 Azcuenaga. Juanita Rozemberg runs another at Arribenos 2148; for reservations call 78-45100 or 78-41377. At El Arca de Noé (Noah's Ark) on Ángel Gallardo, in front of the Museo de Ciencas Naturales, one can dine on knishes, farfel, and blintzes, while enjoying a Jewish show.

PERSONALITIES: When Argentina held its first elections since Alfonsín's Radical Party government took office, the Jewish name on most lips was Marcelo Stubrin's. Stubrin headed the winning party list of thirteen candidates running in the Buenos Aires district. Other Jews who rose to power with Raúl Alfonsín are Marcos Aguinis, a writer who became Argentina's vice secretary of culture, and Bernardo Grinspun, who devised the government's economic reform program.

Also in the public arena—but performing strictly for entertainment's sake—are Berta Singerman, an actress who fills stadiums throughout Latin America with her recitals of Spanish poetry; Dina Rot, a singer beloved for her renditions of Argentine and Ladino songs; and Tato Bores (Borenstein), a popular political humorist seen frequently on nationwide television. Others of note are Kive Staiff, a director at the San Martín Municipal Theater; Bernardo Verbitsky, an author; and César Milstein, who did work in Buenos Aires that contributed to his 1984 Nobel Prize for chemistry. A native *porteño* who achieved world renown is the pianist Daniel Barenboim.

Perhaps the most internationally known Argentine Jew of today, however, is one that few mention unless prompted. When queried about Jacobo Timerman, the former publisher of the liberal newspaper *La Opinión,* and author of *Prisoner Without a Name, Cell Without a Number,* the disdainful reply is always that he is "a case apart," implying that they do not consider him part of the Jewish community or equate his experiences with theirs.

SIGHTS: In keeping with Buenos Aires's fondness for things French, the synagogue housing its oldest congregation was inspired by Paris's great Synagogue de la Victoire. This South American emulation, dedicated in 1932 and popularly known as the Libertad Synagogue, stands at the corner of Libertad and Córdoba streets (Libertad 773), only a couple of blocks away from the Teatro Colón. It is also only a five-minute walk from the 220-foot obelisk on the Avenida 9 de Julio, reputedly the world's broadest boulevard, which informally marks the heart of town.

The synagogue contains the small Museo Judeio de Buenos Aires, which features pictures of the synagogue's founders, memorabilia of native Jewish writers such as Alberto Gerchunoff and Ezekiel Korenblit, photographs of various agricultural colonies, religious objects, and an ivory Purim noisemaker fashioned before the Inquisition. To visit the museum, contact the synagogue's rabbi, Simon Moguilevsky, at 45-2474.

Not far from the synagogue is Once, one of several Buenos Aires neighborhoods where Jews were once concentrated. Though Koreans are now moving in rapidly, even today, in this area roughly bounded by the Avenidas Corrientes, Callao, Córdoba, and Larrea, most of the little shops which sell buttons and linens, shoes and sweaters are owned by Jews. This neighborhood also harbors such institutions as AMIA and the Sociedad Hebraica club.

Here, too, around Lavalle and Junín, was the Jewish red-light district. Should you spot buildings marked with unexplained Stars of David, chances are they had nefarious pasts—though most Jewish porteños are unaware of them, or unwilling to talk of them.

On a loftier level, if the opportunity presents itself, attend a Jewish wedding. They are all-night affairs, with interludes of song-and-dance acts to break up the merrymaking and the eating, which usually does not begin until after midnight.

Also to be seen is the Plaza de Mayo. To this spacious square came the hundreds of thousands of porteños to hear the various Peróns address them from the balcony of the Government House, the pink Casa Rosada. Here, too, on Thursday afternoons, kerchiefed mothers and grandmothers, some Jewish, still march on behalf of the desaparecidos—those who disappeared during the "dirty war."

Of general interest are the old neighborhoods of La Boca, with its gaily colored houses and Italian-style cantinas; San Telmo, birthplace of the tango, with its antique shops and Sunday antique market; and Recoleta, with its French-style buildings and the Recoleta cemetery with its avenue of marble vaults, including Eva Perón's.

Short flights from Buenos Aires go to the Jewish communities in the beach resort of Mar del Plata and Paraná, the latter in Entre Ríos, where many agricultural settlements existed. (Even today, Argentina supplies Israel with much of its kosher beef.) Moisesville is about an eight-hour drive from Buenos Aires.

For all sightseeing, some knowledge of Spanish is important, and Yiddish and Hebrew are helpful, since not much English is spoken.

BOOKS AND MOVIES: A work of fiction that colorfully and humorously combines Jewish and Argentine atmosphere in the world of theater is *Hungry Hearts* (Pantheon) by Francine Prose. For more scholarly reading, there are *The Jews of Argentina: From the Inquisition to Perón* by Robert Weisbrot (Jewish Publication Society) and *From Pale to Pampa: A Social History of the Jews of Buenos Aires* by Eugene F. Sofer (Holmes & Meier). *The House on Garibaldi Street* by Isser Harel (Viking) tells the story of the capture of Adolf Eichmann in the Argentine capital. Excerpts from the writings of six Argentine Jews can be found in *Echad: An Anthology of Latin American Jewish Writings,* edited by Roberta Kalechofsky (Micah Press).

Books of Jewish interest may be purchased from, among others, A. Segal, at Corrientes 2854, and E. Milberg, at Lavalle 2223. Titles range from those of Belva Plain and Amos Oz to the bilingual *Pioneros de la Argentina–Los Immigrantes Judíos.*

Sociedad Hebraica (telephone, 48-5570), the YIVO Library (Pasteur 633, third floor, telephone, 47-6624), and the Seminario Rabínico (José Hernández 1750, telephone, 783-2009) all have libraries worth browsing in. Books to look for include Chaim Avni's *The History of Jewish Immigration to Argentina,* in both Hebrew and Spanish, and Alberto Gerchunoff's *Los Gauchos Judíos* (The Jewish Gauchos), which reportedly exists in English.

The film *The Official Story* offers a good contemporary description of the situation in Buenos Aires before Alfonsín's election. It depicts the story of a family whose child has disappeared, a tragedy which befell many Jews. Precisely because Buenos Aires is now free, the "dirty war" is an issue all *porteños,* Jewish and non-Jewish, will be dealing with for a long time to come.

—PHYLLIS ELLEN FUNKE

Cairo

Shaarei Hashamayim Synagogue *(Egyptian State Tourist Administration)*

Most of us first had our consciousness raised about life for Jews in Egypt when we recited *Avadim hayinu l'Pharaoh b'Mizrayim* (We were slaves to Pharaoh in Egypt) at the Passover Seder. The biblical accounts of the sojourns of Abraham, Jacob, and Joseph in Egypt and the bondage there of the Children of Israel are indelibly imprinted on our collective memory. Succeeding Jewish experiences in the land of the Pharaohs have fluctuated between prosperity and scholarship under tolerant rulers and persecution and decimation under fanatical sovereigns.

The Jewish community of Egypt is the second oldest in the world. There have been Hebrews in Israel since Joshua's conquest, and Hebrews have lived in Egypt since the days of the First Temple, according to literary sources.

Cairo became a must for serious Jewish travelers in 1977, after Anwar Sadat made his historic visit to Jerusalem. Since relations between Egypt and Israel were normalized two years later, tens of thousands of Israelis have also traveled to the capital of the Arab world's largest and most influential country.

Drawing world Jewry to Cairo are not only spectacular antiquities and teeming bazaars of copper and gold. Cairo has had a Jewish population since the city was founded as Fustat more than a dozen centuries ago. Their presence and their contributions to both the city and to Judaism have linked Cairo inextricably to Jewish history.

HISTORY: Physical evidence of three thousand years of Jewish presence in Egypt is scarce. Some tourist guides will take you to a desolate spot along the Nile and show you the ostensible place where Moses was found among the bulrushes. More tangible evidence is the eight-hundred-year-old Ben Ezra Synagogue in old Cairo (the original Fustat), just behind an ancient Coptic church built over a crypt where Joseph, Mary, and the infant Jesus are said to have taken shelter when they fled to Egypt to escape Herod's wrath.

A booklet published by the Cairo Jewish community, available from Natan Avraham Moshe, the shammes of the Ben Ezra Synagogue, deduces from the story of Joseph and Mary continuous Jewish residence in Egypt since biblical times. "Joseph was a Jew," the booklet says, "and the logical thing for him to do was to go to his own people for a refuge."

Jews may have lived in old Cairo since its founding in 641. By the tenth century, there were two Jewish communities in the city, as Mesopotamian Jews joined the Palestinian community. The city became the religious and cultural center of Egyptian Jews, with many noted scholars and yeshivas.

As old Cairo—where Maimonides had lived—slowly declined, Jews moved to new Cairo. As in other Muslim cities, Jews as well as Christians were alternately persecuted and tolerated. Particularly under the Mamelukes, from 1250 to 1517, suffering intensified. In 1301 and again in 1316, Jewish and Christian houses of prayer were closed. In 1354, a mob razed all non-Muslim homes that were higher than Muslim ones. During the fifteenth century, synagogues were inspected to make sure that additions to them, which were forbidden, had not been built. Also under the Mamelukes, the economic situation of the Jews, who had been artisans and merchants, was undermined, as they were barred from trading in spices and other products.

By the 1600s, there were three different Jewish communities: Mustaravim (native, Arabic-speaking Jews), Maghrebim (Jews from North Africa), and Spanish refugees. The Spanish Jews excelled in Jewish scholarship and their halakhic decisions were universally accepted.

The Ottoman Turks followed the Mamelukes, interfering less in the affairs of the Jews than their predecessors—except when incited by Muslim fanatics. On such occasions, synagogues were again closed and burials had to be held quietly or at night to avoid Muslim attacks on the funeral procession. When the Turkish governor—who threatened to slaughter Cairo Jews unless the Jewish director of the mint handed over a huge sum of money—was murdered before he could carry out his threat, the community instituted the celebration of Purim Mitzrayim (Egyptian Purim).

Things worsened for the Jews under the Turks before they improved under an independent Egypt. In the early 1900s, the Jewish community rebuilt itself numerically, economically, politically, and culturally. In 1882, there were five thousand Jews in Cairo; in 1917, there were about twenty-five thousand.

Jews were among the founders of the fashionable residential districts of Zamalek, Heliopolis, and Garden City. The community, most of whom were merchants and industrialists, supported a network of synagogues, schools, charitable institutions, and hospitals; it published newspapers in French, Arabic, and Ladino.

By the end of World War II, there were forty-two thousand Jews in Cairo, about two thirds of all those in Egypt. During the war, many Palestinian Jewish soldiers of the British Army's Jewish Brigade were stationed there, including Royal Air Force pilot Ezer Weizman.

Things began to change after the war. In November 1945, a riot organized by "Young Egypt" seared the Jewish quarter, leaving a synagogue, a Jewish hospital, and an old-age home in ashes. After the State of Israel was declared in 1948, hundreds of Jews were arrested; bombs exploded in Jewish neighborhoods; Jewish businesses were looted. Between 1948 and 1959, some twenty-five thousand Jews took the hint and left Egypt.

This scenario was repeated in 1956, during the Sinai Campaign, and again in 1967, during the Six-Day War, with fewer and fewer Jews to arrest and deport. Most who left had to sign statements agreeing not to return and transferring their property to the Egyptian Government.

COMMUNITY: Today the Jewish community is approaching extinction. It now numbers less than 150, almost all of them elderly. The last bar mitzvah was held in 1980, and the boy is now in Israel. The president of the community, Joseph Dana, has five children, and all of them are in school in Israel. The Jewish community office at 13 Sebil el-Khazender Street is open from 11 A.M. to 2 P.M. (telephone, 824613 or 824885). The Israeli Embassy is at 6 Ibn Malik Street in Giza.

Cairo was once the world center of the Karaite sect of Jews. Now the Karaite center is in Ramle, Israel, and the Karaite community of Cairo has been reduced to fifteen elderly men and women, all of them single except for the Haham (religious leader).

SIGHTS: The Ben Ezra Synagogue (6 Harett il-Sitt Barbara) is officially closed for repairs, which are being financed by Nissim Gaon, a former Cairene who is an international businessman and Sefardi leader. The synagogue has been deleted from the itineraries of old Cairo tours, but any tourist guide in old Cairo will take you there if asked. The exterior walls are covered with scaffolding and adorned with some modern Hebrew graffiti—sorry proof that Israel and Egypt are at peace, and Israelis are free to come and go.

Inside, the synagogue is as dusty as it was on the historic day nearly a century ago when Professor Solomon Schechter, then of Cambridge University, carried a ladder up to the women's gallery and climbed through a trap door into the attic genizah. For a thousand years, this was the burial place for every book, manuscript, contract, letter, will, and any other document containing the name of God. Amid the dust and mold of centuries, Schechter found over a hundred thousand documents, revealing the life and customs of the Jews of Egypt and Palestine for a millennium, plus many hitherto unknown Jewish texts in Hebrew and Arabic.

Another illustrious Cairo synagogue not on any tourist itinerary is the Ben Moshe, or Rambam, Synagogue. It is located in the Mouski Quarter, not far from the Khan el-Khalili market, a section once known as Harat el-Yahud, the old Jewish quarter, where Jews no longer live. Unfortunately, the roof of the main building fell in some years ago. There has been talk of repairing it but, unlike the Ben Ezra Synagogue, no one has provided funds for the repairs.

There is one functioning synagogue in Cairo. It is at 17 Adli Pasha Street, in the heart of the business district, a few blocks from the Nile Hilton. Saturday and holiday services are often attended by Israeli embassy officials and visiting Jewish tourists. The entrance, guarded by local police, is from the alley at the side of the synagogue.

The Egyptian Museum houses some artifacts of Jewish history. On the first floor, in the section dedicated to Akhenaton (Amenhotep IV), are letters from Tell el-Amarna, the capital of Akhenaton's empire, to Jewish cities such as Megiddo and Akko, which were under Egyptian sovereignty. The letters form the most important surviving collection of written sources on the political history of Palestine at the end of the fourteenth century B.C.E. Across the hall from the Akhenaton exhibit is a stele (a stone with a rounded head bearing an inscription) written by Merneptah, the son of Ramses II. The inscription mentions the name Israel for the first time in Egyptian text and places the nation somewhere in Palestine. It is regarded as evidence that the biblical exodus had already taken place, sometime during Merneptah's reign (1236–1223 B.C.E.). The stele was taken from the Great Temple of Amon in Karnak, a mile east of Luxor in Upper Egypt.

PERSONALITIES: Cairo's preeminent Jews were rabbinical scholars. The most outstanding was the Rambam—Rabbi Moses ben Maimon, or Maimonides—who was born in Spain in 1135 and, after a sojourn in Morocco, lived most of his adult life in Cairo, where he was the Sultan's physician. He is revered to this day as the foremost interpreter of Jewish law and philosophy. (His two outstanding works are the encyclopedic legal code of the *Mishne Torah* and the philosophical *Guide to the Perplexed.*) He was also an outstanding medical writer. According to tradition, he wrote his codes and responsa in Hebrew and Arabic in an alcove of the Rambam Synagogue. His son Abraham and grandson David were also negidim (leaders) of the Egyptian Jewish community. Elderly members of the Jewish community still come to the synagogue alcove to light candles and pray.

Though the Jews of Ethiopia were isolated from mainstream Jewry for more than a millennium, there was intermittent contact with Egypt. Rabbi David Ibn Zimra, Chief Rabbi of Egypt in the sixteenth century, was the first to recognize the Beta Israel as Jews.

Gershon ben Eliezer Soncino, the last printer of the famous Soncino family, introduced the first Hebrew printing press in Cairo in 1657. It was also the first one in the Middle East outside of Palestine.

One of Egypt's leading financiers in this century was Victor Harari, a Cairo native who served on the board of governors of Egypt's National Bank. The bank itself was established with the help of Ernest Cassel, a Jewish-born German who is also known for financing the construction of the first Aswan Dam. The Egyptian film industry was pioneered by director Toto Mizrachi, whose son Moshe is a prominent Israeli director. Joseph Cattavi was Egypt's chief revenue officer and his son, Joseph, became minister of finance in 1923; another son, Moses, was president of the Cairo Jewish community for forty years. More recent figures to emerge from Cairo include cartoonist Raanan Lurie and the Israeli poet Ada Aharoni.

SIDE TRIPS: The pyramids and Sphinx are in Giza, about an hour from central Cairo. The sound-and-light show is in English on Saturdays, Mondays, and Wednesdays. Dress warmly even on hot summer days; the desert cools quickly at night. The script of the sound-and-light show has not been changed since Camp David: Islam and Christianity are mentioned as monotheistic religions, but Judaism is not.

Most of the glories of ancient Egypt are an hour's flight from Cairo in Luxor on the site of Thebes, the capital of Upper Egypt, in Aswan, in Abu Simbel, and points in between. The most pleasant way to see everything without strain is to take a Nile cruise which stops at various temples between Luxor and Aswan. The food is good and the guides are informative and helpful.

When you get to Aswan, however, you are on your own. The guides know nothing about the fascinating Jewish community that lived in Aswan even before Ezra and Nehemiah rebuilt the Temple. On Elephantine Island, which is a two-minute ferry ride from the Aswan dock, are the ruins of an ancient Jewish temple. Early in this century, a well-preserved archive of papyri written in Aramaic was discovered there, chronicling the history of this unique Jewish outpost.

The Elephantine community was founded in 525 B.C.E. by a battalion of Jewish soldiers hired by the Pharaoh to protect his frontier against Nubian invaders. The army post existed for hundreds of years, and the papyri document a fascinating exchange of correspondence between the Elephantine community and the Jewish authorities in Jerusalem. One of the customs of Elephantine Jews that differed from current halakhah was that both women and men could divorce their spouses.

In the Great Temple in Luxor are several inscriptions of Jewish historic interest, which guides will point out if asked. One concerns the occupation of Israel by Thutmose III, the Pharaoh who conquered Megiddo, and mentions Jerusalem, Akko, and Eilat. The stele of Sesostris III shows his route to Canaan via the northern Sinai and gives the names of some of his Jewish tribute bearers; during Israel's occupation of the Sinai, many of the sites along Sesostris's route were discovered by Hebrew University archaeologists. The relief of Sheshonk I describes Israel and his pillage of the Temple Mount after King Solomon's death.

RECOMMENDATIONS: Most of Cairo's luxury hotels run Nile cruises between Luxor and Aswan. For more information before you leave home, contact the Egyptian Government Tourist Office, 630 Fifth Avenue, New York, N.Y. 10022, telephone, (212) 246-6960.

READING: To brush up on the history of Arab-Jewish relations in Egypt, read *Jews and Arabs: Their Contacts Through the Ages* by S. D. Goitein (Schocken) and Jacob M. Landau's *Jews in Nineteenth-Century Egypt* (New York University Press). Laurie Devine's novel *Nile* (Simon & Schuster) portrays Arabs and Jews in Egypt since 1948. For a fictional picture of Egyptian life, with a few Jewish characters, try Lawrence Durrell's *Alexandria Quartet* (Dutton).

Of course, you probably don't have to go farther than your own bookshelf to find the most ubiquitous source on Jews in Egypt—the Passover Haggadah. History has its ironies. In 1980, the staff of the newly established Israeli Embassy looked all over Cairo for a hall in which to conduct a Seder for 150 people. They finally found a place that had the space, met the security requirements, and was willing to purchase a new set of dishes for kashrut purposes. It was the Pharaoh Hotel.

—JESSE ZEL LURIE

Charleston

Kahal Kadosh Beth Elohim *(Alan M. Tigay)*

"Historic" and "charming" are the adjectives most often used to describe the beautifully preserved antebellum city of Charleston, South Carolina. Behind the sparkling white piazzas, colorful gardens, and soft Southern accents, however, is a community of sturdy survivors. Through wars, natural disasters, and depressions, Charlestonians persevered and today are proud of their traditions and thriving city.

HISTORY: Charleston's Jewish community of 3,500—in a metropolitan area of 450,000—has a long and rich heritage going back to the late 1600s, almost three centuries during which Jews made great contributions to the city's development. The Jewish immigrants who arrived at the busy seaport of Charles Towne, founded by the English in 1670, were part of successive waves of newcomers—English, Scotch-Irish, French Huguenots, Germans, and others—all seeking religious and economic freedom. Their diverse cultural backgrounds shaped a fascinating and unique city—architecturally, culturally, and religiously. Charleston's Jewish community achieved many "firsts" during those centuries.

The first reference to a Jew in the colony appeared in 1695, the year the diary of Governor John Archdale mentions a Spanish-speaking Jew as his interpreter. In 1697, four Jewish merchants arrived. They were followed by Sefardic Jews from the West Indies, chiefly Barbados, and from Spanish and Portuguese colonies where the Inquisition was in force.

Jews in South Carolina were granted more freedom than in any other British colony under the 1669 Carolina Charter. They were permitted to become merchants, traders, and landowners.

Two remarkable Jews of colonial Charleston were Moses Lindo and Francis Salvador. Lindo, an expert indigo sorter from London, helped develop the growing of indigo in South Carolina's Low Country. In 1763, he was appointed inspector general for indigo, the main crop in the colony after rice. Salvador, son of wealthy English Sefardim, came to Charleston to manage family-owned land. His intelligence and good manners helped get him elected to the first and second Provincial Congresses of South Carolina in 1775 and 1776—the first Jew elected to public office in North America. He helped draft the first state constitution and served in South Carolina's first General Assembly.

In August 1776, Salvador, who was strongly anti-British, fought in a local militia against Cherokee Indians equipped by the Tories. He was shot in an ambush and scalped, the first Jew known to die in the American Revolution.

When Charleston was occupied by the British in 1780, the entire population rose to its defense. All of the city's Jewish men enlisted in military service, with many serving in Captain Richard Lushington's company.

For a generation after the Revolution, Charleston's five hundred Jews constituted the largest, wealthiest, and most cultured Jewish community in the United States. Jews branched out into many trades and professions, including politics. A few wealthy Jews bought land and became planters. The arts flourished and Jews, who were fully integrated into Charleston's lively society, participated in this cultural flowering. Mordecai Manuel Noah and Isaac Harby wrote plays that were produced at the Dock Street Theater (the premiere of Harby's *Alberti* was attended by President James Monroe). Jacob Cardozo edited, and later owned, *The Southern Patriot,* one of Charleston's first newspapers. A talented Charleston painter, Solomon Nunes Carvalho, was official artist on John Frémont's fifth expedition to the West in 1841, afterward writing an account of his adventures on Frémont's last and most dangerous trip.

Penina Moise, born in Charleston in 1797, wrote poetry on Jewish themes even after she became blind later in life. Many of her poems were set to music and are still sung in English-speaking Reform temples. She was the first Jew in the United States to publish a book of poetry, *Fancy's Sketch Book,* in 1833.

It was not just in culture, however, that Jews were well integrated into antebellum Charleston. There were Jewish slave owners (some of whom freed their slaves before it became illegal to do so). There was also at least one Jewish slave auctioneer, Abraham Seixas who was— wouldn't you know it—a New Yorker.

During the Civil War, Jewish men of all ages served in Confederate ranks. Afterward, the South was so impoverished, many Jews left Charleston to earn a living elsewhere. The war marked the end of

Charleston's prominence, but the postwar poverty also helped preserve the city's architecture and ambience.

Charleston's Jewish population increased with the arrival of Russian and Polish Jews between 1880 and 1914. Some Holocaust survivors and, more recently, some Soviet Jews have settled in Charleston. Today many young professionals return to Charleston after completing college. The city is again prospering, from the expansion of its port and military facilities and the growth of industry and tourism.

COMMUNITY: Charleston had enough Jews by 1749 to organize a congregation, Kahal Kadosh Beth Elohim, which built a splendid Georgian synagogue in 1794. After the synagogue was destroyed in the great Charleston fire of 1838, an impressive Greek Revival synagogue was built on the same site. At that time, the Orthodox Sefardic service was liberalized and an organ installed, making Beth Elohim the first Reform congregation in the United States. (Today it is the oldest Reform congregation in the world. Its sanctuary is the second oldest in America, and the oldest in continuous use.)

In 1764, Beth Elohim established its Coming Street Cemetery, America's largest colonial Jewish burial ground. The venerable gravestones with their unique stonecutting relate the saga of the congregation's rabbis and leaders, poets and matriarchs, and soldiers from the American Revolution, the War of 1812, and the Civil War.

Members of Beth Elohim organized the Hebrew Benevolent Society in 1784 and the Hebrew Orphan Society in 1801, the oldest of their kind in the nation and still active today. Beth Elohim's Sunday School, second oldest in the nation, was organized in 1838.

Orthodox Congregation Brith Sholom, founded in 1855 by German and Polish Jews, was the first Ashkenazic congregation in the South. In 1911, Congregation Beth Israel was founded by Russian Jews. The two congregations merged in 1955, becoming Brith Sholom–Beth Israel, with a handsome synagogue on 182 Rutledge Avenue, telephone, (803) 577-6599. The Addlestone Hebrew Academy is next door.

Conservative Synagogue Emanu-El, founded in 1947, now has a new sanctuary at 5 Windsor Drive in suburban West Ashley, telephone, (803) 571-3264.

Some Jews still live in Charleston's old city, which was once, like Jerusalem, surrounded by a wall. In the 1930s, St. Philip Street, in the historic section, was a Jewish neighborhood. Today many Jewish families live in suburban Windermere and neighborhoods west of the Ashley River near the Jewish Community Center.

SIGHTS: Taking one of the informative bus or carriage tours of the historic district is a good orientation. Then put on sturdy walking shoes and go exploring. Plaques identify most buildings of note. Take a stroll down King Street, from Calhoun to Broad, to see prosperous Jewish-owned stores, exactly where Jewish shops have been for centuries.

The sanctuary of Kahal Kadosh Beth Elohim, designated a national historic landmark in 1980, is at 90 Hasell (pronounced "hazel") Street, between King and Meeting streets. Built in 1840 to replace the previous sanctuary destroyed by fire, the Greek Revival temple has withstood much more than its predecessor. It was damaged by Union shells in the Civil War and again by the great Charleston earthquake of 1886.

Beth Elohim's sanctuary is especially beautiful by day when light streams through its pastel stained-glass windows accented with religious symbols. The ornate plaster ceiling is perfectly preserved; the massive Ark is of carved Santo Domingo mahogany. (During the Civil War, when Charlestonians believed their city would be burned like Atlanta, all the city's religious valuables were sent to Columbia for safekeeping. As luck would have it, Sherman burned Columbia instead of Charleston. One Sefer Torah, however, survived the fire and still sits in Beth Elohim's ark.)

The synagogue is open, with guides present, from 10 A.M. to noon, Monday through Friday. Visitors are welcome to worship on Friday at 8:15 P.M. and Saturday at 11 A.M. (no Saturday services in mid-summer).

Beth Elohim's Archives Museum at 86 Hasell Street is open 9 A.M. to 3 P.M., Monday through Friday. The archives display records, paintings, and photographs that document Beth Elohim's history—synonymous with the history of Charleston Jewry—and also beautiful ceremonial objects.

Several points of Jewish interest are located in the City Hall area at the corner of Broad and Meeting streets. In Washington Park, behind City Hall, there is a plaque in memory of Francis Salvador, the only Jewish soldier of the American Revolution to be individually honored in Charleston.

On the second floor of City Hall, another plaque honors Saul Alexander, a rags-to-riches immigrant who left his fortune to local charities of all creeds. Names of several prominent Jewish women of Charleston are included on a plaque called the "Women's Hall of Fame" on the third floor.

Nearby, at 88 Broad Street, is the original building of Charleston's Hebrew Orphan Society, where Judah P. Benjamin, who would one day be Secretary of State of the Confederacy, was a student as a boy. A Hebrew inscription can be seen high on the façade. The house that belonged to Benjamin's father is at 35 Broad Street.

A short walk away, at 89-91 Church Street, is a three-story house which was the model for the "Catfish Row" in George Gershwin's opera, *Porgy and Bess.* Gershwin lived in Charleston during 1934 while he composed the opera.

The Coming Street Cemetery, about two miles away at 189 Coming Street, is always locked, but arrangements can be made for a guided tour by phoning Beth Elohim at 723-1090.

Grace Episcopal Church, at 98 Wentworth Street, features a beautiful stained-glass "Women's Window" with biblical and contemporary heroines. One of those pictured is Hadassah founder Henrietta Szold, shown teaching arithmetic to Jewish children in yarmulkes. Call the church at 723-4575 for information about visiting.

CULTURE: Visitors are welcome at the monthly Sunday breakfast-lectures sponsored by the Emanu-El and Beth Elohim brotherhoods. The Jewish Community Center, at 1645 Wallenberg Boulevard (west of the Ashley River), has lectures, Israeli dancing, square dancing, and events for singles and seniors. Call the center for the latest events at 571-6565.

In 1985, the College of Charleston began a Jewish studies program that includes lectures and concerts open to the public. Call the College of Charleston Office of Special Events at 792-5525.

GENERAL CULTURE AND SIGHTS: Charleston is often called the "cultural capital of the South." Its star attraction is Spoleto U.S.A., begun in 1976, the brainchild of Gian Carlo Menotti. During this lively annual music festival in late May and early June, the city hosts concerts, operas, ballets, and plays with world renowned performers. Free concerts are presented daily in Charleston's historic churches.

The Dock Street Theater at 135 Church Street, restored in 1936, appears as it did when plays of early Jewish playwrights were performed there. In addition to seeing the theater while attending a performance, it can be viewed from 10 A.M. to 6 P.M., Monday through Friday.

The Charleston Symphony performs two concert series a year. Besides the Dock Street Theater, plays are presented at the Queen Street Playhouse and the College of Charleston. There are also two resident ballet companies.

In addition to the many historic houses open for tours, there are nine museums and art galleries, including the new home of the Charleston Museum, 360 Meeting Street; Gibbes Art Gallery, 135 Meeting Street, and the world's largest naval museum, the aircraft carrier U.S.S. *Yorktown* in Charleston harbor. Saturday newspapers carry details.

Charleston's lovely setting lures visitors outdoors—to the harbor, Fort Sumter, and nearby beaches and resorts. Charles Towne Landing, a state park, fifteen minutes' drive from downtown on S.C. 171 is on the site of Charleston's first settlement. Animals and plants then indigenous to the state are seen in their natural setting. Replicas of a seventeenth-century trading vessel and colonial village illustrate life in the colony; an excellent museum traces its history. Visitors may picnic, walk, rent a bike, take a tram. The park is open daily, 9 A.M. to 5 P.M.

No visit to Charleston is complete without a trip to at least one of its gardens, which are at their peak when azaleas and dogwoods bloom in late March and early April. Cypress Gardens, twenty-five miles north of the city, off I-26, is perhaps the best known.

Closer to town along the Ashley River Road (Highway 61) is a cluster of botanic and architectural sights that includes Drayton Hall, Magnolia Plantation and Gardens and Middleton Place. Drayton Hall, built between 1738 and 1742, was the only Ashley River plantation house not damaged by Sherman and the only pre-Revolutionary mansion remaining today. Magnolia Gardens has a section of plants mentioned in the Bible arranged in the shape of a Star of David, clustered around a statue of David as a boy. The area is surrounded by larger trees and shrubs, including palm, olive, Cedar of Lebanon, pomegranate, apple, and Moses's bulrushes.

PERSONALITIES: Charleston Jews gained recognition in diverse fields. Dr. Leon Banov, Sr., was a pioneer in public health, responsible for Charleston becoming the first city in the United States to require pasteurization of milk, introducing measures to eradicate malaria, and opening maternal and well-baby clinics throughout Charleston County. Franklin J. Moses was Chief Justice of the South Carolina Supreme Court during Reconstruction. Willard Hirsch was South

Carolina's best-known sculptor, and William Halsey, of Jewish ancestry, was Charleston's best-known painter. Joshua Lazarus introduced illuminating gas to America's cities; Carrie, Anita, and Mabel Pollitzer were leading suffragettes. Leon Keyserling was chairman of the Council of Economic Advisers under President Truman. Arthur Freed, the songwriter and producer *(An American in Paris, Singin' in the Rain,* etc.), is a Charleston native.

Two of the city's most prominent Jewish citizens today are David Stahl, conductor of the Charleston Symphony, and Reuben Greenberg, the city's black police chief, whose grandfather was a Russian-Jewish immigrant.

SIDE TRIP: The equally historic Jewish community of Savannah, Georgia, only two hours' drive from Charleston on Highway 17 South, dates back to colonial times. Numbering twenty-five hundred today, the community began in 1733 when forty-two Jews, almost all Sefardim, landed there. Two years later they founded a synagogue, Kahal Kadosh Mickva Israel, forerunner of today's Reform congregation Mickve Israel. The impressive synagogue building (dedicated in 1878) and museum at 20 East Gordon Street, faces Monterey Square, one of the many restored city squares in Savannah's large historic district. The synagogue is open Monday, Tuesday, Thursday, and Friday, 10 A.M. to noon. Services are held Friday at 8:15 P.M. (5:30 P.M. in summer) and Saturday, 11 A.M., telephone, (912) 233-1547. A plaque on River Street denotes where the first Jews arrived; a marker at Oglethorpe and Bull streets marks the site of Savannah's first Jewish cemetery.

READING: *The Jews of South Carolina* by Barnett A. Elzas takes readers through 1905. It is available in hardback from Beth Elohim, 86 Hasell Street, Charleston, S.C., 29401, for seventeen dollars, including postage. *The Jews of Charleston* by Charles Reznikoff (Jewish Publication Society) is out of print but may be found in libraries. For a fictional look at early South Carolina Jews, read *This New Land* by Lester Goran (Signet Books). For a more general fictional look at Charleston's history, read *Charleston* by Alexandra Ripley (Doubleday).

RECOMMENDATIONS: The elegant Mills House Hotel, 115 Meeting Street, captures the flavor of old Charleston. King's Courtyard Inn at 198 King Street is one of the many popular small inns in the historic district. The new Omni Hotel, also on King Street, is only a few steps from Beth Elohim. Remember to reserve very early for Spoleto and the peak spring season.

Charleston can be crowded in March and April, and hot in July and August but, like its troubled history, it wears its burdens well. It never loses its charm.

—HELEN SILVER

Chicago

Sears Tower *(Sears Roebuck and Co.)*

Chicago is a city of superlatives—at least that's how Chicagoans think of it. After all, it was bragging, not weather, that earned Chicago the sobriquet "Windy City." Chicagoans boast about having the world's largest exhibition center, the largest hotel, the tallest apartment building, the busiest airport, the busiest street corner. Even the initials of Chicago station WGN-TV stand for World's Greatest Newspaper, *The Chicago Tribune.*

Chicago Jews figure among the superlatives. Take, for example, Julius Rosenwald, remembered as one of the city's retailing geniuses. His bust stands in front of the Merchandise Mart, the world's largest commercial building. Rosenwald, called Chicago's greatest giver, donated three million dollars to create the Museum of Science and Industry, the Midwest's largest tourist attraction. Rosenwald was head of Sears, Roebuck and Company, today the world's largest retailer, headquartered in Chicago in the world's tallest building—110 floors. You might think of Rosenwald when you ride up to the Sears observation skydeck, where on a clear day you'll see as far as neighboring states.

HISTORY: Chicago's history is marked by a series of brash, bold engineering feats that began in the 1840s with the completion of the Illinois–Michigan Canal and the laying of railroad track. By the end of the decade, both of these links provided the connection with the Eastern Seaboard that would cause Chicago's population to quadruple in the next ten years.

Jewish settlement in Chicago also began in the 1840s. The first three congregations—Kehilath Anshe Mayriv (KAM), founded in 1847 by Bavarian Jews; B'nai Sholom, in 1852 by Posen Jews; and Chicago Sinai, in 1861, the first Reform congregation—are all still in existence. The two oldest have since merged into KAM-Isaiah Israel. East European Jews were meeting in small minyans in Chicago during the Civil War. Their first congregation, Beth Hamedrash Hagodol, founded in 1867, continued until recent times and was the progenitor of many others created through splitoffs and geographic divisions.

By 1871, there were ten congregations and several thousand Jews living in Chicago. On October 8 of that year, which was also Simhat Torah, the Great Fire began that destroyed most of Chicago.

Between 1880 and 1900, fifty-five thousand Jewish immigrants poured into Chicago's Maxwell Street neighborhood. By 1910, they began moving from the ghetto outward, most notably to North Lawndale, where as many as a hundred thousand Jews lived at one time and where no Jews live today. Movement has always characterized the Chicago Jewish community. Each summer the Chicago Jewish Historical Society—telephone, (312) 663-5634—conducts bus tours of the old neighborhoods, where dozens of former synagogues still line the once grand boulevards.

Milestones in Chicago's Jewish history include the first Jewish Women's Congress and the founding of the National Council of Jewish Women at the 1893 World's Columbian Exposition; the founding, in 1896, of the Knights of Zion, the first American Zionist organization formed in response to Theodor Herzl's call; the establishment, in 1913, of the B'nai B'rith Anti-Defamation League; and the movement that created the first Hillel, in 1923, at the University of Illinois. An event that both scandalized and pained American Jewry occurred in Chicago in 1924, when Nathan Leopold and Richard Loeb, scions of affluent German Jewish families, murdered fourteen-year-old Bobby Franks.

COMMUNITY: Today, a quarter of a million Jews live in metropolitan Chicago. They represent every variety and nuance, religious and secular, that can be found in a major Jewish center. There are 120 congregations and eight Jewish community centers, plus a myriad of services and agencies. Nearly two thirds of the Jewish population live in suburbs, especially to the north and northwest of the city. They are distributed primarily along Lake Michigan, from Evanston to Highland Park, and to the west of the lakefront area, from Skokie to Deerfield. In Highland Park, Jews comprise over 50 percent of the population. There are smaller Jewish pockets on Chicago's south side—in Hyde Park—in the southern suburbs and, to the west, in Oak Park, a suburb famous for its concentration of houses designed by Frank Lloyd Wright.

Surprisingly, the number of Jews in Chicago has decreased by only five thousand in the last decade, contrary to trends in other northern urban centers, which have been marked by large-scale movement to the Sun Belt. This stability is due to the absorption of six thousand Soviet Jews in recent years and the continuing movement into Chi cago of young, often single, Jews. Statistics indicate there are at least sixty-eight thousand single Jews between twenty-one and sixty-five in the area.

For questions regarding worship and congregations, call the Chicago Board of Rabbis, (312) 444-2896; for kashrut information, call the Chicago Rabbinical Council, 588-1600; for other Jewish communal services, call the Federation, 346-6700.

SIGHTS: Chicago became the architectural center of the country in the late nineteenth century—thanks, in part, to the Great Fire that left lots of room for experimentation—with the development of the skyscraper and the skeleton-frame building. Chicago's first great Jewish architect was Dankmar Adler (1844–1900), son of KAM's rabbi and a partner of Louis Sullivan. Together with Sullivan, he is credited with pioneering the modern office building. The restored Auditorium Theatre, at Congress and Michigan, in the famed Adler and Sullivan Auditorium Building of 1889 (now home of Roosevelt University), attests to Adler's acoustical genius.

KAM's fifth home, now the Pilgrim Baptist Church, at Thirty-third and Indiana in the neighborhood of Michael Reese Hospital, is one of the lesser-known extant Adler and Sullivan works, and its architecture, acoustics, and Sullivan ornamentation inside make it a worthwhile place to see. KAM-Isaiah Israel's current building, 1100 East Hyde Park Boulevard, near the University of Chicago, is also worth viewing, not only for its architecture but also for the small but interesting Morton B. Weiss Museum of Judaica. The Byzantine-style architecture and sanctuary, built in the early 1920s, were based on a second-century synagogue in Tiberias. The building was declared a landmark in 1977.

Another Judaica collection worth seeing is the Maurice Spertus Museum, housed in the Spertus College of Judaica at 618 South Michigan.

Visit the Chicago Loop Synagogue, 16 South Clark Street, for a special treat. The eastern wall of the sanctuary is a magnificent stained-glass window by Abraham Rattner which should be viewed from the inside during daylight hours. Outside, on the façade, is *Hands of Peace,* a sculpture by Henri Azaz.

Several suburban congregations are housed in architecturally significant buildings. The older and major portion of North Shore Congregation Israel, 1185 Sheridan Road in Glencoe, was designed by Minoru Yamasaki.

Another noteworthy building is North Suburban Synagogue Beth El, 1175 Sheridan Road, in Highland Park. Architect Percival Goodman designed the modern sanctuary to incorporate an old estate. There you will find Kol Ami, a Judaica museum with a permanent collection and special exhibits.

Also worth visiting is the modern Joseph and Helen Regenstein Library on Ellis (east of South Woodlawn) at the University of Chicago, which houses the Ludwig Rosenberger Judaica Library of twenty thousand volumes, presented by Rosenberger to the museum in 1980. When the university was founded almost a century ago as a Baptist school, its first president was William Rainey Harper, a world-renowned Hebrew scholar. Today, the university's greatest pride is the ever-increasing lineup of Nobel Prize winners, including Albert Abraham Michelson, the first American to win the prize in physics and, more recently, author Saul Bellow and economist Milton Friedman. The B'nai B'rith Hillel Foundation on the campus of the University of Chicago, 5715 South Woodlawn, is also a center of Jewish life, with many religious, educational, and cultural activities—and kosher meals.

The greatest concentration of Judaica shops, kosher restaurants, and food stores is on the north side of the city in the West Rogers Park section. At the intersection of Devon and California, you will find Gitel's Kosher Bakery, Tel Aviv Kosher Pizza and Dairy Restaurant, and Café Hanegev, all under Chicago Rabbinical Council supervision. A takeout food store, Kosher Karry and Restaurant, is an emporium of old-world smells and tastes.

Devon and Touhy avenues have clusters of kosher restaurants, bakeries, synagogues, and Judaica shops. One of the main Jewish community centers is at 3003 West Touhy. And if you follow Sheridan Road north into Highland Park, you will discover four more congregations, a Habad House, a kosher meat market, deli, and another Jewish center.

The best view of Chicago's skyline is from the front of the Adler Planetarium—a treat that doesn't cost anything. Opened in 1930, the planetarium, endowed by Max Adler, Julius Rosenwald's brother-in-law, was the first in the Western Hemisphere and was one of the few to also house a museum. There you will find one of the three finest collections of antique scientific instruments—the other two being in Oxford and Florence.

The Adler Planetarium and its lakefront neighbors—the Shedd

Aquarium and the Field Museum of Natural History—are on landfill engineered by Jacob Sensibar, a Chicago Jew who earned the title "World's Greatest Earth Mover." Most of Chicago's distinctive twenty-nine-mile lakefront was created by Sensibar's firm, Construction Materials Corporation, between 1914 and 1916. Some of the landfill was sand carried from the other side of Lake Michigan in hopper dredges that Sensibar invented. Later, he was involved in the reclamation of forty-four thousand acres of swampland in the Huleh Lake region in Israel. Nearly every Chicagoan claims the lakefront is the city's greatest natural asset.

North Michigan Avenue—that "Magnificent Mile" from the Chicago River to Oak Street—includes the finest shopping the world has to offer. Among the latest imported specialty shops is Neiman Marcus, opened in November 1983, at Michigan and Superior. The building was financed by Orthodox Jews and constructed with their shomer Shabbat requirements—no Saturday labor.

PERSONALITIES: Aside from Nobel Prize winners, Chicago has also produced "King of Swing" Benny Goodman, the world's greatest clarinetist, cartoonist Herblock, Admiral Hyman Rickover, comedian Shelly Berman, author Meyer Levin, presidential advisers Stuart Eizenstadt and Kenneth Adelman, antiwar activist Daniel Ellsberg, and former Supreme Court Justice Arthur Goldberg. Irv Kupcinet, a former professional football player, is one of the city's most popular columnists (for the *Chicago Sun-Times)* and talk-show hosts.

CULTURE: Chicago has an abundance of Jewish painters, sculptors, weavers, Hebrew calligraphers, paper-cutters, photographers, silversmiths, lithographers, and stained-glass artists. The American Jewish Arts Club (telephone, 761-1382), over fifty years old, is an organization of Chicago-based Jewish artists working in various media and thematic subjects; they mount an annual exhibit at the Spertus Museum.

The Jewish Production Organization for Cultural Events and Theater (POCET) presents the annual Greater Chicago Jewish Folk Arts Festival—usually a jamboree of artists, dancers, musicians, and puppeteers, a juried art exhibit and sale and display of kosher food and Jewish books by Chicago authors.

Chicago is also a major center for the production of Jewish-content cable television, a priority of the Jewish Federation of Metropolitan Chicago. Programs produced in Chicago are marketed to other communities. Cable subscribers in the Chicago area receive over twenty hours of Jewish programing a week on WJUF, the broadcasting arm of the Federation.

Jewish lectures, theater, and other entertainment can be found at a host of synagogues and Jewish centers. Check *The Sentinel,* Chicago's Jewish weekly, for listings.

READING: For a concise history of Chicago's Jewish community, see the chapter "The Jews of Chicago: From Shtetl to Suburb" by Irving Cutler in *Ethnic Chicago,* edited by Melvin Holli and Peter Jones and published by William B. Eerdmans. For the flavor of Chicago's Jewish past, read Saul Bellow's *The Adventures of Augie March* and *Humboldt's Gift* (Viking), or Meyer Levin's *The Old Bunch* and *Compulsion* (Simon & Schuster). For a fictional look at the world of Chicago architecture at the turn of the century, read Meyer Levin's last book, *The Architect* (Simon & Schuster), based on the early years of Frank Lloyd Wright's career. *The Chicago Jewish Source Book* (Follett) is a 330-page guide to all things Jewish in Chicago. Like their city, Chicago's Jews have their share of superlatives.

—RACHEL HEIMOVICS

Copenhagen

Great Synagogue Interior *(Leni Sonnenfeld)*

A large stone from Eilat, whose Hebrew inscription identifies it as a gift of friends of Denmark in Israel, sits in Israels Plads (Israel Square) near the city flower market in Copenhagen. Similarly, a stone from Denmark can be found in Kikar Dania (Denmark Square) in Jerusalem's Beit Hakerem neighborhood. These monuments are symbols of the reciprocal friendship that has existed between Danes and Jews for most of their shared history, particularly in the twentieth century.

HISTORY: That shared history is not very long, however. It was just over three centuries ago—in 1684—that Israel David, court jeweler and unofficial banker to the King of Denmark, and his partner, Meyer Goldschmidt, were granted permission to hold religious services. Though they were limited to the confines of their own houses—where they would conduct them for many years—and though no sermons could accompany them, the act of regal dispensation marked the beginning of organized Jewry in the Danish capital.

The next step, in 1693, was the purchase of land for a cemetery. The following year, Sefardic Jews (David, Goldschmidt, and their fellow congregants were Ashkenazim) were also allowed open worship—a "privilege" that refugees from the Spanish and Portuguese Inquisition had gained in Amsterdam as early as 1608. For the next three centuries, a rich and varied Jewish life would emerge in Denmark, notably in Copenhagen.

There was one significant interruption of that continuous presence: the exodus of all the Jews in Denmark, one jump ahead of the SS commandos dispatched to carry them off to Auschwitz. The Pharaoh was Adolf Eichmann, the Red Sea was the waters of the Øresund, the narrow strait which separates Denmark from Sweden, through which the Danish Israelites made their escape. The Promised Land was Sweden, which offered the refugees not only milk and honey, but housing, education, and jobs till war's end brought a jubilant homecoming to their native country.

The safe journey of seven thousand men, women, and children was made possible by the Christian people of Denmark. On the first day of Rosh Hashanah in 1943, the Nazis, who had occupied the country since 1940, planned a series of roundups of the Jews of Copenhagen, who would be conveniently assembled in the synagogue or in their homes. But these raids were thwarted by the quick action of the Danes. At risk of their own lives, they hid their Jewish fellow citizens in attics and basements, church belfries and funeral parlors, until safe transportation to neutral Sweden could be arranged. During the ten days between Rosh Hashanah and Yom Kippur, the escape was ef- fected.

The events of 1943 were perhaps the most heroic chapter in a history of Danish Jewry that began in 1619, when King Christian IV appointed Albert Dionis, a Sefardi who had established a prosperous import-export business in Hamburg, to operate the royal mint in the newly founded town of Glückstadt. Dionis coined money so effectively —his gold ducats engraved with the Tetragrammaton (the four He- brew letters of the name of God) financed Christian's successful war against Sweden—that the grateful King invited other Sefardim to settle in Glückstadt and Copenhagen, his capital.

The King himself, who had some knowledge of Hebrew and consid- ered it the language of God, had consigned the coins and felt the inscriptions on them had brought him heavenly protection in his victory over the Swedes. Indeed, he placed the same four Hebrew letters on the entrances and pulpits of some of the churches he built, where they are still in evidence.

On a more practical level, Christian IV brought Sefardic Jews from Hamburg and Amsterdam into his kingdom because he hoped that, with their knowledge of languages, their mercantile experience, and their network of familial connections throughout Europe and the Middle East, they could stimulate commerce in Denmark, as they had in the great trading cities of Germany and the Netherlands. The first century of their immigration saw little more than a few scattered minyans throughout the country. As late as 1684, when Meyer Gold- schmidt chanted his first Kiddush, there were only nineteen Jews in Copenhagen.

Today, there are perhaps seventy-five hundred in all of Denmark, their numbers augmented by the fifteen hundred exiled from Poland during the anti-Semitic purges of 1968 and 1969. While nearly all live in the capital, they are so dispersed among its one and a half million inhabitants that nowhere do they form a distinctly Jewish neighbor- hood.

In a national population of five million, the Jews of Denmark have never been a large group, but their impact on the economy, culture, and national well-being has been enormous. Jewish enterprise in the nineteenth century was responsible for the development of brewing, distilling, shipbuilding, and tobacco processing and other important industries which are still basic to the Danish economy.

PERSONALITIES: In this century, Niels Bohr, one of the pioneers of atomic science and a leading figure on the Manhattan Project to develop the atomic bomb, and Victor Borge, the musical comedian who in 1984 celebrated his seventy-fifth birthday with a command performance for his native Copenhagen, spring to mind as outstanding Danish Jews.

There have been many others. In the early nineteenth century, for example, there was Mendel Levin Nathanson, considered the father of Danish journalism. Under his editorship, the *Berlingske Tidende* became the country's leading newspaper, a position it still holds as the voice of conservatism, as opposed to the more radical *Politiken,* whose chief editor is Herbert Pundik. Pundik is a Danish-born Jew who made *aliya* with his family, but still spends three weeks of each month at his office in Copenhagen.

Nathanson was also a prosperous businessman, an economist whose writings are still studied, the author of the standard work on Danish Jewish history, and the organizer of the present well-structured community. He founded the country's first and only Jewish day school, the Caroline School (named after the Danish queen of the time), which still flourishes as a model educational institution.

A later namesake, Henri Nathansen (note the "e"), was the foremost Danish playwright of his time. Born in 1868, he became the director of the Royal Theater in 1909 and wrote works which are still performed. One of them, *Indenfor Murene (Within the Walls),* is esteemed as one of the finest plays in the language. It deals, as do many of his other works, with the problems of intermarriage, and with the questions of assimilation in a free society—like the Danish—where anti-Semitism is virtually nonexistent. As an old man of seventy-five, Nathansen fled to Sweden in 1943 with his fellow Jews; he could not adjust to conditions of life in a new land and committed suicide in 1944.

Another important literary figure was Georg Brandes, a friend of Henrik Ibsen and the most important Danish critic and historian of the late nineteenth century. During that period, his brother, Edvard, led the Liberal Party and served as the Liberal Government's Minister of Finance. Another politician of national stature at the time was Herman Trier, the President of the Parliament.

General C. I. De Meza was commander-in-chief of the Danish Army when Denmark suffered a disastrous defeat at the hands of Bismarck's Germany. Though De Meza was known to be a Jew, there was not even a ripple of anti-Semitism in the expressions of dismay which followed the loss of the war and of the important border territory of Schleswig-Holstein.

Perhaps the most famous Danish Jewish family is the Melchiors, who have given the country generations of bankers and rabbis, statesmen and musicians, since the eighteenth century. Moritz Gerson Melchior was the friend and benefactor of Hans Christian Andersen. In Rolighed, the Melchior home, the world-renowned writer of fairy tales (who, as a child, had studied Hebrew at the Caroline School) passed his declining years and, finally, died.

A descendant of Morris Gerson Melchior was the late Chief Rabbi of Denmark, Marcus Melchior, spiritual leader of the community during its time of exile in Sweden. Marcus's older son, Bent, succeeded his father as the present Chief Rabbi of Denmark; the younger son, Arne, was a member of the national cabinet as Minister of Communication, Transportation, and Public Works, as well as an active member of the Jewish community. Two grandsons of Marcus are also in the rabbinate: Michael Melchior, the sole rabbi in Norway, divides his time between Israel and Oslo, and Uri Schwartz, in his early twenties, is the only rabbi in Finland.

SIGHTS: The Danes have a special way of describing their metropolis; they call it *hyggelig*—cozy. Indeed, the sightseer who walks its streets (the best way to explore Copenhagen) will find that *hyggelig* is the inevitable word for this European capital.

A human scale persists in the Old City. The ramparts of the twelfth-century market town founded by Bishop Absalon live on as street names. The moats which enclosed the medieval castles are now small lakes bordering the ancient quarter; the hunting enclosures of the nobility are small parks. The streets themselves are narrow and gently curving, in defiance of the rigid geometry of nineteenth-century urban planning, as if they had been bent by the prevailing west wind. The seventeenth- and eighteenth-century houses are two and three stories high—gabled, baroque, their façades almost impish in their decorations. There is an abundance of outdoor cafés, flower markets, fruit stands, and young craftsmen displaying handmade wooden toys or jewelry on cobblestoned pavements.

The Round Tower at Købmagergade, built as an observatory in 1637–42, contains a spiraling ramp so wide that Tsar Peter the Great could drive a team of horses from street level to the pinnacle; the Tetragrammaton is inscribed over the entrance. Inside the church next door, the Torahs of the Great Synagogue were hidden from the Nazis.

Around the corner, at 12 Krystalgade, is the synagogue itself, erected in 1833. When it held its one-hundred-and-fiftieth-anniversary service in 1983, it had the Royal Family in attendance. The synagogue's plain exterior does not prepare the visitor for the white-and-gold elegance inside. The magnificent two-story-high sanctuary (a women's balcony rings three sides of the second story, with the Ark occupying the fourth) has tall pillars and a ceiling frieze of gold and blue. Unfortunately, the synagogue and the senior citizens' home adjacent to it sustained structural damage—since repaired—from a terrorist bomb in July 1985.

The Great Synagogue holds daily, Friday evening, and Saturday morning services. In summer, there is a festive Kiddush after Sabbath prayers, and on Sunday mornings, Rabbi Melchior or his colleague, Rabbi Bent Lexner, conducts a study group. The language is Danish, a barrier to most visitors, but there is no difficulty handling the real Danish pastry and schnapps which wrap up the weekly colloquiums.

Since there has never been a ghetto in Copenhagen, the Jewish sights are interspersed among those of general interest. Worth seeing are the Resistance Museum, on Esplanaden (telephone, 01-13-77-14), with its dramatic exhibits of the 1943 rescue; the Royal Library, 8 Christians Brygge, telephone, 01-15-01-11 (ask for Ulf Haxen, the curator, to make an appointment to see the Judaica collection, one of the most important in the world); the community center, 6 Ny Kongensgade (telephone, 01-12-88-68) with its administrative offices, library, *mikva*, small museum, and gift shops; and Israel Square, with its daily fruit and flowers and a weekend flea market.

Also worth seeing are Caroline School, 18 Bomhusvej (01-25-95-00), and Machsike Hadas Synagogue (strictly Orthodox), 12 Ole Suhrsgade.

Tivoli Park, in the very center of town, is even better than the hyperbolic tourist brochures would lead you to believe. Its landscaped gardens are the best in Denmark; there are twenty-five restaurants (of as many different cuisines), a pantomime theater, bands, vaudeville, and, before closing time (which is midnight), a brilliant fireworks display on Wednesday, Friday, Saturday, and Sunday.

EATING AND SHOPPING: Kosher food is available from Arne Cohen Kosher Catering butcher and delicatessen, Rørholmsgade 2 (01-13-30-12); Copenhagen Kosher, Classensgade 5 (01-42-09-81); and Danish Kosher Food, 16 Vendersgade (01-11-70-63). The latter establishment, which supplies prepackaged meals to the airlines and hotels, was also the target of a bomb attack on the eve of Rosh Hashanah 1985. Kosher groceries can also be purchased at I. A. Samson, Rørholmsgade 3 (01-13-00-77). There is also a good vegetarian restaurant, Grøn Mad, 14 Linnesgade, next to Israel Square.

Danish design in furniture, jewelry, silver, porcelain, and furs is perhaps the best in the world; and everything, from class to kitsch, is available on the pedestrian street which cuts through the heart of the Old City. It's the famous Strøget (pronounced "Stroyat"), more than a little honky-tonk these days, though all the best shops, like Illums Bolighus, are still there. Try, also, some of the charming and less frequented side streets like Pistolstraede and Fiolstraede.

READING: There are no English translations of works by Danish Jewish writers. Harold Flender, an American, wrote *Rescue in Denmark* (published by the Anti-Defamation League of B'nai B'rith) and Leni Yahil, an Israeli, wrote *The Rescue of Danish Jewry*, published in English by the Jewish Publication Society, perhaps the definitive work on the subject. A good fictional account of the rescue is Elliott Arnold's *A Night of Watching* (Scribner's). A good travel companion is *Jewish Life in Denmark*, available from the Danish National Tourist Board or local travel agents. It contains a map of the Old City and a block-by-block itinerary of the important sites. The Danes have seen to it that Jewish travelers, no less than any other and perhaps more, will feel cozy in Copenhagen.

—GABRIEL LEVENSON

Denver

Emmanuel Gallery *(Barry Meriash)*

If you are on your way to a music festival in Aspen, to ski in Vail, or to backpack in Rocky Mountain National Park, it is likely that you will also hang your cap in Denver. Once a magnet for health- and wealth-seekers, the capital of Colorado has become, together with the surrounding areas along the Front Range, the eastern chain of the Rockies, a booming metropolis.

Despite industrialization, the majestic mountains can at times still be viewed from the Kansas border, 150 miles away. The celebrated 125-mile skyline from Pikes Peak to Longs Peak is punctuated by skyscrapers and cranes. It was for the once-celebrated clear, dry air that tuberculosis sufferers would flock to Denver "chasing the cure" in the world-class, free National Jewish Hospital for Consumptives (NJHC) or the Jewish Consumptives Relief Society (JCRS).

HISTORY: In the 1859 "Pikes Peak-or-Bust" gold rush, a dozen Jewish men, mostly German immigrants, crossed the plains to the junction of Cherry Creek and the Platte River, where the first gold was found. They were exuberant, hardworking, exemplary in behavior, even elegant. These pioneers served in the city council and territorial government and started the public library and literary societies, including the Denver Club, which later excluded Jews.

Along with the gold-seekers came the health-seekers. The air and sunshine of the city was the popular prescription for tuberculosis. Frances Wisebart Jacobs, wife of Abraham Jacobs, a city councilman and civic leader, was the "mother" or "queen of the charities" and a founder of what is today the United Way. The NJHC, later called the National Jewish Hospital, was originally named for Mrs. Jacobs. Her stained-glass portrait is in the dome of the new state capitol, the only woman so honored.

Tsarist persecution in the 1880s brought a large wave of Russian Jews. Among them was Dr. Charles Spivak, a leader in the early JCRS. Jewish leaders, troubled by the heavy settlement of Jews on the East Coast, devised plans to distribute them throughout the country. Best known among the agricultural colonies that were set up to absorb Jewish immigrants was Cotopaxi. A pious group that was duped into settling there, in the barren mountains near the Arkansas River, was rescued by Denver Jews. The Galveston plan—one of the schemes to distribute Jewish immigrants west of the Mississippi—and Denver's growing reputation as a "kosher" city drew people to the communities along the foothills.

After World War II, many young veterans who had been stationed in Denver returned, but it was not until the energy boom of the 1970s and the discovery of powdered snow by the international jet set that the population exploded. In addition, air and space industries, government agencies, and high technology have created almost unmanageable growth.

PERSONALITIES: The most outstanding Jew in Colorado was Otto Mears, known as "the Hebrew pathfinder" and "the pathfinder of the San Juan," for his network of toll roads and railroads over almost impossible terrain, especially in the San Juan Mountains. His control over the eleven counties he helped to create gave the balance of power in the state to the Republicans. Colorado was admitted to statehood in 1876, and Mears was chosen as the first elector to go to Washington and cast the decisive vote for Rutherford B. Hayes— hence another nickname, "the President-maker." Mears was a treaty mediator who spoke the Ute language with a Yiddish accent. The imaginative creator of gold and silver filigree railroad passes, which are prized by museums, he also proposed covering the state capitol dome with 24-karat gold leaf when he was chairman of the board of capitol managers. His memorials include a stained-glass portrait in the window outside the Senate chamber, the naming of Mears Junction, near the site of his first toll road, and Mount Mears in the San Juan Mountains—not nearly enough to satisfy his admirers, who expected a city or county to be named for him.

Most distinguished of the politically active Jews was United States Senator Simon Guggenheim, who endowed almost every college in the state with a building. He was particularly generous to the Colorado School of Mines. It was in Leadville that the Guggenheim fortune was dug out of the A.Y. and Minnie mines.

Tuberculosis brought many gifted residents to Denver. At the JCRS, H. Leivick and David Edelstadt wrote Yiddish poetry. Golda Meir lived here briefly while her sister was a patient at the sanatorium, and Yehoash (Solomon Bloomgarden) translated the Bible into Yiddish in Denver.

Nationally known business figures were Jesse Shwayder of Samsonite Luggage and David May of the May Company department stores.

COMMUNITY: During the pioneer period there was great cooperation among all groups, but by the 1920s, anti-Semitism was so strong that the city and state governments were taken over by the Ku Klux Klan (members included the governor and other officials). After the scandals that brought down the Klan, there was a tremendous decrease in anti-Semitic activities. In 1984, however, Alan Berg, a Jewish radio show host, was assassinated by a right-wing group in Denver, although only one of his attackers was from the city.

The natives, Jewish and non-Jewish alike, are not entirely happy with the influx of newcomers. Denver is not equipped, physically or socially, to be a big city. However, the community of about forty-seven thousand Jews does offer a full Jewish life.

There are Lubavitch and Reconstructionist institutions, chapters of most major organizations, and five Jewish schools, two of them boarding schools. Judaic studies are taught at the University of Denver. For decades Denver boasted an agreement among the rabbis and B'nai B'rith Anti-Defamation League that no religious ceremony would be performed in a non-Jewish setting. Yet two out of three children receive no Jewish education, intermarriage and divorce are frequent, and social climbing and assimilation are characteristic of the established community and the "boomers."

At one time, rabbis from the various ideologies who were members of the Rabbinical Council conducted joint conversion instruction groups. This unique venture disintegrated in 1984 when the Orthodox, questioning their own standards in accepting converts who would not keep Shabbat or kashrut, withdrew.

SIGHTS AND NEIGHBORHOODS: The early settlers were scattered, the wealthier living east of Cherry Creek, today's downtown. They continued to move east and south. The less affluent lived between the creek and the Platte River. Still in use is the building of Congregation Shearith Israel, now the Emanuel Gallery (at Tenth and Lawrence Street), and the block of restored buildings on Ninth Street which includes a Jewish grocery store on the Auraria Higher Education Center campus.

The only early Jewish neighborhood was West Colfax, west of the river to the city limits. Most of the Yiddish-speaking Jews settled there. One of the largest congregations in West Colfax attracts members from every part of the area. Also located there is a large hasidic community and the two Jewish boarding schools.

A guide to community events, news, and institutions is the *Intermountain Jewish News,* which is available at the Jewish Community Center, 4800 East Alameda Avenue, telephone, (303) 399-2660. To find out about kosher food, contact Rabbi Yaakov Hopfer at (303) 623-6842.

If you stay in a downtown hotel, you can walk or use public transportation to the most interesting sites around the civic center. The state capitol, with the stained-glass windows of Mears and Mrs. Jacobs, are east of the center. A few blocks from there you can catch a shuttle to the restored Larimer Square, once synonymous with Jewish merchandising. A few miles east are the Botanic Gardens at Tenth and York, site of the first Jewish cemetery. The garden has an outdoor exhibit of biblical plants.

Restorations abound. The oldest is the Four-Mile House Historic Park at 715 South Forest. Although its only Jewish connection is that it was on Abraham Jacobs's stage route until the railroad came in 1870, the house and farm are a living museum of life from 1859 and 1883, when the two sections of the house were built.

The modest home in which Golda Meir lived has been moved several times and is now at South Lipan and Louisiana Avenue, where it awaits repair from a recent fire and vandalism. A memorial park to Babi Yar has been dedicated on South Havana, but there is little to see.

DAY TRIPS: Jews lived in practically every Colorado town and mining camp and conducted religious services in them. A trip to Central City, the "richest square mile on earth," can start along West Colfax to I-70, turning off to Black Hawk–Central City, where Jews lived, worked, and attended the noted Central City Opera. There are mine tours, as in most former mining towns.

You can return through Colorado State Park, stopping for spectacular views and nature walks. From the park through Golden Gate Canyon, after about a dozen miles, you will enter the Park of the Red Rocks, with its magnificent natural amphitheater.

The Air Force Academy along I-25 has tours which include the Jewish chapel with its unusual sanctuary. Of special importance are the nine paintings by Israeli artist Shlomo Katz, on the themes of brotherhood, justice, and flight.

After Vail and Aspen, the most popular Colorado destination is Mesa Verde National Park, a worthwhile visit if you want to take a longer trip. In this area are the San Juan Mountains, where Otto Mears built the spectacular Million Dollar Highway from Ouray to Silverton. A marker (not always there) indicates his achievement. A four-wheel drive can be taken into the rugged and historic terrain where Mears lived and worked. The area includes Telluride, today the home of a film festival and ski resort.

READING: Harriet and Fred Rochlin's *Pioneer Jews: A New Life in the Far West* (Houghton Mifflin), Harriet Rochlin's *So Far Away* (Jove), and Kenneth Libo and Irving Howe's *We Lived There Too* (St. Martin's/ Marek) are available in bookstores. You may also try *Pioneers, Peddlers, and Tsadikim: The Story of the Jews in Colorado* by Ida Uchill (795 South Jersey Street, Denver, Colorado 80224). Amy Shapiro's *A Guide to the Jewish Rockies* (University of Denver) and John Dunning's *Denver* (Times), a novel about the Ku Klux Klan and a Jewish family in West Colfax, are out of print but may be available in libraries.

—IDA LIBERT UCHILL

Dublin

James Joyce Bust *(Irish Tourist Board)*

Dublin is renowned for its whiskey, wool, and wearing of the green. What is not as appreciated is that, in Dublin, Abie's red-haired and green-eyed Irish Rose may be neither an O'Reilly nor an O'Grady but a Goldberg.

Yes, there are Jews in Ireland. The settlement of a small Jewish community in Ireland's capital—first Sefardim, later Ashkenazim—amid a Catholic host majority goes back nearly four centuries. And while rocky relations between the two groups sometimes made life difficult for the Jews, their present accommodation is based comfortably on mutual respect for tradition and love of freedom.

HISTORY: The Jewish connection with Ireland reaches back into the country's mythology. The "Shee" fairies that live in castles and sepulchral caverns are believed to be members of the biblical tribe of Dan. According to one legend, the *Lia Fail*—the "Stone of Destiny" used at the coronation of Irish kings—was brought to the country during mythical times and was the pillow on which Jacob had his famous dream.

More rooted in history, according to the *Annals of Innisfallen,* the book of Ireland's legendary figures, are five Jews who arrived from France in 1062, bringing gifts to Turlough O'Brien, King of Munster and a grandson of Brian Boru.

The first Jews to settle in the Emerald Isle in significant numbers were Sefardim fleeing Spain and Portugal in the late sixteenth and seventeenth centuries. Some of those Jews held office in Ireland. In 1591, Trinity College in Dublin began teaching Hebrew.

The community began to dwindle in the mid-1700s. There was some anti-Semitism, and four bills which would have made it easier for foreign Jews to become naturalized citizens were rejected by the Irish Parliament. By 1816, there were only three Jewish families left in Dublin.

But within a few decades the Jewish population began to grow again. This time the immigrants were Ashkenazi Jews escaping Eastern Europe. Today, most of Ireland's Jews can trace their roots to Lithuania.

By 1901, there were more than three thousand Jews in the country. In the ensuing years, they helped fight for Irish independence from Great Britain. Robert Briscoe, a Jewish member of the Irish Republican Army, was sent to the United States in 1917 to raise funds from Irish Americans.

Briscoe (1894–1969) was the first Jewish member of the Dail (the House of Deputies which, together with the Senate, makes up the Parliament) and the first Jewish Lord Mayor of Dublin. He epitomized the quintessential Irish Jew—one who is involved in the country's struggle for freedom, yet remains part of the small but active Irish Jewish community.

Another Irish Jewish luminary was Isaac Herzog. Born in Poland in 1888, he was named Chief Rabbi of the Irish Free State, after serving as rabbi first of Belfast, then of Dublin. He became the Ashkenazi Chief Rabbi of the Yishuv in 1936. His son, Chaim Herzog, is currently President of Israel.

In 1937, the constitution of the new Irish Republic granted Jewish citizens religious freedom. Today Jews say that, in general, this promise has been kept. In Ireland, where tradition—particularly religious tradition—is of considerable interest, there is a constant awareness of the Jewish presence. Books of Jewish content are often reviewed in the Sunday papers, and a handful of Yiddish books are sold in secular bookstores.

COMMUNITY: There are Irish Jewish artists, writers, photographers, businessmen, lawyers, and professors. It is the politicians, however, who are most in the public eye. The Dail has three Jewish members, each from a different party. One of these, Alan Shatter, is a liberal who is often quoted in the newspapers. Gerald Goldberg, the former Lord Mayor of Cork, is a name familiar to every schoolchild in Ireland.

Ireland's Chief Rabbi Ephraim Mirvis—who became the world's youngest Chief Rabbi when he was appointed at age twenty-nine—is invited to state functions and appears on the state-run television station before Jewish holidays. When former Chief Rabbi David Rosen announced that he was leaving to teach in Israel, his picture was on the front page of the *Irish Times.*

"The Jewish involvement is disproportionate," says English-born Rabbi Rosen, who lived in Ireland for five years before making aliyah in 1983. "There's no field of art or culture in which Jews are not involved. Sociologically, it's an almost ideal situation. It's a society that is fundamentally religious and respects religious identity. In fact, you are more respected if you are loyal to your own tradition, and that is expected of you."

If anything, Irish Jews seem to be more cohesive than their counterparts in countries with larger Jewish populations—the result of an effort, perhaps, to retain Jewish identity in a country where the Catholic church is so strong. On the other hand, many young people leave because they find the small Jewish community "claustrophobic."

Dublin's Jewish community, once five thousand strong, has dwindled to about two thousand today. (One of the places they have gone is New York, where members of the Loyal League of Yiddish Sons of Erin march in the annual St. Patrick's Day parade.) Those still in Dublin support a number of religious and social institutions, including four synagogues, a school, a lush golf course at the foot of the Dublin Mountains, and a nursing home. The Dublin Maccabi Sports Center, on Kimmage Road West, is packed with young Jewish athletes on Sunday mornings.

SIGHTS: There are some sights of Jewish interest in Dublin but, like Ireland in general, they cannot be explored or appreciated without talking to local residents. One caveat, however—people appreciate an advance call, so that they can offer you the appropriate hospitality.

One of Ireland's best-known fictional characters, Leopold Bloom, in James Joyce's novel *Ulysses*, was Jewish. He was born in the working-class neighborhood around Dublin's South Circular Road, which used to be known as "Little Jerusalem." Although the city's Jewish population is now scattered into the suburbs of Terenure, Rathmines, and Rathgar, there are still Jewish shops in the old neighborhood, which maintains its nineteenth-century appearance. Perhaps the best way to get a feel for the Irish Jewish community is by taking a long walking tour starting with the Dublin Hebrew Congregation, going through the old quarters of "Little Jerusalem," and winding up in a nursing home in the suburb where many Jews now live.

Start at Adelaide Road, a winding, tree-lined street about a ten-minute walk south of St. Stephen's Green, the city center's main park. The Dublin Hebrew Congregation, an elegant brick Victorian structure built in 1892, is at No. 37. Inside is a beautiful synagogue in the European tradition—polished wooden seats and a women's balcony which wraps around the top.

Then walk west on Adelaide Road, which turns into Harcourt Road and then Harrington Street. One block south of Harrington is Lennox Street, the home of a kosher bakery, "The Bretzel"—perhaps the only place in Ireland that sells bagels.

Continue on Harrington until it becomes South Circular Road. Turn right onto Lower Clanbrassil Street, which used to be the main shopping area of "Little Jerusalem." There is still a kosher butcher at No. 35. At No. 52, there is a brick row house with a brightly painted green door and a polished brass knocker. This is the house where Leopold Bloom was supposed to have lived. A plaque in front says, "Here, in Joyce's imagination, was born Leopold Bloom, citizen, husband, father, worker, the reincarnation of Ulysses."

After Clanbrassil Street, walk over the canal into the Dublin suburbs. Less than half a mile away, on Leinster Road West, is the Old Age Home for the Hebrews. The home's first floor contains a treasure of the community—a replica of a shul which used to stand on Ormond Quay on Dublin's River Liffey. The original shul was built by Abraham Isaac Cohen, a cabinetmaker and antique dealer who felt that Jewish workmen and merchants doing business on the north side of the city should have a place to pray. Thirty years ago, his son, Louis, also an antique dealer, moved the aron kodesh and bimah that his father had made to the nursing home and set up a shul which looks very much like the one he remembers from his childhood.

If you talk to the nursing home residents, some will recount how their parents started out in Eastern Europe and, though bound for America, ended up in the Irish "Little Jerusalem."

Stratford College, a day school, is a good place to get a glimpse of Ireland's Jewish youth. Because there are not enough Jewish students to support the school, there are also Christian pupils. It may be the only Hebrew school in the world at which a nun arrives every morning to teach religion to the Catholic students. A second day school is the Zion Primary School. Half of the Jewish youths are educated in these two schools, while the remainder receive some Jewish education in afternoon Hebrew schools or with private tutors. The Chief Rabbi's office is located in the Stratford College building at 1 Zion Road.

The arts building at Trinity College in Dublin is the home of the Weingreen Museum of Biblical Antiquities. It contains pottery and other archaeological artifacts from Israeli excavations, collected by Professor Jack Weingreen, a fellow emeritus of Hebrew Studies at Trinity. To make an appointment to visit the museum, call J. R. Bartlett (77-29-41).

The Irish Jewish Museum is in the hundred-year-old Walworth Road Synagogue. The upper floor retains the original synagogue interior while memorabilia of the Irish Jewish community is exhibited on the ground floor. (Hours are 11 A.M. to 3:30 P.M., Sundays, Mondays, and Wednesdays.) The museum's curator is Raphael Siev, the only Jew in the Irish diplomatic service. The museum was dedicated in 1985 by President Chaim Herzog of Israel during his first state visit to the country of his birth.

GENERAL SIGHTS: Dublin is an old city, and one of its most venerable treasures is the Book of Kells, an illuminated manuscript of the four Gospels, from the eighth century, reputed to be the most beautiful in the world. Visitors can view the book in the library of Trinity College, which is believed to be the world's largest single-chamber library. Trinity College—part of the University of Dublin—was founded by Queen Elizabeth I of England, and its large arch and cobblestone walks are reminiscent of a time long ago. Its art gallery, however, often exhibits modern works.

Dublin has beautiful squares and parks. Merrion and Fitzwilliam squares are framed by Georgian town houses, with their colorfully painted doors and shiny brass knockers and nameplates. St. Stephen's Green is set on twenty-two acres in the middle of the city, while farther out is the immense Phoenix Park, the largest enclosed urban park in the world.

Dublin is also renowned for its theater and its pubs—the latter seeming, more often than not, to be a form of street theater. Tried and true productions are presented at the Abbey Theater, but experimental plays are staged downstairs at the Peacock, and in small theaters around the city. At Toner's, on Baggot Street, the two traditions are combined: upstairs is a pub; downstairs, a theater company performs plays by Sean O'Casey, John M. Synge, and other Irish playwrights.

EATING: The Maccabi Sports Center has the city's only kosher restaurant. It is open Saturday night and Sunday, but visitors are advised to phone ahead. There are also two vegetarian restaurants—Blazing Salads at Powerscourt Centre and Bananas at 15 Upper Stephen Street—recommended for kashrut observers.

SIDE TRIPS: "If you want to see Jewish Ireland," says former Lord Mayor Goldberg, "Dublin is the place. If you want to see the remnants of Jewish Ireland, you go to Cork and Limerick."

Irish cities are generally more drab than the large cities of Europe.

Outside of Dublin, the real attraction is the countryside. But visitors exploring the natural beauty of County Cork's beaches and cliffs may want to make a quick stop in Ireland's second largest city.

Cork, according to Goldberg, has a Jewish population which is "a minimum of fourteen and a maximum of eighteen." Jewish youths, looking for work, have left Cork for Israel and England. Goldberg suggests that visitors see the city's only shul, which he fears may not be around too much longer if the population keeps declining. The traditional, unpretentious Cork Hebrew Congregation, at 10 South Terrace, was built by Russian Jews almost a century ago.

Limerick is on the way from Dublin to the beautiful and rocky, green hills of western Ireland. It is not only dull; it is also the bleakest place in Irish Jewish history. In 1904, before the formation of the Republic, a Redemptionist priest, perhaps urged on by merchants who were unhappy about Jewish competition, began preaching anti-Semitic rhetoric and instigated a pogrom. Jews were attacked and eventually left the city forever. Interestingly, in 1984 the eighty-year-old incident was discussed and debated in a series of letters in an Irish newspaper as though it had just happened. Dedicated history buffs can walk down Wolfe Tone Street, which used to be the Jewish quarter, or visit the Jewish cemetery, located about half a mile outside the city, on the road to Dublin.

Reports of violence in Northern Ireland scare away many tourists. But parts of Belfast, a city surrounded by mountains, are still lovely, despite the "troubles." The Northern Irish countryside is breathtaking, particularly the Antrim Coast, which has been compared to the Pacific Palisades. There are about five hundred Jews in the province, and the community tends to be more insular and somewhat more prosperous than Dublin's. There are also political differences between the two groups, which are said to be less pointed now than in years past. Dublin Jews generally supported the Republican movement, which fought to free Ireland from Great Britain. Belfast Jews still tend to align themselves with the Protestants, who believe that Northern Ireland should remain forever part of Great Britain. The synagogue in Belfast—the Belfast Hebrew Congregation—is at 49 Somerton Road.

READING: James Joyce's *Ulysses* is both Irish and Jewish. To get a sense of the city, visitors can read Joyce's short stories in *Dubliners* and his novel *A Portrait of the Artist as a Young Man*. Sean O'Casey's *Autobiographies I* (Carroll & Graf) are beautifully written stories about the maturing of a poor Protestant Dubliner. The Irish Tourist Board has published a small pamphlet, "Information for Jewish Visitors," which gives a list of synagogues, with prayer times, restaurants, and institutions.

Ireland is an easy country in which to travel. The people are as friendly as the advertisements claim and the scenery as beautiful. Also special are the unplanned tableaus, the scenes of people going about their daily lives, selling vegetables at the market, drinking at the pubs or bringing a herd of cows home from pasture.

There are even some scenes of Jewish life to watch. One recent Friday afternoon in a kindergarten at Stratford College, two new students were sitting at a small replica of their parents' dining-room table. The little boy wore a yarmulke; the little girl had two silver candlesticks with white candles in them before her. They both sipped cups filled with grape juice. "They are having their Friday night drink," their teacher explained. And the two children of Dublin took another sip.

—BARBARA FISCHKIN

Florence

Santa Croce *(Italian Government Tourist Office)*

A tourist enters a little jewelry store near the Church of Santa Croce in Florence. There is a puzzled look on her face. Why, she wants to know, is there, at the apex of the façade of one of Italy's grandest Gothic churches, a design that looks suspiciously like a Star of David?

The clerk is stumped, as she is every time someone inquires about the six-pointed star adorning this outstanding Franciscan landmark. But she is not alone. There is no mention of it in leading guidebooks. Nor does Florence's official tourist office have a clue.

HISTORY AND SIGHTS: The saga of the star on Santa Croce, however, reposes with the Jewish community in Florence, a community of fourteen hundred that traces its existence to the fourteenth century. It is one of a host of indications of the ongoing Jewish involvement in the fabric of the quintessential Renaissance city of Tuscany. According to Yohanna-Miriam Pick Margolius, former head of the cultural department of Florence's WIZO and niece of Samuel Hirsh Margulies, Chief Rabbi of Florence from 1890 to 1922, the star was mandated by the architect—who just happened to be a Jew from Ancona.

Niccolò Matas, Margolius relates, was one of several architects competing for the commission to design the façade in the late 1850s, when it was decided that the plain brick front of the vast fourteenth-century church should be replaced with the more imposing black-and-white marble. Matas's design won, with no questions asked about the star, because it is regarded as a symbol of Jesus. What is more, a star formed by two superimposed triangles is a mystical sign—the upward-pointing triangle representing man trying to raise himself by praying to God; the one pointing down representing the grace of God descending on man.

Matas's background was not revealed until contract-signing time. Then his origins became clear because, as a presumably observant Jew, he requested Saturdays off. And he had another request. Since Santa Croce is Florence's pantheon, containing the tombs of Machiavelli, Michelangelo, and Galileo, among others, and since all architects who worked on the church were supposed to be buried there as well, Matas wanted his place among the renowned.

But the Franciscan brothers were opposed to burying a Jew on such hallowed ground. And the Jewish community itself was aghast at the thought of a Jew lying in Santa Croce. So Matas was buried under the top steps of the church's entrance, right in front of its massive, sculptured main center door. The burial slab remains today, a white, cracked marble rectangle.

While the Santa Croce star is perhaps the most dramatic and obvious demonstration of the Jewish presence in Florence—indeed, Santa Croce, on the Piazza di Santa Croce, is a sightseeing "must" on all tourist itineraries—a hint of far deeper Jewish involvement may be found by sharply discerning eyes in a fresco on the wall of the Benozzo Gozzoli chapel in the Palazzo Medici Riccardi (Via Cavour 1, up the stairs, immediately to the right of the entrance). Though called *The Journey of the Magi,* this work is said to represent the trip to Florence in the fifteenth century of the potentates of Byzantium. On one side is the entourage from Constantinople. On the other is a portrait of the entire Medici family with court. And among the sages of that court is Elijah Delmedigo, a Jew.

Delmedigo was one of several Jewish men of letters held in esteem by the scholars and humanists of the Renaissance, and it was from him that the thinker Pico della Mirandola learned the Hebrew language, literature, and philosophy—disciplines considered important by the well-educated of that day. Beyond representing the Medicis' appreciation of Jewish thinking, Delmedigo's presence in court also speaks of the position of the Jews in Florence at that time.

Most of them had come from the settlement of Pitigliano, on the edge of Tuscany, which had been established by descendants of Jews brought to Italy as slaves after the fall of Jerusalem in 70 C.E. (The Italian surname Servi, meaning slave, belongs only to Jews.) Though Jews appeared in Florence in the fourteenth century, the first official invitation to them—a group of about a hundred moneylenders—went out in 1430. Bankers themselves, the Medicis appreciated these Jews. Since many records lie unplumbed in the city archives, however, one can only speculate on their help in financing works of the Renaissance.

There were, of course, segments of Florentine society that despised the Jews. A demonstration of this antipathy exists in the fourteenth-century church of Or San Michele, on Via de' Calzaiuoli (Street of Hosiers). On the right, upon entering this sanctuary, stands a statue of

St. Anne and child. On the statue is a Latin inscription phonetically rendered in Hebrew letters. It translates to "I am the light of the world" and is believed to have been engraved there to convey to the Jews the power of Jesus, after a young Jewish boy, in the sixteenth century, allegedly committed a sacrilege against the Church, for which he was executed.

When the Medicis were in power—a situation which seesawed—the Jews were treated well. In fact, the Jewish tenure in Florence was generally fairly comfortable even when they were ghettoized by Cosimo I in 1570. He did so in return for receiving from the Pope the right to absolute rule of Tuscany as its grand duke.

But Cosimo acted reluctantly, and he did not segregate everyone. He chose some families to live near him in the shadow of the Pitti Palace, presumably so he could have moneylenders nearby. Those ten families—enough to form a minyan—lived on a narrow street that, until the Fascists changed its name during World War II, was Via de' Giudei, or Street of the Jews. Today, the street is Via de' Ramaglianti, off Via dello Sprone, and a rough area along the wall is thought to be the remnant of a synagogue.

The ghetto itself, because it could contain no churches, was built in the worst part of town—in the red-light district. Nothing remains today of the ghetto, for the area, known as the Old City, has been completely rebuilt. However, it stood between what are now the bustling Via Roma, Via Brunelleschi, Via de' Pecori and Piazza della Repubblica.

After several false alarms, the ghetto was permanently opened in 1848; some Jews moved across the street to Via dell' Oche, where they built at least two synagogues. Today, near an archway leading to No. 5 on that narrow, cobbled road, a wall plaque commemorates one such site, as well as the liberation of Florence's Jews by the Allies in 1944.

The Jewish community that left the ghetto was not as purely Italian as that which first entered. By the 1600s, encouraged by Cosimo I, Jewish refugees from Spain and Portugal had begun arriving in droves. They were rich, aristocratic, cultured and, unlike the Italian Jews who practiced a religious ritual that derived directly from the Temple in Jerusalem, they followed the Sefardic rite. They established their own synagogue in the ghetto and, by the time of emancipation, it was the dominant one.

Of top priority to the liberated Jews was the building of a synagogue "worthy of Florence." On land purchased at what was then the city's edge, the Jewish community erected a structure inspired by the Byzantine church in Constantinople, Hagia Sophia.

The onion-domed, arabesque-decorated structure, which opened in 1882, stands on Via Luigi Carlo Farini 4 (telephone, 245-252) and is a national monument. Though Florence's Jews now live all around the city, a century ago most clustered within walking distance of the synagogue—the poorer Jews, to its right; the wealthier ones including, reportedly, the Uzzielli family, to the left, in palaces, some of which bordered the exclusive park, Piazza d'Azeglio (Azalea Square).

By the eve of World War II, there were about three thousand Jews in Florence. But many who perceived the threat began emigrating. When racial laws were promulgated in Italy by Mussolini, Florentines tried to protect their Jews. Nevertheless, 243 were rounded up by the Nazis and sent to their deaths, including the rabbi Nathan Cassuto.

PERSONALITIES: Rabbi Margulies (1858–1922), a Polish Jew who immersed himself in the Italian and Sefardic rites, was Florence's Chief Rabbi from 1890 until he died. He founded, in 1899, the Collegio Rabbinico Italiano, reviving Jewish life in Italy, erased some of his community's insularity by establishing contacts between Italian and European Jews, and lifted Florence to the center of Italian Jewry. Rabbi Margulies was a Zionist and in touch with world Jewry, including Theodor Herzl.

Umberto Cassuto (1882–1951) followed in Rabbi Margulies's footsteps. An Italian historian and biblical and Semitic scholar, he was rabbi of Florence and director of the rabbinical seminary. He wrote the history of Florence's Jews in the Renaissance and, in 1939, became a professor of Bible studies at the Hebrew University in Jerusalem.

Another distinguished scholar and ardent Zionist who taught Jewish history, Bible, and Hebrew language at the seminary was Rabbi Hirsch Perez Chajes (1876–1927). He, too, helped propel Florence to the focus of Jewish culture in Italy, before he moved on to become the Chief Rabbi of Vienna.

Also associated with the city is Amadeo Modigliani, the painter and sculptor. He was born in nearby Leghorn, studied in Florence, and later became known as the foremost portraitist among the "Montparnasse Circle" of Jewish artists, who were drawn to Paris at the turn of the twentieth century.

COMMUNITY AND SIGHTS: Today's Jewish community of fourteen hundred supports the massive, Byzantine-style synagogue and museum, elementary and high schools, an old-age home, mikvah, kosher restaurant with Italian-style cooking, and an ad hoc theater group.

The community is well integrated into Florentine society. It has its share of Jewish-owned shops, from Gustavo Melli's antique jewelry store on the Ponte Vecchio to the Diulio 48 department store on Via del Corso in the heart of the city. But unlike Milanese Jews, who are mostly businessmen and industrialists, or Roman Jews, who are primarily merchants and shopkeepers, Florentine Jews can be found in a variety of other occupations as well, ranging from medicine to photography, sculpting (the works of Dario Viterbo are known internationally) to Etruscology (the study of ancient Etruria, today's Tuscany).

Most are well educated; few are needy. But like other Florentines, they tend to be somewhat closed, even to Jews from other cities in Italy. What is more, few among them speak languages other than Italian—though an amateur theatrical group was formed some years ago to perform, on occasion, a comedy, *La Gnora Luna* ("Madame, the Moon") in the Judeo-Florentine dialect that disappeared about two hundred years ago.

Only a handful of Florentines are Orthodox; not many more are observant. And, though the Great Synagogue is officially Orthodox, following an Italo-Sefardic ritual, it permits deviations. Since the war, for example, women have been permitted to join male members of their family downstairs, in the rear, for certain prayers. The synagogue is also distinctive because it reflects the influences of Catholicism—in its pulpit, which is at the top of a winding staircase, and in its use of the organ on some holidays. Though damaged during the war and the Arno flood in 1966, the thousand-seat sanctuary, which sits behind a great wrought-iron gate, in a well-landscaped garden, still has elaborately frescoed walls, Stars of David inlaid in its marble floors, and an Ark with doors of gold.

Upstairs, there is a small museum which contains photographs of the ghetto and brocade Torah covers in carmines, greens, and yellows; old megillahs and the key to the chapel of an association that used to ransom Jews captured by the Barbary pirates. There is also a blowup of Elijah Delmedigo as seen in the Medici court fresco. Call the synagogue number for hours.

Also situated on these communal grounds is the Nathan Cassuto Hebrew School and mikvah. The Home for the Aged is on Via Carducci 11.

EATING: On the second floor of the building immediately adjoining the synagogue is Il Cuscussu (Via Farini 2a, one flight up), the kosher restaurant. It is a bright room, with white-on-red tablecloths, red-and-white checkered lampshades, and specialties of the house that range from a spinach mold iced with tomato sauce to a pâté of olives; from a meat borscht to the couscous that gives the place its name. Its chianti is kosher—indeed, kosher red and white wines are made in Tuscany—and so is its prosciutto. Prosciutto? Yes, made from the dark meat of turkey legs and cured like pork. The restaurant is open every day from 12:30 to 2 P.M. and evenings, except Sundays, 7:30 to 9 P.M. However, on Shabbat and holidays, prepaid reservations are necessary (telephone, 210-670 or 584-631).

SIDE TRIP: Siena, an hour away from Florence, is one of Italy's most beautiful cities. Its synagogue is located near an archway at Vicolo delle Scotte 14, just in from Via del Porrione. A plaque there commemorates those Jews from Siena deported during World War II.

READING: Some of Il Cuscusso's recipes can be found in *The Classic Cuisine of the Italian Jews* by Edda Servi Machlin of Pitigliano (Everest House/Dodd, Mead). Others have been contributed, from her family's legacy, by one of Il Cuscussu's four women owners, Jennie Bassani Liscia—who just happens to be the sister of Giorgio Bassani, author of *The Garden of the Finzi-Continis* (Atheneum), a book about a Jewish family in Ferrara.

Another, perhaps better known, literary tie-in exists in the hills overlooking Florence. There is the Villa I Tatti, once the home of Bernard Berenson, the American art historian and connoisseur who lived most of his life in Italy. This villa, now the property of Harvard University, is said to have been the model for the home of Aaron Jastrow of Herman Wouk's *The Winds of War* (Little, Brown). With its history, style, and understated Jewish connection, the villa is a microcosm of Florence.

—PHYLLIS ELLEN FUNKE

Frankfurt

The Roemer (City Hall) *(German National Tourist Office)*

The position of Frankfurt's Jewish community is perhaps best illustrated by an extraordinary event that took place in 1985. Thirty Jewish protesters marched on stage of the Kammerspiel Theater to prevent the premiere of a contemporary play by the late Rainer Werner Fassbinder that they regarded as anti-Semitic. Instead of booing the demonstrators off the stage, the audience engaged them in an emotional three-hour discussion on anti-Semitism and freedom of expression. "I do not feel myself offended by this play," said Daniel Cohn-Bendit, the Jewish radical who led the 1968 student uprising in Paris and who was sitting in the audience, "but I welcome your protests. You are in the tradition of 1968. This will be the first demonstration in the history of Frankfurt that will not be broken up by the police."

It was an evening of real-life theater. Cohn-Bendit was right; the police didn't intervene. Indeed, the city's mayor and political establishment agreed with the demonstrators. The play was never performed. The Jewish community—sensitive but bold, and widely respected—won its point.

The Jewish community of every German city today is a shadow of what it was before World War II. But one thing has remained constant: Frankfurt-am-Main is, and has always been, the most Jewish city in the country. Though Berlin has had more Jews for most of the last century, Frankfurt has always had at least twice as many on a proportional basis. For influence and depth of history, Frankfurt Jewry cannot be matched. When the Nazis came to power, in fact, Frankfurt was the only major German city with a Jewish mayor. Ludwig Landmann was forced to resign in March 1933, six weeks after Hitler became chancellor.

HISTORY: Frankfurt had a flourishing Jewish community, led by merchants, in the twelfth century and possibly earlier. Between the thirteenth and seventeenth centuries, however, the community lived through repeating cycles of well-being and persecution. There were massacres and expulsions in 1241, 1349, and 1614, but the community always restored itself within a few years. It was in 1462 that Jews were first required to live in the walled Judengasse (Jews' Street).

By the end of the sixteenth century, Frankfurt had a prosperous Jewish community and was also a center of Jewish learning. The eighteenth century saw the rise of Mayer Amschel Rothschild, scion of an old but undistinguished mercantile family. He turned his coin, antique, and money-changing business into one of Europe's leading banking empires.

In the early nineteenth century, Frankfurt established itself as a center of Reform Judaism. By the 1840s, Reform Jews dominated the community, accounting for the large majority of Frankfurt Jewry. The rise of Reform Judaism paralleled the French Revolution, the Napoleonic occupation of Frankfurt, and the German revolution of 1848, all of which contributed to Jewish emancipation. Emancipation, in turn, weakened the authority of the Reform-dominated community board; in 1851 a group of Orthodox rabbis, led by Samson Raphael Hirsch and backed by the Rothschilds, capitalized on the loosening community control and established their own religious association within the community, and eventually their own kehillah. Thereafter, Orthodoxy and Reform coexisted as separate communities in Frankfurt.

From 1900 until 1933—when the community numbered about thirty thousand—Frankfurt's Jews were at the peak of their influence. In 1900, Jewish Frankfurters paid 427 marks per capita in taxes while non-Jews paid 103 marks. Shortly before Hitler's rise, it was estimated that Jews were responsible for 35 percent of the economic activity in Frankfurt, although they were only 7 percent of the population.

Despite the community's history, the fate of Frankfurt Jewry in the Nazi era was no different than that of the rest of Germany's Jews. After Kristallnacht, the night in November 1938 when the nation's synagogues were burned, hundreds of Jewish men were sent to the Dachau and Buchenwald concentration camps. More than half of Frankfurt's Jews emigrated before the war broke out. In 1941, those remaining were deported, first to ghettoes in Poland and Russia and later directly to concentration camps.

PERSONALITIES: Jews had contributed richly to Frankfurt's intellectual life. Among those born in Frankfurt or who worked there in the 1920s and '30s were the social scientists Herbert Marcuse and Teodor Adorno and the theologians Martin Buber and Franz Rosenzweig. Two pioneers of modern psychology, Erik Erikson and Erich Fromm, are both Frankfurt natives, as is the more recently prominent Ruth Westheimer. Also associated with Frankfurt were Nahum Goldmann, the Zionist leader, Moritz Oppenheim, the artist, and Leopold Sonnemann, founder of *Frankfurter Zeitung,* ancestor of the *Frankfurter Allgemeine.* The paper is now one of the leading dailies of West Germany—but if you want a more objective view of the Middle East, read *Die Welt.*

COMMUNITY: There are six thousand Jews in the Frankfurt area today, and the community is characterized by aging, prosperity, and irony. Today's community has only the most tenuous link with prewar Frankfurt Jewry. German Jews who survived the war did not, by and large, return to Germany. Today's community is made up overwhelmingly of postwar refugees from Eastern Europe. The once great Reform Jewish tradition is gone. The one Frankfurt synagogue that survived Kristallnacht—the Liberal Westend Synagogue at 30 Freiherr-vom-Steinstrasse—is today Orthodox, as are the four other synagogues in the city.

The West End has the greatest concentration of Jews, as was the case before World War II, but the area can no longer be called a Jewish neighborhood. There are also Jews in the East End, where most of the other synagogues are. While all the city's synagogues are Orthodox, they vary in ritual from Frankfurter to Mainzer to Polish.

The largest number of Frankfurt's Jews are self-employed, particularly as shopkeepers and real estate brokers. (The character in the Fassbinder play that prompted charges of anti-Semitism was a West End developer named simply "The Rich Jew.") There are no more Jewish bankers. Despite Germany's recent history, and despite the Kammerspiel protest, Frankfurt's Jews feel they are little different from the rest of Western Jewry; their main problem, they say, is assimilation, not anti-Semitism.

Many Frankfurt émigrés maintain ties to the city. Every few years the city of Frankfurt brings over dozens of former Jewish citizens. Visitors are treated to receptions in the fifteenth-century City Hall (the Römer), memorial meetings, and sightseeing. Though many people accept the city's invitations, there are also many who refuse to accept German largesse.

SIGHTS: In Jewish terms, Frankfurt has more sites than sights—places with a Jewish past but no present trace of it. The Judengasse was gone long before Hitler came to power, but you can still stand on the spot. From the Zeil—the pedestrian mall that runs through the center of the city—turn south on Fahrgasse and make a quick left through what was once the wall of the ghetto. You'll be on Bornerstrasse, a narrow, dead-end street of apartments and offices. This is where, for over four hundred years, Jews became victims and million-aires. The only Jewish trace is a plaque marking where the Borner-strasse Synagogue was destroyed on Kristallnacht.

The Westend Synagogue is the only one in the city with any history. The large, gray-stone building is typical of early twentieth-century temple architecture—and certainly a rarity in Germany. If you go there, it is worthwhile to walk through the West End, a hybrid neigh-borhood of stately prewar homes that survived Allied bombings and functional postwar apartment buildings.

Many of the city's Jewish organizations are housed at Hebelstrasse 17 in a former Jewish school. On the first floor of the building—and not yet open to the general public—are the makings of a Jewish museum. A rich collection includes drawings, photographs, books, and artifacts from Frankfurt's Jewish history, but there is a strong emphasis on the Nazi era. This is noteworthy because much of the work on the collection is being done not by the Jewish community but by the city of Frankfurt. Dietrich Andernacht, the city archivist and director of the project, says the museum will be housed in the Roth-schild Palais, at Untermainkai 14, along the Main River. It will, he says, include "Rothschild rooms" and a scale model of the eighteenth-century Judengasse.

News of the community can be found—in German—in the *Frank-furter Jüdisches Gemeindeblatt*. The paper lists weekday and Shabbat prayer times for all the city's synagogues. For questions about kosher meals or what else to see of the Jewish community, call the community center at 59-01-17.

GENERAL SIGHTS: Goethe's house is a faithful reconstruction of the poet's eighteenth-century world. In cobbled Römerberg Square, in front of the City Hall, there is still a medieval feeling, enhanced by new construction of period buildings. The Palmengarten, with its palm trees and rose and alpine gardens, is a pleasant place for a walk.

Across the Main from the center of town is Sachsenhausen which, though it became part of Frankfurt six hundred years ago, maintains an identity of its own. Alt-Sachsenhausen is a part-honky-tonk, part-Middle Ages maze of restaurants and taverns where patrons drink beer and the local brew of apple wine. Also in Sachsenhausen is the Städel, one of Germany's leading art museums.

DAY TRIPS: There are several places that combine Jewish and general interest within easy traveling distance of Frankfurt. Eighty minutes into Bavaria, by train, is Würzburg, a beautiful city noted for the Residenz, the eighteenth-century Baroque palace of its prince-bishops; the Cathedral of St. Kilian, a restored Romanesque church built on the site of a former synagogue; and, facing town from across the Main, Marienberg Castle. The Residenz and the Cathedral, and other buildings in the town, are adorned with the brilliant sculpture of Tilman Riemenschneider. About a hundred Jews live in Würzburg (compared to two thousand before the war). A plaque marks the spot of the Dormerschulestrasse Synagogue, destroyed on Kristallnacht. The community might not have been reconstituted had it not been for David Schuster, a Würzburg native who returned from Israel in the 1950s. In addition to serving several terms in the Bavarian legislature, Schuster oversaw the construction of a new synagogue and home for the aged. The complex at 11 Valentin-Beckerstrasse—particularly the synagogue interior, reminiscent of prewar German sanctuaries—is worth a visit. In 1982, Würzburg gave its annual cultural prize to a native son, the Israeli poet Yehuda Amichai.

About an hour south of Frankfurt is Worms, where Martin Luther refused to retract his beliefs before the Imperial Diet in 1521. There are no Jews in the city today, but the old Judengasse is being restored; many homes have been renovated in the old style and, wherever possible, plaques bearing the names of former Jewish owners posted on the outside.

Adjacent to the Judengasse is an eleventh-century synagogue (which may be the oldest in Europe), restored in 1961. Rashi, the great Talmudic scholar, spent time in the synagogue when he was in Worms. Jews from the surrounding area occasionally use the synagogue for weddings or bar mitzvahs, but it is primarily a tourist sight —and a revered one—in which Gentile guides require Gentile visitors to cover their heads. Behind the synagogue is Rashihaus, the city archive and municipal museum, presided over by Fritz Reuter, who has studied Hebrew and is familiar with Jewish history, local and general. About half the city museum consists of Judaica. Worms also has a well-kept Jewish cemetery dating to the eleventh century.

CHOICES: If you're looking for a hotel that combines modern amenities with old-world charm, the Frankfurter Hof is perfect. It is centrally located and also favored by those who attend the periodic reunions of former Frankfurt Jews. Intercity rail service in Germany is convenient and efficient. Public transportation in Frankfurt works well but can be confusing if you don't know German.

READING: For a good fictional look at Jewish life in Frankfurt

between 1900 and World War II, read *Yesterday's Streets* by Silvia Ten-
nenbaum (Random House). *12 Kaiserhofstrasse* (some editions bear the
title *The Invisible Jew*) by Valentin Senger (Dutton) is the true story of a
Jewish family that managed to live through the war in Frankfurt without being captured. For a four-century biography of Frankfurt's most
famous Jewish family, read *The Rothschilds* by Frederic Morton (Atheneum). For a contemporary picture there is *Strangers in Their Own Land:
Young Jews in Germany and Austria Today* by Peter Sichrovsky (Basic
Books). For an answer to the perennial question of how Jews can live
in post-Nazi Germany, Sichrovsky's book is a good place to start.

—ALAN M. TIGAY

Gibraltar

Samuel Benady, head of Gibraltar Bar, and grandson Julian
(*Leni Sonnenfeld*)

Since Gibraltar, the imposing British bastion on the strait connecting the Atlantic and the Mediterranean, is linked to Spain by an isthmus, it is not really an island. But it might as well be.

Given its location (at the southern European extremity, not nine miles from Africa), its status (a Crown Colony, however autonomous, appended to London), its population (a mélange of thirty thousand mostly Mediterranean peoples), its size (barely two square miles, not all of which is habitable), and its appeal (to Spain, which only recently ended a fifteen-year attempt to cow it by sealing its only border), Gibraltar has—and little wonder—developed its own *modus vivendi.*

It had the advantage of starting from scratch since, after 1704, when England wrested the fortress from Spain, nearly all the Spanish inhabitants left. Apart from the Royal Navy and other garrison members, those repopulating the promontory—forming a city at the Rock's base —included Maltese, Genoese, and Jews. They built a society permeated by Mediterranean warmth but regulated by British discipline.

Faced with the periodically besieging Spanish on one side and the seas that inhibited expansion on the other, Gibraltar's new residents learned, for the sake of survival, to accommodate and tolerate. What is more, with no agriculture, and few resources beyond its harbor, Gibraltar became a largely mercantile community in which Jews, present from nearly the beginning, played such an integral part that at one time almost half the shops on Main Street were Jewish-owned.

The Jewish presence is pervasive, a situation best illustrated by noting that Gibraltar's two highest officials, Chief Minister Sir Joshua Hassan and Mayor Abraham William Serfaty, are Jews. Outside Israel, there is probably no national or colonial entity in the world with such a distinction.

HISTORY: Those Jews who headed for the Rock after 1704 were not the first to set foot on Gibraltar. Historians mention some living there in the fourteenth century who issued an appeal for help in ransoming Jews captured by Barbary pirates, and others purportedly used it as a way station in their flight from the Inquisition. But those who came with British rule were Sefardim living, since the Inquisition, in North Africa, Italy, the Netherlands, and England.

At first they confronted a serious obstacle. According to the 1713 Treaty of Utrecht, in which Spain confirmed Britain's possession of the Rock, neither Moors nor Jews could live in Gibraltar under any circumstances. Jews quickly made themselves useful to the British, however, by negotiating with Morocco for goods whenever Spain threatened to, or actually did, cut supply lines. By 1717, there were probably three hundred Jews on the Rock, but they lived under the threat of expulsion and, after several token attempts by the British to enforce the treaty's terms, the Jews were, during a moment of British-Spanish détente, evicted.

Had Spain and Britain remained friendly, the Jews would probably have remained barred. But when the Spanish embargoed Gibraltar again and Britain needed help from Morocco, the Moroccan King—who had at least one Jewish confidante—intervened. Morocco, he said, would supply Gibraltar only if it were open to all his subjects, both Moors *and* Jews. Britain continued trying to dance at two weddings, but by the siege of 1727, during which the Jews stood fast, it was clear they were in Gibraltar to stay.

They began obtaining property grants, including one for the first officially sanctioned synagogue, Shaar Hashamayim. By 1739, all the family names still prevalent today were present—Hassan, Benady, Serfaty, and Benyunes. By 1753 there were six hundred Jews in the enclave, making up a third of the civilian population. The community included not only the wealthy merchants who dealt with Morocco, but also small traders, shopkeepers, laborers, boatmen, tailors, shoemakers, peddlers, and porters. The largest property owner on Gibraltar also came from their ranks. Isaac Aboab was referred to as "the king of the Jews," both affectionately and otherwise.

Indeed, occasionally, the fine houses of Gibraltar's Jews were targets of resentment and once, in 1780, they were subjected to a mild pogrom during which doors and windows were broken and the Jewish cemetery desecrated. But, comparatively speaking, Gibraltar's Jews encountered few internal difficulties.

Though the Great Siege of 1779–83 drove some Jews to London, others stayed on, working as privateers or in other defense-related positions. Abraham Hassan so distinguished himself in the army that he was granted land. Later, during the Napoleonic Wars, Aaron Núñez Cardozo, who enjoyed the friendship of Lord Nelson, discovered a conspiracy that threatened the fortress. He too was granted land in the heart of town, on which he built a grand house which is now the City Hall.

Midway through the nineteenth century, when the Rock was at the pinnacle of its strategic importance, most retail trade was being handled by the two thousand Jews then living in Gibraltar. They were attending new synagogues formed to handle the overflow, publishing a paper in Ladino, *Cronica Israelita,* and patronizing the theater in numbers sufficient to darken the stage on Friday nights.

Their presence in Gibraltar continued with little interruption until World War II when all civilian residents were evacuated to Madeira, Tangier, and England. After the war, some did not return.

During the war, Gibraltar became a conduit for some refugees escaping from Hitler; later, with the establishment of Israel, it became a staging ground of Moroccan Jews bound for the new state. There has been no great aliyah among Gibraltarians, however, and the size of the Jewish community today is about six hundred.

COMMUNITY: The Jews of Gibraltar, says James Levy, president of the community, are "integrated but not assimilated." By this he means they live happily and comfortably among other Gibraltarians, work and play with them, yet maintain a decidedly—and overtly— Jewish way of life.

Indeed, the Gibraltar community—almost entirely Sefardic and assertively proud of it—is known for its religious conservatism and cohesiveness. While estimates vary, and range widely, from 20 to 90 percent, a large number of Jewish Gibraltarians are shomrei mitzvot. No Jewish shops open on Saturdays or Jewish holidays. Almost every Jew is kosher, at least at home (using meat imported from the Netherlands and Britain). Many attend daily services. Children wear kippot in the streets, and more women than fifty years ago are covering their hair according to strict Orthodox observance. In addition, despite the community's appreciation of new blood, its conversion rules are so strict that it recognizes only those performed in Gibraltar or the United Kingdom, and decidedly not those of Morocco.

Not surprisingly, though, there are chinks in this apparently solid front. With time, there have been intermarriages—enough so that one community member comments, "There are Cohens on Main Street who haven't been Jews for a hundred and fifty years." Meanwhile, another Jewish observer notes that if the Jews do not "cheat" on their diet in Gibraltar, probably a good third do when they get to Spain, not to mention those who ride on Saturdays.

Nevertheless, according to Chief Minister Hassan, in Gibraltar each religious group expects others to practice their tradition, which makes it relatively easy to be observant. (Jewish officials, for example, are usually asked before official functions what they can eat; such events are carefully set with an eye to religious calendars.)

Besides crediting Gibraltar's scant size and deep Jewish roots for this tolerance, one Jewish businessman thinks that such détente exists because, while the Jews form a minuscule minority, and the Roman Catholics the overwhelming majority, they unite since neither is part of the small Protestant Establishment. From another viewpoint, Gibraltar's Jews can mix yet maintain their Jewishness, because the Sefardim, more than the once-ghettoized Ashkenazim, are used to adapting themselves to their environment.

Gibraltar's little community supports four rabbis and four synagogues, all of which operate on Shabbat and holidays, but only one of which is used—on a quarterly rotation basis—for daily services. The leading synagogue, from which the entire community is addressed, is Shaar Hashamayim. A small synagogue, for children up to twelve, has also been established in Gibraltar's Jewish school, with services conducted by the students. And, in all, "God Save the Queen" is sung, in Hebrew, on holidays.

The community also maintains a club, an old-age home, and various social service operations, taking pride in its ability to look after its own.

While it has no spectacularly rich members, the community is reasonably prosperous, with about 20 percent of Main Street's establishments still in its hands. This represents a recent decline, since some shopkeepers have sold to incoming Indians, and more in the current generation are pursuing professional careers instead. Gibraltarian Jews, though, are involved in all fields—from police work to surveying. And they live all over Gibraltar—if for no other reason than that housing is so scarce.

For all its remoteness, insularity, and inbreeding—it seems as if everyone is related to everyone else—and for all the pettiness this engenders, James Levy asserts that the community is healthy. Furthermore, though the community has been static for some years, Levy now sees renewed growth, as young couples have larger families and expatriates return.

The latter stems largely from the opening of the Spanish border. Once cause for concern—lest young people spend their weekends "over there" and undesirable elements (that is, terrorists) enter—the recently revived freedom is now viewed as a positive factor that could lead to contact with other communities. In fact, the primary worries of Gibraltarian Jews today seem to be the loss of status they may suffer when Sir Joshua is no longer in office and the problems the public wearing of kippot could cause—since this, in some eyes, underscores their difference from the rest of the population.

PERSONALITIES: The most outstanding Jew in Gibraltar is Sir Joshua, who was first elected mayor in 1945 and has gone on to win elections in all but one term since. In 1964, he was chosen Chief Minister and, as such, pleaded Gibraltar's case for remaining British before the United Nations. Abraham Serfaty followed him to the mayoralty in 1979. Solomon Seruya, a Main Street proprietor, divides his time these days between Gibraltar and Jerusalem, where he is vice president of the Sefardic Council and where, in 1976, he was appointed Israel's ambassador to the Philippines. Samuel Benady is the head of the Gibraltar Bar.

SIGHTS: Though Gibraltar may be a ministate—with no one of its attractions more than minutes from the other—it has managed to cram a fair number of sights and sites into a small area. Its four synagogues, in fact, exist on the very fringes of the bustling Main Street area.

Of prime interest is Shaar Hashamayim, behind an unprepossessing wall at 47-49 Engineer Lane. As Gibraltar's principal Jewish place of worship, the synagogue is known both as the Great Synagogue and the Cathedral Synagogue. The congregation generally dates its founding to 1724 and claims to be the oldest such Sefardi institution in Europe after the Portuguese Synagogue in Amsterdam and Bevis Marks in London.

Originally, the synagogue property was entered from a road that juts off Engineer Lane at a right angle, running past the red-and-white wall of Macs Corner, a restaurant. Once called Synagogue Lane, this curving way is now Serfaty's Passage, one of several streets named for Jews. (Among others are Bensimbra's Alley, Serruya Ramp, Abecasis's Passage and Benoliel's Passage—where the houses of the namesakes once stood.)

When a storm destroyed the first Shaar Hashamayim in 1766, adjacent land was purchased for the construction of a larger, more elegant edifice. The synagogue, entered today from Engineer Lane through an elaborately decorated tiled courtyard, is quietly dignified, with its marble pillars, its traditional central pulpit, and its mahogany trim— for the walls, the Ark, and the gracefully carved pews—all accentuated by an impressive collection of silver lanterns.

Gibraltar's largest synagogue, however—and its only free-standing one—is Nefusot Yehuda, a three-hundred-seat structure towering above a beige stucco wall on a corner plot at 65 Line Wall Road. Built for a congregation established around the start of the nineteenth century, Nefusot Yehuda exhibits a Moorish influence, its galleries and walls covered with intricate arabesques. It also boasts ornate chandeliers and Torah crowns.

Discreetly located behind a brown door in a gray wall next to a Barclays Bank and opposite the police station is the little, second-floor synagogue, Etz Hayim, at 91 Irish Town. Opened for prayers in 1759, it is Gibraltar's oldest extant Jewish worship hall; even before then, though, it was a yeshiva.

Gibraltar's newest—and smallest—synagogue is Abudarham, its name in gold letters on a black door on the alley-like Parliament Lane at No. 20.

Like Etz Hayim, this can be entered only during services. Arrangements can be made to view the two larger synagogues in off hours, however, by contacting Solomon Benady, secretary of the Jewish Community, mornings at 72606. The number rings in the Jewish community offices at 10 Bomb House Lane, the address, as well, for the Jewish school and mikvah. Across the street, at 7 Bomb House Lane, is the Jewish Club, with rooms for card-playing and a kosher restaurant which tourists can use.

The kosher bakery, a pink stucco building with "Chalah" written in blue letters above "Croissants," stands near Nefusot Yehuda on Line Wall Road, while the kosher butcher is located just off John Mackintosh Square, next to the Bacchus Restaurant, in the heart of town.

The square is bordered on one side by the massive white City Hall, once Aaron Cardozo's home. And, opposite, at the Main Street side of the square, stands the House of Assembly. In its central passageway— called here the lobby—is a sculptured wall plaque honoring Gibraltar's World War I dead. Its list of names is headed by a medallion of a Jewish soldier, "Lieut. S. Benzecry," and a notation calling him "The Hero of Bourlon Wood."

Away from the town center, where Line Wall Road elbows around to the city walls, is the Jewish old-age home. The eight-room institution, named for the benefactor who provided homes for all faiths, is called the Mackintosh Jewish Home.

Much farther out of town, halfway up the Rock, is the area known as Jews' Gate, in honor of the gate that once stood there leading to the old—and still extant—Jewish cemetery.

GENERAL SIGHTS: Though Jews' Gate can be reached from the midstation of the cable car up the 1,398-foot Rock, it is, perhaps, better visited by car, on a tour that includes the stalactites and stalagmites of St. Michael's caves, the tunnels of the gun emplacements, the Galleries, and of course the entrancingly playful Barbary apes of the Rock. (With luck, from there one will see a plane land on Gibraltar's east-west runway, which completely crosses the isthmus and extends into the sea, running right over the main road into town.)

But for most, the chief attraction of Gibraltar is Main Street's shopping where, though it no longer enjoys free-port status, bargains still can be found. Among the prominent Jewish-owned shops here are The Red House (cameras, watches, electrical appliances), S. M. Seruya Ltd. (jewelry, perfumes), Benamor's (luggage), Princess Silks (fabrics), Janine (boutique), Teo (clothing), Attias (toys), and Benzaquen (antiques).

DAY TRIPS: With the Spanish frontier now open, the entire Costa del Sol and even Granada are within a day's reach of Gibraltar. Here and there along the coast are signs of a renewed Jewish presence in Spain, primarily exhibited in shop names, occasionally accompanied by a Magen David. In Marbella, Torremolinos, and Málaga, there are synagogues. In addition, in the garden of Alcazaba Castle in the heart of Málaga, stands—his head bowed in contemplation, his cloak pocked by the weather—a statue of Ibn Gabirol, the poet-philosopher born there in 1021. Granada features the Alhambra, whose oldest sections were built by the Jewish prime minister of a Moorish caliph. It was also there that King Ferdinand and Queen Isabella, on March 30, 1492, signed the order expelling the Jews from Spain.

RECOMMENDATION: The Rock Hotel, just beyond town, defines "luxury" in rather Spartan terms, but offers acceptable accommodation—and vegetarian or fish diets if desired.

READING: Among the fiction set in Gibraltar are Paul Gallico's *Scruffy* (Doubleday), about one of Gibraltar's apes; John Masters's historical novel *The Rock* (Putnam); John D. Stewart's *Gibraltar: The Keystone* (Murray); and Warren Tute's *The Rock* (Ballantine). For factual works on Gibraltar's history, look for the books of local author George Palao and *Gibraltar—The History of a Fortress* (Harcourt, Brace, Jovanovich) by E. Bradford. The Gibraltar Bookshop, at 300 Main Street, managed by Anita Benady, stocks many of these volumes. Her brother, Mesod "Tito" Benady, wrote the pamphlet, "The Settlement of Jews in Gibraltar, 1704–1783," as well as the popular *Guide-book to Gibraltar.*

—PHYLLIS ELLEN FUNKE

Hong Kong

Star Ferry *(Ray Cranbourne/Hong Kong Tourist Association)*

Hong Kong's Jewish community has thrived since the mid-nineteenth century when merchant-prince David Sassoon and his Baghdadi family came to settle. Following him later to the Orient was the global migration of Jewish merchants from Russia, Poland, Austria, Germany, Syria, Iraq, and other corners of the world. They came to Hong Kong—sometimes after difficult journeys, many times after outbreaks of religious persecution—to find their fortune.

HISTORY: Although today a center of world commerce, the tiny island just south of the Tropic of Cancer was, less than a hundred and fifty years ago, an undeveloped fishing village. But it was only a matter of time before Britain, then the world's greatest shipping power, would seek to grab the Far East's best and most convenient harbor.

The British brought opium from India and used it to pay for Chinese goods—silk, porcelain, tea, and spices. The Chinese, who preferred silver currency, viewed opium as "foreign mud" and attempted to stop the import of the evil drug by restricting trade with the West. When China forbade the import of the poppy in 1838, British attacked and the Chinese, unable to resist modern arms, were defeated. The Treaty of Nanking, in 1842, opened several Chinese ports to Western trade and ceded Hong Kong Island and mainland Kowloon to the British. That status is due to change in 1997, when Great Britain's ninety-nine-year lease on the mainland New Territories, adjacent to Kowloon, expires. The Chinese and British governments have already negotiated the return of the entire self-governing colony to Chinese sovereignty.

When the British took control of Hong Kong, the Sassoon family—already long-standing, flourishing traders throughout India and China—moved immediately along with other opium dealers into the crown colony. "You can't be too proud of it," notes Sir Lawrence Kadoorie, philanthropist and pillar of the Hong Kong Jewish community, "but there it was." Kadoorie's father, Sir Elly, and his uncle, Sir Ellis, settled in Hong Kong and developed business interests there and in Shanghai. They established their family as commercial barons and the Sassoons' successors to the title of "Rothschilds of the Far East."

Wherever the Sassoons set up shop, Jewish employees from Baghdad followed, so that by the turn of the century, nearly a hundred Sefardim were living in Hong Kong. With the advent of the Russian Revolution, Ashkenazim also began to arrive.

Several thousand had fled through Siberia by way of the Manchurian Railway, to Harbin in northeast China. Although some sought business opportunities in Hong Kong, most joined the largely Sefardic population in Shanghai, which was then China's mercantile, industrial, and financial center.

Two waves of German Jews also infiltrated China. The first, in the early 1930s, included mostly professionals—doctors and lawyers. The bulk, perhaps as many as twenty thousand, escaped in 1938 and 1939. A few thousand Austrian and Polish Jews likewise sought refuge in the Orient, but they had little time to get settled before the outbreak of the Pacific War, and most remained in transit camps.

By the end of World War II, there were nearly thirty thousand Jews in Shanghai and several hundred in Hong Kong. Ever riding the coattails of history, many Shanghai Jews would make their way to Israel during the Chinese Revolution, although the diehard "Asia hands" preferred to remain in the Far East and relocated to Hong Kong.

COMMUNITY: Today there are roughly five hundred Jews in Hong Kong. A handful, such as the Kadoories, have been in the Far East for decades. Mostly of Iraqi or Russian descent, they consider themselves permanent residents. The transient population, posted to Hong Kong for stints of several years, comes from all over the world. Consequently, the ethnic makeup of the community is always changing. A few years ago, nearly half were Israelis, many of whom were involved in the diamond business. Today Americans, South Africans, and West Europeans compose the majority. Like many Asian countries, Hong Kong has little notion of anti-Semitism which, according to Syrian-born Ezra Sassoon, may explain why "about half of the Jews here don't feel the need to be with other Jews." But at least two hundred families do, and they are the active members of the Hong Kong Jewish Recreation Club at 70 Robinson Road (telephone, 5-490981).

SIGHTS: Although there is talk of redeveloping the recreation center property into two high-rise residential blocks—with sports facilities, restaurants, and a synagogue—at the moment the small, squat clubhouse in the heart of Hong Kong's Midlevels, built fifty years ago by Elly Kadoorie, is the hub of most Jewish activity.

Sunday-school classes are held in the small room upstairs, while on the main floor, in the warm, friendly if unassuming lobby and coffee shop, bagels and lox, borscht, and other Jewish fare are regularly enjoyed. The club also features a kosher restaurant with a Chinese menu. Foreign visitors are welcome, and the club will arrange presentations on the history of Jews in Hong Kong and Kaifeng for larger groups.

The weekly 1 P.M. Sunday brunches are held in the adjoining auditorium which, during the week, serves as the site for bridge games, exercise classes, meetings of the hundred-member Jewish Women's Association of Hong Kong, as well as for editing and assembling the center's magazine, *The Jewish Chronicle.*

Space of any sort is a rare commodity in Hong Kong and the center is fortunate to have a lawn large enough for a tennis court. At the far end of the sloping lot is the Hong Kong Jewish community's stellar feature: the Ohel Leah Synagogue, which opened its doors in 1900.

Sir Jacob Sassoon hired a Baghdadi architect to build the graceful, Oriental-style synagogue, with its marble floors, mahogany bimah, antique wooden paddle fans, and stained-glass windows. Orthodox Sabbath services are held and, after Saturday prayers, all are invited to the lovely Kiddush and luncheon in the center.

Except for the quaint Jewish cemetery tucked behind an orange Buddhist temple in the shadow of the towering apartments of Happy Valley, Hong Kong boasts little else of specifically Jewish heritage. The historic cemetery at 13 Slan Kwang Road is shaded by bamboo, jacaranda, and hibiscus trees on land donated in 1855 to the Jewish community by David Sassoon. It is the burial place of the last Jew from Shanghai, Russian-born Max Leibovich, who died in 1982.

But if Jewish institutions are rare, institutions with Jewish roots are everywhere: the legendary Star Ferry which crosses the harbor, linking Hong Kong to mainland Kowloon; the Peak Tram that climbs the 1,818-foot high Victoria Peak, with its superb view of the island; indeed, every light bulb in the city is, in effect, the handiwork of the Kadoorie family. Some people go so far as to say that the Kadoories own Hong Kong; that, of course, is an exaggeration. But the adventurous merchant Kadoorie family, which is the major shareholder in the

China Light and Power Company, ranks today among the top banking, real estate, and industrial mandarins in Hong Kong.

Hotels, too, are part of the Kadoorie empire. They include the eight-hundred-room Hong Kong Hotel, next door to Ocean Terminal at the tip of the Kowloon Peninsula, and the grande dame of deluxe hostelry, the Peninsula Hotel, also in Kowloon, with its mix of Old World elegance and personalized service. Though built in 1928, the Peninsula still is one of the most gracious hotels in the East.

DAY TRIPS: With a picnic basket in tow is the best way to visit the Kadoorie Experimental Extension Farm off Paak Ngau Shek in the Lam Tsuen Valley of the New Territories. Although officially a center for agricultural and livestock research—the unique swayback-free hog was bred here—the farm, overseen by Lawrence Kadoorie's brother Horace, seems more like a giant manicured park extending for thousands of acres. Hire a car and make the long drive into the country when your wallet or feet cannot take shopping any longer.

You can rent a converted Chinese junk or motorized "wallah wallah" to explore Hong Kong's nearly two hundred outlying islands. Nearby Lamma and Lantao islands claim fine seafood restaurants, while the island of Cheung Chau, once a pirate's haunt, is one of the few remaining signs of an older China, with narrow lanes and charming Asian ambience. There is an hour-long ferryboat with a wonderful view of Hong Kong's skyline that regularly departs for Cheung Chau from Star Ferry Pier.

Unquestionably, however, the most popular pastime here is racing. Elly Kadoorie, in fact, was one of the stalwarts of Hong Kong's early horse-racing fraternity, which today goes under the name of the Royal Hong Kong Jockey Club. Sellout crowds attend twice-weekly race meets, at the old track at Happy Valley on Hong Kong Island and at the new course at Shatin in the New Territories.

Sun Dynasty village at Laichikok in Kowloon is another sight worth visiting for more than one reason. The village is a replica of Kaifeng and the atmosphere of old China is apparent in the pinewood, stone, and tile architecture and authentic costumes. For the Jewish tourist, however, it brings to mind the once flourishing community of Chinese Jews which existed in Kaifeng between the twelfth and nineteenth centuries. After centuries of mingling, the Kaifeng Jews bore distinctly Chinese physical characteristics and held influential positions, yet they retained their Jewish identity and traditions.

EATING: Rabbi Mordecai Avtzon, who has volunteered to update those curious about kosher dining, can be reached at the Jewish Recreation Club (594-872). All major hotels will serve prepacked kosher "airline" food on request, or contact M. A. V. Hofstein at 3-679087. The Beverly Hills Restaurant in the New World Center near the Regent Hotel reportedly has a kosher deli.

Even if you are staying elsewhere, head for the corner of Salisbury and Nathan Roads in Kowloon and take tea or a light meal in the Peninsula's gilt-columned lobby, once described as the crossroads of East and West and, in truth, the meeting place for Hong Kong society.

Two other culinary landmarks, Landau's near the Excelsior Hotel and Jimmy's Kitchen at 1 Wyndham Street, Hong Kong-side, are also owned by a Jewish family who came to China from Poland in the early 1900s. Both restaurants serve international cuisine in classic surroundings at reasonable prices.

READING: Hong Kong is the ultimate example of what happens when the inscrutable East meets the technological West. Thus, as might be expected, any number of novels use this South China island as their setting. *The World of Suzie Wong* by Richard Mason (World Publications) explores the colorful Wanchai District, while James Clavell's best-selling Asian sagas, *Tai-Pan* and *Noble House* (Delacorte), fictionalize the wheelings and dealings of the trading companies. Falling into the spy genre is John le Carré's *The Honourable Schoolboy* (Knopf). A classic on the Jews in Kaifeng around the eighteenth century is Pearl Buck's *Peony* (John Day). A more recent novel on Jews in Hong Kong and Kaifeng is *East Wind* by Julie Ellis (Arbor House). For the flavor of Jewish life in Shanghai—the destination of Jews from the fourteenth century until after World War II—add two books to your reading list: *Deliverance in Shanghai* by Jerome Agel and Eugene Boe (Dembner Books) and *Mandarin* by Robert Elegant (Simon & Schuster).

For a place so far from the mainstream of Jewish history, China has more than its share of Jewish literature. And Hong Kong, as the last outpost of the Chinese-Jewish encounter, has more than its share of attractions.

—DEBRA WEINER

Houston

Kinky Friedman *(Courtesy of Kinky Friedman)*

"Houston is *the* city of the second half of the twentieth century," Ada Louise Huxtable wrote in *The New York Times,* describing the oil industry capital that skyrocketed to become the fourth largest city in the United States. She made her observation before the oil bust, but it is still true enough. If palatial suburban shopping malls, spaghetti-bowl freeways, and Astroturf are the symbols of contemporary culture, then Houston embodies the ethos of late twentieth-century America—slick yet spirited, entrepreneurial yet small-town friendly. And Houston's Jewish community is likewise a microcosm of American Jewry in its diversity of origins, its religious and organizational patterns, and its once-concentrated and now dispersed neighborhoods.

HISTORY: Both Texas and Houston celebrated their one-hundred-fiftieth birthdays in 1986—the state marking its independence from Mexico and the city the purchase of the first plot of land by Augustus and John Allen and the naming of the city in honor of General Sam Houston, who had just won the battle of San Jacinto nearby. Texans pride themselves on their history perhaps more than citizens of any other state (where else must every public school teacher pass a course in state history and government to be licensed to teach, say, chemistry?) and the sesquicentennial observances were lavish. Jews, too, recalled with pride their role in the founding and development of the state and city.

A Jew by the name of Samuel Isaacs was among the "Old Three Hundred" who came with Stephen F. Austin to Texas in 1821, when the territory was under Mexican rule. Before independence fifteen years later, there were Jews living in Velasco, Nacogdoches, San Antonio, and Bolivar. Jews fought with Houston at San Jacinto, with Colonel William J. Fannin at Goliad, and two Jews died at the Alamo. During the nine years that Texas was an independent nation, Henry de Castro, a French Jew from a Marrano family, brought five thousand people from Alsace-Lorraine to Medina County and had the town of Castroville and Castro County named in his honor.

Houston was founded four months after independence and the French-born Eugene Chimene, who had fought at San Jacinto, was the city's first Jewish resident; by 1837, there were enough Jews for a minyan. In the early days, Jacob de Cordova, a Sefardic Jew from Jamaica, was a city alderman; he also helped lay out the plan for the town of Waco and introduced the Order of Odd Fellows to Texas. A member of Houston's first Chamber of Commerce, Cordova also wrote books about Texas and, in 1858, toured the East Coast of the United States and England to attract settlers to Texas. Two early Jewish entrepreneurs were Morris A. Levy, who helped organize the Houston Ship Channel Company, which made Houston a port for oceangoing vessels, and Henry S. Fox, one of the founders of the Houston Cotton Exchange.

Despite the prominence of some of its members, the Jewish community of Houston grew slowly at first, from seventeen adults in 1850 to sixty-eight (plus forty children) a decade later. A plot of land was purchased for a cemetery in 1844. In 1854 a home was converted to a synagogue—the first in Texas—and the Orthodox Beth Israel Congregation was formed. Zacharias Emmich was its first spiritual leader, acting as rabbi, cantor, and shohet.

While Houston had the first Jewish cemetery and synagogue in Texas, Galveston, fifty miles southeast on the Gulf of Mexico, had a larger Jewish community until 1880. Galveston was the cultural capital of Texas for much of the nineteenth century; while people were still shooting each other in gunfights elsewhere in the state, the citizens of Galveston were going to the opera. It remained one of Texas's major cities until it was devastated by a hurricane in 1900. German Jews rose to great prominence in Galveston. In 1866, twenty-one out of twenty-six Galveston merchants were Jewish. While New York didn't have a Jewish mayor until 1975, by 1915 Galveston had had three.

After 1880, East European Jews began following their German coreligionists to Texas and to civic prominence. One Russian Jew became a director of the Houston Gaslight Company and another was president of the Houston Light and Power Company. The new wave of immigrants founded two Orthodox synagogues, the largely Galician Dorshe Tov and the Russian-Polish Adath Yeshurun, which merged into Congregation Adath Yeshurun in 1891. Meanwhile Beth Israel came under liberal influences and became classically Reform.

The influx of East European Jews was greatly swelled, after 1907, by the Galveston Plan, the brainchild of philanthropist Jacob H. Schiff and writer Israel Zangwill, to divert the masses of East European Jewish immigrants from New York and the East Coast to the sparsely settled areas between the Mississippi and the Rockies. Galveston, already a minor port of entry, was chosen because there was a Bremen-to-Galveston passenger line, run by the North German–Lloyd Shipping Company, and because of the presence in the city of a dynamic circuit-riding rabbi, Henry Cohen, who could provide community leadership and support for the plan.

Houston was one of many cities that benefited from the program, which settled ten thousand Jews before it ended on the eve of World War I. Though statistically the Galveston Plan was a failure—thousands and thousands of Jews continued to pour into the East—the program may have had a subtler success. Scholars point out that it did more than anything else to create a Jewish presence throughout the country, a situation that undoubtedly contributed to the ultimate acceptance of Judaism as one of America's three major religions.

The East Europeans who settled in Houston, unlike their counterparts in the East, accommodated themselves to and were absorbed into the culture of the German Jews. Not crowded into tenements, they found opportunities to prosper quickly, mixed with non-Jews socially and in business, and adopted the courtesy and friendliness of the southern milieu. The newcomers did add their own institutions, however, founding, among other things, a Zionist organization in 1903 and a Workmen's Circle in 1915. *The Jewish Herald-Voice,* which is still the chief community newspaper, was founded in 1908. In 1924, Beth El, Houston's first Conservative synagogue, was formed.

The leading figure in the community during the early decades of the twentieth century was Rabbi Henry Barnston, who occupied the Beth Israel pulpit from 1900 to 1943 and helped found the Houston Symphony and the Museum of Fine Arts. Jewish participation in civic and political life was less visible between the wars, however, because Ku Klux Klan activity made Jews wary.

Many German refugees arrived in the 1930s, to be followed by more East European refugees after World War II. In 1943, as the call for a Jewish state grew, anti-Zionist sentiment grew in Houston, led by the American Council for Judaism. Temple Beth Israel adopted a set of "basic principles" excluding from membership anyone who professed a belief in Israel as the homeland of all Jews. "We consider ourselves no longer a nation," the principles stated. "We are a religious community, and neither pray for nor anticipate a return to Palestine . . ." A minority of dissenters from the principles withdrew to form another

Reform congregation, Emanu-El. (Today, of course, it is perfectly kosher to be a Zionist at Beth Israel.)

COMMUNITY: Houston's Jewish community of thirty thousand, like the city itself, has a high proportion of newcomers; the Jewish population has doubled since the early 1960s. Houston Jews come from all parts of the United States as well as from Russia, South America, South Africa, Iran, and Israel. Fast as it has been, however, Jewish growth has not kept pace with the phenomenal burgeoning of the city as a whole. While Houston recently passed Philadelphia to become the fourth largest American city, metropolitan Philadelphia has some 280,000 Jews while Houston has little more than one tenth that number. Jews form only about 1.6 percent of Houston's population, below their proportion in the U.S. population and well below the urban average. These figures give a clue as to why Jewish Houston is such a mix of big city and medium-sized shtetl.

In its early days, Houston was, of course, much more shtetl-like than it is today. Initially, most Jews settled in First and Second Wards, later moving on to Third Ward, near the first site of Congregation Beth Israel, a frame building on LaBranch Street. The East European immigrants at the end of the nineteenth century tended to move into Fifth Ward, around Franklin and Navigation, or Sixth Ward, around Houston and Washington streets—areas now without Jews.

The second area of settlement, beginning in the 1920s and '30s, was in Washington Terrace and then Riverside Terrace, along North and South MacGregor. This area, more spread out than the first area of settlement, was home for most of the synagogues and the Jewish Community Center through the end of the 1950s.

Then the Jewish population shifted to the southwest, first to the subdivisions along North and South Braeswood Boulevard and later to Meyerland. The congregations and the Jewish Community Center rapidly followed the people in their southwestwardly movement. In the seventies this move continued into Fondren Southwest and the Memorial–Spring Branch area. Today Jews can be found sprinkled in suburbs that surround the city—with synagogues opening in Kingwood and the Woodlands to the north and in Clear Lake, near Galveston Bay and the NASA Space Center. For the first time, Houston has not one area of Jewish settlement but many, although the southwest is still the "Jewish core of town"—if not exactly an ethnic stronghold.

As in many middle-sized Jewish communities, Houston's Jews affiliate in sizable proportions with their many Jewish institutions, both religious and secular. Religiously, Houston follows the national pattern of Reform and Conservative predominance, with the largest synagogues being Temples Beth Israel and Emanu-El (Reform) and Congregation Beth Yeshurun (Conservative). Orthodoxy remains a small minority, although more visible since the arrival of a Habad Lubavitch Center and a Sefardic congregation founded by Iranian immigrants.

Economically, Jews are predominantly merchants in direct retail or businesses supporting retail. Secondarily they are strongly represented in the professions.

Given the importance of the oil industry to Houston's economy, Jews have had to overcome some discrimination in hiring from companies that do business with Arab countries. This economic anti-Semitism is not limited to the oil companies but also affects construction and engineering firms that have Arab clients.

A pro-Arab, subtly anti-Israel bias can be felt as well in the Houston newspapers. On the day that the Egypt-Israel peace initiative began via television between Anwar Sadat and Menahem Begin, the evening *Houston Chronicle* carried two stories, both a few days old, about an Israeli air strike into Southern Lebanon—"The Town That Is No More" and "Israel Hits Lebanon Again"—but no mention of the peace feelers. If you want to distinguish between the two, the morning *Houston Post* is more balanced in its Middle East coverage.

On the other hand, Houston has one of the most successful programs around for promoting a positive image of Israel in the black community. Mickey Leland, a black congressman, runs the Youth Kibbutz Internship, which takes ten minority children to Israel every summer and encourages them to speak about their experience when they return.

SIGHTS: The major Jewish institutions in Houston—the synagogues, Jewish Community Center, and Jewish Home for the Aged—are built Texas-style: big, spread-out, commodious, and pleasant to look at. Temple Beth Israel, at 5600 North Braeswood, for instance, is an ultramodern structure which was expanded to house a day school after the temple was built. In its lobby are twelve needlepoints based on the Chagall Windows at the Hadassah-Hebrew University Medical Center in Jerusalem.

Temple Emanu-El, at 1500 Sunset Boulevard, across from Rice University, has in its lobby a three-figure bronze statue called *The Bar Mitzvah.* A museum named for the synagogue's first rabbi, the Robert

I. Kahn Gallery, includes a Leonardo Nierman tapestry called *Genesis* and a bronze sculpture by Alexander Liberman called *Sacred Precincts.*

Congregation Beth Yeshurun, at 4525 Beechnut, also houses a synagogue museum, the Isaac Toubin collection of Judaica and ritual objects. The walls of the social hall are decorated with needlepoint recreations of a series of biblical lithographs by Israeli artist Reuven Rubin.

The United Orthodox Synagogues of Houston, at Greenwillow and South Braeswood, has a Holocaust memorial glass sculpture by Herman Perlman. Altogether there are thirteen synagogues in Houston proper, and another six in adjacent suburbs.

The Jewish Community Center at 5601 South Braeswood brings together all elements of the community for cultural, educational, and recreational events. It offers extensive sports facilities—two pools, a health club, tennis and racquetball courts, and ball fields. Its Kaplan Theater is used for artistic and educational events, and its halls, classrooms, and library serve everybody from preschoolers to senior citizens. The JCC has branches in the Memorial area and West Houston, and a new addition is being planned in the Fondren section. Next door to the JCC are the offices of the Jewish Federation of Greater Houston, the Bureau of Jewish Education, and the Jewish Community Relations Committee.

Seven Acres, the Jewish Home for the Aged, is worth seeing for its Texas scale. The 281-bed facility at 6200 North Braeswood provides the most up-to-date medical and social service care for its residents as well as outreach to the community by supplying "meals-on-wheels," a large-type library, and its Klein Eye Clinic.

There are Jewish day schools on the elementary level from all the major Jewish religious movements: the Irvin M. Shlenker School at Beth Israel (Reform), the William S. Malev Schools at Beth Yeshurun (Conservative), the Hebrew Academy (independent, but with Orthodox leanings) going up to high school, and the Torah Day School, sponsored by Lubavitch. In addition, the I. Weiner Secondary School, a community-based junior high school, takes a centrist philosophy.

GENERAL SIGHTS: After you've seen the Astrodome, Astroworld, and the Transco Waterfall, step back and look for the contributions Jewish Houstonians have made to the institutions of their city. Near the University of St. Thomas is the Rothko Chapel, the last major work of Jewish abstract artist Mark Rothko. The chapel displays fourteen expressionist paintings by Rothko, and in front, facing a reflecting pool, there is a twenty-foot steel obelisk dedicated to the memory of Dr. Martin Luther King, Jr. At the Texas Medical Center, a five-hundred-acre, twenty-nine-institution complex, is the twelve-story Jewish Institute for Medical Research, an affiliate of Baylor College of Medicine.

Worth the hour's drive out of the city is a visit to the Lyndon B. Johnson Space Center, where you can see displays of spacecraft, moon rocks, a lunar roving vehicle, and a lunar module.

After visiting the NASA space center, continue on to Galveston to look at the beautiful Victorian homes along Broadway, which look much the way they did when German Jews played a leading role in what was then a major city. The city is still home to about seven hundred Jews, as well as a Conservative synagogue, Beth Jacob, on Avenue K and a Reform temple, B'nai Israel, on Avenue O. If you make Galveston a day trip, stay for dinner at one of its fine fish restaurants.

CULTURE: Despite rumors to the contrary, there is culture in Houston beyond Gilley's, the beer and barbecue bar immortalized in the movie *Urban Cowboy.* Houston has long had a noteworthy ballet company. The Houston Symphony, whose past conductors include Leopold Stokowski and André Previn, is now under the direction of Sergiu Comissiona, who is Jewish. The De Menil art collection, one of the last great private art collections, recently opened to the public. And the Houston International Film Festival, held annually, is the world's largest in number of films submitted.

Jewish culture, too, is rich if sporadic. The high point of the year is the November Jewish Book Fair, sponsored by the JCC, and one of the best of its kind in the country. Speakers in recent years have included Elie Wiesel, David Wyman, Martin Gilbert, Camelia Sadat, Yael Dayan, Erica Jong, Isaac Bashevis Singer, and Chaim Potok. In addition to the speakers, the array of some fifteen thousand books is truly impressive.

Jewish Education Week, in February, sponsored by the Bureau of Jewish Education and the Federation, has brought noted Jewish scholars such as Eli Grad and Isadore Twersky to Houston.

Elijah's Cup, a gallery at 12306 Meadow Lake Drive, carries original Judaica by known and soon-to-be-discovered artists. The Source, at 9760 Hillcroft, is the local Jewish bookstore.

A folk singer who blends his Jewish and Texas heritages in unique ways is Kinky Friedman ("the first Texas-Jewish country-music star") who had the audacity to name his group "The Texas Jewboys."

The best place to look for what is happening in the Jewish community is still *The Jewish Herald-Voice*—telephone, (713) 630-0391.

PERSONALITIES: Houston's Jews have excelled in many fields. In education, Norman Hackerman retired in 1985 after serving as president first of the University of Texas and then of Rice University. Joseph Melnick, a leading virologist, became dean of graduate research at the Baylor College of Medicine. Aaron Farfel was chairman of the Board of Regents of the University of Houston from 1971 to 1979, and Alfred R. Neumann was the founding chancellor of the University of Houston–Clear Lake.

In politics, Billy Goldberg was chairman of the state Democratic Party. In music, Fredell Lack is an acclaimed violinist. In space, Jeffrey Hoffman, the first Jewish astronaut, took four mezuzahs with him on the Space Shuttle Discovery. Judith Resnik, who died on the Space Shuttle Challenger in 1986, also made her home in the area.

On the literary scene, both Max Apple, author of *Free Agents* (Harper & Row), winner of the 1985 Harold U. Ribalow Prize for fiction, and Rosellen Brown, author of *Tender Mercies* and *Civil Wars* (Knopf), write and teach at Houston universities. Julia Wolf Mazow has anthologized Jewish women's fiction in *The Woman Who Lost Her Names* (Harper & Row). Charles Hoffman, a Houston native who made aliyah, is a reporter for *The Jerusalem Post.*

EATING: Excluding the snack bar at the Jewish Community Center and the possibility of getting a corned beef sandwich at one of the two kosher butchers, there is no kosher restaurant in Houston. There is a non-kosher, "kosher style" restaurant, Alfred's, at 9123 Stella Link, which serves both blintzes and pastrami. Several bakeries and bagel shops, including the excellent Three Brothers bakery on South Braeswood, are under rabbinical supervision, and many top hotels do kosher catering. For kashrut information, contact the Houston Kashrut Association at 723-3850.

GETTING AROUND: Houstonians don't believe in walking, except around shopping malls and through the tunnels that link many of Houston's downtown office buildings. The best way to get around is by car on the excellent freeways—and despite the stereotype of cowboys behind wheels, Houston drivers are generally courteous, obeying the signs that admonish them to "Drive Friendly."

READING: After you've read James Michener's blockbuster *Texas* (Random House), you may be Texased out, but you'll need to read on to get the Jewish dimension. For a sketch of suburban life in the most

Jewish of Houston suburbs, read Max Apple's vignette, "This Land Is Meyerland," published in the literary magazine *Antaeus*. For an informative portrait of Houston Jewry, read Elaine H. Maas's chapter on Jews in *The Ethnic Groups of Houston,* edited by Fred R. von der Mehden (Rice University Studies). The history of the Galveston Plan is detailed in Bernard Marinbach's *Galveston: The Ellis Island of the West* (SUNY Press). The film *West of Hester Street,* produced by Allen and Cynthia Mondell, also tells this fascinating story. And after that, listen to Kinky Friedman's album, *Sold American,* to get the full flavor of Jewish Texana.

—ROSELYN BELL

Istanbul

❧❦

Istanbul's Hagia Sophia *(Pan American World Airways)*

Istanbul—once Constantinople and before that Byzantium—is an uncommon city. Straddling the Bosporus Strait, with one foot in Europe and the other in Asia, its geography loudly bespeaks the duality of its heritage. Even today, as it politically and intellectually aligns itself with the West, the myriad minarets spiking the city's skyline and the mournful, rhythmic "belly dance" music emanating from its windows suggest a soul still nourished by the East.

That this soul is, at once, hospitable and xenophobic, complicates matters for Istanbul's Jews. They generally feel welcome in this environment, where they thrive and prosper. Yet, as a minority in a Muslim country, they feel it best to maintain a low profile. As one young Jew says, "Istanbul may seem like any other European city. But this is, after all, the Middle East."

HISTORY: When Sultan Bayazid II, who ruled the Ottoman Empire from 1481 to 1512, heard that Spain had expelled its Jews, he reportedly said, "You call Ferdinand a wise king, he who has made his country poor and enriched ours!" Such was the attitude welcoming those refugees who, in droves, made their way, at the close of the fifteenth century, to Constantinople.

Jews had been in the region for centuries, having established a synagogue in the Byzantine capital by 318. But conditions were variable. At times they prospered, as coppersmiths, silk weavers, and even, despite church disapproval, as court physicians. At other times they were persecuted. Venetian and Genoese Jews came to the city and lived in enclaves, as did the Byzantine Jews. Following the Ottoman conquest in 1453, many Ashkenazim from Central Europe arrived, largely in response to a letter by Rabbi Isaac Sarfati of Adrianople, telling of the salubrious conditions for Jews in Ottoman lands.

Nevertheless, today's Jewish community in Istanbul really dates its establishment—whose five hundredth anniversary it is preparing to celebrate—from the expulsion from Spain. Together with Jews from Portugal, the Spanish refugees helped swell Istanbul's Jewish settlement to more than thirty thousand—the largest in Europe—and earn for the city, in sixteenth-century responsa literature, the title of "Jewish mother-city."

The Jews flourished to such an extent that, in 1551, Niccolo Nicolia, a French diplomat visiting Istanbul, wrote: "They increase daily through the commerce, money-changing, and peddling which they carry on almost everywhere on land and on water; so that it may be said truly that the greater part of the commerce of the whole Orient is in their hands. In Constantinople, they have the largest bazaars and stores, with the best and most expensive wares of all kinds."

This same chronicler credits—as do other sources—the Jews with bringing the printing press to the Turks, plus the know-how to make and use firearms. This knowledge, among other factors, helped the Turks defeat the Mamelukes in 1515 and take control of Israel.

Jews in Istanbul had always felt Israel's proximity. In the sixteenth century, Joseph Nasi, a Portuguese Marrano banker who had come to Istanbul to practice his Judaism openly, gained such favor at the courts of Sultan Suleiman the Magnificent and his son, Selim II, that he was granted the concession to rebuild Tiberias. Little, ultimately, came of his effort, but the tie to Eretz Israel was renewed and Istanbul thereafter became the major conduit for funds headed to Jerusalem.

Nasi was otherwise so influential that Europe's Christian leaders often negotiated through him to gain the ear of the Sultan—who gave Nasi several Mediterranean islands and named him the Duke of Naxos. Among other Jews who made their marks in sixteenth-century Turkey were the physicians of the Hamon family—father, son, grandson, and great-grandson—who served a succession of sultans.

The era's one jarring note was a decree issued during Murad III's reign (1574–95), ordering the Jews to death for wearing rich clothing and jewelry in the streets. A Jewish court physician got the decree rescinded, but the Jews were compelled to stop dressing ostentatiously. (They would be reprimanded again, in the eighteenth century, when they were forbidden to wear silks and fancy shoes in the streets and were ordered to don tall, pointed hats. To this day, Turkish Jews have a tendency to criticize their housewife neighbors who go to the morning market, according to one resident, wearing their jewels and mink coats "as if they were bathrobes.")

In the seventeenth century, fires that burned the Jewish quarters caused the beginning of the end of the kehalim—the separate communities to which Jews belonged according to their origins. When the fires caused them to change neighborhoods, they started joining synagogues near their new homes, regardless of their background.

During the same period, the Jews of Istanbul also found themselves competing with each other to redeem Jewish captives from the Cossacks, Tatars, and Ukrainians who, after the massacres in Poland of 1648–49, were selling Jews in Turkey.

The most striking occurrence of the period, however, was the emergence of Shabbetai Zevi. From Izmir (then Smyrna), he gained a large following by claiming to be the Messiah. Bothered by his popularity, the Sultan gave him the choice of conversion to Islam or death. Zevi chose conversion—and many followers did likewise, thus originating the sect of "Jewish Muslims" called the Dönmeh—"the turned"— which still exists. The Dönmeh, who only marry among themselves, formed a secret society whose practices are only now being revealed by today's more open younger generation. According to reports, the group, which claims a membership of fifteen thousand, uses tefillin, circumcises in the Jewish manner, observes a seven-day mourning period, has a twenty-four-hour fast day (albeit in January), and follows various other Jewish-type rituals, while praying in a mosque. In Istanbul, their house of worship is referred to as "the Jewish mosque."

The Ottoman Empire began its decline in the seventeenth century, and with it came the economic and cultural decline of Istanbul's Jewish community. By the nineteenth century there was little Torah study and books were being printed in Spanish and Ladino, since Hebrew was no longer widely read. The community received a boost when Russian refugees from the 1905 revolution swelled it to a hundred thousand. But nothing quite prepared it for the jolt it took when Kemal Atatürk created the secular and national Republic of Turkey in 1923. (The Dönmeh were supporters of the Young Turk revolution, and several of them were ministers in Atatürk's first post-revolution cabinet in 1909, including Finance Minister Djavid Bey.)

In his determination to yank Turkey into a Western version of the twentieth century, Atatürk, among other Draconian moves, separated church and state so completely that Turkish was mandated as the language of prayer even in mosques and clergymen were prohibited from wearing clerical garb in public. To build a national spirit, Atatürk banned all organizations with international ties.

While these measures were aimed at the entire Turkish population, certain provisions strongly affected the Jews, who could no longer easily study Hebrew or belong—officially, at least—to such groups as the World Zionist Congress or even B'nai B'rith. The Jews, who under the sultans had generally been treated with favor, now found themselves scrambling with everyone else. And though they formally renounced their minority status for Turkish citizenship, as Turkish nationalism intensified they found themselves, however intangibly, regarded as outsiders.

Turkish citizenship did help when World War II came and Turkey, in its neutral position, was able to extract its citizens, even Jews, from various hot spots. But it didn't help when, in 1942, the government levied a tax that hit Jews so much more heavily than others that many were financially ruined; or in the 1950s and '60s, when anti-Turkish outbreaks on Cyprus provoked retaliation against *all* minorities in Turkey. Coupled with the political upheavals Turkey experienced periodically between 1950 and 1980, the climate created was conducive to Jewish emigration. About a quarter headed for the United States, France, and Canada, while half—mostly the poorer ones—went to Israel.

Turkish Jews are not demonstrably Zionistic. Israel is, in fact, a subject about which they have "learned to play down feelings," as one explains, or a subject on which the comment for the record is often, "No comment." These ambiguous reactions stem not only from Ottoman days, when a Jewish state meant cutting off a piece of the Empire, but also from Young Turk philosophy, which saw Zionism as a threat to Turkish nationalism. Nevertheless, Turkey does, with varying degrees of cordiality, maintain diplomatic relations with Israel.

COMMUNITY: The young man who appeared for the meeting was, by all accounts, a prominent professor and writer. Almost the first thing he told the reporter was, "Don't believe anyone who tells you otherwise. This is a secular state, not a Muslim one, and there is no trouble for the Jews here at all—no segregation, no censoring, nothing." But almost in his next breath, he said that he did not wish to be identified. Nor would he name other prominent Jews in the city—lest they not wish their names in such print, either. Thus, he epitomized the ambivalent feelings of the Jewish community in today's Istanbul.

After the years of political instability and street terror which, in the 1970s, afflicted the entire country, Turkey's return to democratic government made its Jews feel comfortable once again and comparatively safe—at least until the bloody attack on the Neve Shalom Synagogue in August 1986. The terrorists were Arabs; Istanbul's Jews do not fear such attacks from Turks. Still, some change their names—because, it is explained, "if a Turk and a Jew are up for the same job, the Turk, of course, will get it." None runs for office because "no one would vote for you." As one resident puts it, "While we might have among us a thousand-dollar-a-plate dinner to support our hospital or old-age home, we would not, as Americans would, think of having a big thousand-dollar-a-plate dinner for Israel. There is no palpable anti-Semitism in Turkey. But it is best, in Jewish activities, to be prudent."

Nevertheless, for a community of twenty thousand—there are probably about twenty-two thousand Jews in all Turkey today—Istanbul Jewry keeps itself fairly active. In addition to maintaining the hospital and home, it keeps alive a high school, a primary school, one legal young people's social club (there are hints of "illegal" ones, with foreign ties), a summer camp, and the community operation itself— not to mention the fourteen functioning synagogues of the twenty-seven or so still extant.

While 98 percent of the Jews today in Istanbul are Sefardim and all their synagogues are Orthodox, most probably would be regarded as Conservative in practice. According to one estimate, only about 20 percent observe kashrut and refuse rides on Saturday. Younger people tend to be more observant; the older ones grew up in an era of secularization, when religion was downplayed. Istanbul's largest synagogue today is Neve Shalom; its busiest—and most "in," at the moment—is Sisli, though Caddesbostan, in the Erenkoy section of Istanbul's Asian side, where the city's Yuppies are now moving, has the largest congregation.

The majority of Istanbul's Jews are in business, primarily textiles, though the community does boast a fair number of engineers, lawyers, and some doctors. Most are in Turkey's upper income brackets. The younger generation speaks Turkish as its first language and English is generally second. Everyone over forty, however, speaks Ladino and, usually, French.

Istanbul's Jews live together from choice, not necessity, but move readily—virtually as soon as others "invade" their enclaves. Over the centuries they have wandered all over Istanbul, establishing themselves in the most desirable areas. When the waves of refugees from Spain first arrived, they settled in Galata, on the northern side of the Golden Horn where it curves away from the Bosporus. Next they moved up the then-fashionable Horn to two areas that face each other across the water—Hakoy and Balat. Then they spread up the Bosporus itself, on both sides, to Ortakoy, in Europe, and Kuzguncuk, in Asia. They even have been trend-setters in resort areas, with synagogues on two of the Princes Islands in the Sea of Marmara, Buyukada, the largest, and Heybeli, and have built a summer camp for underprivileged children on Burgaz. Among the other neighborhoods in which they live today, albeit in a somewhat more integrated fashion than previously, are, on the Asian side, Yeldegirmen, Kadikoy, Haydarpassa, and Suadiye; on the European side, Harbiye, Gayrettepe, Nisantas, Sisli, Esentepe, Etiler, and Bebek (the last two, extremely wealthy areas). They have also moved as close to the Black Sea as the pleasant, country-like Buyukdere. And many still live in Galata.

SIGHTS: Reflecting its low profile, Istanbul Jewry does not play up its attractions. Synagogues may or may not be open when visitors want to see them; other sights may not be talked about at all. And calling the Chief Rabbinate of Turkey (Turkiye Hahambasiligi, Yemenici Sokak 23, Beyoglu, telephone, 144-87-94/5) for assistance may not produce someone speaking English. However, the community is delighted to welcome visitors and is becoming more aware of their needs —particularly with the five hundredth anniversary of Sefardi presence approaching.

The big synagogue, Neve Shalom, where major functions are held, is in the old Galata area, not far from the rabbinate and the Galata Bridge. At 67 Buyuk Hendek Caddesi, a street along which horse-drawn carts occasionally still rumble and milk cans may still roll, it is designed like a theater-in-the-round, with the bimah and ark in front, and seating on the three sides. Also in this area is the Italian Synagogue, 29 Okcu Musa Caddesi, which has a black-and-white-tiled, vine-covered courtyard—that serves as a natural sukkah—and an interior decorated with crystal chandeliers, velvet draperies, and worn Turkish carpets. On a steep, narrow, cobbled street, behind an iron gate, stands the only Ashkenazi synagogue operating today (37 Yuksek Kaldirim).

Across the Golden Horn, in Balat, a jumble of low buildings and market stalls on cobbled streets overhung with vines, is the Achrida Synagogue, 15 Kurtci Cesmi Sokak. Built around 1470 by Jews from Macedonia, it is the oldest in Istanbul that can now be entered—if the caretaker with the keys is around. It features an elaborately carved women's gallery and pews and a pulpit shaped like the prow of a ship —allegedly commemorating the vessel in which the Sefardim arrived from Spain. Shabbetai Zevi preached there in 1655. On the Golden

Horn itself, at 162-54 Dibbek Caddesi Karabas Mahalesi, is Or Hayim Jewish Hospital, a 120-bed facility staffed by Jewish physicians. It sits in a pretty garden, which also boasts its own synagogue.

The old-age home—where residents are generally most anxious to chat—is in the Haskoy area, along with the below-ground-level synagogue, at 3 Mahlul Sodak, of the hundred Karaites, whose ancestors came to Istanbul in Byzantine times. In the same area are two reminders of Abraham de Camondo who, in the nineteenth century, because of his great wealth and banking ability, was dubbed "the Turkish Rothschild." Near the water rises a great white palace-like building, once Camondo's home and today owned by the military. And on a hill overlooking the new Londra Asfalti superhighway (one of the main routes to the airport), stands Camondo's mausoleum, on an isolated patch of land. Slated for demolition, along with the rest of the cemetery in which it stands, to make way for the new road, the highway's route was altered out of respect for Camondo. (Another structure erected by Camondo is a flight of graceful, curvy stairs running up an incline off Bankalar Caddesi—the Bank Street.)

Moving north along the Bosporus to Ortakoy, on a plot of land in the shadow of the bridge across the strait, is Etz Haim Synagogue, at 38 Mullim Naci Caddesi. Since the spot was designated for synagogues, it once held three—two Sefardic and one Ashkenazic. One Sefardic building burned down, but there is still a Sefardic prayer hall and an Ashkenazic chapel. Embedded in the courtyard wall is the marble ark that remained after the fire. Its date: 5666.

Crossing the bridge to the suburban-looking Kuzguncuk, one finds two more synagogues. Though officially called the Merkez Synagogue, at 8 Icadiye Caddesi, and Virane Synagogue, at 8 Yakup Sokak, they are popularly known as "Kal de Abaso" and "Kal de Arive" for the former is on a major street down a hill, while the second is hidden away *up* a hill. Although almost all their congregants have moved away, they still return regularly on Saturdays. The larger one, with frescoed walls and paintings of Israeli scenes on the ceiling, has its pulpit at one end, facing the ark, across the synagogue, at the other end. The smaller one has seats covered with rose brocade ringing its walls and its floors are covered with a riot of Oriental rugs. This homey place is used when the weather is cold—because it is more easily heated.

For a change of pace, there is "the Jewish Mosque," spiritual home of the Dönmeh. The beige structure is located in Tesvikiye, an area adjoining Nisantas.

GENERAL SIGHTS: The first "must" of Istanbul is the Topkapi Palace, a great conglomeration of buildings containing not only the jewels of the treasury (with the emerald dagger featured in the film), but also the harem quarters, sultan's garments, and a variety of pavilions and kiosks. Next is the Blue Mosque, covered with blue-glazed tiles and uniquely boasting six—not four—minarets. Not far from the Blue Mosque is the Hagia Sofia, the domed Byzantine church which was converted to a mosque. The Hagia Sofia has been a model for synagogues as well; Temple Emanu-El in San Francisco and the synagogue in Florence both have architectural features inspired by it.

Suleymaniye Mosque is also considered one of Istanbul's masterpieces, and the white marble Dolmabahce Palace, where the sultans lived from 1854 on, is a startling mix of Turkish, Hindu, and Italian styles. For browsing—and bargaining, if you wish—there's the covered bazaar, with its four thousand tiny shops, a number of which are Jewish-owned.

DAY TRIP: By car or public bus, Turkey's old capital of Edirne (formerly Adrianople) can be reached in a day. Its synagogue, outwardly glorious, is a facsimile of Vienna's Great Synagogue. Inside, it's a shambles; there are only about ten Jewish families left in the city.

PERSONALITIES: However bashful Istanbul's prominent Jews may be, certain names are, nonetheless, known throughout the city—if not the country—and even beyond. Sami Kohen is an internationally known journalist based with the Istanbul daily *Milliyet.* Habib Gerez is an artist and poet whose works have been exhibited and published in Western Europe. Izzet Kehribar is a prize-winning photographer. Two major Turkish industrialists are Jak Kamhi, head of Profilo, which makes, among other things, boats, refrigerators, and televisions; and Uzeyir Garih, head of Alarko, whose construction projects have included the lighting and air-conditioning for Istanbul's splendid new airport. Istanbul natives who have achieved prominence on other shores include Meshulam Riklis, the American financier; and the Gazit brothers—Mordecai, whose political career in Israel has included such posts as director of the prime minister's office and ambassador to France, and Shlomo, the former director of military intelligence who is now president of Ben Gurion University.

CULTURE: The newspaper *Salom,* which has known other incarnations, has recently been revived as a weekly in Turkish and Ladino.

Several amateur theater groups exist in the community, presenting plays in Turkish; a favorite subject is the Marranos. Ladino music is currently undergoing a resurgence in Turkey, where Jewish composers once had a strong influence on Ottoman music—and vice versa—and concerts are given primarily in Jewish clubs but also, on occasion, in state theaters. Among the leading performers are the Yeshua Aroya Chorale, and Karen Gershon and Izzet Bana. Advertisements for such concerts can be found in *Salom* and daily Turkish newspapers, and cassettes exist of such performances. The best way to get information on events is probably to call the Chief Rabbinate or inquire at one of the city's Jewish bookstores—Hachette's at Istiklal Caddesi 469 or Kohen's at Tunel Pasaji 13.

READING: There is little available in English on Turkish Jewry, but *Strolling Through Istanbul* by John Freely and Hilary Sumner-Boyd (Redhouse Press) gives a good sense of the city. If you can't see the film version of *Topkapi* before you go, try the Eric Ambler novel on which the movie was based.

RECOMMENDATION: The Istanbul Sheraton, which is used by the Jewish community for many of its weddings and bar mitzvahs, is planning to install a kosher kitchen. Meanwhile, it will happily cater to dietary needs on request.

—Phyllis Ellen Funke

Jerusalem

The Cardo *(Israel Government Tourist Office)*

Jerusalem is a modern city suffused with its past. It is, above all, a city of contrasts—between ancient, old, and new, between a polyglot of living and dead cultures, and between traditional and secular ways of life. It lies at the crossroads of East and West and at the juncture of three continents. Capital of an industrialized and technologically sophisticated nation, it is steeped in spirituality and trapped in its turbulent history.

Jerusalem is a place where the melting pot never took hold. It remains today, as always, a mosaic of peoples, faiths, and ideas—inwardly troubled, outwardly serene, and unexpectedly resilient.

HISTORY: Just over three thousand years ago, an obscure warrior-king called David captured a small settlement, high up in the Judean Hills. Its name was Jeru-Salem, meaning the "foundations of wholeness" or "peace." David kept both the settlement and its ancient name. Bringing the Ark of the Covenant to Jerusalem, he turned his mountain conquest into the national and religious capital of Israel—an act that was to echo through the centuries.

David's city was no larger than two football fields laid side by side. His son Solomon extended the city northward, launching a massive building program that included the Holy Temple. He turned the "city of David" into a center of international renown, which has attracted conquerors from his day to ours.

Jerusalem has been conquered thirty-six times, besieged more than fifty times and destroyed ten times. Egyptians, Assyrians, Babylonians, Persians, Greeks, Romans, Muslim caliphs, Crusaders, Mamelukes, Ottoman Turks, and, finally, the British all fought for the city, ruled over it, and met defeat in their turn. Each of them contributed to Jerusalem. They built palaces, temples, churches, mosques, water channels, and thick defensive walls, administrative, commercial, and legal systems—layer upon layer, through culture and time.

It was not until the 1860s that Jerusalem overflowed the confining and protective Old City walls. Driven by overcrowding and filth, Jewish neighborhoods began to rise westward along Jaffa Road toward the Mediterranean coast. The Christian Arabs built southeast toward Bethlehem and the Muslim Arabs north in the direction of Damascus.

When Israel fought its War of Independence in 1948, the cease-fire line sliced through the city. Jewish Jerusalem, now perched on Israel's eastern frontier, became the capital of the re-created State, and Arab Jerusalem was annexed by the Hashemite kingdom of Jordan. A wall divided the two halves of the city for the next nineteen years.

Despite the wall and international refusal to recognize the city as Israel's capital, Jerusalem rapidly became the center of Jewish national life. Reunified during the Six-Day War of 1967, it began a meteoric growth, almost doubling its population during the next two decades.

COMMUNITY: Since King David stormed Jerusalem, there have always been Jews in the city. Through starvation and disease, persecution, war and devastation, the city's Jewish population has dwindled but never ceased to exist.

Today it numbers 306,000—71 percent of Jerusalem's 428,000 residents. They come from all 101 nations of the exile—merchants from Iraq, craftsmen from Yemen, farmers from Ethiopia, and professors from the universities of Europe. They come from the great cities of North America, collectives of Soviet Russia, remote reaches of Kurdistan, and isolated villages high in the Atlas Mountains.

In the time-honored tradition of "two Jews, three opinions," Jerusalem's Jewish community contains almost every shade of Jewish affiliation and nonaffiliation. Dozens of hasidic dynasties have followers in Jerusalem—golden-coated descendants of those who came in the seventeenth century when the movement was born and black-coated Hasidim who escaped the flames of Nazi Europe.

Jerusalem's Orthodox Jews also embrace a variety of traditions—molded in Germany, the Netherlands, Morocco, India, Iran, North America. Their hats and knitted, embroidered, or cloth head-coverings identify their ideologies. Conservative, Reform, and Reconstructionist Jews from the West are growing in number in Jerusalem, earnestly pursuing an elusive dialogue.

And there are the Jerusalem Jews who claim no religious affiliation. They regard their observant co-religionists with detachment, disinterest, bewilderment, and increasingly with hostility.

The cultural and ethnic boundaries between Jerusalem's Jews remain in place, but somehow the intricate mosaic usually works. The community is unself-conscious and cosmopolitan, displaying—more often than not until now—a sympathetic curiosity in the customs and practices of their fellow citizens.

SIGHTS: Jerusalem grew by neighborhoods. Each preserves its own special flavor and traditions—and to see only one or two is to miss what the city is about.

There are Jerusalem-lovers, scholars, and tour guides who maintain that a lifetime is insufficient for seeing the city. But to dip into a panorama of neighborhoods is to glimpse beneath Jerusalem's grand exterior and into its complex inner life.

The Old City is chronologically and emotionally the first of Jerusalem's neighborhoods, boasting Mount Zion and the Jewish Quarter, with its Western Wall. Entering Jaffa Gate will bring you directly to two multimedia presentations in the Citadel (erroneously called the Tower of David)—one in the northeast tower and one in the western tower—which will provide a partial introduction to Jerusalem's thickly layered and multifaceted history. For hours call the Government Tourist Information Office (telephone, 241-281) or visit the branch just inside the Jaffa Gate.

The Dung Gate is nearest to the Western Wall and the Temple Mount. From there you can go to the rebuilt Jewish Quarter by crossing the plaza and ascending the steps at the farthest side from the Wall. As you wander the gleaming white stone streets and courtyards, you will delight in the beautiful reconstructed synagogues, the new modern apartment buildings and yeshivas. There are also museums, such as the Old Yishuv Court Museum, at 6 Ohr Hahayim Street, and the Burnt House, with charred remains from the time of the Second Temple's destruction. Walk through the rebuilt Cardo, a shopping area on what was once the main thoroughfare during Roman times.

The first neighborhoods outside the walls mark the beginning of the modern city. These include Yemin Moshe, between David Hamalekh (King David) Street and Mount Zion, financed by Sir Moses Montefiore in 1868, now a restored artists' quarter; Mahane Yehuda, next to Jaffa Road and four blocks north of Herut Square, in 1887, now a bustling open-air market; and Mea Shearim, the "walled-in" city of the ultra-Orthodox, which you can enter through Rabbi Avraham Mislonim Street. Mazes of narrow lanes, arches, and courtyards, and houses with outdoor cisterns, make their charm greater for the visitor than for the resident.

The Bukharan Quarter, founded in 1891 by wealthy Jews from Russia, was the first to be built with Jerusalem stone. One is still able to see residents wearing the national costumes of their ancestors on special occasions.

In the 1920s and '30s, Jerusalem began expanding both east and west. Mount Scopus, from where would-be conquerors from Alexander the Great to Jordan's Arab Legion looked down on Jerusalem, became a hill of science. The Hebrew University opened there in 1925, followed by Hadassah Medical Center in 1939. Both have been rebuilt since the 1967 reunification of Jerusalem.

During this time, the Jewish Agency compound on King George Street, the King David Hotel on King David Street, and the Rehavia neighborhood rose in central Jerusalem. The city also moved west. New garden suburbs were built in Kiryat Moshe and Bet Hakerem. In Bayit Vegan, the Holyland Hotel displays a meticulous 1:50 scale model of Jerusalem in Second Temple times.

The showpiece buildings of the western city were built during the first nineteen years of statehood. The Hebrew University and Hadassah Hospital, banished from Mount Scopus, built new facilities at Givat Ram and Ein Karem—the medical center including a synagogue with luminous windows, designed by artist Marc Chagall.

The Knesset moved into its permanent home in 1966, part of a complex including government buildings. In the complex is the Israel Museum, the country's largest, with its classical art and sculpture, gems of Jewish history—including the complete interiors of synagogues from seventeenth-century Italy and nineteenth-century Germany—Jewish art and folklore and, in the separate Shrine of the Book, some of the Dead Sea Scrolls. A formal residence for Israel's President was completed in Talbieh in 1973.

Two neighboring hilltops on the western edge of the city were set aside as memorials in 1953: Mount Herzl, to the visionary Theodor Herzl and other Jewish and Zionist leaders who came after him; and the Hill of Remembrance, to the six million Jewish victims of the Nazi Holocaust, their memory preserved in the Yad Vashem Museum.

Following the Six-Day War of 1967, Jerusalem strove to sew up the seam between its reunited halves. Residential neighborhoods were built across the old border in Ramat Eshkol and French Hill. The bitter battle for the city is commemorated at Ammunition Hill, now a park and museum.

Jerusalem's population rocketed after reunification, and huge satellite suburbs were built at Gilo, Ramot, East Talpiot, and Neve Yaakov to accommodate the influx. Jobs were needed for the new Jerusalemites, without destroying the city's unique fabric and history. To this end high-tech parks are being developed—notably on Mount Scopus, where research and assembly plants are creating space-age medical, communications, and solar technologies.

CULTURE: Jerusalem has some two hundred parks and gardens, three world-class museums, two orchestras, an international book fair, a music festival, movie festival, and thriving cinema center.

The Friday *Jerusalem Post* lists events for the week ahead. Jerusalem's musical tastes stretch from the Jerusalem Symphony Orchestra and chamber music at the Targ Center in Ein Karem to western pop and rugby songs in the downtown bars and cafés, hasidic songfests, Christian hymnals, and Sefardi and Arab-style music-making.

Jerusalem's half-dozen theaters and theater clubs enthusiastically produce everything from Shakespeare, in Hebrew, through Broadway hits to the works of local playwrights—often with simultaneous translation into English. Samples of a recent representative week of events include Sholem Aleichem stories (in English) at the Hilton and King David hotels; the Diaspora Yeshiva Band at the Mount Zion center; the Jerusalem Symphony at the Jerusalem Theatre; *The Dead Bride,* a play on Anne Frank, at the Khan Theatre; and Beckett's *Waiting for Godot* at the Gerard Behar Theatre.

Lectures—academic, religious, and political—and study groups are offered all over the city most evenings of the week. There is usually folk dancing, to watch or to join, at the International Cultural Center for Youth (12 Emek Refaim), the Hebrew University, or one of the hotels. Local arts and crafts are made and sold in the House of Quality and Hutzot Hayotzer—both just outside the Old City walls.

One of the greatest joys of Jerusalem is sitting in the cafés and taking in the atmosphere. Three particularly good spots are the terrace café of the Cinematecque, the film center on Hebron Road overlooking the Valley of Hinnom and the Old City wall; the garden of Beit Ticho (7 Harav Kook Street), the former home of artist Anna Ticho, now a museum in a shaded, secluded corner just steps from busy Jaffa Road; and Café Atara, a journalists' hangout, on Ben Yehuda mall in the center of the new city.

Food culture reflects two thousand years of diaspora—kosher and nonkosher versions of Hungarian, French, Russian, Chinese, Japanese, Indian, Moroccan, Iranian, and plain heimish cuisine.

READING: Books about Jerusalem fill libraries. A ruthlessly selective list for the visitor includes Kathleen Kenyon's *Digging Up Jerusalem,*

(Praeger), among the most enjoyable and readable archaeological studies of the city. Martin Gilbert's *Jerusalem History Atlas* (Macmillan) is a digestible and painless way of following the city's serpentine history since 70 C.E. *O Jerusalem* by Larry Collins and Dominique Lapierre (Pocket Books) is a lengthy but fast-moving street-by-street account of the city during the siege and battles of 1948. *Footloose in Jerusalem* by Sarah Fox Kaminker (Crown) may offer the best guide to seeing Jerusalem on your own. *Jerusalemwalks* by Nitza Rosovsky (Holt, Rinehart & Winston) can also help you find your way to the must-see sites of the city.

PERSONALITIES: Jerusalem has been home to or destination of the molders of Jewish history and destiny: King David made it his capital and King Solomon ruled there. Herod built it up and Jesus led his followers there. The giants of contemporary Israel, like David Ben Gurion and Golda Meir, fought for and lived in Jerusalem. But one name stands out today from among Jerusalem's myriad sons and daughters of fame: the city's mayor since 1965, Teddy Kollek. Every place in the city—old and new, Arab and Jewish, center and suburb, parks and industrial areas—bears his touch. The son of an assimilated Viennese family, Teddy is the first and only mayor of reunified Jerusalem. Under a now-legendary gruff and often downright rude exterior, it is his dynamism, sensitivity, and supreme pragmatism that have normalized life in the capital—and won not only the support of the city's Jewish and Arab residents, but worldwide acclaim.

DAY TRIPS: On King David Street, roughly at the traffic lights after the King David Hotel, lies part of the watershed which Jerusalem straddles. Rain falling west of it finds its way to the Mediterranean; rain on the east trickles into underground springs that feed the Dead Sea.

Even with all there is to see in Jerusalem, it is worth fitting in at least two out-of-town trips—one east and one west—to understand what the watershed means to Jerusalem and its history. Twenty minutes westward, toward Tel Aviv, are the well-watered slopes and woods of the Judean Hills. By road or by the slow-but-scenic railway, there are kibbutzim to visit, with guesthouses and public swimming pools: Maalei Hahamisha, Kiryat Anavim, and Shoresh. Stop at the ruined Crusader convent of Ein Hemed (also called Aqua Bella—both names meaning "beautiful waters"). The Martyr's Forest, with its monumental sculpture *Scroll of Fire,* and the Avshalom Stalagmite Cave (Mearat Hanetifim) near Bet Shemesh should also be seen.

To the east, the picture changes dramatically. Jerusalem lies on the edge of the Judean Wilderness, an austere moonscape whose sparse winter rains produce delicate desert flowers and deadly flash floods. This is where prophets, hermits, and fugitives roamed throughout millennia. Here in the dusty heat lies the Dead Sea, at the lowest point on the earth's surface; the flower-filled oasis town of Jericho—perhaps the oldest town in the world—with blocks from its massive walls still lying where they came tumbling down; and the oases of Ein Gedi and Nahal Arugot, their springs and waterfalls coursing through steep rocky gorges into pools where hyena and desert ibex gather to drink.

RECOMMENDATIONS: For history and style, the King David Hotel is unsurpassed. For contemporary luxury, try the Jerusalem Hilton or the Jerusalem Plaza. For the best location and views, try the less expensive Eilon Tower.

TRIVIA: The living Bible is the theme of two parks—one in Jerusalem and one outside the city. The Biblical Zoo in western Jerusalem has collected almost all the mammals, birds, and reptiles mentioned in the Bible. It displays them, wherever it can, in biblical tableaux—encouraging, for example, the lion to lie down peaceably with the lamb. A half-hour drive west of Jerusalem, toward Ben Gurion Airport, is Neot Kedumim, a park where the Bible's landscapes are re-created with all the biblical trees, flowers, herbs, and spices that its dedicated botanists can identify.

—Wendy Elliman

London

The Royal Exchange *(British Tourist Authority)*

Walk along the Thames, attend one of the many excellent theatrical productions that London always seems to offer, enter the lobby of one of the city's magnificent hotels, go shopping on Oxford Street. You cannot fail to notice the effect of the pipeline of money that seems to flow from the oil sheikdoms of Arabia to this great city. In this atmosphere of economic boom, Jack is still doing all right, living in London. And Yankel, his Jewish counterpart, is not doing badly either.

HISTORY: When William the Conqueror arrived on British shores in 1066, he opened the gates as well for what was to become the first Jewish community in England. Refugees from anti-Semitism on the Continent and seekers of economic opportunity settled first in the area of London now known as Old Jewry. While the Jews of England in medieval times continued to suffer the "slings and arrows" of anti-Semitic caricature, blood libels, wholesale massacres such as the one at York in 1190, and the Crusades undertaken by Richard the Lion-Hearted, their presence—because they contributed to the "outrageous fortune" of the ruling classes—was nevertheless tolerated. On Tisha B'av in the summer of 1290, however, no longer perceived as economically necessary to the Crown, the Jews were unceremoniously expelled from England.

The resettlement of the Jews in England, accomplished largely through the efforts of Rabbi Menasseh Ben Israel (known to us mainly from Rembrandt's portrait) did not come until 1665. That Shakespeare found it artistically necessary to dramatize the story of a Jewish moneylender named Shylock for an English society that was virtually *Judenrein* is one of the curiosities of literary history. It is possibly due to an atmosphere such as the one portrayed in *The Merchant of Venice* that the readmission of the Jews was never formalized. They were simply allowed, by Oliver Cromwell, to return. Sefardim first, then Ashkenazim, they came, and they built one of the most highly organized Jewish communities the Western world has ever seen.

Limitations placed on Jewish activity in England were never as strict as on the Continent, but spurred by the emancipation in France and the Catholic emancipation in Britain in 1829, Jews agitated for their own official equality. The first emancipation bill passed the House of Commons in 1833 but it was consistently defeated by the House of Lords. In 1847, the city of London elected Lionel de Rothschild its parliamentary representative, but continued opposition in the House of Lords blocked the legislation that would have allowed him to take the required oath on a Hebrew Bible. Repeatedly elected by his constituency, Rothschild was finally able to take his seat in Parliament in 1858 when a compromise allowed each house to set its own form of oath. Twenty-seven years later, Lionel de Rothschild's son, Nathaniel, joined the ranks of Lords himself—the first professing Jew raised to peerage. One of Lionel de Rothschild's most ardent supporters in Parliament was Benjamin Disraeli; although baptized, the future Prime Minister never hid his Jewish origin and, in fact, took pride in it.

In 1863, Rothschild and Isaac Goldsmit, the most prominent members of the Ashkenazic community, joined with Sir Moses Montefiore, the recognized head of the Sefardim, to solidify the Board of Deputies of British Jews. To be sure, the Sefardim still had their Haham (leading rabbinical authority) and Mahamad (communal council) firmly entrenched in the Bevis Marks Synagogue. These were eclipsed by the Board of Deputies and by the vision of Rabbi Nathan Marcus Adler, who united all Ashkenazic congregations in the London metropolitan area into a United Synagogue and created the Chief Rabbinate of England, on the model of the Anglican Church, with its Archbishop of Canterbury.

The modern history of the Jews of London is a story of stability and volatility. During a period when the great masses of Jews were distinguished by their ability to avoid calling attention to themselves, and were simply living out their lives in a comfortable environment, many individual Jews with ambition were able to rise meteorically.

Sir David Salomons became the first Jewish Lord Mayor of London in 1855; Disraeli, of course, was one of the great Victorian prime ministers. In addition to Montefiore and the Rothschilds, there were the *nouveaux riches* of later waves of immigration, like Sir Isaac Wolfson and Lord Israel Sieff, who learned the lessons of *noblesse oblige* from their predecessors and used their fortunes to support the Jewish communities of both England and Israel. Wolfson, by the way, is the only man besides Jesus to have a college in both Oxford and Cambridge named after him. Sieff's monumental contribution to the Zionist cause is emblematic of that of both Britain and English Jewry.

It was George Eliot's nineteenth-century novel *Daniel Deronda* that explained to the world the Jews' longing for a homeland in Palestine. It was England's Lord Balfour who issued the 1917 declaration that recognized these aspirations officially. And it was England that gave the new state its first President, Chaim Weizmann.

Other Jews born in or associated with London include the pioneering economist David Ricardo; Harold Abrahams, the Olympic runner whose story is told in the film *Chariots of Fire;* Harry Marks, founder and first editor of the *Financial Times;* Brian Epstein, manager of the Beatles; anthropologist Ashley Montagu; playwright Harold Pinter; hair stylist Vidal Sassoon; and comic actors Marty Feldman and Peter Sellers.

COMMUNITY: London, with about 240,000 Jews, is the center of the Anglo-Jewish community of 350,000. It has perhaps a hundred synagogues of every denomination. London's East End, adjacent to the financial district known as the City, was once a neighborhood teeming with Jewish immigrants. They have all since moved up and out, mainly to London's suburbs. There, in the serenity of Golders Green—particularly the Finchley Road section—Edgware, Stamford Hill, Hendon, and Ilford, you will see comfortable middle-class homes, neatly designed synagogues, and Jewish day schools.

Statistics cannot begin to give an idea of the vibrancy of this community. If you look at the numbers, you might, as many London Jews do, despair for the future. If you look at the people and what some of their leaders are doing, you take hope. In Jewish education alone, the efforts are impressive. Jews' College (11 Montagu Place), the oldest rabbinical seminary in England, trains religious leaders. The Ilford Jewish Primary School (Carlton Drive, Barkingside, Essex) and the Jewish Free School (175 Camden Road) reach out to all segments of the population. Then there is Yakar, a new center for adult Jewish learning in Hendon, which offers more than twenty weekly classes and monthly forums on a wide range of Jewish topics, from Mishnah to modern Hebrew, and from practical Judaism to Jewish philosophy. Wealthy London parents who once would have sent their kids to Harrow and Eton send them instead to Carmel College, a Jewish prep school in Wallingford, near Oxford.

SIGHTS: The heart of London is the square mile called "The City," where there is still a street called Old Jewry. There were synagogues in Old Jewry as well as on Gresham and Coleman streets. A synagogue also stood on the site of the present National Westminster Bank, at 52 Threadneedle Street.

At the corner of Threadneedle and Cornhill is the Royal Exchange, with its murals by Solomon J. Solomon, once president of the British Royal Society of Artists. Among the Solomon works in the Exchange is a portrait of Nathan Mayer Rothschild, founder of the London house of the family banking firm. The southeast corner of the Exchange was once known as "Jews' Walk."

If you are interested in Jewish architecture, the splendid Spanish and Portuguese Bevis Marks Synagogue on St. Mary Axe (pronounced "Simmery Axe") should be on your itinerary. Modeled on the Portuguese Synagogue in Amsterdam, it was completed in 1701 and is the oldest synagogue in the British Commonwealth (telephone, 289-2573).

A synagogue convenient to the tourist area is the Central Synagogue on Great Portland Street. It has twenty-six exquisite stained-glass windows depicting the range of Jewish culture.

There is a great deal of Jewish art to be seen in London, at the Tate Gallery on Millbank, the National Gallery on Trafalgar Square, the Courtauld Institute Galleries on Woburn Square and the Rothschild headquarters in St. Swithin's Lane, among others. If your time is limited, you might want to concentrate on the library of the British Museum and the "must see" Jewish Museum.

The British Library's exhibit hall has a case of ornately illustrated Hebrew manuscripts, including Maimonides's *Mishneh Torah,* a fourteenth-century Pentateuch with illustrations of the tribes of Israel dressed in Crusader garb, and the Golden Haggadah, dated roughly to 1320. The British Museum is on Great Russell Street.

The Jewish Museum is located in Woburn House (Upper Woburn Place, telephone, 387-5937), a complex of several Jewish organizations, including a well-stocked bookshop. Don't be put off by the drab entryway to the museum—the collection is first-rate. It contains the earliest dated Purim Megillah (1647), with engraved illustrations by Salom Italia. On the far wall is a magnificent sixteenth-century Venetian Aron Kodesh, which was inadvertently used as a wardrobe by the Earl of Tankerville. Solomon Hart, a nineteenth-century English artist, painted many canvases on Jewish themes; the museum features his richly colored, highly detailed *Simhat Torah.*

Another museum of Jewish interest is the North London house in which Sigmund Freud spent the last year of his life. Two days after the Germans marched into Vienna in 1938, he told his disciples, "After the destruction of Jerusalem by Titus, Rabbi Jochanan ben Zakkai asked permission to open a school at Yavne for the study of Torah. We are going to do the same." Freud's "Yavne," at 20 Maresfield Gardens, has many of his personal effects, including his collection of classical and Egyptian antiquities.

Two non-Jewish sights that you might have missed are the Southwark Cathedral at London Bridge near the site of Shakespeare's Globe Theatre (which is scheduled for reconstruction), and the Royal Festival Hall on the South Bank of the Thames. This concert hall is also a convenient place to step indoors, away from London's weather, and to stroll, snack, attend a free lunchtime or evening jazz concert, buy souvenirs, and, above all, rest your feet.

Three activities that you'll not want to deny yourself are shopping at London's many department stores—the bargains are terrific in January—catching a play or two (or three) at one of the many inexpensive theaters, and walking, strolling, or sauntering.

EATING: There is a vast network of kosher restaurants, serving tasteful and tasty dinners every evening. Bloom's in Golders Green (130 Golders Green Road) and in the East End (90 Whitechapel High Street) are still reliable standbys. For something more exotic, Zaki's at 634 Finchley Road offers kosher Middle Eastern food in a refined atmosphere, with fresh flowers, candlelight, and courteous service. Reuben's (20a Baker Street), not far from the shopping district, offers an elegant dining room upstairs and an "eat it and beat it" kosher delicatessen downstairs. (There's a lot of rhyming in London. "Marks & Sparks" is the nickname of Lord Sieff's department store, Marks and Spencer.)

READING: Read London's *Jewish Chronicle* for an idea of what Jewish life in London is like as well as for listings of Jewish theater, film, radio, and lectures. For a historic view of Jews in England, read Sir Walter Scott's *Ivanhoe;* the movie version of this classic starred a London-born actress who would later convert to Judaism—Elizabeth Taylor. To go from the sublimely serious to the sublimely hilarious, you need to read only two books. The first is Cecil Roth's *History of the Jews in England* (Clarendon); the other is *The King of the Schnorrers* (Dover), Israel Zangwill's side-splitting tale of Jewish communal life in London's East End at the turn of the century.

—JOSEPH LOWIN

Los Angeles

Bay Cities Synagogue in Venice Beach *(Bill Aron)*

Hasidim and Hollywood, blintzes and beaches—Jewish life in the land of mellow.

Only three decades ago, Los Angeles was the place to which Jews escaped as they ran from old neighborhoods on the East Coast, helter-skelter toward assimilation. Basking in the golden sun, scattered between mountain and beach, they could disappear in the California melting pot, masked as if by cinematic illusion.

Today, however, Los Angeles Jews are visible, powerful, and at the cutting edge of American Jewish life—not too shabby for a locale often called a collection of suburbs in search of a city. Los Angeles is home to the third largest Jewish community in the world, trailing only New York and Tel Aviv. Los Angeles Jewry has left its mark on the city's politics, real estate development, and, those quintessential California endeavors, Hollywood and the music business.

Like the city's semidesert terrain, made green by water imported from the Sierra Nevada, Jewish life in Los Angeles has flowered from arid assimilation to vibrant, lush vitality. Influential centers of Jewish culture, learning, and activism have sprouted where once it was difficult to find a kosher restaurant.

Still, the community lacks roots. While increasing numbers of Jewish Angelenos are native-born, most still come from someplace else. Ironically, the growth of Los Angeles Jewish life has made it easier to remain uninvolved; the external signs of Yiddishkeit are so manifest that it is unnecessary to affiliate institutionally.

HISTORY: Los Angeles's birthname, El Pueblo de Nuestra Señora la Reina de Los Angeles (the City of our Lady, Queen of the Angels), bespeaks the city's Spanish roots. Founded by Spanish colonists in 1781, Los Angeles was nearly sixty years old when Jacob Frankfort, a tailor and the city's first Jewish resident, arrived.

In 1850, according to a Federal census, the city was home to fewer than two thousand souls; of those, a scant eight were Jewish. All but Frankfort were merchants; all were unmarried; six were German. They lived next door to one another in a downtown commercial building—the city's first Jewish neighborhood.

The city's first charitable organization was the Hebrew Benevolent Society, founded in 1855 to establish a Jewish cemetery. Congregation B'nai B'rith, organized in 1862, ultimately evolved into the present-day Wilshire Boulevard Temple.

By the turn of the century, Jews numbered about twenty-five hundred of Los Angeles's hundred thousand citizens, and Los Angeles Jewish life took off. Fueled by an influx of Eastern European Jews, including many tuberculosis victims escaping East Coast sweatshops, Jewish social services began to develop.

The Kaspare Cohn Hospital, founded in 1902, ultimately evolved into the world renowned Cedars-Sinai Medical Center. The Duarte Sanitarium, founded in 1914 by the Jewish Consumptive Relief Association, became the City of Hope respiratory center. The Federation of Jewish Charities, founded in 1911, was precursor to today's Jewish Federation Council, an umbrella organization that represents nearly five hundred groups.

COMMUNITY: There are about a half million Jews in Los Angeles County, out of a total population of seven million. Neighboring Orange County has an additional sixty thousand Jews out of two million people. One thing constant about Los Angeles Jewry is change. Many of the Iranians who have settled in Los Angeles since the Khomeini revolution are Jews. More recently, Latin American and South African Jews have arrived. Los Angeles is also home to thousands of Soviet Jewish immigrants, a growing hasidic community, and as many as a hundred thousand Israelis.

Jews occupy prominent positions in politics, law, medicine, and science, in the aerospace, high-tech, home electronics, and construction industries, and on college campuses such as the University of California at Los Angeles and the University of Southern California. Jews founded several local banks, and Jewish developers built many of the housing tracts that transformed the San Fernando Valley's orange groves into subdivisions. Jews founded the Columbia, Universal, Warner Brothers, Paramount, Twentieth Century-Fox, and MGM film studios and are prominent in television production. Ditto popular music, Los Angeles's other garrison of glitter and glamour.

Los Angeles Jews do not merely relate to the community at large; they lead it. Six out of fifteen Los Angeles City Council members are Jewish. Two of them, Joel Wachs and Zev Yaroslavsky, are potential mayoral candidates. In fact, Yaroslavsky's political base grew out of the Southern California Council for Soviet Jews, which he directed.

Jews were among the major supporters of Los Angeles's Mayor Tom
Bradley, who is black, although Jewish relations with the black and
Chicano communities are more respectful than loving. In addition,
five members of the city's congressional delegation are Jewish, as are
the Los Angeles County sheriff, the city superintendent of schools, the
district attorney, one county supervisor, and four state legislators.

Totaling close to one hundred and fifty congregations, Los Angeles
synagogues include tiny storefront shtiebls, huge "temple-plexes"
with thousands of members, and more conventional Reform, Conservative, and Orthodox congregations. Alternative Judaism is well
represented by havura-type minyans, such as the Westwood Free
Minyan, which meets at UCLA Hillel; the Library Minyan, affiliated
with Temple Beth Am in the Pico-Robertson area; and Minyan Ariel,
which meets every other week at Adat Ari El in North Hollywood.
Several batim, Jewish student collectives near major college campuses, add to the variety.

Los Angeles's Jewish news is covered by *The Jewish Journal of Greater
Los Angeles,* published by the Jewish Federation Council, and three
independent newspapers—*Heritage,* the *B'nai B'rith Messenger,* and
Israel Today. UCLA is home to *Ha-Am,* one of the oldest Jewish student
papers in the country.

The thirteen-story Jewish Community Building—known locally as
the "Jewish Pentagon"—is located at 6505 Wilshire Boulevard, near
Fairfax Avenue. The building is home to the Jewish Federation Council, which asserts itself as the communal and political voice of Los
Angeles Jewry, as well as most of the major Jewish organizations with
offices in Los Angeles.

SIGHTS: Jews long ago left their early settlements in Boyle
Heights and downtown, making Fairfax Avenue the traditional heart
of Los Angeles Jewish life. Fairfax is a polyglot community of elderly
Europeans, Israelis, recent Soviet immigrants, Holocaust survivors,
and Hasidim. With their gift shops, bookstores, kosher markets, and
kosher and nonkosher restaurants, featuring delicatessen, Israeli,
Hungarian, and other foods, the blocks between Third Street and
Melrose Avenue are still where Los Angeles Jews go when they want to
feel ethnic.

But Fairfax has been supplanted as the area where most Jews live by
thriving and ever more visible Jewish neighborhoods throughout the
city. Just southwest of Fairfax, the blocks surrounding the intersection
of Pico and Robertson boulevards recently have become a center of

modern Orthodoxy. Pico is lined with kosher markets and nearly a dozen kosher restaurants, including fast-food fried chicken and hamburgers, pizza, Middle Eastern, meat, and dairy. The last is the Milky Way, owned by director Steven Spielberg's mother, Leah Adler, and likely the only kosher restaurant anywhere decorated with E.T. and Indiana Jones posters.

Hancock Park, to the east of Fairfax, was once known primarily for the mansions of its (emphatically not Jewish) wealthy residents. This past decade it has had an influx of hundreds of Hasidim, refugees from the Frost Belt, who have established storefront shuls, stores, restaurants, and a large yeshiva on La Brea Avenue.

Santa Monica and rapidly gentrifying Venice are seeing a resurgence of Jewish life focused on two beachfront synagogues, Mishkon Tephilo (Conservative) and Bay Cities Synagogue (Orthodox), both led by dynamic young rabbis.

With more than two hundred thousand Jewish residents, the San Fernando Valley by itself would rank among the top ten Jewish communities in the world. Valley neighborhoods such as North Hollywood, Van Nuys, Sherman Oaks, and Encino, bedroom communities that form the city's Jewish backbone, are becoming more visibly Jewish. Valley synagogues tend to be large—several have two thousand or more member families. Stephen S. Wise, a Reform temple overlooking Sherman Oaks, is a mountaintop complex that spreads over several acres. The Conservative Valley Beth Shalom in Encino is known for its dozens of synagogue havurot, an idea originated by its rabbi, Harold Schulweis. The Aish HaTorah Yeshiva and a number of bustling Lubavitch minyans are helping Orthodox neighborhoods grow in North Hollywood and Encino.

Several synagogues and buildings formerly used as such are architecturally noteworthy. Wilshire Boulevard Temple, the descendent of Los Angeles's first congregation and still among the city's largest, is an example of the "synagogue as cathedral" mode once favored by Reform congregations. Located at 3663 Wilshire Boulevard, the building features a mosaic-inlaid dome, a large rose window, Byzantine columns in black marble, and several murals. The Sephardic Temple Tifereth Israel at 10500 Wilshire Boulevard is a beautiful stone structure that would not be out of place in Jerusalem. The temple features a traditional Sefardic interior and an outdoor Spanish garden. Congregation Talmud Torah, known to almost everyone as the Breed Street Shul, is among the few remaining symbols of the once-thriving Boyle Heights neighborhood. A large brick structure featuring polished wood interior fixtures, the synagogue was featured in both the 1927 and 1980 versions of *The Jazz Singer.* Located at 247 N. Breed Street, the congregation still holds services on Shabbat and Yom Tov and sometimes on weekdays.

Los Angeles is also home to a network of seven Jewish community centers. One, the Israel Levin Senior Adult Center, on Ocean Front Walk in Venice, was the subject of *Number Our Days,* the Academy Award-winning documentary which examines the lives of Venice's elderly Jewish community—an old-country haven in the midst of Los Angeles's beachfront glitz.

Because Los Angeles Jewry's greatest growth has taken place during the last fifty years, historical sites are few and not terribly dramatic. A plaque in the sidewalk near 214 S. Broadway, now one of the Hispanic community's major shopping streets, commemorates Congregation B'nai B'rith's first building. Another plaque, on Lilac Terrace near Dodger Stadium, marks the former location of the first Jewish cemetery. A statue of American Revolution financier Haym Solomon stands in MacArthur Park at Seventh and Park View streets.

Los Angeles is home to several museums and galleries featuring Judaica and Jewish art. The Skirball Museum at Hebrew Union College (3077 University Avenue near the University of Southern California) offers outstanding exhibitions of Judaica, art, and antiquities, as well as a lovely gift shop. Both the Jewish Community Building and the University of Judaism (15600 Mulholland Drive) mount frequent art exhibits. The Martyrs Memorial at the Jewish Community Building and the Simon Wiesenthal Center (9760 W. Pico Boulevard) house museums devoted to the Holocaust and do ongoing Holocaust education. The Wiesenthal Center produced the Academy Award-winning documentary *Genocide.*

The Michael Hittleman Gallery (8797 Beverly Boulevard) showcases exclusively Israeli art and the work of Marc Chagall. Gallery Judaica (1312 Westwood) features fine arts and ritual objects, ketubahs, watercolors, and sculpture. The latest addition to Los Angeles's growing Jewish art scene is the Jewish Quarter (8685 Wilshire Boulevard in Beverly Hills) which, under one roof, features shops and galleries selling fine art, antiquities, Roman glass, antique and modern silver, Jewish folk art and crafts; it also has a photography studio and a travel agency specializing in Jewish-interest and kosher tours.

J. Roth Bookseller (9427 Pico Boulevard) is Los Angeles's finest Jewish bookstore and one of the most beautiful Jewish bookstores in the country. Its soft-spoken and charming proprietor, known to all simply as Jack, oversees all measure of holy books, as well as the latest Jewish spy thrillers. Upstairs there is a small gallery for art and fine ritual objects.

CULTURE: Los Angeles's Jewish renaissance has spurred the growth of serious Jewish institutions and culture. The California branch of Reform Judaism's Hebrew Union College moved in the 1970s to a modern campus adjacent to USC, where it trains rabbis, Jewish educators and communal workers. On the crest of the Santa Monica Mountains, the University of Judaism, the western branch of the Jewish Theological Seminary, has a beautiful facility where Conservative students can learn while surrounded by some of the city's most beautiful vistas. Yeshiva University's West Coast branch shares Pico Boulevard quarters with the Simon Wiesenthal Center. Lubavitch runs a growing empire of shuls, schools, and counseling programs throughout the city. In Simi Valley, just outside Los Angeles, the Brandeis-Bardin Institute runs a "laboratory for living Judaism" that offers lectures, weekend programs, and summer sessions for children, college students, and adults. And a smörgåsbord of Jewish curriculum is available at the local secular universities, especially at UCLA and USC, where students can earn degrees in Jewish studies.

Virtually every Jewish institution, synagogue and campus Hillel organization in Los Angeles sponsors lectures and other cultural events. The Streisand Center for Jewish Cultural Arts at the UCLA Hillel Foundation (900 Hilgard Avenue), sponsors an annual lecture and concert series that has featured such luminaries as Elie Wiesel, Isaac Bashevis Singer, and Chava Alberstein. Jewish arts festivals, generally held in the spring, bring other lectures and concerts to area campuses.

The University of Judaism sponsors lectures at Sinai Temple in West Los Angeles and Valley Beth Shalom in Encino and has showcased such musicians as Yitzhak Perlman in its campus auditorium. The Brandeis-Bardin Institute sponsors a lecture series in the city, and most of the larger synagogues also run lectures and concerts. Keeping track of them is no mean feat, but a good way to start is to read the local Jewish newspapers, check posters in Jewish neighborhoods, or call the Community Calendar at the Jewish Community Building.

A variety of radio and television programs feature Jewish content. Most notable is the Jewish Television Network, which airs entertainment, children's shows and programs on Jewish thought and affairs. JTN programs appear on Group W Cable, Sunday through Thursday from 6 to 8 P.M., and on Communication Cable from 7 to 9 P.M. Check the papers for other TV and radio offerings.

PERSONALITIES: Los Angeles Jews number in their midst prominent politicians, presidential advisers, industrialists, writers, musicians, and, of course, movie stars and Hollywood moguls.

In Hollywood's pioneer era, the Warner brothers—Albert, Harry, Jack, and Sam—founded a movie studio of the same name and made the first sound film, *The Jazz Singer.* Louis B. Mayer and Samuel Goldwyn shaped MGM, Harry Cohn ran Columbia Pictures, Adolph Zukor founded Paramount, and William Fox, né Fuchs, pioneered Twentieth Century-Fox. Today, Lew Wasserman, head of the Universal Studios/MCA (Music Company of America) empire and a Democratic insider, though not especially active in Jewish community affairs, is widely regarded as the most economically and politically powerful Jew in the city.

Local household words include director Steven Spielberg, actors Dustin Hoffman, Richard Dreyfuss (who reportedly made his debut in a Hanukkah play at the Westside Jewish Community Center), and Debra Winger. Norman Lear, Ed Asner, Barbra Streisand, and Herb Alpert are all active in community affairs.

In addition to City Councilmen Yaroslavsky and Wachs, there are two rising congressional stars in the political arena—Henry Waxman and Mel Levine.

Local Jewish industrialists include Armand Hammer, head of Occidental Petroleum; Simon Ramos, the "R" in the TRW engineering operation; and Norton Simon, whose empire at one time included food and soft drink processing, packaging, printing and publishing, but who now concentrates on philanthropy.

Writers who make Los Angeles their home include Irving Wallace and family members Sylvia and Amy Wallace and David Wallechinsky. Michael Medved, who co-authored *What Really Happened to the Class of '65* with Wallechinsky, is partly responsible for the Jewish renaissance in Venice and Ocean Park.

GENERAL SIGHTS: The typical Los Angeles travel itinerary of Hollywood, Disneyland, and the beaches often leaves out some of the city's most charming attractions. The Children's Museum (310 N.

Main Street) is an exciting, hands-on education for both youngsters and their parents. The museum is hard by Union Station on Alameda Street, Los Angeles's rail terminal and a beautiful example of early California mission architecture. Also nearby is Olivera Street, a cobblestone block done up as a typical Mexican marketplace, said to be the oldest street in the city.

Ocean Front Walk on Venice's beach is a carnival combining every California stereotype—and some not so stereotypical. Tanned sun-worshippers, teenyboppers on roller skates, musicians, street-corner preachers, and hedonistic yuppies strolling with perfect children gather in sidewalk cafés. At the same time, Orthodox members of the Bay Cities Synagogue conduct services, and the elderly Jews of the Israel Levin Senior Citizens Center sit on their benches watching the parade go by.

If you wish to avoid the hoopla of a Universal Studios tour and still get an inside view of a working film factory, try the Burbank Studios VIP tour. For twenty dollars a person, visitors are escorted through the studio in small groups. Tour offerings vary according to what is in production. Reservations are necessary (telephone, 954-1744).

DAY TRIPS: The picturesque seaside community of Santa Barbara is eighty scenic miles up the Pacific Coast Highway. About thirty miles beyond that is Solvang, a Danish village in the middle of California. For a seagoing adventure, try a trip to Catalina Island, with its rugged coast line, buffalo herds (brought to the island when Westerns were being filmed there) and flying fish. The Catalina Express runs daily round trips (telephone, 519-1212).

READING: The great Jewish novel of Los Angeles has yet to be written. One small slice of Jewish life in the movie business can be found in *The Return of Mr. Hollywood* by Josh Greenfeld (Doubleday). For a general look at Hollywood by a Jewish author, see Nathaniel West's 1939 classic *The Day of the Locust. Number Our Days,* the documentary film on elderly Jews in Venice, is also an enthralling book by anthropologist Barbara Meyerhoff (Dutton). In 1982, the Federation published *Jewish Los Angeles, A Guide*—available for $5.95 from the Federation and at many local bookstores—which includes a self-guided tour of historic Jewish Los Angeles.

RECOMMENDATION: While most local hotels offer kosher TV dinners to guests who request them in advance, Los Angeles also boasts one strictly kosher hotel. The Beverly Grand at 7257 Beverly Boulevard, telephone, (213) 939-1653, caters to observant Jewish visitors and features L'Orient, a glatt kosher restaurant serving traditional continental and Chinese dishes. Jewish travelers seeking general community information or in need of assistance can call the Jewish Community Building at (213) 852-1234.

TRIVIA: Where is the first solar-heated mikvah in the country? Los Angeles, of course—the Teichman Mikva (12800 Chandler Boulevard) in North Hollywood.

—NEIL REISNER

Madrid and Toledo

Prado Museum *(Spanish Ministry of Tourism)*

The man at the airport's government tourist office insists on telling a Jewish visitor about all his Jewish friends. The hotel concierge proudly reveals he knows the synagogue's address by heart. And the shopkeeper reports, in detail, about a television program he saw on Ladino music. Thus Madrid—in the name of Spain—informs Jews that, five hundred years after expelling them, they are welcome back.

Not just welcome, but wanted. In the flurry of festivity marking the establishment of diplomatic relations with Israel in 1986 and, two years earlier, marking the nationwide observance of the 850th anniversary of the birth of Maimonides, dozens of newspaper articles and media presentations celebrated the Sefardic contribution to Spain, while Spaniards, aware that multitudes descended from Marranos and Conversos have Jewish blood, hurried to check out their roots.

This is not all that is hurrying Madrid these days, of course. After years of isolation from mainstream Europe, Madrileños rush to catch up with the late twentieth century. Hence, their city—a stylishly contemporary one of broad boulevards and grand plazas, of fashionable new neighborhoods and atmospheric old ones—hums, at almost all hours, with action.

Madrid's three thousand Jews are also caught up in this. While too new to have a definite place yet in the scene, they go with the flow, happy to participate and happy, once again, to be Spanish.

HISTORY: Contrary to popular conception, Madrid, although it did not become Spain's capital until after the Jews' expulsion, did, even as an eleventh-century Moorish stronghold, have a small Jewish community. There was also a town nearby called Alluden—from the Arabic *al-Yahudiyin*, "the Jews." The Madrid community flourished in the thirteenth century, until the imposition of restrictions on usury rates, real estate dealings, and relations with Christians.

But in the days when Spanish Jewry knew glory, Toledo—forty-five miles south of Madrid, about an hour by today's transport—was Spain's capital and a leading Jewish center. By the twelfth century, twelve thousand Jews lived there; in 1391, it had Spain's largest Jewish population.

Under Muslim rule, Toledo grandly contributed to the Golden Age, becoming a headquarters for both religious and secular scholarship, a place where Jews, as intermediaries between Muslims and Christians, translated Arabic works on mathematics, astronomy, and Greek philosophy into the vernacular and Latin—works that would reappear with the Renaissance. After the Christian reconquest, Jews remained undisturbed for a while, and rose to such high state positions as diplomat, financier, interpreter, adviser, even royal scribe; in addition, they owned land, vineyards, and slaves.

According to tradition, Toledo's Jewish community was the oldest on the Iberian peninsula, having descended from exiles from the tribes of Judah and Benjamin who fled the destruction of the First Temple. More likely, however, they arrived with the Visigoths during the fourth or fifth century, and were discriminated against until the Muslim invasion of Spain in 711 under Tarik (who, some say, may have been a Jew).

Among the outstanding Jews from Toledo during the Middle Ages were: Meir Ibn Megas, who established a Talmudic academy there; Abraham Ibn Ezra, a witty, peripatetic translator, grammarian, and biblical expert whose commentaries accompany most scholarly Hebrew Bibles today; Joseph Ferruziel (Cidellus) a member of the Royal Court, from a family that considered itself of the House of David—and behaved accordingly; and Judah Halevi, physician, philosopher, and poet, whose religious poems have become part of the High Holy Day prayerbook, and whose passion for Zion is best represented by the poem that begins, "I am in the West but my heart is in the East."

One Spanish Jew who was not universally revered in Toledo was Maimonides. The city was a center for challenging the writings of the Rambam (a native of Córdoba) on the grounds that they were undermining the faith.

From the twelfth until the mid-fourteenth century, the Jews of Toledo were occasionally attacked or harassed and, on one occasion, imprisoned in their synagogues until they paid a special tax. The real trouble began in 1366, when a vicious, three-year civil war began between Pedro the Cruel and his bastard brother Henry. Perhaps because Pedro had used Jews to execute his tyrannical policies—they were, particularly, his tax gatherers—they were turned upon with a vengeance and, as the city changed hands several times, the Jews not only were forced to raise one million gold coins, but also suffered the death of eight thousand of their community.

Next, the Jews were forced to wear identifying badges and give up their Spanish names. In 1391 riots against the Jews of Seville spread throughout the country. In Toledo, almost all the synagogues were burned and the Jewish quarter was ravaged. Many abandoned Judaism for conversion—becoming Conversos.

Until then, Jewish converts had been eagerly welcomed. But suddenly there were far too many to be easily absorbed. They began marrying into the Spanish aristocracy and occupying the country's best positions. Some even turned against other Jews; Pablo de Santa María, né Solomon Levi, did a brilliant job of forcing Jews to convert. But many grew jealous of the roles now played by the Conversos and in Toledo, as elsewhere, Conversos were persecuted—and often slaughtered. Churchmen began to question the purity of their faith and, in 1480, established the Inquisition to root out heretics. One of the instigators of the Inquisition was the infamous Tomás de Torquemada, said to have descended from Jews himself.

There remained only one further step for Spain to take to rid itself of its Jews. On March 31, 1492, King Ferdinand (also said to have had Jewish blood) and Queen Isabella, gave the Jews four months to leave Spain, under the pain of death.

After Philip II made Madrid the Spanish capital in 1561, it became the scene of numerous autos-da-fé—including some for Portuguese Conversos who had made the city the principal center for their activities. During the seventeenth century, when Portuguese Conversos were influential in the royal court, the possibility of readmitting Jews was raised, but rejected because of opposition from Inquisition authorities.

Only after 1869, when Spain received a new constitution, could Jews begin to return to the city in safety. By then the secret practices of Marranos who had stayed in Spain had, for the most part, been dropped and the Conversos become Christian in memory as well as in practice. Madrid did attract Jews from North Africa in the nineteenth century and, during World War I, gave refuge to Jews from Eastern Europe, among them the Zionist leader Max Nordau. There was little community organization until the passage of a law, in 1924, granting citizenship to individuals of Spanish descent. During the Spanish Civil War the community dispersed.

In Francisco Franco (another said to have Jewish blood), the Jews found great ambivalence. Franco outwardly decried what he called the universal "Anglo-Judeo-Masonic conspiracy" and allied himself with

Arab causes (particularly after Israel and other democracies denied his bid for United Nations membership because of his fascism). However, as leader of a country not overrun by Germany in World War II, he gave asylum to some Eastern European refugees; in 1967 he provided passports for Egyptian Jews on the run.

COMMUNITY: The Spanish Jewish community of today began forming after World War II and now numbers about fifteen thousand. In 1967, along with other non-Catholic groups, it was given legal status, allowing it to create associations and own property. In 1980, Spain abolished the concept of a state religion. And with the establishment of diplomatic relations with Israel, some see the closing of a circle that began with the expulsion of 1492.

After five hundred years, Jews named Salama, Castile, and Toledano are back in a Spanish capital. And some young, idealistic members of the community are already dreaming of a presence as rich and significant as the one in Maimonides's time. Meanwhile, the primary thrust in Madrid is to keep its small community of three thousand united.

Madrid's Jews hail from three backgrounds. The first—a fairly small contingent—came from Eastern Europe during or immediately following World War II. In the 1950s and '60s, as Morocco gained its independence and incorporated Tangier, Jews, primarily from the northern cities, arrived and now constitute about 70 percent of the community. Also during the 1960s, Madrid saw an influx of Latin American Jews, fleeing that region's upheavals. Together with a handful from Israel, England, Hungary, and the United States, they comprise the community's remainder.

Jewish Madrileños work in fields ranging from high-tech electronics to commerce, with many professionals among the younger generation.

Culturally, the community considers itself Sefardic—and makes a decided distinction between its heritage and that of Jews who truly intermingled in the Diaspora with Arabs. Religiously, though, it is reluctant to define itself—lest it alienate even one precious member. It has sought a common denominator, described by one cautious leader as "mildly Orthodox." Samuel Toledano, secretary-general of Spain's Federation of Jewish Communities, says of the Madrid contingent, "Since everyone disagrees, we think we are on the right course."

Beth Yaacov Synagogue, to which 525 families belong, opened in 1968. The Jewish community, which has its headquarters in the synagogue building, supports a variety of institutions, including a day school in the fashionable Madrid suburb of Moraleja (where many Jews live) attended by 160—or 25 percent—of the children in grades one through ten, a youth camp about twenty miles from Madrid, two kosher butchers, a cemetery, and a new country club, still under construction.

Spanish Jews say they are free to socialize as they choose; in fact, these days—perhaps because they are still novelties—they even find themselves lionized.

MADRID SIGHTS: Beth Yaacov, Madrid's first synagogue since 1492, is down a little street that looks like an alley. It's at Calle Balmes 3, near Plaza de Sorolla, in Madrid's downtown area.

The discreet building—guarded by a police car day and night—also houses a small chapel, two social halls, a Talmud Torah room for Sunday classes, a mikvah, a library, and facilities for kosher catering. (In fact, a section of one hall can be blocked off as a kosher restaurant, if tourists call in advance.)

The synagogue itself boasts marble floors covered with Oriental-style runners and, in its one wall open to the light are modernistic red, white, and blue stained-glass windows. As part of a university course in the humanities, Spain's Queen Sophia studied Judaism and attended services here in May 1976. The office numbers are 445-9843 and 445-9835. Be prepared for a security check on entering.

At Calle del Duque de Medinaceli 4, near the American Express office, is the Arias Montano Institute for Jewish Studies, a government-sponsored center, founded in 1941 for research in Hebrew, Sefardic, and Near East studies. It is known for its library of more than sixteen thousand volumes and rare manuscripts (recently damaged by fire) and publishes a semi-annual journal called *Sefarad.* Bear in mind that nonresearchers and tourists without credentials are dissuaded from visiting. The same applies for the Jewish Studies Department at the University of Madrid.

Visitors are more than welcome, however, at Sefarad, the one Jewish-owned shop on the Gran Vía, Madrid's primary shopping street. Located at No. 54, it features, along with other Spanish gift items, antique Mediterranean menorahs, contemporary Jewish-themed tiles, and a porcelain rabbi originally made exclusively for the store by Lladro.

In areas not far from the Gran Vía once existed Madrid's Jewish neighborhoods. One judería is believed to have stood where fashionable homes and apartment buildings now rise near the Royal Palace. It was bordered by the Calle de Bailen, the Plaza de Isabel II, the Calle Mayor, and the Calle Santiago, and included the Plaza de Oriente, which was, until the nineteenth century, a maze of alleys. Another judería may have been on the Calle de la Fe, now a dark, narrow street in the old town, not far from the Atocha Railroad Station; a synagogue situated next to the Church of San Lorenzo was destroyed in the riots of 1391.

GENERAL SIGHTS: The Prado, with its matchless collections of masterpieces by Velázquez, Ribera, Murillo, Goya, El Greco, Rubens, Titian, Raphael, Correggio, Tintoretto and others, is one of the world's great art repositories. What is more, a number of its works have a particular attraction for Jews. Some are of interest not because of the theme, but because of the faces, which often seem decidedly ethnic. Others present relevant—if not necessarily pleasant—subjects, such as money-changers and autos-da-fé. And still more—often by the masters—arc on Old Testament themes. Among those to look for are Veronese's *Moses Rescued from the Nile;* Ribera's *Jacob's Dream* and *Isaac and Jacob;* Poussin's *The Triumph of David;* Caravaggio's *David Victorious Over Goliath;* Bassano's *Entrance of the Animals to the Ark;* Murillo's *Rebecca and Eliezer;* Tintoretto's *Moses, Esther Before Ahasuerus* and *The Queen of Sheba's Visit to Solomon;* Dürer's *Adam and Eve;* Berruguete's *Auto-da-Fé Presided Over by St. Dominic de Guzmán;* and Reymerswaele's *The Money-Changer and His Wife.*

In the heart of the old town, surrounded by a network of narrow streets, is the expansive, portico-encircled Plaza Mayor, scene of countless autos-da-fé. Also in the center of town is the Puerta del Sol, near which may have been another judería. The Archaeological Museum, at Calle de Serrano 13, has a collection of Jewish artifacts from Toledo—worth visiting, but hardly a substitute for a visit to Madrid's older neighbor.

TOLEDO SIGHTS: Toledo is one of those places in Spain where the reminders of the country's Jewish past still stand. Built of golden-hued limestone, the walled city, set high on a cliff, has been compared to Jerusalem. Its streets are narrow, steep, cobbled, and laid out like a Minotaur-maze, with so many blind alleys it is a cinch to get lost.

The primary judería was in the city's southwest quarter. (A small Jewish enclave called the Alcana also existed nearer the Cathedral, where a Calle de la Sinagoga still runs.) The main area stretches as far north as the Cambrón Gate, formerly named "Gate of the Jews," and is bisected by Calle del Ángel, once Calle de la Judería (now the name of a small branch street). Even before the Middle Ages, the quarter was walled and had its own fortress—which made it something of an independent town.

Records indicate the existence, at one time or another, of ten synagogues and five chapels. Only two major synagogues still stand (though the church, Posada de la Hermandad, is said to have been a Jewish chapel).

On the Calle de los Reyes Católicos, near the city's wall, in the heart of the old judería, is the oldest of Toledo's Jewish monuments, the synagogue-turned-church, Santa María la Blanca, built in 1203. It stands off the street in a garden where, even in winter, birds chirp in the tall trees.

Built in the *mudéjar*—or Moorish—style, the interior is a chorus of columns topped by the swirls of arches which, from different perspectives, form a variety of overlaying patterns with each other. The capitals are delicately molded in pine-cone motifs and some old tile work remains on the floor. In addition to having been a church, this structure—too dimly lit for proper viewing—knew incarnations as a dance hall, a barracks, a carpenter's workshop, and a refuge for reformed prostitutes. Not far from it have been found the remains of a mikvah.

Just down the street, beyond the square now called Plaza de Barrio Nuevo, is the second synagogue, El Tránsito. Its entrance is on Calle de Samuel Levi, named for Samuel Levi Abulafia who built the structure as a private chapel for his family. Abulafia, a shrewd politician, allied himself with Pedro the Cruel, and was his treasurer until his enemies denounced him as a traitor and he was tortured to death.

The synagogue was finished in 1357, four years before Abulafia's death. Designed by Rabbi Meyer Abdeli from Granada, the most renowned architect of the time, it is reminiscent of the Alhambra. The interior is rectangular with a seemingly soaring forty-foot-high ceiling, elaborately carved from cedars of Lebanon. The walls are covered with intricate filigree representing grape leaves, palmettos, and lilies of the valley, while circling the walls is a band of Hebrew lettering with quotations from the Bible and the Psalms. (Similar inscriptions have been included in Madrid's new Beth Yaacov.) One wall is dominated by a recessed window panel in front of which stand three foliated arches that cast delicate, lacy shadows on the opposite wall. On another wall, windows alternate with closed-in arches. El Tránsito is considered one of the best preserved pre-Inquisition monuments but it too is not shown off to best advantage.

The adjoining Museum of Sefardic Culture has a collection of ancient tombstones and inscribed stones from synagogues, pre-Inquisition Jewish jewelry, nineteenth-century Moroccan wedding outfits, fifteenth-century amulets, and various holiday-related objects. The museum's single drawback is that its exhibits are labeled only in Spanish.

A few steps from El Tránsito is the Casa del Greco, where the painter once lived. It stands on the site of Samuel Halevi Abulafia's palace, which supposedly had a tunnel leading under the walls to the nearby Tagus River. An underground passage is also said to have existed along the outer edge of the judería. At a site now the Plaza de Zocodover, several autos-da-fé were held.

DAY TRIPS: In Segovia, the Castilian city of moats and castles, the Church of Corpus Christi was originally the main synagogue. Built in the thirteenth century in the *mudéjar* style, it resembles Toledo's Santa María la Blanca. It was converted into a church in 1420, after Jews were accused of desecrating the Host and, in 1572, became the property of Franciscan nuns. The judería was originally situated around the Calle de la Judería and, later, around the Barrio Nuevo or Judería Nueva, where the church of La Merced, probably once a synagogue, stands today.

The medieval walled city of Ávila was the birthplace in 1515 of the religious educator Santa Teresa. The descendant of a Converso silk merchant from Toledo, she attempted, with San Juan de la Cruz, probably of similar background, to reform the Carmelite order. The town's Church of Todos Los Santos and the Chapel of Mosen Rubi (Calle de López Núñez) are thought to have originally been synagogues. Torquemada is buried in the Sacristy of Ávila's Convent of Santo Tomás.

El Escorial is the site of the monastery of San Lorenzo and the summer palace of King Philip II, completed in 1584. Effigies of the six Kings of Judah are sculpted on the walls of the palace's Patio of Kings, while the monastery contains a superb collection of medieval Hebrew Bibles and illuminated manuscripts. These were assembled in the sixteenth century by a Converso, Benito Arias Montano. He traveled through Europe to save Bibles banned by the Church and offered them to Philip as the foundation for a royal library, of which Arias Montano became the director. The library is open to visitors but few, if any, Bibles are on display and may generally be seen only by researchers.

PERSONALITIES: Since Madrid's Jewish community is young, there has not been much time for luminaries to emerge. However, on the national board of the Socialist Party is Enrique Mujica Herzog, who is half-Jewish and openly identifies with his origins. He was a strong advocate of the establishment of relations with Israel. Jacob Hassan is a professor of Sefardic Culture at Madrid University and Elena Benarroch is developing an international reputation as a fur designer. Another international reputation is that of Lita Milan Trujillo, the widow of Rafael Trujillo, the dictator who admitted many Jewish refugees to the Dominican Republic during World War II. Mrs. Trujillo is a Hungarian Jew from Jaffa.

READING: For contemporary history, see Haim Avni's *Spain, Franco and the Jews* (Jewish Publication Society). For the past, the JPS has published Yitzhak Baer's *History of the Jews in Christian Spain* and E. Ashtor's *History of the Jews in Moslem Spain.* For an overview of Spain in general, Spanish Jews and non-Jews suggest James Michener's *Iberia* (Random House). To recommend Hemingway is to state the obvious.

RECOMMENDATIONS: The Villa Magna is a new, ultra-elegant, ultra-fashionable hotel conveniently located just beyond Madrid's commercial heart on the broad, north-south boulevard, Paseo de la Castellana. The travel agency Viajes Transit, Fernando el Católico 12 and Vallehermoso 40, (telephone, 447-7916), handles kosher requests, while the travel agency, Viajes Day, General Orgaz 3, (telephone, 270-4612), handles Jewish travel to and from Spain and, when large groups are involved, can arrange special events, such as services in Toledo's El Tránsito Synagogue. Not everyone in Spain's travel industry knows synagogue addresses by heart, but in the country's desire to welcome Jewish visitors and explore its own Jewish past, you may be left with that impression.

—PHYLLIS ELLEN FUNKE

Melbourne

Melbourne Trams *(Australian Tourist Commission)*

If it's Monday in New York, it's Tuesday in Melbourne. That's the time differential between these two cities at opposite ends of our globe. As one Melbourne rabbi put it: "On that great day, when the Messiah comes to lead all the Jews out of exile and back to Jerusalem, we Australians—with a twenty-four-hour head start—will already be settled in."

Meanwhile, pending the Messiah's arrival, the seventy-five thousand Jews of the island continent are making do. If cosmopolitan Sydney is their Tel Aviv (to offer neat, simplistic analogies), the more conservative Melbourne is their "Down Under" Jerusalem.

HISTORY AND COMPARISONS: Sydney's founding fathers were convicts, sent to remote Australia from the slums of London for such crimes as stealing bread. In their initial landing at Botany Bay in 1788, there were at least six Jews. Sydney's Jewish population of twenty-seven thousand is largely derived from central European forebears: Germans, who managed to escape their homeland just before World War II, when Australia allowed seven thousand to enter; Hungarians, fresh from the displaced persons camps, or, a decade later, refugees from the Russian invasion of their country in 1956. Their religious commitment tends to be less zealous than that of the Melbourne Jews, the schism between Orthodoxy and Liberal (Reform) Judaism much less marked. Melbourne's thirty-two thousand Jews are of largely East European origin.

Modern Sydney, with a romantic nod toward its scarlet past, is rather laid-back, free-swinging, open-minded (it is presumed to have the largest homosexual population in the world, after San Francisco's). Perhaps the key adjective for Sydney is "secular."

By that token, the word for Melbourne would be "religious." Named for the Tory Prime Minister at the time of Queen Victoria's coronation in 1837, the city has retained, until now at least, a certain nineteenth-century formality. The early settlers were respectable yeomen and merchants, adherents of the Anglican Church. Among the group of 145 good citizens who established Melbourne in 1835, there were two Jews—no less Orthodox than their fellow pioneers and as obedient to the authority of the Chief Rabbi of Great Britain as the Christians were to that of the Archbishop of Canterbury.

John Levi, the country's first native-born rabbi and the head of Liberal Judaism in Melbourne, foresees an increased polarization in the city's Jewish community. Presently, it is 20 percent liberal and 80 percent traditional, including a good many we would call Conservatives, who have no choice but to observe Orthodox ritual. The rabbi predicts that the religious center, "lacking any firm principles or philosophy, will not hold" and that "by the end of the century, only Hasidism, on the denominational 'right,' and Reform Judaism on the 'left,' will survive."

But such a process is a decade or so into the future, even if Rabbi Levi's prophecy is fulfilled. At the moment, modern Orthodox Judaism is alive and well in Melbourne—together with the Hasidim and the Liberal movement. Despite the divisions among the three, they offer the community a variety and an intensity of Jewish life unequaled on the continent.

Such qualities reflect their East European origin. To the genteel Judaism of the early immigrants from England, these new Australians brought the assertive Yiddishkeit of the shtetls. They came to Melbourne in two successive waves—the smaller, in the 1890s, fleeing the pogroms of Tsarist Russia; the larger, after the Holocaust, composed of the homeless remnants who chose Australia because of its relatively open immigration policies, or simply because they wanted to put the greatest distance between themselves and the horrors they had experienced in Europe.

COMMUNITY: Since World War II, the Melbourne community has more than doubled its numbers. It supports some two hundred organizations, among which are sixteen Orthodox and three Liberal synagogues, two homes and a sheltered workshop for the aged, three foster homes, four migrant hostels, seven day schools, eighteen part-time schools, ten kindergartens, a museum, art galleries, libraries, a publishing house, a weekly newspaper, a monthly literary magazine in English and Yiddish, a Yiddish theater and choir, sixteen Zionist groups, seventeen youth clubs, sixteen sports organizations, and twenty-one landsmanschaften.

With so broad a range of structures and activities, it is no wonder that Australian Jews look to Melbourne as their spiritual center, their Jerusalem, the very core of continuing identity.

One indication of Melbourne's central role is the phenomenon of attendance in full-time religious day schools. Eighty percent of Jewish children go to one or another of the kindergarten-through-high school institutions. Mount Scopus, the first in the country, founded in 1948, has twenty-five hundred students and is said to be the largest in the world.

Isi J. Leibler, a leading Melbourne businessman and Jewish community leader, ascribes this extraordinary enrollment to what he calls "the tyranny of distance." His Jewish countrymen are so far removed from the Jewish mainstreams in the United States and Israel, he says, that they feel the urgent need to give their children an unassailable identity in a distant land where Jews make up less than .5 percent of the total population and which, moreover, tempts them with the assimilationist seductions of an open, egalitarian society, virtually free of anti-Semitism.

PERSONALITIES: There is also the phenomenon—not unusual in Jewish history—of upward mobility. The early arrivals from Poland and Russia were itinerant peddlers or workers. The peddlers settled down and became merchant princes. The watchmakers opened jewelry factories. The tailors became the clothing manufacturers. The carpenters and the cabinetmakers turned to the mass production of furniture.

Their children and grandchildren, enacting a scenario parallel to the American one, are "overrepresented," they proudly assert, in the arts and the professions. Melbourne Jews have held every political post, from city councilman—including a number of lord mayors—to cabinet minister. Indeed, two of their number have won recognition as the outstanding Australians of their time.

Sir Isaac Isaacs, born in Melbourne in 1855 to a Polish immigrant family, became the nation's Chief Justice and the first native to serve as Governor General. Like James Madison in the constitutional struggles in early United States history, Isaacs was the major figure in the development of an Australian constitution which would assert the sovereignty of a federal government over its component states.

He was a practicing Jew, but one who saw his Judaism only as a religion, rejecting completely its national, cultural, and political aspects. A staunch Anglophile and anti-Zionist, he strongly defended Britain's role in Palestine. At the age of ninety, Isaacs was still appearing in public, eloquently supporting the policies of Ernest Bevin, the British Foreign Secretary who fought Jewish immigration to Eretz Israel and deported "illegals" to the detention camps in Cyprus.

A thoroughgoing Zionist, quite to the contrary, was Isaacs's contemporary, Sir John Monash, also a native son of Melbourne and, indeed, one of the most revered figures in Australian history. Monash is best known as the Commander in Chief of the combined Australian-New Zealand Armed Forces, the Anzacs, in World War I. Lloyd George, Great Britain's wartime Prime Minister, called him the finest military leader in the British Empire.

Despite the honors heaped upon him by the British Government, Monash—a religious Jew all his life—was also a political activist. As early as 1930, he was the president of the Zionist Federation of Australia and a vigorous proponent of a Jewish state in the British Mandate of Palestine. Shortly before his death, he was named a full general. Named in his honor, Monash University in Melbourne is one of Australia's leading educational institutions.

The achievement of an Isaacs or a Monash is not unique among Australian Jews. They have always enjoyed a climate of acceptance and a freedom from anti-Semitism—except in the hallowed precincts of one or two of Melbourne's private social clubs, where the good, old-fashioned, kid-gloves Judeophobia of the British upper classes still prevails. Their membership committees routinely turn down the application of the heir to one of Australia's biggest department store chains. Like the Goldwassers of Arizona, who became the Episcopalian Goldwaters, the applicant's family has long since converted to the respectability of the Anglican Church, but the dip into the baptismal font was all in vain.

One of Melbourne's most prominent Jews today is Sam Lipski, a television newsman who also edits the *Australia/Israel Review.*

NEIGHBORHOODS AND SIGHTS: If, however, a department store magnate still cannot make the climb of his choice, he may find solace in the luxury of an estate beyond the confines of the old neighborhood. The same mobility that has characterized the economic life of Australian Jewry applies equally to its Lebensraum; but the direction is not so much upward as it is southward.

The impoverished immigrants settled initially in the working-class districts of Melbourne, such as Balaclava and St. Kilda, north of the Yarra River, which bisects the city. With prosperity, their descendants have moved south of the Yarra, to such elegant suburbs as Caulfield and Toorak—easily the equivalents of Beverly Hills and Scarsdale.

In a city of two and a half million, the Jews of Melbourne are hardly visible any longer, but a real and heimish presence lingers in the concentration of kosher restaurants, butchers, and groceries on Carlisle or on Acland Street in the city's St. Kilda district.

For travelers from abroad, Melbourne, no less than Sydney, is a wonderful place to visit, both Jewishly and generally. You can eat the best latkes in the Southern Hemisphere in Scheherazade's at 99 Acland Street, or have kosher haute cuisine at Goldman's, 58 Hawthorn Road, in North Caulfield.

The key sight of Jewish Melbourne is the Melbourne Hebrew Congregation (oldest and largest in the city), Toorak and St. Kilda roads, South Yarra. Founded in 1841, the Orthodox congregation moved to its white Victorian structure in 1930. In the synagogue complex is the Australian Jewish Museum, which features a slide-and-sound show, *Arrival and Survival,* about the 150-year history of Jews in Melbourne. Temple Beth Israel (headquarters of Liberal Judaism), 76-82 Alma Road, St. Kilda, is also worth a visit.

CULTURE: The Kadimah Cultural Centre, 7 Selwyn Street, Elsternwick, shows Yiddish plays and films and has a large library of works in Yiddish and English. Melbourne's B'nai B'rith office also offers a range of activities, most notably its Thursday lecture and kosher lunch (99 Hotham Street, East St. Kilda, telephone, 527-4491).

Melbourne's ethnic radio station, 3EA, features daily programs in English, Hebrew and Yiddish.

For Jewish events in Melbourne, write or call the Victorian Jewish Board of Deputies. The address is 401 Swanston Street, Melbourne 3000; the telephone number is 67-5341. Their annual directory is also useful as a guidebook.

GENERAL SIGHTS: Get around town by a wonderful trolley network reminiscent of Judy Garland's St. Louis. Stop at the municipal zoo and see such unique "Down Under" creatures as kangaroos, koala bears, and duck-billed platypuses.

Only God could make these animals, but the city affords such spectacular manmade wonders as the Collins Place complex, designed by I. M. Pei. The tallest structure in Australia, it encompasses a glass-covered acre of shops, boutiques, and restaurants. One of its fifty-story towers houses the five-star Regent Hotel, with 377 rooms built around an atrium, a hollow interior core fifteen stories high. Each room faces outward, offering views as superb as the hotel's food and services.

READING: There are many good works of fiction by Melbourne Jews about the Jewish experience in their city, although they are generally available only in Australia. Look for *On Firmer Shores* (Globe Press) by Serge Liberman, a prize-winning collection of short stories about growing up Jewish in a poor, Gentile neighborhood. Judah Waten's *Love and Rebellion* (Macmillan) is another volume of short stories dealing with immigrant adjustments to the country. Morris Lurie (a kind of Australian Philip Roth) is the author of *Running Nicely* (Thomas Nelson), frenetic short stories about a variety of restless protagonists—who are really variations of Lurie himself. Harry Marks's *Unicorn Among the Wattles* (Hyland House) is a novel about a Jewish soldier's painful readjustment to civilian life in Melbourne. Nancy Keesing's *John Lang and the Forger's Wife* (John Ferguson) is a study of Lang, a Jew and the first native-born Australian novelist.

Though the Jewish communities of Melbourne and Sydney are nearly equal in size, Melbourne's Jewish literature is considerably richer. Melbourne's history isn't any longer, but in the most Victorian Jewish community in the world, the past and present co-exist very nicely.

—GABRIEL LEVENSON

Mexico City

Palace of Fine Arts *(Pan American World Airways)*

Mexico City is the ultimate urban experience. It has bustle worthy of New York, sprawl worthy of Los Angeles, crowding worthy of Tokyo, squalor worthy of Bombay, and a friendly demeanor worthy of Rome. With sixteen million people, it is fast on its way to becoming the world's largest city—and in terms of people within the city limits, it probably already has that distinction. Amid such numbers, the city's Jews are a mere speck, but a speck that flourishes like no other in the diaspora.

Though Mexico has an identity all its own, there is one area, particularly evident to tourists, in which it is similar to Israel. That is in the national interest in archaeology. And just as Israel sometimes focuses on its biblical history at the expense of the two-thousand-year diaspora, so Mexico has a tendency to focus on its Indian heritage at the expense of its Spanish colonial past.

HISTORY: There were "New Christians" (nominal Catholics of Jewish birth) with Hernán Cortés, who conquered the Aztecs in 1521, and Marranos made up a large portion of the Spanish settlers in the sixteenth century. By 1550 there were probably more crypto-Jews in Mexico City than Spanish Catholics, and the Judaism of Mexico's Marranos is believed to have been closer to normative Jewish practice than that of Marranos in Spain.

Marranos prospered in early Mexico and the development of the country's trade and commerce was largely due to their efforts. They were not immune to the Inquisition, however, even though it was imposed less harshly than in Spain. Mexican Marranos were burned at the stake as early as 1528, when the conquistador Hernando Alonso was among the victims. Throughout the colonial period, about fifteen hundred people were convicted of following Jewish practice, of whom about a hundred were executed.

The Marranos had assimilated by the nineteenth century, although many prominent Mexicans have claimed Jewish descent, including Presidents Porfirio Díaz, Francisco Madero, and José López Portillo, and the great muralist Diego Rivera. "My Jewishness is the dominant element in my life," Rivera wrote in 1935. "From this has come my sympathy with the downtrodden masses which motivates all my work."

Modern Jewish settlement began in the 1820s, when a small number of German Jews arrived in Mexico City. In the 1860s, Emperor Maximilian brought with him from Europe many Belgian, French, and Austrian Jews. Syrian Jews began arriving in the 1890s and were followed by Jews from other parts of the Ottoman Empire. Immigrants from Eastern Europe came after World War I, particularly after the United States closed its doors to large-scale immigration in 1924.

Jewish merchants in the early twentieth century had an impact similar to that of their Marrano brothers of the sixteenth. They introduced to Mexico the system of buying on credit, which raised the living standard of the lower classes. A campaign against immigrant merchants, many of them Jewish, in Mexico City's Lagunilla Market in the 1920s, had the effect of improving the Jewish economic condition. Jewish stall owners responded by opening private stores, most of which prospered.

COMMUNITY: There are about forty thousand Jews in Mexico City—making up about 80 percent of the Jews in the country. The main areas of Jewish settlement are in Condessa, an older neighborhood just east of Chapultepec Park; Polanco, a newer section north of the park; and the suburb of Tekamachalco. There are still many Jews in commerce, particularly the garment trade, but more and more Jews are entering the liberal professions. Among the prominent Jewish names from Mexico City are Jacobo Zabrudovsky, the television anchorman known as the Walter Cronkite of Mexico; Sergio Nudelstejer, one of the Spanish-speaking world's leading biographers; and Leon Dulzin, now of Israel, head of the Jewish Agency.

Mexico City Jewry is a study in contrasts—close-knit yet diverse, a part of the Mexican fabric and yet a community apart. Unlike the usual pattern, the community's great wealth does not seem to be a prelude to assimilation. Intermarriage is about 5 percent, and Jewish families are large, perhaps because relatively few women work outside the home; the vast majority of Jewish children attend one of the city's nine Jewish day schools.

Historically, the community has been fragmented, and its various parts—Polish, German, Hungarian, Syrian (with separate communities from Damascus and Aleppo), American—have their separate synagogues. Zionism, acculturation, and Mexican xenophobia have helped unify the communities, but perhaps the biggest unifying factor is the Centro Deportivo Israelita, or Jewish Sports Center. A combination country club and community center, it is the one organization to which virtually every Jew in Mexico City belongs. The sports center is to Mexican Jewry what the army is to Israel—the place where all the communities meet. On any given Sunday, a visitor can be forgiven for thinking that every Jew in Mexico City is at the center's sprawling complex on Avenue Ávila Camacho.

In addition to the Ashkenazi and Sefardi communities, there are two groups of indigenous Mexicans practicing Judaism. In the city's Vallejo section is a group of mestizos—people of mixed Spanish and Indian descent—who claim Marrano ancestry. In the village of Venta Prieta, about sixty miles north of Mexico City, another mestizo group practices Judaism. Although the Jewish origins of the Venta Prieta group seem less clear, visitors have noted that their commitment to Jewish life and to Israel is firm.

SIGHTS: Two spots in central Mexico City have Jewish associations that are far from apparent. The Plaza Santo Domingo, at the corner of Brazil and Venezuela streets, is today a picturesque square filled with sidewalk typists and printers. Three hundred years ago, however, it was the site of autos-da-fé, the trials of the Inquisition, at which many Marranos were condemned. Alameda Park, adjacent to the beautiful Palace of Fine Arts (Bellas Artes), was where executions were carried out during the Inquisition.

Three blocks south of the Plaza Santo Domingo, and about five blocks east of Alameda Park, is the Zócalo, the huge open plaza that is the city's heart. A visitor can spend an entire day seeing sights within five minutes of the Zócalo. At the top of any list would be the Rivera murals in the National Palace (Palacio Nacional), the seat of Mexico's government, on the east side of the plaza. Among the panoramic wall paintings that depict the country's entire history, Rivera included scenes from the Mexican Inquisition. Also worth seeing in the area of the Zócalo is the Templo Mayor, a recently excavated Aztec temple one block north of the National Palace. Perhaps the best part of the area, however, is its ambience, with street vendors and street life to the north and east of the plaza and shops to the west. The best view of the area is from the rooftop restaurant of the Hotel Majestic, where Madero Street meets the Zócalo.

Of more specific Jewish interest is Nidhei Israel, the community center at 70 Acapulco Street. It houses the city's only kosher restaurant, its most attractive synagogue, a library, and a Holocaust museum (which is open by appointment only). The center is also the headquarters of several Jewish organizations and of *Tribuna Israelita,* the country's Jewish feature magazine. It is also the best place to call for information on Jewish events or sights in the city (211-08-74).

The most Jewish atmosphere is to be found in Polanco, a neighborhood of elegant Spanish-style homes mixed with less elegant high-rise apartment buildings. Stroll along shady Horacio Boulevard on a Saturday and you'll see families walking to and from the synagogues that dot the area, as well as newsboys with distinctly Indian features delivering Yiddish papers.

The Sports Center, or Centro Deportivo, is worth a visit, not only because it is the "in" place among Mexico City's Jews, but because of its cultural attractions. It houses a theater, which usually runs plays on Jewish themes during the summer, an excellent photo gallery, and a small art gallery. Foreign visitors are welcome. The Sports Center's huge grounds were used as a storage and staging area for relief supplies after the earthquake that devastated parts of Mexico City in 1985. For information on Sports Center events, call 557-30-00.

The Jewish cultural event of the year is the annual music festival, usually held in October and November, at which world-class Jewish artists perform at the Palace of Fine Arts.

For those interested in archaeology and ethnohistory there are two places that must appear on any itinerary: the National Museum of Anthropology in Chapultepec Park, which Mayor Teddy Kollek of Jerusalem has praised as "probably the greatest museum created in our generation," and the pyramids at Teotihuacán, about forty-five minutes north of the city. The seventh-century pre-Aztec structures are spectacular, but for all that is known of the area's ethnic history, little is known of the civilization that built what may be the Western Hemisphere's most impressive ancient buildings.

RECOMMENDATIONS: If you want elegance, modernity, and a Jewish neighborhood to stay in, the best place is the Hotel Presidente Chapultepec, on the edge of Chapultepec Park in Polanco. Mexico City's subway is one of the world's bargains, but beware. Most subway maps published in Mexico and in American guidebooks show Line 7 running through Polanco; what they don't say is that the line is under construction. Taxis are plentiful and relatively cheap. Instead of giving your driver the name of your hotel, give him the intersection at which it is located; the fare will be considerably less.

If you are interested in local culture but put off by the lang barrier, don't give up so easily. Mexico City's theater life is good and lively and often features Spanish versions of Broadway shows; if you see one with which you are already familiar, it can be quite enjoyable. A recent run of *Joseph and His Amazing Technicolor Dreamcoat* was particularly popular.

Mexico City's seven-thousand-foot elevation makes it an ideal vacation spot in any season. It can be combined with a trip to one of the country's coastal resorts or be a trip in itself. A good companion to take on the plane is *Aztec* by Gary Jennings (Avon), the great Mexico City novel.

There are still some travelers who avoid Mexico out of the belief that it is anti-Israel. This belief stems from the country's 1975 vote in the United Nations for the infamous "Zionism-is-racism" resolution. A Jewish boycott of travel to Mexico had a tremendous impact on the country and, coincidentally, hurt a good number of Mexican Jews in the travel industry. The Government apologized for its vote, and it is worth noting that all of the recent Mexican presidents, with the exception of Luís Echeverría, who was in office at the time of the UN vote, have had good relations with the Jewish community. A few years ago, when a senator gave an anti-Semitic speech in the Mexican national assembly, he was kicked out of the ruling party.

Still, Mexico is not a melting pot like the United States, and there is a certain xenophobia directed against all immigrant groups. This can best be seen in Carlos Fuentes's novel, *The Hydra Head*, in which most Mexican Jews are depicted as Israeli agents. Nevertheless, Mexico has been kinder to Jews than most societies, as the vibrancy of Jewish life in Mexico City demonstrates.

—ALAN M. TIGAY

Miami

Beth David Synagogue *(Courtesy of Beth David)*

Quick—what's the most Jewish city in America? If you had asked the question any time between 1800 and 1980, the answer would have been New York. But this is the decade in which the demographic honors have shifted to Miami. The four hundred thousand Jews in Miami's two-county (Dade and Broward) metropolitan area constitute more than 14 percent of the general population. The 2.1 million Jews of metropolitan New York are more than a percentage point behind.

That Miami is Jewish in the first place should hardly come as a surprise. Amid the Yiddish banter on Miami Beach's Collins Avenue and the condos of Fort Lauderdale, the tropical architecture that looks vaguely like Tel Aviv's and the synagogues that dot the landscape, it is Gentiles who feel like a minority—unless they are Hispanic.

But if everyone knows how Jewish Miami is, few know the details. Contrary to popular belief, Miami Jewry is not overwhelmingly a community of retired people, as its extensive Jewish school network, from elementary school to university, testifies. It is a lively collection of people of all ages that has produced one of the most richly diverse Jewish communities in history.

HISTORY: Although the Miami area has the large majority of Florida's Jews, it is also the youngest Jewish community in the state. Jews had made their mark on Florida history long before anyone had dreamed that Miami would amount to more than an isolated trading post. David Levy Yulee, son of a Caribbean lumber magnate, was instrumental in attaining statehood for Florida in 1836 and became the state's first U.S. senator; he later served in the Confederate Congress. Colonel Abraham Myers, after whom the city of Fort Myers is named, was one of at least half a dozen Jewish officers who served in the Florida Indian Wars of the 1830s and '40s.

The first Jew in Miami was Samuel Singer, who came from Palm Beach in 1895. That was the same year in which a freeze that killed citrus and sugarcane crops as far south as Palm Beach convinced Henry Flagler, the railroad and resort developer, to extend his tracks to Miami. But most of the Jews who arrived in Miami before the turn of the century were moving north from Key West, which had imposed a discriminatory tax on itinerant peddlers. The first ad hoc congregation was organized for the High Holidays in 1896, but it wasn't until 1912 that the first permanent congregation, B'nai Zion, was founded.

The Florida land boom of the 1920s brought more Jews to the area, but as late as 1940 the permanent Jewish population was only seventy-five hundred. The real acceleration began after World War II.

COMMUNITY: Miami was the first American Jewish community in which most of the people came not from Europe but from elsewhere in the United States. Instead of landsmanshaften from Bialystok and Berdichev, it has associations of Jews from Chicago and Cleveland. New York high schools have been known to hold their reunions in Miami Beach. This situation has produced a community which lacks roots. A Jew from Europe cut his ties with the old country, but a settler in Miami generally does not, even if his move is permanent. Jewish fund-raisers in Miami rarely hear "I gave at the office." What they hear, according to an official of the Great Miami Jewish Federation, is "I gave in Philadelphia."

A unique element of Miami Jewry is the Latin community. There are about five thousand Cuban Jews and about an equal number from a variety of Latin American nations—Chile, Peru, Argentina, Nicaragua, etc.

Jews have played a major role in the industries for which the Miami area is best known—tourism and real estate. There was a time when the vast majority of the Miami Beach's hotels were Jewish-owned, although they are now increasingly controlled by national chains and outside syndicates. Later generations of Miami Jews have also followed in the footsteps of David Yulee. Abe Aronowitz became Miami's first Jewish mayor in 1953; Miami Beach has had many. Richard Stone became Florida's second Jewish senator in 1974. Hank Meyer, perhaps the only public-relations man in the Florida State Hall of Fame, got there largely through his successful efforts to make Miami Beach world-famous.

SIGHTS: Miami Beach is still the most predominantly Jewish part of the metropolitan area. South Beach, best known today for its crime rate, is the old neighborhood, and it retains much of its Jewish character. Washington Avenue has been referred to as the Orchard Street of Miami Beach; it's an exaggeration, but the atmosphere is distinctly Jewish. The atmosphere actually extends most of the length of Miami Beach, from the beautiful, small Art Deco hotels in the south to the imposing high-rises in the north. Most of the commercial strips along Collins Avenue have Jewish stores and restaurants.

Other areas of heavy Jewish settlement are the Kendall section in southwest Miami, Coral Gables, North Miami, North Miami Beach, Hollywood, Hallandale, and western Fort Lauderdale. In many ways, the Fort Lauderdale area is a separate urban unit from Miami-Miami Beach, and some would argue that Fort Lauderdale is eclipsing Miami and Miami Beach as the Jewish population and cultural center of south Florida.

The Miami area has more than its share of attractive and unusual synagogues. Most worth seeing in Miami itself is the tropical-classical Beth David (2625 S.W. Third Avenue), the successor congregation to the pioneering B'nai Zion. In Miami Beach are the Cuban Hebrew Congregation (Ashkenazi, at 1700 Michigan Avenue) and Temple Moses (Cuban Sefardi, 1200 Normandy Drive). Also in Miami Beach are the stately Temple Emanu-El (1701 Washington Avenue), Beth Raphael (1545 Jefferson Avenue), dedicated to victims of the Holocaust, and Beth Sholom (4144 Chase Avenue), with its domed sanctuary designed by Percival Goodman and its garden with plants from the Bible.

Beth Sholom, which started as a soldier's congregation in World War II, and Emanu-El are both noted for their lecture and entertainment series. Among the recent lecturers at Beth Sholom have been Elie Wiesel, Simcha Dinitz, and Wolf Blitzer. The temple's artists series has recently featured Mikhail Baryshnikov with the American Ballet Theatre, Isaac Stern, Itzhak Perlman, José Carreras, Plácido Domingo, and Kiri Te Kanawa, as well as the Israel Philharmonic and the Montreal Symphony. The temple also has a film series and one of the Miami area's best known art galleries.

For popular entertainment, the best place to look is at the hotels that line Collins Avenue. There are comedians, cabarets, and theaters and, often as not, the performances are on Jewish themes. The entertainment—like the hotels and condos—tends to be fancier above Forty-first Street, where most of the street movement is in cars. But the atmosphere is more heimish below Forty-first Street, where most of the traffic is on foot.

For tours of Jewish Miami, contact Sam Brown at (305) 421-8431. For questions on the community, call Nancy Zombek at the Federation, 576-4000.

READING: Most of the Jewish entertainment listings run in the

Miami and Fort Lauderdale dailies, and in the monthly *Miami-South Florida Magazine*. To put you in the mood, novels with a Miami setting include *Sadie Shapiro in Miami* by Robert Kimmel Smith (Simon & Schuster) and *No Enemy But Time* by Evelyn Mayerson (Doubleday).

GENERAL SIGHTS: The attraction of beaches is obvious, but there are things to see and do in the Miami area that escape the attention of many. The Cuban quarter, Calle Ocho (S.W. Eighth Street in Miami) is well worth a visit, as is the Villa Vizcaya, Miami's Italian Renaissance palace. Boat rides on the intercoastal waterway offer pleasures not experienced in the Atlantic or in Biscayne Bay. And the Everglades is an easy day trip.

RECOMMENDATIONS: The Miami area has hotels for every budget, taste, and level of kashrut observance. Without prejudice to the others, one that seems to combine modern sophistication with an old-fashioned resort feeling is the Fontainebleau Hilton. There are also at least a dozen kosher hotels along Collins Avenue in Miami Beach.

Most travelers avoid Miami in the summer, when the weather is sultry and hurricanes hover offshore. But the old saw that "Miami is dead after Pesach" applies mainly to the hotel business, and to a lesser extent to the entertainment circuits. The Jewish presence is a permanent, year-round proposition. In America's most Jewish city, you'll always feel at home.

—ALAN M. TIGAY

Montreal

Richard Dreyfus as Duddy Kravitz (*The Museum of Modern Art/Film Stills Archive*)

The decade from 1975 to 1985 saw an outflow of both capital and English speakers from Montreal, mostly in the direction of Toronto. According to legend, some apartment buildings in the Jewish sections of Toronto shake when, during a televised hockey game, the Montreal Canadiens score a goal. But the anecdote obscures two important points: Montreal still has a large, vibrant Jewish community; and the exodus of English-speaking Ashkenazim has been partly offset by the influx of twenty thousand French-speaking Sefardim during the last twenty years.

HISTORY: Jews were not permitted to live in Quebec under French rule. The first Jews arrived in Montreal in 1760 as civilians attached to the British Army, which had conquered Quebec the previous year; ever since, Anglophone and Francophone Montrealers alike have regarded the Jews as a segment of the English-speaking community.

Montreal's first synagogue, Shearith Israel, was founded in 1760 by Jews of Spanish and Portuguese origin, some of whom had belonged to the synagogue of the same name in New York. It wasn't until 1831, however, that the congregation, along with Jewish communities in Quebec City and Trois Rivières, received legal recognition from the Legislative Assembly of Quebec. Thereafter, the Jewish community played an increasingly active role in the affairs of the city. Abraham de Sola, who became haham of Shearith Israel in 1847, was also a professor of Hebrew and Oriental literature at McGill University and a longtime president of the Natural History Society of Montreal.

The Jewish community grew slowly, however, and numbered only seventy-six hundred in 1901. Large-scale immigration from Eastern Europe—spurred by Tsarist pogroms, persecution in Romania, and, finally, the imposition of restrictive immigration quotas in the United States—brought the Jewish population to eighty thousand on the eve of World War II; postwar refugee immigration brought the numbers to a peak of 120,000 around 1970.

COMMUNITY: Today, the community numbers a little over a hundred thousand. Montreal is unique for the relationship between its

Jews and its majority culture, the French Canadians. Quebec has a history of anti-Semitism, although it is not always easy to distinguish animosity toward Jews as Jews from resentment toward Jews as merely one of the more successful elements of the Anglophone population. Even the nonbigoted often view Jews as Anglophones first. *La Presse,* one of Montreal's French dailies, ran a feature article not too long ago on the overwhelmingly Jewish suburb of Côte St. Luc. The article never mentioned Jews; it referred to the community simply as an English-speaking enclave.

Many Jews are ambivalent about the cause of their French Canadian neighbors. Jews tend to be more sympathetic than other English speakers to the French Canadians' effort to protect their cultural heritage, and of all the segments of the Anglophone community, the Jews have the highest proportion of bilingualism. But the Jewish community took offense at Quebec's language legislation, such as the law requiring that all commercial signs be in French. While most Jews insist that the Jewish exodus of the late seventies and early eighties was not a result of the separatist Parti Québécois's rise to power, they agree that the economic conditions brought on by a separatist provincial government pushed a lot of people out. Since the Parti Québécois began to mute its separatist rhetoric, and since the return to power of the Liberal Party in 1985, a few departed Montreal Jews have returned.

The arrival of French-speaking Jews from North Africa, however, has transformed the Jewish community from an entirely Anglophone group to one that has roots on both sides of Montreal's linguistic track. Francophone Jews now make up about 20 percent of Montreal Jewry.

Montreal's Jewish community structure is, in many ways, a reflection of the structure of Quebec society. Unlike the rest of Canada and the United States, public schools are something new to Quebec, and even today the churches play a prominent role in public education. Traditionally, most Jews attended Protestant (and English-speaking) schools; today, 40 percent of Montreal's school-age Jewish population attends Jewish day schools—by far the highest percentage of any North American Jewish community. And because Montreal didn't have, until recently, its own public library system, an extensive Jewish Public Library, with its own branches, grew to serve both the Jewish and general community.

The main concentrations of Jews are in the suburbs of Côte St. Luc,

Westmount, Hampstead, and Outremont and in the Côte des Neiges area inside the Montreal city limits. There are also communities in Dollard des Ormeaux and Chomedy.

Jews have always exerted an influence beyond their own neighborhoods in Montreal. They have traditionally been highly visible in commerce, particularly in the garment industry, and they show up frequently in French Canadian literature, like the novels of Gabrielle Roy. Canada's former Prime Minister, Pierre Elliott Trudeau, grew up among Jews in Montreal and is said to speak fair Yiddish. At one time in the 1970s, Montreal's three major sports teams—the Canadiens of hockey, the Expos of baseball, and the Concordes of football—were all Jewish-owned. The Expos are still owned by Charles Bronfman.

Montreal has produced more than its share of Jewish talent and personalities. The atmosphere of the old Jewish neighborhood around St. Viateur Street is captured in the novels of Mordecai Richler and Saul Bellow and in the poems of A. M. Klein and Leonard Cohen. Also from Montreal are comedian Mort Sahl, actor William Shatner, journalist Elie Abel, David Lewis, the late head of Canada's New Democratic Party, and Eric Berne, the psychologist who founded transactional analysis. Jews returned to the Quebec cabinet with the election of Robert Bourassa as provincial premier in 1985; Herbert Marx is his justice minister.

SIGHTS: For a community of its size, it is surprising that Montreal has no synagogues of architectural distinction. There were some classical buildings—long since abandoned—in old neighborhoods; most of the more modern buildings are utilitarian. But what the city lacks in aesthetics it more than makes up for in variety. The flagships of Montreal Jewry are Shearith Israel—the Spanish and Portuguese Synagogue (4894 St. Kevin Street), the oldest congregation in Canada, which is today predominantly Moroccan—and Shaar Hashomayim (450 Kensington Avenue, Westmount), a huge, Orthodox-leaning Conservative synagogue and the city's oldest Ashkenazic congregation.

The main drags of Jewish Montreal are Côte Ste. Catherine Road and Victoria Avenue. On these streets, and some of the streets that radiate from them, can be found Jewish institutions, bookstores, butchers, cafés, and restaurants.

If there is a nerve center to the Jewish community it would have to be the 5100 block of Côte Ste. Catherine Road. On the south side of the street is the Saidye Bronfman Center, the place to find art exhibits, theater, concerts, and lectures. Among the recent events have been Yiddish productions of *The Jazz Singer* and *The Megillah of Itzak Manger* and English-language productions of *The Diary of Anne Frank* and the Broadway hit *For Colored Girls* . . . For information on events at the Saidye Bronfman Center, call (514) 739-2301.

For listings of other cultural events, the best places to look are the *Canadian Jewish News* (Montreal edition) and *The Suburban,* both weeklies.

Across the street from the Saidye Bronfman Center is a building housing the Jewish Public Library, the Holocaust Museum and Research Center, and a variety of Jewish welfare organizations. It also houses the Allied Jewish Community Services, the place to call (735-3541) with any questions about Jewish sights or events that your guidebook doesn't answer. If you have a question about kashrut, call the Jewish Community Council (739-6363). If you have a question about Shabbat or weekday services, call the JCC or one of the synagogues.

The old neighborhood is one of the best parts of the Jewish Montreal tour. Although it is now more Greek and Portuguese than Jewish, the area between St. Louis Square and Outremont, and running down Boulevard St. Laurent almost all the way downtown, still has many reminders of its Jewish soul.

For a three-hour tour of Jewish Montreal, contact Allan Raymond at 489-8741 or write to him in advance at 5475 Rosedale Avenue, Montreal H4V 2H8.

The Bagel Bakery, on Fairmont west of Clark Street, and the nearby Wilensky's were both used in filming for the movie *The Apprenticeship of Duddy Kravitz,* based on one of Richler's novels. Richler himself lived in the 5700 block of St. Urbain, a typical street of Montreal row houses. St. Louis Square was the center of the Jewish neighborhood in the 1940s; today it is frequented by Haitian and Vietnamese immigrants. St. Viateur Park, farther to the west, still turns into a hasidic center on summer weekends. Throughout the area are delicatessens (such as the popular, nonkosher Charcuterie Hébraïque, otherwise known as Schwartz's, at 3895 St. Laurent), former synagogues, and Jewish schools.

EATING: There are many Jewish eateries around the city, but some of the best known (like the Brown Derby, a popular breakfast spot, and the Ben Ash chain) are not kosher. Most of the city's half-dozen kosher restaurants are Moroccan-owned, which means a kosher meal in Montreal is more likely to include couscous than cholent. The consensus among locals is that the best of the kosher restaurants is El Morocco, at 3450 Drummond Street. A popular neighborhood spot is the kosher restaurant in the Snowdon YMHA.

READING: There is a wealth of literature with Montreal's Jewish community at the center. Those of Richler's novels most evocative of the city are *St. Urbain's Horseman* and *The Apprenticeship of Duddy Kravitz* (Bantam). Bellow's *Herzog* (Avon) also has a Montreal setting. A work of nonfiction worth looking at is *Bronfman Dynasty* by Peter Newman (McClelland & Stewart). By far the best guidebook is a poorly printed forty-two-page pamphlet put out a few years ago by the Canadian Jewish Congress; it has seven walking tours of Jewish Montreal and lots of practical information. If you can't get a copy from the Congress, try the Allied Jewish Community Services.

GENERAL SIGHTS: Montreal, of course, has more than Jewish sights. Any visit is likely to include dining and strolling in Old Montreal, a walk or calèche ride up to Mount Royal Park for its spectacular view, shopping in the extensive underground city, theaters and museums. What many travelers miss, however, is the "Latin Quarter," along Boulevard St. Denis, an area of cafés, bistros, and restaurants where little English is heard. Also, Prince Albert Street between St. Denis and St. Laurent is a particularly quaint pedestrian mall of restaurants in restored row houses.

SIDE TRIP: Quebec City is a three-hour drive up Route 20, and it is as different from Montreal as New York is from Nieuw Amsterdam. Like Jerusalem, the town's old city is surrounded by a wall; inside there are narrow, winding streets that seem little changed from the eighteenth century. Below the walled city, on the bank of the St. Lawrence, the restored buildings date back to the seventeenth century.

Quebec City's Jewish community was never large. Two Jews settled there in 1767, and in 1790 John Franks was appointed the first chief of the Quebec Fire Brigade. In the nineteenth century Jews served in city government and were prominent merchants. Sigismund Mohr, an electrical engineer from Germany, was the pioneer of hydroelectric development in Canada; his work not only lit Quebec City, but put the province on the road to becoming, literally, a North American power broker.

The Jewish community, which peaked at about five hundred in 1961, today numbers no more than a hundred, and there is no guarantee that the one synagogue (Beth Israel, 939 Salabery Street) will have a minyan, even on Shabbat.

RECOMMENDATIONS: Montreal has no shortage of hotels for all tastes and budgets, but particularly noteworthy is the Hyatt Regency (777 University Avenue), which is centrally located, luxurious, and provides kosher meals on request. The trip to Quebec City is worth it if only to stay at the Château Frontenac, a huge Victorian hotel that dominates the cityscape and has no peer.

Much of Montreal, from the centrally located tourist attractions to the Jewish neighborhoods in the west, is easily accessible by Métro, the city's subway system. The best way to see Quebec City is on foot.

While it may seem obvious that summer is the only season in which to visit a Canadian city, in fact, Montreal and Quebec City deal admirably with the coldest of temperatures. Quebec City has a winter festival that is one of the year's biggest draws, and Montreal's extensive underground transport and shopping network make it possible to cover much of the city in winter without stepping into the cold. Outdoor strolling is certainly easier from April to October, but if you go to Montreal during the hockey season there are still enough Jews left that you might feel an apartment building shake.

—ALAN M. TIGAY

Nairobi

〽〽

Nairobi Hebrew Congregation *(Alan M. Tigay)*

Nairobi, Kenya—it almost was the Jewish homeland. Though most people tend to identify Kenya chiefly with wildlife and safaris, in 1903, fourteen years before the Balfour Declaration, the British Foreign Office offered to the Zionist movement a vast tract of fertile East African highlands to populate as a nation.

HISTORY: Theodor Herzl warmed to the suggestion of Kenya as the new Zion and, expecting the World Zionist Congress to follow suit, a dozen Russian Jews who had made their way to South Africa decided to trek the additional distance north—to the rich Uasin Gishu Plateau in what then belonged to the Uganda Protectorate but now is part of Kenya. They had intended to move in as Canaan's founding settlers, only to discover on their arrival that Colonial Secretary Joseph Chamberlain's gift had in fact been declined.

Most of these pioneering spirits returned to South Africa. Abraham Block, however, stayed on—farming, trading, cattle ranching, speculating where and when he could. (Block would one day become Kenya's Conrad Hilton, owning nine hotels including the classic Norfolk Hotel in Nairobi and the Mawingo Hotel in Nanyuki, which actor William Holden later purchased and renamed the Mount Kenya Safari Club.) Eventually he brought his family over from Lithuania, and a wife from Palestine. Along with other Jewish colonists who, hoping to find their fortune in Africa, had drifted in over the years, he "begat" Nairobi's Jewish community.

Timberwork is all that remains of the first synagogue, built by nineteen Jewish families in 1913 when Nairobi was an infant town of red dust and papyrus swampland. Although South Africa and Zimbabwe would attract sizable Jewish populations, Kenya's community would always be small by comparison.

Still, it was influential. Lawyers, doctors, architects, hoteliers, traders, and businessmen have always been counted among its Jewish inhabitants and, in the late 1950s, when the Nairobi Jewish community was at its peak of a thousand, the president of the Board of Kenya Jewry, Israel Somen, was elected Nairobi's mayor.

The greatest influx of Jews into Kenya arrived immediately after

World War II. Mostly Holocaust survivors, these Central European Jews moved to the Great Rift Valley (where Louis Leakey discovered most of his finds of early man), settling around the town of Nakuru where, as coffee and crop farmers, they worked the luxuriant land. The Nakuru synagogue no longer exists, but in the Nakuru cemetery a Holocaust memorial plaque still stands.

A less permanent group of Jews who spent time in Kenya were the members of the Irgun Zvai Leumi and Lohamei Herut Israel, including three men who would later become ministers in Menahem Begin's Cabinet. Captured by the British, they were sent by train to Kenya in March 1947, and imprisoned in the town of Gilgil. Though several escaped, most remained behind bars until Israel's independence. Today the detention camp at the foot of the Knayamwe Hills serves as an army barracks and can only be visited with government permission.

When, sparked by Kenya's independence in 1963, the sun began to set on Britain's East African Empire, many Jews left for Israel.

Although in 1973 Kenya, like most African countries, severed official relations with Israel, political ties with this key East African nation prior to the Yom Kippur War were strong. Israel helped establish Kenya's School for Social Workers in Machakos, and numerous Israeli agricultural and irrigation experts assisted in various development projects.

Two Israeli construction companies, Solel Boneh and H and Zed, have between them built much of modern Kenya—highways, water supply projects, pipelines, airstrips, housing and office buildings, government ministries—and continue to do so.

COMMUNITY: Though Israeli-Kenyan diplomacy fluctuates with the political barometer, the government of President Daniel arap Moi maintains unofficial links with Israel. Many Kenyans still study in Israel, participating in programs in labor, cooperatives, soil management, and the like, while a transient community of several hundred Israelis, most of whom work for Israeli companies, small-scale industries, or in private enterprise, lives in Nairobi. These Israelis make up a large portion of Kenya's Jewish population of four hundred and fifty.

SIGHTS: Originally built as the British protectorate headquarters, an "irreputable place in the sun for shady people" (at least for the immigrant population) in the 1920s and '30s, Nairobi is a bustling urban center today with nearly a million people and all the problems of most third-world capitals.

Slum communities lie adjacent to neighborhoods with elegant villas; modern architectural wonders tower above the sprawl of poverty. One of the poorer nations in the world, Kenya is also one of the most prosperous in Africa. Replete with contradictions, Nairobi is always interesting and its languid pace should be enjoyed.

Members of the Jewish community uphold the Jewish traditions, and services are held Friday evenings and Shabbat mornings in the white-brick Nairobi Synagogue built in 1955. The synagogue, in the center of Nairobi, at the corner of University Way and Uhuru Highway, has stained-glass windows and pieces of wood from the old temple decorating the entranceway.

Nairobi Synagogue claims distinction as the synagogue with the most beautiful garden in the world. Sharing the landscape of jacaranda and flame trees, hibiscus, and other flowering bushes and plants is the synagogue's Vermont Memorial Hall, a community center where religious classes, social events, as well as Israeli celebrations are held.

Although it is possible to charter a plane and fly directly to one of Kenya's thirty-seven protected wildlife areas, most visitors begin their safari at Nairobi's Jomo Kenyatta International Airport. While there are no telltale signs, it was here that the Israeli rescue teams stopped to refuel on their way home from Entebbe on July 4, 1976.

Two other Nairobi landmarks—the Kenyatta International Conference Center and the beautiful University of Nairobi—have a place in recent Jewish history. In 1985, the last in a decade-long series of UN-sponsored conferences on the status of women took place in Nairobi. Though most of the conferences had been characterized by resolutions attacking Israel and equating Zionism with racism, the Nairobi conference marked a turning point. Third-world delegations, led by Kenya's, resisted Arab pressure in favor of discussing real women's issues, even when the discussions included Israelis. Government delegations met at the Kenyatta Center while nongovernment organizations met at the university.

GENERAL SIGHTS: Hunting was banned from the wildlife areas several years ago, but countless exotic species can be captured with the camera lens. It is only a short hike from the center of town to Nairobi National Park—a fine introduction to the wildlife and game runs to come. At the front of the park is the Animal Orphanage where stray animals are brought and sick ones cared for. Safaris to the game parks in and around Nairobi, and to anywhere in the country, can be easily arranged in advance of your trip or after you arrive.

The Nairobi National Museum has the finest collection of fossils from Leakey's anthropological finds, as well as many original artifacts from Kenya's more than fifty tribes. Nearby is Snake Park, and every afternoon, traditional dances can be seen at Bomas of Kenya, one kilometer from the park off Langatta Road.

For those who prefer more down-to-earth entertainment, Sunday is racing day at the Nairobi Horse Club, with what must be the loveliest track in the world. Nairobi's casino is noted for more than gambling; inside the antique wood-paneled "den," beneath its whirling paddle fans, a bit of the British Empire somehow endures.

The pace of a bygone era is in evidence at the elegant stone-built Norfolk Hotel which, since opening its doors in 1904, has served as home for romantics and adventurers. Abraham Block, who by the 1920s had been involved in nearly every sort of adventure—including a spell in jail for having sold a cow improperly—purchased the place in 1924. During the ensuing decades and to the present, he and his two sons—Jack, recently deceased, and Tubby—would play host to the wild happenings and mischief of royalty, heads of state, visiting dignitaries, authors (Hemingway stayed there during his Kilimanjaro days), celebrities, and notorieties alike.

Over the years, Block expanded his holdings into a hotel empire, purchasing the New Stanley Hotel in the center of Nairobi; the world-renowned forest lodge, Treetops, in the reserve at Nyeri; and the Nyali Beach Hotel at the coastal resort town of Mombasa. His holdings also included Samburu Game Lodge, in the most northerly of the popular parks, and the Keekorok Lodge, in what is considered Kenya's finest park, the Masai Mara Game Reserve, where elephants, lions, rhinoceros, buffaloes, and leopards all abound. Now, however, only the Norfolk remains under direct Block management.

On New Year's Eve 1981, Arab terrorists blew up the dining wing of the Norfolk, killing sixteen people and injuring more than a hundred. Since restored to its grandeur, the Norfolk, with its covered verandas and garden cottages, reigns as the grande dame of Nairobi.

For those with families or those on a modest budget, the Fairview Hotel, owned and run by Charles Szlapak, the synagogue's current rosh kehillah (only President Moi is permitted to use the title president), is recommended. Only a kilometer from the city center, off Bishops Road, the Fairview, with its five acres of garden, offers the atmosphere of a residential country hotel. Mrs. Szlapak reputedly makes the best borscht as well as the best homemade cream cheese in all of East Africa. Both the Norfolk and the Fairview are walking distance from the synagogue.

Kosher restaurants are not to be found in Nairobi, but all of the hotels offer salad bars, and many of the city's Indian restaurants (the Minar off Banda Street is particularly noteworthy) have vegetarian menus. For Middle Eastern cooking, try the Supreme, behind the fire station off Tom Mboya Street, or the Paddock, in the ICEA building off Kenyatta Avenue.

READING: Pick up a copy of *The Lunatic Express* by Charles Miller (Macmillan). Included in this story of the building of the six-hundred-mile railway across Queen Victoria's Africa is a section on the British plan to establish the Jewish nation in Kenya. More difficult to locate is *The Jews of Nairobi* by Julius Carlebach. Had Kenya become the Jewish homeland, such a book might have been in greater demand. You should, however, be able to find a copy at the synagogue.

—DEBRA WEINER

New Orleans

Al Jaffe's Preservation Hall *(Greater New Orleans Tourist and Convention Commission)*

New Orleans is really two cities. On the one hand, it's a world-class tourist spot with Creole and Cajun culture, Mardi Gras and the French Quarter, Antoine's and pralines; a city of quaint street names, Dixieland jazz, and legends of decadence and pleasure. But New Orleans is also a major mercantile and maritime center, where an affluent and generous citizenry has filled its streets with art and architecture, schools and museums, libraries and parks. Though they are few in number, New Orleans Jews have lavished money, energy, and ingenuity on their city. For over a hundred and fifty years, Jews have helped make New Orleans not only a good place to visit, but a good place to live as well.

HISTORY: New Orleans was established by the French in 1718 and seesawed between French and Spanish rule until the French sold Louisiana to the United States in 1803. In the 1750s, Jews began to arrive from the Caribbean. Under the French they suffered restrictions from the Black Code; under the Spanish from the more repressive Inquisition.

Newport-born Judah Touro arrived in the sweltering bayous shortly before the Louisiana Purchase. He did what any enterprising Yankee might have done. He went into the ice business—and many other commodities as well. His beneficence to all is legendary. Besides a hospital and gifts to Jewish and non-Jewish congregations, he willed the city money to beautify Canal Street, which, in the 1850s, was briefly renamed Touro Street.

Touro was wounded in the Battle of New Orleans in the War of 1812. That's the battle and war that elevated pirate Jean Laffite to patriot. Scholars are undecided whether to believe a purported memoir by Laffite, published in the 1950s, claiming he was reared by his Marrano grandmother. He also claimed never to have been a pirate. In any case, he is New Orleans's greatest folk hero. Another legend is Adah Isaacs Menken, born in a suburb of New Orleans in the 1830s. She was one of the leading American actresses of the nineteenth century, as well as a poet. An attractive woman who was a practicing

Jew, she now and then scandalized her public. Her relationships with Swinburne and Dumas père were well known.

The first Jewish congregation, Gates of Mercy, was founded in 1828 and later merged with another to become the present Touro Synagogue. Of today's eight congregations, five were founded before 1900 and one in 1904. It was also in 1828 that Judah P. Benjamin arrived to begin a career that led to the U.S. Senate and, eventually, to his appointment as Secretary of State for the Confederacy. During the occupation of New Orleans, feisty Eugenia Levy Phillips was imprisoned for laughing during a funeral procession for a Union soldier and Rabbi James K. Gutheim chose to leave New Orleans rather than sign the oath of allegiance to the Union.

Yellow fever decimated the local population at frequent intervals. In 1853, 137 Jews succumbed. As a direct result, New Orleans Jewry founded one of the first Jewish orphanages in the United States. The Touro Infirmary, today a leading medical teaching and research center and a constituent agency of the New Orleans Federation, dates from the same period. In 1881 New Orleans Jews settled over a hundred and fifty newly arrived Russian immigrants in Sicily Island, Louisiana—the first in a series of American Jewish agricultural experiments. These poor victims of the Tsar now found themselves in mosquito-ridden isolation, replete with rattlesnakes and disease, with little drinking water and former slave quarters for housing. When the Mississippi flooded a few months later, the experiment was over.

A historic moment occurred in December 1949 when Rabbi Julian Feibelman of Temple Sinai opened the doors of his synagogue to the first integrated audience in New Orleans. Two thousand blacks and whites sat down together to hear Ralph Bunche of the United Nations, who had been denied a public hall for the meeting.

COMMUNITY: There are about twelve thousand Jews among approximately one million New Orleanians. The Jewish population is slowly increasing. Slightly more than half of New Orleans Jews live within the city limits, mainly in the Uptown area that lies between the Garden District and Tulane University; there is a smaller enclave in the Lakefront area. However, there's a growing movement to suburban Metairie, where the young, upwardly mobile families are heading. Metairie is also the locale of the only Conservative congregation (Tikvat Shalom, at 3737 West Esplanade Avenue), the Orthodox Young Israel congregation (4428 Courtlands Road), and the Reform Gates of Prayer (4000 West Esplanade Avenue).

New Orleans Jews have always gotten along quite well with their non-Jewish neighbors. Today, the only time there's a problem is at Mardi Gras. Jews (and many others) are excluded from the three or four most socially prominent "krewes," the clubs that sponsor balls and parades. Not that the carnival is so important, but the dining clubs associated with those krewes are also closed to Jews, and that's where important business transactions occur. It doesn't matter that these clubs, the Boston and the Pickwick, had Jewish members in the nineteenth century—or that the first king of Mardi Gras was a Jew. That was in 1872, when Louis J. Salomon, great-grandson of Haym Salomon, became the first carnival Rex. Apart from this, Mardi Gras today is enjoyed by all. The biggest extravaganza is the Bacchus parade which does have large Jewish participation.

PERSONALITIES: One of the nineteenth century's leading concert pianists and composers was a Jewish native of New Orleans, Louis Moreau Gottschalk. Jews associated with New Orleans in this century include Martin Behrman, mayor of the city from 1904 to 1920; Allan Jaffe, founder of Preservation Hall, the great Jazz Center in the French Quarter; and Joe Cahn, who heads the New Orleans School of Cooking in the city's newly remodeled Jackson Brewery. Two Jewish daughters of New Orleans who made their marks elsewhere are Lillian Hellman and Kitty Carlisle.

SIGHTS: The two best ways to see New Orleans as a tourist are to walk through the French Quarter and to ride one of the St. Charles streetcars. Places of Jewish interest in the French Quarter include the Hermann-Grima House, 820 St. Louis, built in 1831 by Samuel Hermann, a Jewish commission merchant of substantial importance. Open to the public and on the National Register of Historic Places, Hermann-Grima has fine antiques, an inner courtyard, and a separate kitchen house—all restored. At 900–910 Royal, the Miltenberger Mansions were built by a wealthy Jewish widow in 1838 for her three sons. Their descendants became Catholic, but one married Michael Heine, who remained a Jew and who was a cousin of poet Heinrich Heine. Michael's daughter Alice, raised a Catholic, became the first American Princess of Monaco, when she married Prince Albert.

The Historic New Orleans Collection at 533 Royal has within its private collection several items of Jewish interest. Enter the interior courtyard and you will find a plaque, in English and Hebrew, commemorating Judah Touro's gift of a vacated church to a Jewish congregation in 1850. In the library, ask to see two rare books on the history of Jews of New Orleans that date from 1903 and 1905.

Nearby, at 540 Royal, is Nahan Galleries which features, among its general display, several Jewish artists including Théo Tobiasse, Leonardo Neirman, Yaacov Agam, Shalom of Safed, and Marc Chagall. The gallery has also cosponsored numerous exhibits with local and out-of-town Jewish organizations.

On Chartres Street, facing Jackson Square, you will find the Louisiana State Museum, where the New Orleans Tourist Office is now located. The museum includes both the Cabildo at 701 Chartres and the Presbytère at 713 Chartres, where there are galleries devoted to the history of the area, including artifacts pertaining to Judah P. Benjamin and Judah Touro. Both extremely important historically, the Cabildo and Presbytère date from 1795. The Cabildo housed the Spanish municipal government and later was the site of the signing of the Louisiana Purchase agreement. The Presbytère, originally built as a rectory, became instead a city courthouse.

The St. Charles streetcars will take you from the French Quarter through the Garden District and uptown to the campus of Tulane. The streetcars, now a National Historic Landmark, run around the clock. Fare is sixty cents and day passes are available. (It is, by the way, the only remaining streetcar line in the city; the streetcar named Desire is now a bus.) On the St. Charles route you will pass many of the homes and institutions, past and present, of New Orleans Jews. Before you reach the Garden District, at Lee Circle, you will catch a close view of the Greater New Orleans Mississippi River Bridge, the only bridge spanning the river from within the city limits. The bridge was opened in 1958 thanks to the efforts of one man, Captain Neville Levy, a Jewish shipbuilder.

Touro Synagogue, at 4338 St. Charles, was designed in 1909 by a leading Jewish architect, Emile Weil, and still uses the altar from the original Dispersed of Judah Synagogue, given to the congregation by Judah Touro.

At 5120 St. Charles, the Milton H. Latter Public Library honors a Jewish World War II hero killed on Okinawa and is a gift to the city by his family. The beautiful mansion was built in 1907 by Marks Isaacs, a Jew who owned a department store—and one of the city's first autos. Two blocks farther uptown is the Jewish Community Center, at the corner of Jefferson. This full-service center, built in the 1950s, is on the site of the former Jewish orphanage. When you visit the JCC, cross the street and walk two blocks toward the lake on Jefferson, to the Newman School. Founded in 1903 by Isidore Newman as a manual training school for children of the Jewish orphanage, Newman today is regarded by many as the best college preparatory school in the south.

Continuing toward Tulane, just off St. Charles at 1630 Arabella, is a private home, dating from the 1840s, that once belonged to Judah P. Benjamin and was used by the Union Army as a hospital during the Civil War.

At 6227 St. Charles is Temple Sinai, New Orleans's first Reform congregation. Visit its Barbara Weintraub Collection of Art for a good representation of modern Jewish artists including Shlomo Katz, Chaim Gross, Yaacov Agam, and Marc Chagall. The Julian Feibelman Chapel includes a tapestry sculpture made by the women in the congregation—and two stained-glass windows made from windows salvaged from a former Sinai building.

Tulane University begins at 6400 St. Charles. At St. Charles and Audubon Place stands the President's Mansion, a magnificent example of classical revival architecture. This was the home of Samuel Zemurray who gave this and many other gifts to Tulane. The third-floor ballroom with its Aeolian organ was the locale for parties attended by Jewish teens in bygone days. Doris Hall at Newcomb College (part of Tulane) was provided by Zemurray in honor of his daughter. Zemurray arrived in this country penniless. Soon after, when he noticed large quantities of bananas rotting in port, he went into the banana business and eventually became the head of United Fruit.

Walk down Audubon Place from St. Charles and at the corner of Freret is the Howard Tilton Memorial Library. The archives of the Southern Jewish Historical Society are there as well as records of the New Orleans Port of Entry. For information about the archives and about the Judaic Studies Program on campus, contact Professor Joseph Cohen of the English Department, (504) 865-5585.

CULTURE: Adult education lectures and series are offered by congregations, the JCC, and the Tulane Jewish Studies Program. Tulane, for example, marked the 850th birthday of Maimonides in 1985 by featuring two Maimonides scholars. There are weekend seminars for adults at the Henry S. Jacobs Camp, sponsored by the Union of American Hebrew Congregations, in Utica, Mississippi.

The Klezmania Jewish Music Orchestra performs for public and private events, as does a local folk dance troupe offering Israeli dance concerts. For details of events, call the JCC, at 897-0143, or look at the biweekly *Jewish Times,* available at the JCC or New Orleans Federation office.

GENERAL SIGHTS: The New Orleans Museum of Art was founded seventy-five years ago and was known until recently as the Isaac Delgado Museum of Art, named for its original benefactor, a Jewish sugar merchant. The museum is open Tuesday through Sunday at Lelong Avenue in City Park, 488-2631. Longue Vue House and Gardens is the eight-acre estate of the late philanthropists Edgar B. Stern, a cotton broker, and his wife, Edith Rosenwald Stern, daughter of Sears, Roebuck founder Julius Rosenwald. If you enjoy seeing estates and gardens, by all means visit this nationally recognized showcase. Open daily except Mondays at 7 Bamboo Road in Metairie, (504) 488-5488. A treat that doesn't cost anything is the Algiers Ferry at the foot of Poydras Street. Take your car with you across the Mississippi.

LAGNIAPPE (New Orleanese for an extra treat):   No visit to New Orleans can be complete without considering food. Unfortunately, there is no New Orleans-style kosher restaurant. But you are in luck if you can find a copy of Mildred L. Covert and Sylvia P. Gerson's *Kosher Creole Cookbook* (Pelican). There are recipes for Oysters Mock-a-Feller (made with gefilte fish), Cuzzin Caledonia's Chicken-Fried Steak, and Baleboosteh's Bouillabaisse, plus other marvelous delicacies. The foreword is written by Rabbi Jonah Gewirtz, who is also the head of the New Orleans Orthodox Rabbinical Council.

Serio's Kosher Delicatessen, 133 St. Charles, just outside the French Quarter, is not kosher, but kosher-style. In Metairie, Fortuna's Cuisine, 4241 Veterans Boulevard, serves Israeli food. The Bagel Factory, 3113 North Causeway in Metairie, has received Rabbi Gewirtz's stamp of approval. Contact Rabbi Gewirtz at (504) 283-4366 for information regarding Orthodox resources. For newcomers, there's a Shalom New Orleans kit available from the Federation, 1539 Jackson Avenue, New Orleans, 70130, telephone, 525-0673.

READING: Bertram Wallace Korn's *The Early Jews of New Orleans* (American Jewish Historical Society) remains the definitive history but only takes the reader to around 1840. David Max Eichhorn's *Joys of Jewish Folklore* (Jonathan David) includes wonderful tales about New Orleans Jewry, part history and part legend. A recent popular novel of New Orleans Jewry is Belva Plain's *Crescent City* (Delacorte). A general, and hilarious, novel set in the city is the Pulitzer Prize-winning *A Confederacy of Dunces* by John Kennedy Toole (Louisiana State University Press). Among the many New Orleans guidebooks, probably the most enjoyable and unusual is the delightful and informative *Frenchmen, Desire, Good Children and Other Streets of New Orleans,* by John Churchill Chase (Collier/Macmillan.) Like everything else from New Orleans, from jazz to Jews, the city's literature is a bit offbeat, and the richer for it.

—RACHEL HEIMOVICS

New York

Scene from a nineteenth-century Purim "fancy dress" ball.
(Courtesy of the New York Public Library)

New York, New York—the town so good they named it twice. Not only the hub of America, it is also the epicenter of American Jewry. Harry Golden called New York "the greatest Jewish city in the world." His point was that Jews have had a greater impact on New York than any other ethnic group on any other American city. When the New York Mets won the World Series in 1969, the headline of *The Daily News* said, "Mazel Tov." When a TV reporter asked the mayor why he didn't turn the other cheek in a political squabble, Ed Koch deadpanned, *"I'm* not a Christian."

There is a vibrancy and intensity of Jewish life in New York that is found nowhere else outside of Israel. Many Jewish men proudly wear yarmulkes on the street; advertisements on subway-car billboards remind Jewish passengers to light Shabbat candles; some coffee shops serve matzo brei on Passover; and the Empire State Building is bathed in blue and white during Jewish holidays.

HISTORY: In 1654, twenty-three Jews, mostly Sefardim, fled the newly imposed Portuguese Inquisition in Brazil. Originally bound for the Netherlands, they were waylaid by Spanish pirates, captured by the French, and ultimately found themselves en route to New Amsterdam. The governor of the colony, Peter Stuyvesant, wrote to his superiors at the Dutch West India Company, "praying most seriously that the deceitful race not be allowed to further infest and trouble this new colony." Many of the company's stockholders were Jewish, however, and the Jews were allowed to stay.

While the general population of the colony accepted the Jews, Stuyvesant established landowning, residential, and occupation restrictions on the Jews. Jacob Barsimon (who had arrived in New Amsterdam a month before the refugees from Brazil) and Asser Levy led the fight against the governor, filing lawsuits and petitions. Many of the restrictions had been lifted by the time the colony was taken over by the British in 1664 and renamed New York. Even with restrictions, Jews prospered quickly. In 1655, Jewish taxpayers paid 8 percent of the cost of the *Waal* built on what is now Wall Street, though they accounted for only two percent of the assessed population.

New York's first congregation, Shearith Israel, was organized around 1706, but the first synagogue building on Mill Lane wasn't erected until 1729 and the community grew slowly. Many of the original settlers returned to the Netherlands and, of those who remained, intermarriage was high. Rodrigo Pacheco attained the highest office of any colonial Jew in 1731 when he became the agent representing New York's interests in Parliament.

Between 1768 and 1770, eleven Jewish merchants signed the Non-Importation Resolutions, one of the measures that protested Britain's policy of taxation without representation. When the British occupied New York in 1776, many of the city's Jews fled to Philadelphia.

Gershom Mendes Seixas, cantor of Shearith Israel, was one of fourteen ministers who participated in George Washington's first inaugural in 1789, when New York was the capital of the United States. Three years later, Benjamin Seixas and Ephraim Hart were among the founders of the New York Stock Exchange.

With the arrival of English, French, and newer Dutch immigrants, New York Jewry had an Ashkenazi majority by 1825, the year in which the city's first Ashkenazi congregation, B'nai Jeshurun, was formed. Even then, however, the Jewish community numbered only six hundred, no more than in Charleston, South Carolina.

Heavy taxes in Europe after the Napoleonic Wars caused an increase in Jewish immigration, chiefly from Poland and Bavaria; by 1840, New York's Jewish population had jumped to ten thousand. By midcentury, the community was large enough to have its own flourishing social and cultural life. Young men's clubs stressing social, literary, or communal interest were formed; one of them, the Harmonie Club, still exists. Various Jewish organizations held elaborate balls, particularly at Purim, which were highlights of the Jewish social season.

The Purim balls became a vehicle for raising funds to aid the sick and wounded during the Civil War. One of the chief northern fundraisers was Joseph Seligman, whose New York firm sold two hundred million dollars in war bonds. While Jewish soldiers were spread widely among the Union forces, they predominated in Company D of the 8th New York National Guard. During the war, Samuel and Myer Issacs led the successful effort to install Jewish chaplains in the service.

By 1880, New York was home to an established, predominantly middle-class, Reform, German (with smaller numbers of English, Dutch, Bohemian, and Polish) Jewish community of sixty thousand. Then came the immigrant waves from Eastern Europe. Over the next fifty years, the community would increase to two million. Never before had so many Jews lived in one place.

As each wave of Jewish immigrants established itself, it tended to view newcomers as inferior. Eastern European doctors, for example, established their own hospital, Beth Israel, when they felt discriminated against at Mt. Sinai Hospital. Established Jews attempted to have their East European brethren settled in less densely populated areas like the Catskill Mountains, rural New Jersey, and the Plains states. The efforts were mostly in vain. Of all the immigrants who poured into the United States between 1881 and 1924, Jews ranked highest in their preference for New York. More than 70 percent got off the boat and stayed put.

The first stop for most Jews was the Lower East Side, which Jews helped make the most densely populated neighborhood in America. The neighborhood became the center of a flourishing Jewish community, with sweatshops and synagogues, Yiddish theaters and newspapers. The Jewish reading market was so lucrative that even William Randolph Hearst published a Yiddish paper for a time.

It was on the Lower East Side that establishment Jews made another stand against the orientalization of American Jewry by opening the Educational Alliance, the neighborhood's largest and most influential community center, to make the newcomers more like them. Orthodox leaders viewed the center as a bastion of Reform Judaism in their midst, and radicals viewed it as the establishment's use of charity to silence social protest. But the masses took advantage of the English classes, naturalization courses, and the wide-ranging cultural activities offered.

The fear that the large numbers of Jewish immigrants from Eastern Europe would increase anti-Semitism were somewhat justified. Social barriers increased in the late nineteenth and early twentieth centuries and German Jews sometimes found themselves barred from membership in clubs their grandparents had been instrumental in founding. Jews were certainly one of the groups in mind when Congress put a halt to large-scale immigration in 1924.

German Jews had already moved up Fifth and Lexington avenues before the onset of mass immigration. One of the more obscure facts of New York's Jewish history, however, is the speed with which the East Europeans left the old neighborhood for greener pastures. Between 1910 and 1920, the population of the Lower East Side declined by about 25 percent.

As they prospered, Jews moved out; the new subway system facilitated their exodus to the Upper West Side, Harlem, and the Bronx, or to Williamsburg and Brownsville in Brooklyn. Later on, prosperity meant moving to the suburbs of Long Island and Westchester County. Like other American cities, New York's demographic evolution has resulted in many synagogues moving, closing, or remaining open to a diminished congregation. On the other hand, because of the sheer size of its Jewish community and its ability to recycle neighborhoods, New York has more functioning old synagogues than any other city.

COMMUNITY: There are 2.1 million Jews in the New York metropolitan area, almost evenly divided between the city and its suburbs. About 275,000 live in Manhattan, the organizational core of both New York and American Jewry.

Modern Jewish enclaves in Manhattan are to be found in the Lower East Side, the Upper West Side—now experiencing a renaissance—and the stalwart Washington Heights area, home to many refugees from Nazi Germany. The 1970s and '80s saw a large influx of Russian, Syrian, Iranian, and Israeli Jews. For the most part, recent Jewish immigrants live in the less expensive outer boroughs.

There are 96,000 Jews left in the Bronx—down from a peak of 590,000 in the 1930s; the borough's Jewish strongholds are in Pelham Parkway, Riverdale, and Co-op City. The presence of Montefiore and Jacobi hospitals and the Albert Einstein Medical School of Yeshiva University has kept many Jewish doctors in the area. In the South Bronx, notorious for its resemblance to the bombed-out cities of postwar Germany, one synagogue remains—the Intervale Jewish Center at 1024 Intervale Avenue.

Home to 317,000 Jews, Queens, second in Jewish population to Brooklyn, boasts some of the most conspicuously Jewish neighborhoods of New York. The Forest Hills-Rego Park section, an established Jewish neighborhood, has recently seen a wave of immigration from the Soviet Union and Israel. Kew Gardens Hills is a bastion of Orthodoxy in a borough community dominated by Conservative Jewry.

The list of Jewish concentrations in New York's suburbs is virtually endless. A highly selective list of the most Jewish areas includes Great Neck and the Five Towns area on Long Island; Scarsdale and White Plains in Westchester County; and Monsey and Spring Valley in Rockland County. In neighboring New Jersey there are large communities in Englewood, Teaneck, Fair Lawn, Highland Park, Livingston, Short Hills, and Lakewood.

That the Jewish community is politically involved is hardly surprising, though it is but one small example of its influence. In addition to producing New York's last two mayors (Koch and Abraham Beame), the community is represented by City Controller Harrison Goldin, City Council President Andrew Stein, and many other elected officials.

Jews are at the top of the professions for which New York is known best. The city's two greatest publishing institutions, *The New York Times* and *The New Yorker,* are Jewish-owned. Random House, Alfred A. Knopf, the Viking Press (now part of Viking Penguin), and Simon & Schuster are among the publishing houses started by Jews. Many publishers of Jewish or Hebrew books are located in New York—Herzl Press, Behrman House, Phillip Feldheim, Bloch, and the Union of American Hebrew Congregations, just to name a few.

At the turn of the century, 85 percent of those employed in the garment industry, New York's largest, were Jewish. Through the efforts of such groups as the Bund and the Workmen's Circle, and encouraged by the premier Yiddish newspaper, the *Forward,* Jews were instrumental in the formation of many unions, including the International Ladies' Garment Workers' Union. Ironically, much of the struggle of the Jewish garment unions was against the Jewish manufacturers who employed them. Though union ranks have since been filled by newer immigrant groups, much of New York's labor leadership is still Jewish, from Sol Chaikin of the ILGWU to Victor Gotbaum, head of the municipal workers union.

While Jews are still associated with the garment industry, there are other occupations, ranging from cigar making to the manufacture of carousel horses, in which the predominance of New York Jews has long since been forgotten.

Most of the occupational barriers have been breached, but Jews were traditionally barred from shipping, port, and transportation concerns, and from large banks and insurance companies. Closed doors in these areas contributed to the heavy Jewish concentration in other businesses, such as investment banking (Kuhn Loeb, Lehman Brothers, Bache), retailing (B. Altman, Bloomingdale's, Gimbels, and Macy's), real estate, and building.

Nowadays, New York Jews are employed in virtually every occupation, from doctor to dockworker, chemist to cabdriver. There is even an organization of Jewish police officers, the Shomrim Society. Most

Jews, however, have fulfilled the dreams of their immigrant parents or grandparents to whom education was the key to success. Jews took advantage of the free public education offered in New York and at one point accounted for 90 percent of the students at City College. Jews now constitute between 35 and 40 percent of the student bodies of such colleges as Columbia and New York University (whose initials, NYU, are sometimes referred to by New Yorkers as standing for "New Yeshiva University"). About half of all Jewish children in New York attend either yeshiva or Hebrew school, in contrast to only 25 percent at the turn of the century.

Because New York has such a large Jewish community, there is no one central organization that represents them all. New York Jewry covers the spectrum from total nonaffiliation to ultra-Orthodoxy. Important religious organizations include the Union of American Hebrew Congregations (Reform) at 838 Fifth Avenue, the United Synagogue (Conservative) at 155 Fifth Avenue, and the National Council of Young Israel (Orthodox) at 3 West 16 Street. The list of national Jewish organizations *not* based in New York is much shorter than the roster of those that are. In addition to Hadassah, at 50 West 58 Street, New York is home to the United Jewish Appeal, the National Conference on Soviet Jewry, the American Jewish Committee, the American Jewish Congress, the Anti-Defamation League of B'nai B'rith, and the American Jewish Joint Distribution Committee. Many Zionist organizations are located under one roof, at 515 Park Avenue.

SIGHTS: What better place to start your tour of Jewish New York than a trip to the Statue of Liberty, the first glimpse immigrant Jews had of "the golden land" on their way to Ellis Island. On the base of the recently renovated monument is the poem "The New Colossus," by the Jewish poet Emma Lazarus. Ferries to the statue, with its Museum of Immigration, leave from Battery Park.

In Battery Park itself is a plaque in honor of Lazarus. At the corner of State and Whitehall Streets is another plaque, at the base of a flagpole, commemorating the first twenty-three Jewish settlers in New York.

A short subway ride puts you in the middle of the twenty-block area known as the Lower East Side. At the turn of the century, it was the first stop for new immigrants—replete with workshops, sweatshops, tenements—and six hundred thousand Jews. The population now includes Chinese, blacks, and Puerto Ricans, but there are still Jews and Jewish bookstores, sofrim, kosher delis, and Jewish shopkeepers along Essex, Grand, Canal, Delancey, and Orchard streets. Visit Orchard Street on a Sunday, its sidewalks bursting with clothing displays and shoppers, to get a taste of what the Lower East Side was like at the turn of the century. The street is closed to traffic and bargains abound.

The Lower East Side has many important Jewish sites—too many to mention. The first Jewish cemetery in the United States, dating back to 1682, can be found near Chatham Square, off St. James Street. Nearby is the hundred-year-old Khal Adath Jeshurun, also known as the Eldridge Street Synagogue, at 12 Eldridge Street. A New York landmark, it was the first synagogue in the city built by Eastern European Jews. (Earlier congregations merely took over Protestant churches, a practice condoned by Orthodox rabbis because there had been no religious statues present.) Recently, the synagogue has been renovated and hosted its first wedding in fifty years. The synagogue is also part of the Lower East Side Historic Conservancy program to trace and recreate the experiences of Jewish immigrants. For a "Peddler's Pack Tour," sponsored by the Conservancy, or for information about its activities, call (212) 219-0888. The Conservancy's most unique fundraising innovation was the revival, in 1986, of the "fancy-dress" Purim Ball, hosted by New York's glitterati.

Along East Broadway, you can find many important Jewish landmarks. The *Forward,* still the largest Yiddish newspaper in America (although its prominence has declined as its readership has dwindled, and it is now a weekly rather than a daily) and literary home to Isaac Bashevis Singer, has moved from its original location at 175 East Broadway to the Workmen's Circle building uptown. The former Forward Building, which once housed Jewish labor and political offices as well as the newspaper, is now a Chinese church, but the Hebrew lettering is still visible at the top. Next door is a Bank Leumi branch with Chinese lettering, a sign of the changing character of the Lower East Side. Seward Park, located across the street, also bears testimony to the changing neighborhood. Once a gathering spot for Jewish immigrants, it is now drug-infested. The Educational Alliance Building (known in local parlance as "the Edgies"), at 197 East Broadway, houses a successful immigrant absorption institute. Started in 1883 in an attempt to Americanize Jewish immigrants, it now provides vocational training and English lessons to its Jewish and non-Jewish clientele. The Henry Street Settlement (265 Henry Street), founded in

1893 by the pioneering social worker Lillian Wald, now has a large Puerto Rican clientele in addition to the Jews it serves.

Two nearby synagogues hold special distinctions. The Bialystoker Synagogue, at 7 Willett Street, built in 1826, was originally a Methodist church; its building is the oldest structure in New York housing a synagogue. Nearby Congregation Anshe Slonim, at Norfolk and Stanton streets, is the oldest original synagogue structure in New York, built in 1849. Abandoned for many years and in disrepair, the building was recently purchased by a private developer.

Rivington Street boasts both the only matza factory and the only kosher winery in Manhattan. The Streit's matza factory at 150 Rivington does not allow visitors (you'll need to go to Brooklyn for that) but the Schapiro winery—makers of the "Wine You Can Almost Cut with a Knife"—at 126 Rivington offers free tours as well as Sunday wine tastings.

Take a walk along what used to be known as the "Jewish Rialto"— Second Avenue. Once stars such as Boris Thomashefsky and, later, Molly Picon and Edward G. Robinson, graced the stages of the many Yiddish theaters. A few remain, including the Yiddish Art Theater on East Twelfth Street and the abandoned Anderson Yiddish Theater on East Fourth Street. Second Avenue is still home to many avant-garde theaters.

Behind the bustle of midtown Manhattan you can find literally dozens of places to daven. There are occupation-based shuls, such as the Millinery Center Synagogue at 1025 Avenue of the Americas and the Garment Center Congregation at 205 West 40 Street, that are convenient for daily services, and a host of minyans that meet in offices and stores. A list of Manhattan minyans may be obtained from Agudath Israel, 5 Beekman Street, telephone (212) 791-1800.

Midtown Manhattan boasts two institutions which would barely exist without Jews—the diamond and jewelry business and the Broadway stage. The Forty-seventh Street diamond center, between Fifth and Sixth avenues, is dominated by Hasidim and has a growing influx of Russian, Persian, and Israeli Jews. Some deals are still made outdoors and sealed with a handshake; don't worry, security is very tight.

New York and theater are synonymous. Jews played, and continue to play, important roles in both the Jewish and mainstream theaters, as actors, producers, writers, and directors. Vaudeville and early radio spawned such talents as the Marx Brothers, George Burns, Fanny Brice, and Milton Berle. David Belasco and Florenz Ziegfeld were among the premier producers in the early days of theater and they have been followed by today's theater moguls like Alexander Cohen, Gerald Schonfeld, and the Shubert Organization. The great names of the Broadway musical—Irving Berlin, George Gershwin, Rodgers and Hammerstein, Lerner and Loewe, Stephen Sondheim—are Jewish, as are many of the leading directors and playwrights like Joseph Papp, Arthur Miller, Lillian Hellman, and Harold Pinter. At any given time, there are at least ten Broadway and Off-Broadway shows of Jewish interest, ranging from the subtly Jewish plots of Neil Simon to the surviving Yiddish stage.

The United Nations, along First Avenue between Forty-second and Forty-seventh streets, belongs in both the asset and liability columns of Jewish history. Though in recent years its General Assembly has been a forum for anti-Israel resolutions and propaganda, it is also the institution that gave birth to the Jewish state in 1947 and whose peacekeeping forces patrol the frontiers of the Middle East. Across from the UN at Forty-third Street is the Isaiah wall, with its inscription of Isaiah's prophecy about beating swords into plowshares. On Forty-seventh Street, on the south side of Dag Hammarskjöld Plaza, gathering place for the annual Soviet Jewry rally, is Arbit Blatas's Holocaust memorial, consisting of six bronze plaques. A six-block stretch of First Avenue north of Forty-second Street is called Raoul Wallenberg Walk, after the Swedish diplomat who saved tens of thousands of Jews during the Holocaust.

One midtown sight not to be missed is the Central Synagogue (Reform), at 652 Lexington Avenue (Fifty-fifth Street). The Moorish-style structure, modeled after Budapest's Dohany Synagogue, is the oldest in New York still in use (since 1872). It is a city, state, and national landmark. Park East Synagogue at 163 East 67 Street (the Central Synagogue's rival for distinction as the most beautiful in New York) is located across the street from the Soviet mission to the UN; on its Moorish Revival façade is a plaque bearing a message to its neighbor: "Hear the cry of the oppressed. —The Jewish Community of the Soviet Union."

Though small and unassuming, the Fifth Avenue Synagogue, at 5 East 62 Street, is known as the "Millionaire's shul." The name comes not only from its location in one of Manhattan's most exclusive neighborhoods and the income level of some of its congregants, but also from the many dignitaries who come from the nearby luxury hotels to pray. The Orthodox synagogue was once headed by Immanuel Jakobovits, now the Chief Rabbi of Great Britain.

Built on the location of the Astor Mansion (complete with intact wine cellar), Temple Emanu-El, at Fifth Avenue and Sixty-fifth Street, is the world's largest synagogue. A massive cathedral-like building, the main sanctuary, with its Tiffany windows, can seat thirty-five hundred. First organized in the Lower East Side by German Jews in 1845, the flagship of the Reform movement is now in its fifth location. Radio station WQXR broadcasts the temple's Friday night services. Emanu-El is also one of the few Reform synagogues to hold daily services.

The world's largest continuous stained-glass façade can be found in the Milton Steinberg building adjacent to the Conservative Park Avenue Synagogue at 50 East 87 Street. The ninety-one panes portray Jewish holidays and traditions. On the Madison Avenue side of the Park Avenue Synagogue is Nathan Rapoport's sculpture dedicated to the Jewish children who perished in the Holocaust.

First located in the Chelsea district in Manhattan, Mt. Sinai hospital moved to its present location, Fifth Avenue between 99th and 101st streets, in 1904. This renowned hospital was started in 1853 and originally named "Jews' Hospital." It treated only Jews until 1864; in 1866 its name was changed to Mt. Sinai.

The Stephen Wise Free Synagogue, named for the pioneering Reform rabbi, is at 30 West 68 Street. Before the congregation settled into its own building in 1922, it held services in Carnegie Hall.

One of the most unique Orthodox institutions in New York is Lincoln Square Synagogue (200 Amsterdam Avenue). Best known for its programs of outreach to the nonaffiliated, it is frequented by Jewish singles and baalei teshuva. The modern structure has a circular interior and a see-through, plexiglass mehitza; the bimah is in the middle, to symbolize the centrality of the Torah in Jewish life.

Shearith Israel (8 West 70 Street), commonly known as the Spanish and Portuguese Synagogue, was the first congregation in New York, founded by the twenty-three original Sefardic settlers. Originally located on Mill Street (now South William Street), it moved to its current site in 1897. The small, colonial-style chapel, with its Tiffany windows, is used for daily services and is especially impressive. It has a camouflaged havdala set and some candlesticks from the Inquisition period, as well as furnishings from the original synagogue. (A replica of the Mill Street synagogue can be found on the roof of the Wall

Street Synagogue at 47 Beekman Street.) Shearith Israel sponsors a Sefardic Fair in May. Call 873-0300 for details.

Reform Congregation Rodeph Sholom, founded in 1842 (the first congregation on the Lower East Side), has been at 7 West 83 Street since 1930. Its ornate sanctuary is highlighted by a beautiful ceiling with a Magen David motif. Rodeph Sholom also has the only Reform day school in Manhattan. One of the congregation's previous buildings still stands at 8 Clinton Street. Built in 1853, it is the second-oldest surviving synagogue structure and home now to Congregation Chasam Sofer.

The Jewish Center at 131 West 86 Street was organized by Rabbi Mordecai Kaplan to fulfill his concept of a multifaceted gathering place for Jews, providing social, cultural, and recreational facilities as well as a place to pray. Although it has served as the model for Conservative Jewish centers, this center is Orthodox.

Kaplan himself eventually moved down the block to form the Society for the Advancement of Judaism (15 West 86 Street), the center of Reconstructionist Judaism. The society's synagogue features murals depicting the rebirth of Israel.

B'nai Jeshurun, at 270 West 89 Street, is the city's oldest Ashkenazi congregation, having seceded from Shearith Israel in 1825, the first of many splits that gave rise to twenty-seven different congregations in the following thirty-five years. Its first home was a former Presbyterian church at 112 Elm Street (no longer standing); its present structure, featuring a beautiful baroque interior, is its fifth home, built in 1918.

To the west, at Riverside Drive and Eighty-ninth Street, is the Chofetz Chaim Yeshiva, housed in a mansion. Its recent designation as a landmark received a mixed reaction: the neighbors, many of them Jews prominent in the music world and in the media, rejoiced that their river view would not be blocked by a proposed high-rise building; the yeshiva is now saddled with the cost of upkeep.

Ansche Chesed Temple, at 100th Street and West End Avenue, was founded in 1876 and has been at its present location since 1921. The now-thriving synagogue was saved by the marriage between several neighborhood havuras, whose members used to daven in private homes, and the aging congregation which had a large building but not enough people to pray in it or keep it up. Ansche Chesed figured prominently in the book *An Orphan in History* by Paul Cowan (Doubleday).

Probably the leading collection of Jewish and Hebrew books in the world can be found at the Jewish Theological Seminary, the Conservative rabbinical training institute at Broadway and 122nd Street. A manuscript in Maimonides's handwriting is on display there. The library, with more than a quarter million volumes, serves scholars daily and has also been used by moviemakers. Norman Jewison did research at the seminary in preparation for the film version of *Fiddler on the Roof.*

Harlem was once a Jewish neighborhood and it still has one synagogue—the Ethiopian Hebrew Congregation, at 1 West 123 Street. Though many of the black congregants are not halakhically Jewish, there is no doubt about the Jewishness of the ritual and the sincerity of the worshippers. Call 534-1058 for information on services.

Yeshiva University, at Amsterdam Avenue between 183rd and 187th streets in Washington Heights, is the oldest and largest Jewish university in America (seven thousand students). In addition to its high school, college, and seminary, it has an excellent museum; Mayor Koch used an antiquarian Bible from the museum at his swearing in ceremony in 1986.

Khal Adath Jeshurun (85 Bennett Avenue), not to be confused with the Eldridge Street synagogue with the same name, is the mainstay of the Orthodox German-Jewish community that lives in Washington Heights.

For guided tours of Jewish New York, contact Oscar Israelowitz, author of several travel books, at (718) 951-7072.

CULTURE: Located at 1395 Lexington Avenue, the 92nd Street Y (Young Men's and Young Women's Hebrew Associations) offers a wealth of Jewish—and secular—culture and education. Lectures, films, concerts, dance, and Yiddish theater abound, with such notables as Elie Wiesel, Isaac Stern, Isaac Bashevis Singer, and Itzhak Perlman. Call 427-6000 for current events. The Y also offers sleeping accommodations for young adults—the only Jewish Y in the country to do so.

Your next cultural stop should be the Jewish Museum, three blocks west of the 92nd Street Y, at Ninety-second Street and Fifth Avenue. Housed in the elegant, turn-of-the-century Warburg mansion, the Jewish Museum is the largest in the Western Hemisphere devoted to Judaica and Jewish artists. A branch of the Jewish Theological Seminary, the museum's permanent collection is augmented by several special exhibitions each year. Recent offerings have included "The Jewish Heritage in American Folk Art," "The Precious Legacy: Judaic

Treasures from the Czechoslovak State Collections," "The Circle of Montparnasse: Jewish Artists in Paris, 1905–1945," and "Jews of India." The National Jewish Archive of Broadcasting is also on the premises. Call the Jewish Museum at 860-1888 for details.

One of the finest collections of Jewish scholarship is at the New York Public Library, at Forty-second Street and Fifth Avenue. The collection includes 125,000 books, as well as microfilm and Jewish publications. Another important collection is at the New York University Library of Judaica and Hebraica at 2 Washington Square North, in Greenwich Village.

The YIVO Institute for Jewish Research (1048 Fifth Avenue) contains many original documents on Jewish life, in addition to three hundred thousand volumes, photographs, music sheets, and recordings.

In addition to the Broadway theaters, there are three companies that regularly produce Jewish works: the American Jewish Theater at the 92nd Street Y, the Folksbiene Theater at 123 East 55 Street, and the Jewish Repertory Theatre at 344 East 14 Street.

You can hardly find an art gallery in New York that doesn't feature some Jewish artists. There are several stores featuring Jewish collectibles on the Lower East Side. One particularly good place uptown is In The Spirit, at 460 East 79 Street (call 662-6693, as the hours are irregular). New York's leading auction houses, Sotheby's (1334 York Avenue) and Christie's (502 Park Avenue), both have Judaica departments and periodic Judaica auctions.

Check *The Jewish Week* for Jewish cultural offerings, including radio and television listings of Jewish interest. Radio stations WEVD and WNYM have especially extensive Jewish programming. *The New York Times* and *New York Magazine* are also rich sources of information regarding Jewish events.

EATING: New Yorkers love to complain about their city, but no one can complain about a dearth of kosher restaurants. There are as many kosher restaurants in New York as there are in Tel Aviv. One of the most famous is Bernstein-on-Essex, popularly known as Shmulke Bernstein's (135 Essex Street), which features deli and Chinese menus. Another culinary institution is Ratner's (138 Delancey Street), the Lower East Side's and New York's most famous dairy restaurant. Ratner's, by the way, is open on Shabbat. At 22 Wooster Street, near Canal, is New York's kosher Japanese restaurant, Shalom Japan, replete with such items as sushi, tempura, and chopped liver (known here as "Karate Choppe"). Moshe Peking, at 40 West 37 Street, is an elegant kosher Chinese restaurant. Benjamin of Tudela at 307 Amsterdam Avenue, near Seventy-fourth Street, features an international kosher menu. Every kashrut-observing New Yorker has a vegetarian restaurant to recommend. Some of the city's Indian restaurants offer vegetarian menus as well. Check *The Jewish Press* for the wide variety of other restaurants—dairy, meat, or the numerous pizza and falafel joints.

GENERAL SIGHTS: Most of New York's general sights have their Jewish elements or connections. The Museum of Modern Art has works by many Jewish artists—Marc Chagall, Camille Pissarro, Amadeo Modigliani, Raphael Soyer. The Guggenheim Museum, designed by Frank Lloyd Wright, is named for its Jewish patron, Solomon Guggenheim. The Metropolitan Opera House at Lincoln Center features Chagall paintings.

Everyone has a few selected tips to offer for New York sightseeing. A Circle Line Tour around Manhattan provides a good orientation for the city. (The boats leave from Forty-second Street and the Hudson River.) As important as its sights are the city's events, many of which are free. Street fairs abound in late spring and early fall; during the summer, New Yorkers enjoy concerts and plays in Central Park at the Delacorte Theater (near the West Eighty-first Street entrance); October brings the New York Marathon, managed by Fred Lebow, a Rumanian Jew; to accommodate observant runners, a Shaharit service is held near the starting line in Staten Island. If you're in New York in December, be sure not to miss the lighting of the world's largest Hanukkah menorah (thirty-two feet high) at Fifty-ninth Street and Fifth Avenue. If you run out of ideas or find no free events scheduled, there's always Greenwich Village, with its outdoor cafés and sidewalk artists; the Village is home to the New York branch of Hebrew Union College (the Reform seminary) at 1 West 4 Street.

A novel way to find information regarding the almost two hundred and fifty museums and cultural institutions in New York is to visit the IBM Center at Fifty-seventh Street and Madison Avenue. With the help of an electronic billboard that responds to the slightest touch, you can find a museum for just about any interest.

PERSONALITIES: New York Jews have made their mark in government, science, business, the literary scene, and entertainment. In addition to city leaders, New York has produced Governor Herbert Lehman, Senator Jacob Javits, Supreme Court Justice Benjamin Cardozo, and far too many members of Congress to mention. Mayor Fiorello LaGuardia's mother was Jewish and he was a cousin of Luigi Luzzatti, the first Jewish prime minister of Italy. New York has also been home to Jonas Salk, developer of the polio vaccine, and astronomer Carl Sagan. Intellectual lights with roots in New York include Hannah Arendt, Lionel Trilling, Susan Sontag, E. L. Doctorow, Ben Hecht, Bernard Malamud, Cynthia Ozick, Chaim Potok, J. D. Salinger, and Herman Wouk, along with singers Robert Merrill, Jan Peerce, Roberta Peters, Beverly Sills, and Richard Tucker.

READING: For a historical look at New York, try *Our Crowd, The Grandees* (both Harper & Row), and *The Rest of Us* (Little, Brown) by Stephen Birmingham, which deal, respectively, with the wealthy German Jews, the Sefardim, and the East Europeans of New York. More general background can be found in *World of Our Fathers* (Simon & Schuster) by Irving Howe and *The Greatest Jewish City in the World* (Doubleday) by Harry Golden. The trilogy by literary critic Alfred Kazin—*A Walker in the City* (Harcourt, Brace, Jovanovich), *Starting Out in the Thirties* (Little, Brown), and *New York Jew* (Knopf)—provide an autobiographical look at growing up Jewish in New York. Novels by Herman Wouk—*Marjorie Morningstar, City Boy* (Doubleday), and *Inside, Outside* (Little, Brown)—and E. L. Doctorow—*The Book of Daniel* (Modern Library) and *World's Fair* (Random House)—are set in New York, as is Abraham Cahan's *The Rise of David Levinsky* (Harper & Row). Other New York classics include Henry Roth's *Call It Sleep* (Avon) and Paul Goodman's *The Empire City* (Macmillan).

RECOMMENDATIONS: If money is no object, stay at the Waldorf-Astoria (Park Avenue and Fiftieth Street), where the Israeli Prime Minister stays when he is in town, or at the elegant Plaza Hotel (Fifth Avenue and Fifty-ninth Street). The New York Hilton, at Sixth Avenue and Fifty-third Street, is luxurious and particularly convenient to the theater district. A good value is the small and artsy Wyndham Hotel at 42 West 58 Street, next door to Hadassah House. Wherever you stay in New York, you'll be near something Jewish. Peter Stuyvesant's loss is your gain.

—PEARL WEISINGER

Nice

Hotel Negresco on the Promenade des Anglais
(French Government Tourist Office)

There are many good reasons to go to Nice—the sun, the beaches, luxurious casinos, carnivals, festivals, and some of the prettiest sights you may wish to see. And if you look around, you will even find the Jewish community.

Of the 750,000 Jews in France, about 25,000 are in Nice—capital of the Riviera and of international tourism. Jews may well be perfectly integrated in this large resort city, but their community is nevertheless active.

HISTORY: The first mention of Jews in Nice was in the fourteenth century, when an edict compelled them to wear distinguishing badges. After the first settlers from Italy, the influx of Jews followed the ebb and flow of anti-Semitism. Jews arrived from Rhodes, expelled by the Turks in 1499. Marranos came by way of Italy and Holland in the mid-seventeenth century. Jews from Oran (Algeria) were allowed to bring in their slaves when they settled some years later. By the early fifteenth century, a synagogue and Jewish cemetery had been established.

When the Count of Savoy took control of Nice in 1430, he offered Jews protection from baptism, yet instituted various prohibitions and restricted them to a separate quarter, the Giudaria. Over the years, ghetto living was alternately abolished and reinstituted. Not until 1848, when Nice became permanently French, did the ghetto disappear, its inhabitants emancipated. Today the rue Giudaria no longer exists, but some believe that the house at 18 Rue Benoît Bunico was once the ancient synagogue.

The advantages of a free port with trading access to the Mediterranean and a geographical location near the crossroads of France, Italy, and Spain were not lost on homeless Jews looking for a place to settle. Add the comfortable climate and the easygoing nature of Nice denizens, and one wonders that the community did not grow faster. Even as late as the early 1900s there were only five hundred Jews in Nice.

The ensuing catastrophes brought drastic changes, however. Many Jews who had escaped to sunny Nice from Nazi-occupied France during World War II at first enjoyed the security of the occupying Italians' relatively lenient rule. But after 1943, when the Nazis invaded Nice, thousands were deported, many martyred. The bulk of the twenty-five thousand Jews living in Nice today (more than 80 percent) arrived in the early 1960s as refugees from the French territories in North Africa.

COMMUNITY: The Jewish community is scattered yet extremely organized. Direct contact can be established through Jean Kling, the regional chief rabbi (telephone, 85-82-06).

There is no Jewish quarter nowadays, mostly due to the variety of occupations in which Jews engage. But many are connected through one of the numerous Jewish groups. There are four B'nai B'rith lodges, a central fund that disperses aid to Jewish schools, youth groups, rest homes, and social causes, not to mention support for Israeli causes. As Nice is a twin city of Netanya, one of the most active clubs is the Netanya Club.

Nice has a Jewish day school, two yeshivas, and a Jewish bookstore (Librairie Tanya, 2 Rue Gramont). Thirty miles out of town there is a Jewish sports center open all year long, combining camping, sports, and religious courses. There is also Centre Michelet, a modern, elegant facility in the northern part of the city (22 Rue Michelet) that can cater a Riviera wedding or bar mitzvah; it even has a mikvah on the premises. The building also houses the Centre Consistorial, the central body of Nice Jewry.

L'Arche, a monthly published in Paris, has a special Nice edition six times a year. A fortnightly, *Nitzan,* covers the activities of the community and has articles of general interest. The newsletter, *L'Atis,* serves the traditional Sefardi community. *Shalom Nitzan,* a weekly half-hour program on a radio station owned by Nice Mayor Jacques Médecin, is dedicated to Jewish topics.

SIGHTS: Most prominent of Nice's eight synagogues is the Sefardi synagogue, located at 7 Rue Gustave Deloye (telephone, 85-44-35). Built in 1890, with a splendid walk-in Ark that contains twelve Torahs, it is the spiritual center of the North African community. During the summer it boasts a full house at its services. Not far away, on 1 Rue Blacas, is the smaller Ashkenazi synagogue, lately enjoying the support of the Lubavitcher Rebbe. Synagogues are open only two hours daily for services.

Since terrorist attacks against synagogues some years ago, there is heavy security at all French synagogues during Sabbath services and synagogue-goers are advised not to congregate outside the buildings.

The old Jewish cemetery in Nice, located in a spectacular spot called Le Château, is one of four denominational burial grounds atop the main hill on which the city is built, with a picturesque panorama beneath. The cemetery dates to the sixteenth century, and there are family vaults of old Italian Jewish families, reminiscent of non-Jewish tombs in Florence and Genoa. On the four-century-old sepulchral vault of the Landau family, an Italian architect, Romanelli, has left not only his name but also his address in Florence, for prospective clients.

There are also testimonials of the Nazi scourge. As you enter the cemetery, there are two memorials, one containing an urn of ashes, the other a receptacle full of soap, the remains of the many deported Nice Jews. Higher up on the hill is the Château, now a military school, and every day at 1 P.M. a naval gun is fired, as if in homage to the dead.

CHAGALL MUSEUM: Nice is the home of the renowned Musée National Message Biblique, Marc Chagall. If you have time to visit only one place in town, this is it. Located in the poshest part of Nice, on the corner of Avenue Docteur Ménard and Boulevard Cimiez, on land supplied by the city and in a building erected by the government, it houses a collection donated by the artist to France, where Chagall "was born a second time." Some eighty thousand people visit every year, and with the recent death of Chagall, the museum has assumed added importance.

It was of Chagall that Picasso once remarked, "He must have had an angel in his head somewhere." That angelic touch is in the twelve spectacular paintings of scenes from Genesis and Exodus, the preparatory sketches (forty-five oils, ninety-one pastels), gouaches, lithographs, sculptures, and tapestries. Particularly breathtaking are the stained-glass mosaics and painted glasses. The light of the French Riviera, Chagall's home for many years, illuminates the stone and glass complex. Less well known is a unique library located in the museum, dedicated to the history of religions. For information, call 81-75-75.

RESTAURANTS: Not far from the main synagogue, there are several kosher restaurants, Le Roi David (9 Rue Clement Roassal; telephone, 87-65-25) and Chez David Guez (26 Avenue Pertinax; telephone, 85-70-16). There is also Restaurant Universitaire Cacher (31 Avenue Henri Barbusse; telephone, 51-43-63). Ask at the Community Center, 1 Rue Voltaire, for more information on kosher foods, or call the office of Rabbi Kling.

GENERAL SIGHTS: From the Chagall Museum, walk farther up

the hill, on Boulevard Cimiez. It is the central artery of a hill in the aristocratic quarter of town and has some of the most opulent private residences of the Riviera. There you will find the Matisse Museum, which offers insight into the creative process of this renowned painter.

But the obligatory visit, without which no one can really say he was in Nice, is a walk down the Promenade des Anglais, the wide seashore avenue, which has been the traditional parade ground of the rich and famous of Europe for over a century. Nowadays, although the traffic is rather heavy, the scene is still impressive and stimulating on a summer afternoon. And sipping coffee at the Negresco, probably the finest and best-known hotel on the Riviera, is no less of a tradition. If you have no budget limitations, stay there and enjoy the treatment reserved for kings and magnates.

SIDE TRIP: Saint Paul de Vence is a medieval hill town about a half hour from Nice. Not only is it worth the trip to walk the twisting, narrow streets, but it is also an important artists' colony. Chagall lived there for the last twenty years of his life. Matisse had a home there as well. A contemporary Jewish artist who lives in the town is Théo Tobiasse.

READING: Documentation on the Nice community is scarce, because Nice was never a leading spiritual center or cultural fountainhead in the Jewish tradition. There are several books in French, but for English readers there is Paula Hyman's *From Dreyfus to Vichy* (Columbia University Press), which embraces the entire twentieth-century history of the Jews in France and has a considerable chapter dedicated to Nice.

—EDNA FAINARU

Paris

Grand Synagogue Interior *(Leni Sonnenfeld)*

Paris, the city of fashion, has a new rage—Jewishness. There is a return to Jewish roots, not only among Jews, but also among Catholics. As a local observer put it, Paris is the only city in the world where both the chief rabbi and the archbishop (Cardinal Jean-Marie Lustiger) are Jews.

On the surface, one wouldn't expect Judaism to flourish here at all. Paris has cafés where one can commune over a cup of coffee for hours, bridges that invite leisurely strolls across the Seine, eye-arresting museums and monumental edifices which say "stop and look," and an evening culture of dining, opera, theater, and hundreds of cinemas. French culture is so attractive, stimulating, and absorbing that it demands an almost total devotion from Parisians. Yet the Jews of Paris have found a way to be French—a little less French than Emancipation might have envisioned—but increasingly and authentically Jewish.

HISTORY: According to legend, the first Jews to arrive in France were exiled there from Palestine by the Romans. Not much is known about Jewish life in Paris before the Middle Ages, although there is evidence of a synagogue in Paris in 582 C.E. As elsewhere in Europe, medieval Jews were welcomed—or, more accurately, their presence was tolerated—because they were perceived as economic assets to the king, who needed the income from their taxes. When the royal treasury required more than taxes, the Jews were routinely expelled from France and their belongings seized. The first expulsion was caused by a Host-desecration case against the Jews of Paris in 1290. Their "definitive" expulsion took place in 1394, and there is no evidence of Jews in Paris during the next two centuries.

The modern settlement of Jews in the French capital dates from the beginning of the eighteenth century. On the eve of the French Revolution there were forty thousand Jews in France, mostly German-speaking Jews living in Paris. In 1790, Jews became citizens of France, although, according to the often-quoted statement by the Count of Clermont-Tonnerre, they were to be given "everything" as individuals and "nothing" as Jews. Napoleon's ascendancy was a mixed blessing for the Jews. Yet by creating the Consistoire Central Israélite in

1808, he gave them the "everything" they needed to survive as a Jewish community: self-government.

The nineteenth century saw the rise of the middle class in France and with it the elevation of Jews to the bourgeoisie. Their vilification toward the end of the century by anti-Semite Edouard Drumont in his scurrilous *La France Juive* led directly to the trumped-up charges of treason against Captain Alfred Dreyfus in 1894. In Paris, one thing always leads to another, and among the results of *L'Affaire Dreyfus* was the conversion to Zionism of journalist Theodor Herzl and—equally important for French Jewry—the passing, in 1905, of the law separating church and state. The Dreyfus Affair was of importance not only to Jews, however. It was a seminal event in French history that, to this day, symbolizes the struggle between justice and generosity on the one hand and order and respect for established institutions on the other. According to Jean-Denis Bredin, author of the most recent in a ninety-year stream of books on Dreyfus (*The Affair*, published by George Braziller), this struggle is not always between two French camps but something that runs within each Frenchman, producing an inner conflict that offers some explanation of France's modern history.

In 1939, there were 150,000 Jews living in the French capital. The roundup of Paris Jews during the summer of 1942 sent many who had escaped deportation into the Resistance or into the arms of sympathetic Christians. Postwar Paris was home to many East European refugees, increasing the Jewish population even as Ashkenazi Jews raced to assimilate. In the 1960s, with the dismantling of the French colonial system in North Africa, a vibrant, exciting Sefardic community arrived in Paris, indelibly changing the face of French Jewry.

COMMUNITY: The Jewish community of three hundred thousand is organized around three principal institutions. The Fonds Social Juif Unifié is the fund-raising arm, with social and educational activities. The Conseil Représentatif des Institutions Juives de France, born of the Resistance, is the major Jewish defense and umbrella organization. The most important organization for Jewish life, however, is the Consistoire Central Israélite de France. According to Émile Touati, president of the Paris branch, French Judaism is neither Orthodox, Conservative, nor Reform, but "Consistorial," the center of which is roughly between left-wing Orthodox and right-wing Conservative Judaism. Locally, the *consistoires* are in charge of synagogue life and kashrut supervision. On a national level, under the leadership of

Grand Rabbin René-Samuel Sirat, the *consistoire* has been a force in enriching Jewish life in all areas. There are now enormous Jewish communities in the suburbs of Paris—Sarcelles, Créteil, La Varenne—with synagogues, Talmud Torahs, and community centers.

Jews count politically in Paris and are able to influence legislation, Touati says. Jewish education is a very high priority in the community; there are waiting lists to get into the better Jewish day schools, such as the École Maimonide and École Lucien de Hirsch. Young Jews, members of the Renouveau Juif (Jewish Renewal) movement, have also contributed to the renaissance of Jewish culture.

Most French Jews are Zionistic and often send their children to summer camp in Israel and to eventual aliyah. Among the youth groups is a prestigious scouting organization, the Éclaireurs Israélites. There is a rabbinical school in Paris, and all the major international Jewish organizations have offices there, including, most recently, Hadassah.

CULTURE: One thing the children of Abraham have in common with the descendants of Charlemagne is their love of reading. Book publishing is a major industry in France and bookstores can be found in every quarter. It only *seems* that most of the books on their shelves are by Jews or on Jewish topics. Your best bets are the PUF Bookstore on the Boulevard Saint-Michel in the Latin Quarter or the FNAC Department Store in the Montparnasse section, where books are sold at a handsome discount. There are several Jewish newspapers and magazines. *L'Arche,* a four-color glossy, is the best known; the Consistoires's *Information Juive* is among the most literate, and one of the most prestigious scholarly journals in the world is the *Revue des Études Juives,* published in Paris.

Aside from books, the most important cultural phenomenon taking place today is the growth of Jewish radio stations. It seems that every major city has at least one, offering courses on a wide variety of Jewish topics.

Adult education courses are held in many localities. The activities at the Centre Rachi (30 Boulevard de Port Royal, telephone, 331-98-20) —which include lectures, Jewish plays, choral groups, and Bible classes—are reminiscent of those at New York's 92nd Street Y.

PERSONALITIES: Paris has several prominent Jewish daughters and sons in all fields of endeavor. In the second half of the nineteenth century, Sarah Bernhardt reintroduced French classical theater to a dazzled populace. One of the greatest statesmen France has ever had was Léon Blum, its first Jewish Prime Minister and a clear voice for liberal and Jewish causes. Today, among the best known Jews are Simone Weil, former President of the European Parliament, and Jack Lang, President François Mitterand's Minister of Culture.

Most of the Jewish glamor in Paris is in the field of culture. Marcel Marceau is the world's premier mime. Probably the best-known French Jews are Josy Eisenberg, a television rabbi with a national pulpit, and Bernard-Henri Lévy, leader of the school of New Philosophers, author of the prize-winning novel *Le Diable en Tête* (Grasset), and often talked about as future presidential material. One of France's most important filmmakers is Claude Lanzmann, best known for his nine-and-a-half-hour Holocaust documentary, *Shoah.*

Singer Enrico Macias, whose son's bar mitzvah at the Western Wall in Jerusalem was reported in the French media, is one of France's most popular TV and cabaret entertainers. Other Jews associated with Paris, past and present, include the writers Marcel Proust, André Maurois, and Albert Memmi, artist Camille Pissarro, and André Citroën, the pioneer French automaker.

SIGHTS: The most interesting Jewish neighborhood in Paris is the Pletzl, in the Marais section (Métro Saint-Paul). Located not far from the Notre Dame Cathedral, the Marais section has quaint, narrow streets with colorful names, such as the Rue des Mauvais Garçons (Bad Boys Street) and the Rue des Rosiers (Street of the Rose Bushes).

The Pletzl is not far from some of the most distinguished monuments in Paris. The architecturally elegant Place des Vosges, which houses both the Victor Hugo Museum and a synagogue, and the Hotel Carnavalet, former home of Madame de Sévigné, are within walking distance. In the Pletzl itself, you will find a synagogue designed by Art Nouveau architect Hector Guimard at 10 Rue Pavée. (The ornate *Métro* entrances around the city and some beautifully proportioned private houses bear his unmistakable signature.) The Pletzl also has a plethora of Jewish bookstores and souvenir shops, kosher restaurants, bakeries, butchers and *charcuteries,* and, of course, Jo Goldenberg's restaurant. There you can ask for information, get directions, reminisce about prewar Europe, and buy Israeli takeout foods. Many of Goldenberg's clients are non-Jews, and he views himself as a public relations man to the Gauls. Goldenberg, whose restaurant is not kosher, beams with pride when he announces that his son is a Lubavitcher Hasid.

Another restaurant that should not be missed is the strictly kosher and posh Le Chandelier, 4 Rue Paul-Valéry (telephone, 704-55-22 for reservations, closed Friday and Saturday), which is housed in a former upscale brothel. For a traditional North African meal, go to the Sefardi equivalent of the Pletzl, the Boulevard de Belleville, to enjoy kosher couscous at the Dar Djerba (110 Boulevard de Belleville).

All is not food in Paris, however. Not far from the Pletzl, at 17 Rue Geoffroi l'Asnier, is a Memorial to the Unknown Jewish Martyr (Métro Pont-Marie). Equally moving is the museum upstairs dedicated to the Jewish partisans and Resistance fighters of every European country; there are enough Jewish heroes for several books. If you are inclined to do a bit of Jewish research, the museum also houses a Jewish archive, which browsers will find rewarding.

Several synagogues—like the Synagogue de la Victoire at 44 Rue de la Victoire—are worth a visit, although it is impossible to enter them other than during services. Often called the "cathedral," as well as the "Rothschild synagogue," the Synagogue de la Victoire was built in 1874 in Romanesque Revival style. Its lavish decor features marble and stained glass.

Warmly recommended for praying is the synagogue at 14 Rue Chasseloup-Laubat. This is a hidden jewel of synagogue architecture, with a friendly "Ashkesfard" minyan and possibly the best cantor in Paris.

Take the *Métro*—clean, efficient, and with easy-to-read maps—to the Lamarck-Caulaincourt station for a visit to the Museum of Jewish Art (42 Rue des Saules). It has a permanent exhibit of Chagalls and Pissarros, models of wooden Polish synagogues, shofars, and matza covers, and an ornate Ark curtain. One of the most curious objects is an egg with the 1789 Declaration of the Rights of Man inscribed in both French and Hebrew. The museum is not a pretty place; its collection, together with that of the Musée de Cluny, off Boulevard Saint-Michel in the Latin Quarter, is scheduled to form the basis for a magnificent new Municipal and National Museum of Jewish Art and Culture.

Parisians love to complain about their architecture. They did so when the Eiffel Tower and, more recently, the Pompidou Center were built. Today, the major controversy surrounds American architect I. M. Pei's plans for renovating the Louvre, complete with a glass pyramid in the palace's main courtyard. For a fascinating explanation of the issues involved, don't miss the exhibit on the Grand Louvre, at the Orangerie only yards away.

READING: In preparing for your trip you might read Ernest Hemingway's *A Movable Feast* (Charles Scribner's Sons) about bohemian life in prewar Paris. A description of Jewish life in the Marais is found in Cynthia Ozick's novel *The Cannibal Galaxy* (Knopf, Dutton). The breathtaking story of the fate of wartime Paris, narrated by Larry Collins and Dominique Lapierre in *Is Paris Burning?* (Simon & Schuster), gives another perspective.

DAY TRIPS: France is a relatively small country, and its efficient rail system makes day-tripping out of Paris a breeze. One hour to the north is the picturesque city of Rouen where, underneath the Palace of Justice, was discovered recently an eleventh-century yeshiva, complete with students' Hebrew graffiti.

Another city worth a day's trip—for one thing, you can try out the French National Railroad's high-speed train (the TGV)—is Lyon, an ancient Gallo-Roman city with a vibrant Jewish community of twenty thousand. It is also the place where Klaus Barbie, the "Butcher of Lyon," was, at this writing, imprisoned and awaiting trial.

Not to be missed in Lyon is Neve Shalom, the beautiful new Sefardi synagogue and community center (317 Rue Duguesclin); a kosher restaurant where you will meet Jewish students from the university; and the main synagogue at 13 Quai Tilsitt, about which edifying and miraculous legends have been woven. For details, contact the chief rabbi of Lyon, Richard Wertenschlag, at 837-13-43.

Once back in Paris, make one last stop at the magnificent new Forum des Halles, not far from the Pompidou Center, near the Marais. Across the street, in the Jardin des Halles, is the recently dedicated René Cassin Square, named for the French-Jewish human rights activist who won the Nobel Peace Prize in 1968. The Forum itself is a glass-and-chrome complex with shops, galleries, restaurants, and an outdoor café that has the most refreshing view in all of Paris. The setting is perfect for appreciating the convergence of Jewish and French life in this most attractive of cities.

—JOSEPH LOWIN

Philadelphia

Elfreth's Alley *(Alan M. Tigay)*

"Philadelphia—Get to Know Us" is both the City of Brotherly Love's latest slogan and a good motto for its Jewish community. With its treasure of historic sites and myriad other attractions, America's fourth-largest Jewish community, and fifth-largest city, are worth getting to know.

Unlike the very visible communities of New York or Los Angeles, Jewish Philadelphia does not wear its ethnicity on its collective sleeve. But with a history reaching back to colonial times, Jews are inseparably linked to the city. And Philadelphia Jewry has been powerful in national Jewish affairs, both past and present.

HISTORY: Jews visited Philadelphia as early as 1706, but permanent Jewish settlement dates to 1737, when Nathan and Isaac Levy arrived. Jewish communal activity began in the 1740s when Nathan Levy secured land for Jewish burial and informal religious services were held. While the first Jewish congregation can be traced to this period, there is no record of the congregation's name, Mikveh Israel, prior to 1773.

The early Jewish residents, most of Sefardic Dutch background, flourished under the liberal influence of the dominant Quakers and played important roles in colonial Philadelphia life. In 1748 Jews were among the founders of the Dancing Assembly, an exclusive social club that still exists.

In August 1752, what was to become the symbol of freedom known as the Liberty Bell arrived aboard the ship *Myrtilla,* owned by Nathan Levy and his partner David Frank, provisioner for the British army during the French and Indian Wars. The bell was cast to commemorate the fiftieth anniversary of William Penn's Charter of Liberties of Pennsylvania.

Jewish patriots, merchants, and financiers were among the leading supporters of the coming Revolution. Mathias Bush, president of Mikveh Israel and leader of the community, was the first merchant to sign the Non-Importation Resolutions against British goods, designed to protest the Stamp Act. Other signatories included Barnard and Michael Gratz, of the same family that later produced Rebecca

Gratz, the beautiful philanthropist thought to be the model for Rebecca in Walter Scott's *Ivanhoe.*

The majority of Philadelphia's Jews supported the Revolution, although a few were Tories and at least one was expelled by the Continental authorities. Mikveh Israel's first rabbi, Gershom Mendes Seixas, was a leading revolutionary patriot. The merchant and banker Haym Salomon helped finance the Revolution. With Levy, the Gratz family, and twenty-one revolutionary soldiers, Salomon is buried in the Mikveh Israel cemetery at Eighth and Spruce streets.

In 1802, German Jews who had broken away from Mikveh Israel formed congregation Rodeph Shalom, making Philadelphia the first city in the Western Hemisphere to house Sefardi and Ashkenazi synagogues. By 1830, the two-minhag community numbered between five hundred and a thousand.

From 1846 to the eve of the Civil War, the city's Jewish community grew from fifteen hundred to eight thousand. As the community leadership passed from descendants of the Sefardic colonists, the mostly German new arrivals found themselves as welcome as their predecessors had been. By 1880, the preponderance of German Jews made the community a fairly homogeneous one of twelve thousand.

Well integrated into community life, the German Jews viewed later Jewish arrivals as embarrassingly backward. But in great waves the Russians came after 1881, bringing the city's Jewish population to seventy-five thousand by 1900 and two hundred thousand by the early 1920s.

COMMUNITY: Metropolitan Philadelphia has a Jewish population of about two hundred and eighty thousand. Despite all the changes it has gone through since the days when it numbered a few hundred, the tone of Philadelphia Jewry's relations with the general community remains what it was in the eighteenth century when Benjamin Franklin organized three lotteries to raise money for the construction of Christ Church. Members of Mikveh Israel were among those who purchased tickets. During the Revolution, Jewish refugees came to Philadelphia from areas of the country occupied by the British and, in 1782, Mikveh Israel dedicated its first real synagogue building to serve the swollen community. When the refugees returned to New York, Charleston, and elsewhere after the Revolution, the small Philadelphia community was left with a big mortgage. Franklin and other Christ Church parishioners participated in the Mikveh Israel lottery to raise the not inconsequential sum of eight hundred pounds.

Aside from social barriers, the pattern of generally smooth relations was seriously disturbed only once, in the 1930s, by the anti-Semitic Father Charles Coughlin, whose Sunday radio broadcasts attracted a small following in the Irish community, and by the strong presence of the German-American Bund. Responding to these threats, city Jews established the Philadelphia Anti-Defamation Council, which evolved into the present-day Jewish Community Relations Council.

Philadelphia Jews have occupied virtually every public office in the city and state, including governor (Milton Shapp), U.S. senator (Arlen Spector), congressman, judge, city council member, and district attorney. Jewish prominence in the business world has continued unabated through the centuries as well. The seven sons of Adam Gimbel, a Bavarian immigrant who settled in Philadelphia, found the renowned department store dynasty in 1894. Albert M. Greenfield was the real estate and banking magnate known for the restoration of Society Hill and other downtown projects.

Philadelphia has had a disproportionate impact on American Jewish life. Local Jews were instrumental in founding the American Jewish Committee and B'nai B'rith. The Jewish Theological Seminary, in New York, was founded by Sabato Morais, an Italian-born Philadelphia rabbi.

Notables include Isaac Leeser, appointed as leader of Mikveh Israel in 1829, who sought to reconcile tradition with American ways, thus becoming a forerunner of Conservative Judaism. (While Orthodoxy and Reform Judaism can certainly be found in Philadelphia, it is today perhaps the most predominantly Conservative of America's major Jewish communities.) Through Leeser's translations of traditional texts, he introduced English into Jewish ritual and founded the *Occident and American Jewish Advocate,* the country's first Anglo-Jewish newspaper.

In 1864, a group of Philadelphia Jews established Maimonides College, the first rabbinical seminary in the United States. Maimonides closed after six years, but one of the founders, Moses Dropsie, later endowed Dropsie College, a nonsectarian institute for graduate study in Judaica and related fields. Rebecca Gratz's brother Hyman endowed what became, in 1897, Gratz College, the first Hebrew teacher training school in America.

Dropsie's first president, Cyrus Adler, also served as president of the American Jewish Historical Society and as librarian of the Smithsonian Institution. In addition, he served as president of Mikveh Israel and the Jewish Theological Seminary and was a founder of both the Jewish Publication Society and the American Jewish Committee.

SIGHTS: As it aged, Philadelphia suffered the fate of many older American cities, but in recent decades much of its colonial real estate has been lovingly restored by community groups and the National Park Service. Mikveh Israel returned to the area after following various Jewish population shifts and now shares quarters at one end of Independence Mall with the Museum of American Jewish History, built during America's Bicentennial. The synagogue and museum building, on Commerce Street between Fourth and Fifth, is just a short walk from Independence Hall and the Liberty Bell. It houses many personal and religious items that belonged to colonial Jews.

Nearby, between Front and Second, is Elfreth's Alley, the oldest colonial street in the city and among the oldest continuously occupied residential streets in the country. Jews have lived on the street throughout its history. Moses Mordecai, a merchant who signed the Non-Importation Resolutions in 1765, lived at No. 118. His widow married Jacob I. Cohen, an Indian trader, peddler, and revolutionary leader, who lived at No. 124. Cohen is thought to be the hero of Stephen Vincent Benet's story "Jacob and the Indians." Cohen's holdings in Kentucky were surveyed by Daniel Boone. German Jews lived on the street close to the city's second synagogue, Rodeph Shalom, in the mid-nineteenth century. With the influx of East European Jews in the 1880s, the street became something of a sweatshop district for the nascent garment industry.

The Walnut Street Theater, at Ninth and Walnut, was built in 1809 and is the oldest surviving theater in the United States. In the early twentieth century, after the Arch Street Theater was razed, Yiddish theater impresario Maurice Schwartz transferred his Yiddish Art Repertory Theater to the facility.

There is a sizable Jewish presence in Society Hill, an area of restored colonial town houses in Center City. Some of the synagogues themselves are in restored buildings and are convenient for visitors staying at downtown hotels. In addition to Mikveh Israel, neighborhood synagogues include the Society Hill Synagogue (Conservative) at 418 Spruce and B'nai Abraham (Orthodox) at 527 Lombard.

On Benjamin Franklin Parkway at Sixteenth Street is the Martyr's Monument to the Jewish victims of the Holocaust. The eighteen-foot bronze sculpture was created by Nathan Rapoport, who designed the monument to the Warsaw Ghetto fighters in Poland, as well as many other memorials in Israel, Europe, and the United States. Dedicated in 1964, the Philadelphia monument was the first in America commemorating the Holocaust.

Outside the colonial area, at 2010 Delancey Place, is the Rosenbach Museum, established by bookseller A. S. Wolf Rosenbach, a president of Gratz College, and his brother Philip. They established a foundation to maintain their nineteenth-century town house as a museum, which houses an eclectic collection of rare manuscripts, fifteenth-century Judaica, art, and books. The museum houses a copy of the Bay Psalm Book of 1640, the first use of Hebrew type in the Western Hemisphere, and the original manuscript of James Joyce's *Ulysses.*

South Philadelphia, now home to many of the city's Italians, and location of the colorful outdoor Italian market, was a port of entry for East Europeans. It featured a thriving Yiddish-speaking Bohemian community and was home at one time to Naphtali Herz Imber, who received two bottles of wine as payment for composing *Hatikva.*

Today Jews are spread throughout the city and suburbs. About a third of Philadelphia's Jews live in "the Great Northeast," a sprawling series of neighborhoods that spreads roughly from Oxford Circle to the Bucks County line. The area includes some of the most identifiably Jewish neighborhoods in the city, especially in the shopping district around Castor and Cottman avenues, with its kosher butchers and other shops.

Jews first moved to the Northeast section in the nineteenth century when they settled a section of Port Richmond that became known, alternately, as "Jewtown" and "Jerusalem." Within two generations, however, they moved to rowhouse developments such as Oxford Circle, Mayfair, and Bustleton. The spread ultimately extended beyond the city limits into Elkins Park, Cheltenham, Abington, and other suburbs. Jewish institutional life followed, as synagogues once closer to downtown relocated. One, Beth Sholom, at Old York and Foxcroft roads in Elkins Park, was designed by Frank Lloyd Wright. The first synagogue designed in the United States by the legendary architect, it is known, at Wright's request, as "The American Synagogue."

Northwest Philadelphia, particularly the Mount Airy and Germantown sections, has in recent years become home to much of the city's Jewish counterculture. The area contains some of the city's most integrated neighborhoods, which are characterized by a high degree of community participation. Jewish life is anchored by the Germantown Jewish Center. A Conservative synagogue, the center is also home to several havura-style minyans which meet in various class-rooms and chapels. The area is also home to B'nai Or, a fellowship which meets for prayer and study under the guidance of Zalman Schachter-Shalomi, a charismatic rabbi and mystic.

The Merion-Wynnefield area straddling Philadelphia and neighboring Montgomery County is home to many Jewish families, as well as a black middle class. Many elderly Jews live in Wynnefield which, along with Overbrook Park, is also home to a thriving Orthodox community. Farther west, the Main Line communities of Bala Cynwyd, Havertown, Wayne, and Wynnewood are home to affluent Jewish families in single-family homes. There are also significant numbers of Jews to the southwest, in Delaware County communities such as Media, Springfield, and Broomall.

On the New Jersey side of the Delaware River, the heaviest Jewish concentration is in Cherry Hill.

Philadelphia has two kosher restaurants, and some hotels can provide kosher TV dinners with advance notice. The European Dairy Restaurant is at Twentieth and Sansom streets in Center City. Pitom Pizza, in the Northeast at 7638 Castor Avenue, delivers.

The Jewish Information and Referral hotline at (215) 893-5821 can provide answers to travelers' questions.

CULTURE: Jewish cultural activities—concerts, films, plays, lectures—are often sponsored by the Jewish Community Centers of Greater Philadelphia, located throughout the city. The most versatile JCC's are the Center City branch, at Broad and Pine (telephone, 545-4400); the Klein branch at Red Lion Road and Jamison Avenue (698-7300); and the Kaiserman branch at City Line and Haverford Avenue (896-7700).

Art and other exhibitions are regularly mounted by the National Museum of American Jewish History (55 North Fifth Street) and the Philadelphia Museum of Judaica at Congregation Rodeph Shalom, 602 North Broad Street.

The Reconstructionist Rabbinical College, located in a former estate at Greenwood Avenue and Church Road in Wycote, sponsors frequent lectures, seminars, and exhibits, as do many of the larger synagogues. Gratz College, at Tenth Street and Tabor Road, sponsors occasional programs. So do the city's two Jewish day schools, Akiba Hebrew Academy, in Merion, and Solomon Schechter, with facilities in Bala Cynwyd and Abington.

The best source of information on Jewish Philadelphia is the *Jewish*

Exponent, a century-old weekly now published by the Federation of Jewish Philanthropies. Providing in-depth coverage of Israeli and American Jewish issues and a variety of features, the *Exponent* is among the best Jewish newspapers in the country.

"The Barry Reisman Show," broadcast on WIBF-FM, 103.9, features Jewish music and topical programming. It is on every day between 3:30 and 5:30 P.M., and Sundays from 9 A.M. to 1 P.M.

PERSONALITIES: Philadelphia is not solely populated by the ghosts of important Jewish figures from centuries past. The twentieth century has also produced its share of prominent Jewish Philadelphians in the arts, business, and politics. William Paley, whose creative and business genius produced the CBS television network, is the son of Philadelphia cigar maker Sam Paley. Former Ambassador to the United Kingdom Walter Annenberg, philanthropist, friend of presidents, publisher of *TV Guide,* and former owner of *The Philadelphia Inquirer,* is also involved in the Jewish life of the city. Siegmund Lubin, who was a rival of Thomas Edison in producing the first motion pictures, was based in the city; a more recent Philadelphia-born filmmaker is Sidney Lumet.

The liberal politics of playwright Clifford Odets, journalist I. F. Stone, and linguist and philosopher Noam Chomsky were the product of Philadelphia upbringings. Two who still make their home in the city are Ted Mann—who has served as chairman of the Conference of Presidents of Major American Jewish Organizations and headed both the American Jewish Congress and the National Conference on Soviet Jewry—and the author Chaim Potok. David Brenner, the comedian, peppers his material with references to his Philadelphia childhood. Two native Philadelphians who made their marks in music are singer Eddie Fisher and jazz artist Stan Getz.

The Pennsylvania Ballet was founded by Barbara Weisberger and the longtime conductor of the Philadelphia Philharmonic was Eugene Ormandy, who had Jewish roots. Three of the city's four major sports teams—the football Eagles, the hockey Flyers, and the basketball 76ers—are Jewish-owned. For much of the last fifteen years the University of Pennsylvania and Temple University have both been headed by Jews.

GENERAL SIGHTS: Throughout the city there are reminders of Jewish contributions to the community at large. The beautiful building housing the Free Library of Philadelphia, located on Benjamin Franklin Parkway at Nineteenth and Vine streets, was dedicated in

1927 while Simon Gratz was the Library's president. Cyrus Adler served as the facility's librarian and later as president.

The Rodin Museum, on the parkway at Twenty-second Street, was endowed in the 1920s by Jules E. Mastbaum, a theater owner who became one of the city's most prominent and generous Jewish citizens.

Also on the parkway, whose sights are easily worth an entire day, is the Academy of Natural Sciences. Located at Nineteenth Street, the Academy was founded in 1812 and is the oldest scientific institution of its kind in the country.

The Franklin Institute, at Twentieth Street, is a popular museum dedicated to the mechanical and applied sciences. Its Fels Planetarium was endowed by Samuel S. Fels, a Philadelphia soapmaker and philanthropist.

At the top of the parkway, at Twenty-sixth Street, is the Philadelphia Museum of Art, an imposing temple-like structure that houses one of the finest collections in the country. It periodically mounts exhibits of Jewish interest, such as the huge 1985 show of Marc Chagall's work that included several pieces from the museum's own collection.

Fairmont Park, one of the largest urban parks in the world, is dotted with mansions that were the homes of Philadelphia's elite as far back as colonial times. A day spent touring the mansions can be a refreshing respite from the city's bustle. Information on docent-led tours is available at local tour agencies or from the city's tourist center at 1425 John F. Kennedy Boulevard. The tourist center is a good stop for information on other city attractions as well.

Fairmont Park is also home to the Philadelphia Zoo, the nation's oldest, and a child's paradise.

DAY TRIPS: Philadelphia is a perfect jumping-off point for a grand variety of day trips in all directions. It is two hours from the Jersey Shore, which includes the casinos of Atlantic City and the quaint atmosphere and restored Victorian houses of Cape May. Along the way, travelers can stop in some of the former Jewish agricultural colonies of South Jersey such as Rosenhayn or Roosevelt. To the west, in Lancaster County, is Pennsylvania Dutch country, home of the Amish. Upstate from the city are the Pocono Mountains, with colorful scenery in any season and a large array of resort hotels, not to mention Jewish summer camps.

READING: *Jewish Life in Philadelphia, 1830–1940* (Institute for the Study of Human Issues), an anthology edited by Murray Friedman, is a

fascinating collection of essays that describe the growth of Philadelphia Jewry. In articles covering such diverse topics as Jewish women
and philanthropy, Irish-Jewish relations, national Jewish leaders born
locally, and conflicts between German and Russian Jews, the book
weaves a detailed portrait.

The Sun in Mid-Career by Christopher Davis (Harper & Row) is a
biographical novel based on the life of Marc Blitzstein, librettist, composer, and creator of such works as *The Cradle Will Rock.* The Davis
book is as good a place as any to start getting to know Philadelphia.

—NEIL REISNER

Prague

Prague's old Jewish Cemetery *(Leni Sonnenfeld)*

Prague is one of Europe's most spectacular cities, a well-preserved showcase of history—and Prague's Jews helped make it so. The city is replete with Romanesque, Gothic, Renaissance, and baroque architecture. And many outstanding examples are in the city's Jewish Quarter.

To the credit of the Communist government, much time, effort, and money have been invested in renovating the castles, monasteries, palaces, cathedrals, and magnificent residences that reflect a millennium of construction. The center of the city has been kept amazingly free of unsightly neon lights, billboards, and twentieth-century highrises. Many streets are still cobblestoned.

This emphasis on history seems to suit the Czechs well. In these often gloomy days, which are difficult economically as well as politically, the local population tends to live a lot in the past. This is a real boon to the Jewish traveler, for the Jewish community of Prague, one of the oldest in Europe, has made very real contributions to the city. And unlike other Eastern Bloc countries, Czechoslovakia has chosen to emphasize the fact.

One of Prague's main tourist attractions is the ghetto, site of the State Jewish Museum complex, which includes five well-preserved ancient synagogues, a remarkable cemetery, Europe's largest and best collection of Jewish religious art (which was the source of "The Precious Legacy" exhibit that toured the United States in 1984), and a tasteful tribute to the 77,297 Czech Jews who died in the Holocaust. The ghetto was, in its day, virtually a separate city, with its own mayor and town hall.

HISTORY: By 1091, Jews were already living in Prague. They probably first arrived as traders, from the east and west, in the middle of the tenth century. The Jews were concentrated in two districts: in the vicinity of the ninth-century Prague Castle, today the seat of the Czech presidency; and near the castle Vysehrad, today a national cultural monument located on the cliffs above the Moldau River and the site of the Church of St. Peter and St. Paul. Also on the Vysehrad site is the "new" Jewish cemetery where many prominent figures of Czech culture are buried, including the writer Franz Kafka.

For the next seven centuries, the size and well-being of Prague's Jewish community fluctuated continually, depending on the goodwill of the ruling regime. The community endured murders at the hands of crusaders, persecution, forced baptism, and banishment; it also flourished during favorable times. During one period in the thirteenth century Jews were granted special privileges by King Premsyl Ottokar II in return for payment of high taxes; this encouraged Jews, especially from Germany, to settle in Prague. The city also became the first north of the Alps where Hebrew books were printed.

Among the illustrious rabbis in Prague was Judah Loew ben Bezalel (1525–1609). Known as the Maharal of Prague, he was a scholar, thinker, author, pedagogic reformer, head of a Talmudic academy, and a mystic to whom the creation of the golem is attributed. The golem, according to legend, was a clay creature who stalked the Jewish Quarter to protect its inhabitants against anti-Semitic attacks until it had to be destroyed. The golem was immortalized by Czech writers Gustav Meyerink in a nineteenth-century psychonovel and by H. Leivick in a 1920 poetic drama which is still part of Israel's Habima Theater repertoire.

Jews were granted equal rights in 1848; the ghetto was abolished four years later and united with the rest of the city. Today it is part of the city's Josefov section. Emancipation saw Jews integrated into the work force, and the process of assimilation and secularization brought them prominence in cultural and literary life. Jewish intellectuals tended to use German and the contribution of Czech Jews to German-language literature was enormous. The group of authors which achieved international recognition as the "Prague Circle" included Kafka, Max Brod, and Franz Werfel. Jewish poets and novelists also contributed to Czech literature. Important scientists taught at Prague universities, including Albert Einstein, who was a professor of physics there from 1910 to 1912. Jews were also among the most celebrated actors of the German- and Czech-language stage. Composer Gustav Mahler, a native of Bohemia, spent several years in Prague as a conductor.

Czechoslovakia was among the first countries to recognize the State of Israel and, during Israel's War of Independence, was one of its chief arms suppliers. But, following the Soviet line, it no longer has diplomatic ties with the Jewish state, and official Czech policies are stridently anti-Israel and anti-Zionist.

COMMUNITY: The Jewish Town Hall at Maislova 18 is headquarters of the remaining Prague Jewish community. Before the Germans invaded in March 1939, there were fifty-six thousand Jews. Three years after the war there were eleven thousand. By 1950, after the Communist takeover, at least half had left for Israel and the West. Approximately three thousand residents of Prague today identify themselves as Jews, but only a few hundred attend High Holiday and Passover services, and only a few dozen come regularly to pray on Shabbat, most of them elderly. Rabbi Daniel Mayer arrived in 1984, the first rabbi to serve the community in twenty years.

Because of the deteriorated relations between Czechoslovakia and Israel, some Jews who frequent the synagogue may be reluctant to speak with visitors from the West. It is known that the synagogue is watched by the Czech secret police. There is a younger generation, however, which has discovered Judaism in recent years; most are the offspring of mixed marriages in which the Jewish spouse was once a loyal Communist. They generally speak some Hebrew (study of Hebrew is not forbidden in Czechoslovakia) and either English or French, and are easy to approach. In this group are people who are trying to emigrate, without much success. Don't be surprised if they suggest meeting in a restaurant or park, and not on the synagogue premises.

SIGHTS: The Jewish Town Hall is easily recognized by the clocks on its tower—one with Roman numerals that runs conventionally, the other with Hebrew letters that runs counterclockwise. The building was refurbished a few years ago with contributions from the American Jewish Joint Distribution Committee.

Most of the Jewish sights in Prague are part of the State Jewish Museum, open daily except Saturday from 9 to 5. Tickets, which cost about fifty cents, can be purchased at the individual buildings and are valid for a week. The services of English-speaking guides are available at the buildings and can also be reserved in advance.

The sixteenth-century Maisel Synagogue, on Maisel Street, houses a fabulous collection of Czechoslovakian Judaica, including 5,400 religious objects of historical value which were brought to Prague from 153 communities by the Nazis, who intended to create a "central museum of the defunct Jewish race." Also displayed there are silver, brass, copper, bronze, tin, and iron crafts, most of them in eighteenth-century baroque and rococo styles. Particularly impressive are the silver Torah breastplates, crowns, headpieces, and pointers, as well as havdalah spice containers, candlesticks, menorahs, and wedding and holiday plates.

The High Synagogue, on Maisel Street, and the Moorish Spanish Synagogue, on Dusni Street, contain the State Museum's textile collection: synagogue curtains, draperies, Torah mantles, and pulpit coverings. The most valuable date from the late sixteenth century and are richly embroidered in gold and silver. The Spanish Synagogue is also noted for its stucco interior patterned after the Alhambra. Still more Judaica, including Hebrew manuscripts, Haggadas, and ketubahs are in the seventeenth-century baroque Klausen Museum.

The Pinkas Synagogue, on Valentinska Street, was completed in 1535, and is an example of late Gothic and Renaissance styles. Originally a private residence, it underwent several reconstructions in the seventeenth century. After World War II, the synagogue became a memorial to the victims of the Nazis; the names of all Czech Jews killed in the Holocaust are inscribed on the synagogue's walls.

The positive attitude of the Czechs toward Prague's Jewish past is dramatized by the permanent exhibit devoted to the concentration camp art rescued from nearby Theresienstadt. The drawings and poems are exhibited in the State Jewish Museum's most contemporary structure, Cemetery Hall, the former ritual hall which adjoins the cemetery, built in pseudo-Romanesque style in the early twentieth century.

The Old Jewish Cemetery, adjoining the ghetto, is one of the most remarkable historical monuments in Prague. Founded early in the fifteenth century, the irregularly shaped ground includes twelve thousand tombstones dating from 1439 to 1787, when a decree ended burials in residential quarters. The Jews of Prague coped with scarce burial space by burying in layers. In some areas, there are as many as twelve burial layers, with the twelve tombstones clustered on top.

Along with the usual inscriptions on the tombstones, there are often poetic epitaphs, reliefs illustrating the name of the deceased (a bear for Dov), his profession (medical instruments, tailor's scissors), and other symbols (hands raised in blessing, Levite jugs, crowns, pine cones, grapes). The oldest tombstone is that of Avigdor ben Isaac Kara, a Prague judge, kabbalist, and poet. Also buried in the cemetery is Mordecai Maisel (1528–1601), mayor of Prague's Jewish town during a cultural renaissance. He built the Maisel Synagogue, the High Synagogue, and the adjacent Town Hall.

Two synagogues belong to the Jewish community. The Altneuschul, located at Cervena 2 and completed in 1270, is the oldest still functioning in Europe, and one of two in Prague where Shabbat and holidays are still observed. In the early Gothic synagogue is the original and official emblem of the community—a Swedish cap in the center of a shield of David—presented by the emperor in 1648 after the Jews' distinguished defense of Prague against invading Swedes. (Despite the popular misconception that "Altneuschul" simply means "old-new" synagogue, it actually takes its name from the Hebrew words *al t'nai,* "on condition." The synagogue was built on condition that when the messianic age arrives it would be torn down and rebuilt, brick by brick, in Eretz Israel.) Prague's other functioning synagogue is the Moorish Revival Jerusalem Synagogue, at Jerusalem 7.

GENERAL SIGHTS: There are many other sites to visit in this picturesque capital, which Goethe called, "the most beautiful gemstone in the world's jewelled crown." There is the Charles Bridge, one of thirteen that span the Moldau River, which is still illuminated at night by ornate lanterns casting a soft glow on the marble statues. The exquisite Tyl Theater is almost as it was when Mozart premiered his new opera *Don Giovanni* there in 1798. Every hour on the hour, as they have since they were created by a whimsical watchmaker in the fifteenth century, twelve apostles march past a skeleton which strikes the time on the Old City Hall's astronomical clock.

Jewish topics, particularly the history and legends of Prague Jewry, became a common theme in the work of non-Jewish authors and artists. The statue of Rabbi Loew stands at the entrance to the new City Hall, and a statue of Moses near the Altneuschul, both works of Czech sculptors commissioned by the Prague municipality.

EATING: The Jewish Town Hall has the city's only kosher kitchen and a large dining room where foreign visitors can eat with local Jews on the eve of every holiday and Shabbat, as well as noon every day except Sunday. The price for guests is approximately $2.50 (25 crowns). Meat is slaughtered by the community's one remaining shohet. Wine and, during Passover, matza, are imported from Israel via Hungary.

There is a restaurant called the Synagogue operated by the State Jewish Museum, but it is not kosher.

RECOMMENDATION: Jewish travelers interested in exploring the ghetto thoroughly and in participating in synagogue services and meals, might consider staying at the Intercontinental Hotel which, although Prague's most expensive, is located right in the Jewish Quarter.

SIDE TRIP: Theresienstadt, which the Czechs call the "Museum of National Suffering," is a short drive from Prague. Originally an old fortress town built by Queen Maria Theresa, its Czech population was evacuated by the Nazis in 1941, who remodeled it the following year into a showcase ghetto—for the Red Cross and other international observers—with Jewish officials and a semblance of community life. Writers, artists, and scholars, wealthy Jews who could buy "protective custody," and German Jewish veterans of World War I were interned there. The showcase, of course, was a sham; 33,500 died at Theresienstadt and 84,500 were shipped from there to other concentration camps.

READING AND FILM: To prepare for a journey to Czechoslovakia, the traveler should try to see two movies: *The Shop on Main Street,* winner of the 1965 Academy Award for Best Foreign Film, based on a novel by the late Ladislav Grossman, describes persecution of Jews in Slovakia during World War II; *Confession,* by Costa-Garvas, re-creates the ordeal of Artur London, one of the Jewish Communist officials seized as a traitor in the Rudolf Slansky plot against the state in 1951.

To get a feel for Jewish life in prewar Prague, two books are recommended: *When Memory Comes* by Saul Friedlander (Farrar, Straus & Giroux) and *Golem* by Gustav Meyerink (Dover). To understand Prague today, read *So Many Heroes* by Alan Levy (Second Chance Press), which vividly describes the rise and fall of the Dubcek government.

Despite the current regime's anti-Israel policies, the Czech people are not considered anti-Semitic by local Jews. To illustrate Czech indifference to religion and race, the story is told of workmen who, during World War II, were instructed by the Nazis to climb to the top of the House of Artists and remove from among the weatherbeaten busts of great composers the head of Felix Mendelssohn. "What does he look like?" asked the workmen. "He is a Jew with a long nose and Semitic features," replied the Nazis. When the Czech workmen returned from the roof they had the bust of Richard Wagner with them.

—JOAN BORSTEN

Rio de Janeiro

One of Rio's beautiful beaches. *(Brazilian Government Trade Bureau)*

Imagine a cosmopolitan city filled with Parisian-style buildings and avant-garde fashion, plunked down on a ribbon of endless beaches with mountains rising up behind them. Add to that samba music and the warm and easygoing spirit of the Cariocas—what the city's residents are called—and you have Rio de Janeiro. No wonder Jews have lived in the city since the sixteenth century and thrived there.

Rio is known for its hospitality and integration of races and nationalities that might clash anywhere else. In fact, it's one of the only cities in the world where Arab and Jewish storeowners have formed an organization to promote their businesses. Its name? S.A.A.R.A.—pronounced like the desert.

HISTORY: When Pedro Alvares Cabral, a Portuguese explorer, landed in Brazil in 1500, he was accompanied by his personal secretary who also commanded the provisions ship—Gaspar da Gama, the first Jew in Brazil. Two years later, a group of Marranos—known as *Cristãos Novos,* or New Christians—arrived to start the export of brazil, a dyewood: hence, the country's name. Another Marrano, Diego Dias Fernando, was one of the first owners of a sugar mill and plantation; others planted the first cotton, rice, and tobacco fields in the country. Gradually, some of the Marranos drifted to Rio de Janeiro and assimilated into the city's population. What is surprising is that today, several descendants of these original Marrano families have discovered their hidden Jewish roots and have converted back to Judaism.

In 1654, the Dutch, who had taken over part of Brazil, were defeated, and the Portuguese demanded that the Jews leave the country. One group of twenty-three Jews fled from the northern port city of Recife to the Dutch colony of New Amsterdam to become the first Jewish settlers of New York.

The first great wave of Jews to arrive again in Brazil did not occur until the 1820s, when religious liberty was established in the country. These Jews came from Morocco and Turkey and settled in the city of Manaus, on the Amazon River, where they traded in rubber. Some left the jungle for the growing city of Rio and started the first Jewish community center in 1846. Known as União Israelita Shel Gemilut

Hasadim, this Sefardic synagogue still thrives today, now located on Rua Rodrigo de Brito 37. Another wave of Sefardic Jews would come from Egypt a century later, after the 1956 Sinai War with Israel.

Jews from Eastern Europe began to arrive in Brazil toward the end of the nineteenth century. Encouraged by Jewish agricultural projects, they settled in farms in the south. Others headed straight for Rio and gathered in the center of the city, around a plaza called Praça XI. By the start of World War II, over thirty-thousand East European Jews had arrived. Some went into typical Jewish retail businesses such as clothing and jewelry. Others started furniture stores; some guess that the Jews must have felt secure enough in Brazil to think about home furnishing. Jews are still active in these industries.

COMMUNITY: The Jewish population of Rio today is about fifty thousand. The other large concentration of Brazilian Jewry is in São Paulo (seventy thousand), and Jewish communities are also found in Recife, Pôrto Alegre, and Belo Horizonte.

In Rio, the Jews are evenly divided among Sefardim and Ashkenazim. And, while there may be Sefardi-Ashkenazi tensions in Israel, none exist in Rio, reflecting the city's melting-pot ethic. Jews, like all other Cariocas, are more fun-loving than their Jewish countrymen in São Paulo. Jewish life in Rio, therefore, tends to be more recreational and beach-oriented and less religiously observant. The Lubavitch hasidic community tried twice to open a Habad house in Rio and failed—while their Habad house in São Paulo does well. As one Carioca Jew observed, "The Jews in Rio are like those in Tel Aviv: on Shabbat, they go to the beach."

Like other Cariocas as well, social life for Jews centers around their clubs. These nonexclusive clubs offer meeting places and facilities for their Jewish members. The largest Jewish club in Rio, Hebraica (Rua das Laranjeiras 346), has a pool, soccer field, a restaurant (albeit nonkosher), and sponsors Jewish cultural events throughout the year.

SIGHTS: Integration into the community was hardly a problem for Rio's Jews, who quickly dispersed throughout the city. The old Jewish neighborhood around Praça XI is gone, but the city's first Ashkenazi synagogue, Beit Yaakov, still stands. It is an imposing white building with a colorful, tiled mosaic of Mt. Sinai and the Ten Commandments on the outside front wall. The synagogue, now called the Grande Templo Israelita, is rarely used, however, since all its members have moved out of the area. Its address is Rua Tenente Possolo 8.

For a look at what the old Jewish neighborhood might have been like, visitors should go to the area around Rua Alfándega in downtown Rio. Here is the heart of S.A.A.R.A., the Arab-Jewish retail organization founded in 1958, linking stores selling everything from rich coffee to sequined and feathered carnival costumes. S.A.A.R.A. members often meet in Restaurant du Nil on Rua Alfándega to eat hummus and pita and discuss business—not politics.

The largest active synagogue in the city is Associação Religiosa Israelita on Rua General Severiano 170. Known as German Liberal, this congregation also has its share of Carioca idiosyncracies: men wear kippot and sit separately from women, but there is a mixed choir and an organ.

The small Orthodox Ashkenazi community in Rio is centered around the Bar Ilan school in—where else?—Copacabana. The five-hundred-student school has a kosher restaurant that serves lunches and Sunday brunches featuring gefilte fish and other traditional Jewish fare. Bar Ilan is also the only facility in Rio to bake and sell hallah and provide kosher catering. The school's phone number is 257-4299 and it is located at Rua Pompeu Loureiro 48. The hospitable school administration can also provide information about Rio's kosher butcher services and mikvah. (The Associação Religiosa Israelita uses an outdoor *mikvah*—the ocean.)

GENERAL SIGHTS: No visitor to Rio can afford to miss the spectacular panorama from the top of Corcovado, the highest hill in the city. This hilltop is also the home of a statue of Jesus with his arms outstretched. At night, the statue is lit and shines like the cross above Montreal. Another view is from the top of Pão de Açúcar (Sugarloaf), which can be reached by cable car and overlooks the beaches of Copacabana, Botafogo, and the Guanabara Bay.

For those who prefer to see the natural beauties of Rio from the ground, there's Tijuca Forest, with innumerable waterfalls and lush greenery. Plant lovers should also tour through the Jardim Botanico, which contains tropical flowers and an abundance of plants and palms.

The former palace of Brazilian Emperor Dom Pedro I is now the Museu Nacional which displays jewels, coins, and uncut stones dating to 1500. More up-to-date art can be found in the Museu de Arte Moderna, whose trustees include Samuel Malamud, a Rio lawyer and the first representative of Israel in Brazil.

The beaches of Copacabana and Ipanema should also be part of a tourist's circuit for a plunge into real Carioca life. Be prepared for the hot sun and the itsy-bitsy, teeny-weeny bikinis. Afterward you can sit at one of the cafés along Copacabana Beach.

CULTURE: The Biblioteca Bialik, at Rua Fernando Osorio 16, (telephone, 245-5272), sponsors a Sunday morning lecture series in Yiddish on literature and other topics. Rio's clubs and synagogues also sponsor cultural events. For further information, call Federação Israelita do Rio de Janeiro at 240-6278.

PERSONALITIES: Turn on Brazilian television, buy a magazine or a book, and chances are you'll be tuning into the multimedia company, Manchete, owned by Adolpho Bloch, who some say is Brazil's Jewish Hearst. Jews are also prominent in acting and music: Teresa Racquel, a leading lady, has her own theater in Rio; Flora Purim is internationally known as a singer and musician. Walter Burle Marx was the founder and long-time conductor of the Rio de Janeiro Philharmonic. The mayor of Rio in the mid-seventies was Israel Klabin, who is still active in Brazilian politics and Jewish affairs. And one descendant of the Morrocan rabbinic Azulay family—founding members of Rio's first Sefardic synagogue, Gemilut Hasadim—is Daniel Azulay, seen every day on Brazilian television in a children's program. Rio was also the final home of Stefan Zweig, one of the most prominent playwrights in prewar Europe, who left Austria in 1935 and, in his depression over the war, committed suicide outside Rio in 1942.

DAY TRIPS: In the mountains surrounding Rio is a small town about an hour away called Petrópolis. It is the site of Dom Pedro I's summer palace, now a museum of art objects and furniture. (Visitors are given slippers to wear so that they won't scratch the floors.) During January and February, Brazil's summer season, Petrópolis has a sizable Jewish weekend population. The city has one synagogue— Sinagoga Israelita Brasileira, at Rua Aureliano Coutinho 48—and the Machane Israel Yeshiva.

If one day trip is by land, another is by sea. You can book passage on a boat that leaves from Rio and tours the tropical islands off the coast of the city. These tours can be arranged at your hotel.

RECOMMENDATIONS: One of the grand old dames of Rio hotels is the Gloria. It used to be right on the water until Rio's government reclaimed land to build a park and highway. The view is still lovely, however. Another grand dame is the Copacabana Palace, right on the beach of the same name. A newer hotel in a newer part of town is the Caesar Park, located on Ipanema Beach and near the trendy clothing stores along Rua Visconde de Pirajá. Less expensive in the same neighborhood is the Sol Ipanema.

WHEN TO GO: Carnival time, usually in late February or early March, is when all of Brazil goes wild: its New Orleans-style Mardi Gras runs nonstop for three days, culminating Brazil's summer and marking the start of Lent. If you want to travel to Rio then, book your trip well in advance. If you prefer to go during a calmer time, you can still catch the carnival spirit at clubs like Asa Branca, Rua Mem de Sá (telephone, 252-4428), which features samba bands and famous Brazilian musicians. You can also attend rehearsals of samba schools, such as Unidos da Tijuca (Rua São Miguel 430). They exhibit the dances to be performed at carnival parades throughout the year. You can dance all night in Rio, as the saying goes, and many Cariocas actually do.

—DIANA KATCHER BLETTER

Rome

Michelangelo's Moses *(Italian Government Travel Office)*

They have seen republics and empires rise and fall, Caesars and popes come and go—but throughout the turbulent centuries, Rome's Jews have maintained their persistent presence along the banks of the Tiber, almost as eternal as the Eternal City itself. Of the approximately thirty-two thousand Jews who live in Italy, twelve thousand live in the capital.

Today, after a two-thousand-year presence, the Jews of Rome are well integrated into the city's irreverent and bustling atmosphere. In the contemporary environment, which casually absorbs ancient ruins and priceless monuments amid snack shops and newsstands, Roman Jews are nonetheless conscious of their special history.

In the shadow of St. Peter's, under the always pervasive, sometimes oppressive, and lately fraternal force of the Vatican, the Jews of Rome have carved out a place for themselves in the life of the city. The descendants of the original Judeo-Italian stock, who later mixed with Sefardic and Ashkenazic immigrants, have always been an adaptive community.

HISTORY: The Jews of Rome constitute the oldest Jewish community in Europe and one of the oldest continuous Jewish settlements in the world. Jews first arrived in Rome in 139 B.C.E. as the Maccabees' emissaries to the Senate. The early ambassadors were followed by enterprising merchants who saw rewarding trading opportunities between Rome and the Middle East. More permanent residents came as Jewish slaves who had been taken prisoner during the military campaigns of Pompey and Vespasian; it was they who established a community across from the Trastevere section (along the right bank of the Tiber River), an area that is still a Jewish neighborhood. Their ranks were swelled by refugees who came to Rome after the fall of Jerusalem in 70 C.E. (Indeed, Roman Jews pride themselves on the historical purity of the Italian liturgy, which they claim is the authentic rite used during the days of the Temple.)

At the height of Roman power, the Jewish community was not simply another diaspora outpost. If a transmillenial parallel can be drawn, it had similarities to the American Jewish community of today.

The empire may have had as many as five million Jews (although the city of Rome probably never had more than forty thousand). They were influential enough to obtain guarantees of personal and religious freedom from Julius Caesar and the Emperor Augustus and prosperous enough to buy the freedom of Jewish slaves brought from Judea.

The Jewish condition began to deteriorate when the emperors adopted Christianity in the fourth century. There was pressure to convert, and periodic anti-Jewish violence. The fortunes of the Jews declined further with the decline of the empire.

After the fall of Rome in 476, the Jewish condition was largely a reflection of papal policy. Though many popes issued anti-Jewish edicts, there was a tendency for such pronouncements to be enforced less strictly in Rome itself than by zealous ecclesiastics abroad. During the eleventh and twelfth centuries there were three "Jewish" popes— Gregory VI, Gregory VII, and Anacletus II, all members of a Roman Jewish family that adopted Christianity in 1030.

After the expulsion of the Jews from Spain in 1492, many exiles came to Rome, where they added their customs to those of the existing Italian community. During the following centuries, Jews also arrived from North Africa, the Middle East, and, after the Holocaust, from Poland and Germany, each group assimilating into the Roman community while maintaining its individuality.

However much a sanctuary Rome may have appeared to Jews fleeing persecution, the history of the Jews in Rome has hardly been characterized by security or serenity. Protected by Julius Caesar and tolerated to various degrees by the emperors who followed, Roman Jews were subjected to the caprices of the later Christian emperors and suffered considerably during the papal period. From the Middle Ages on, various papal bulls restricted the Jews to the trades of moneylending or dealing in old clothes. They were made to wear distinguishing signs on their garments, suffer the deprivation of the study of the Torah (small wonder that the Vatican has one of the world's largest collections of Judaica), and listen to conversion sermons in Christian churches.

During the centuries after their arrival in Rome, Jews had been at liberty to live in the Trastevere or any other section of the city they chose. In 1556, however, Pope Paul IV confined the Jews to the ghetto —an edict that remained in force through 1847. In that narrow scramble of close, crowded streets—remnants of which can be seen today—

extending barely four blocks in either direction, the Jews built "sky-scrapers" of seven or eight stories on top of ramshackle buildings to house their families.

COMMUNITY: After the ghetto was abolished, most of Rome's Jews continued to live nearby, as they do today. Between three hundred and four hundred Jews live in the ghetto area proper. The main addition to the community's native Italian Jews in recent years has been a sizable immigration from Libya. Many of the stores on Rome's Via del Corso are owned by Libyan Jews.

Despite centuries of deprivation and isolation, many of Rome's Jews have achieved prominence. Outstanding Jews include Bruno Zevi, a leading Italian architect, Giorgio Bassani, the author of *The Garden of the Finzi-Continis,* and Alberto Moravia, whose novels include *Two Women,* the film version of which won an Academy Award for Sophia Loren. Other Jews have made their mark in business: the Stock liquor company is owned by a Jewish family and Olivetti, the office equipment firm, is managed by a Jew. And of course, there is a steady stream of Jewish doctors, lawyers, and academics who hold prestigious positions in Roman society. Not surprisingly, perhaps, the Vatican has always had five or six Jewish doctors on call, even during the worst anti-Jewish persecutions.

Some distinguished past residents of the ghetto were Ernesto Nathan, the first Jewish mayor of Rome (1907–13), and Emanuele Conegliano, who wrote the librettos for three of Mozart's operas. In the early part of this century Rome hosted not one but two successive Jewish prime ministers—Sidney Sonnino and Luigi Luzatti.

SIGHTS: Roman Jewish life today is played out against a background of historic sites. Like the rest of Rome, where Renaissance palaces bump up against ancient ruins at almost every turn, Jewish Rome is omnipresent but sometimes invisible to the untrained eye.

The easiest place to discover Jewish Rome is in the ancient ghetto. A ten-minute walk from the Roman Forum, the ghetto lies opposite Tiber Isle (site of the Jewish Hospital and Home for the Aged), just behind the main synagogue. The Via Portico d'Ottavia marks the major boundary of the ghetto, and is still the principal shopping street of the Jewish quarter, with dry goods shops and kosher butchers lining the way.

At one corner of this street, where one of the seven ghetto gates once stood, is a plaque commemorating the two thousand Roman Jews who perished in the Holocaust. A more substantial monument is the Fosse Ardeatine, just outside the Porta San Paolo, a few yards from the synagogue. The monument memorializes 335 Jewish and Christian Romans massacred by the Nazis in 1944.

The synagogue itself, Tempio Israelitico, at Lungotevere Cenci 9, is an imposing and impressive structure that is one of Rome's distinctive landmarks. It was here that Pope John Paul II made his historic visit in April 1986, embracing Rome's Chief Rabbi Elio Toaff and declaring to the Jewish community, "You are our dearly beloved brothers and, in a certain way, it could be said that you are our elder brothers."

Designed by a Christian architect in 1904, the building conveys a sense of Byzantine splendor with its gilded dome and massive structure. Oddly enough, the Orthodox synagogue is in the shape of a cross. A museum attached to the synagogue details Roman Jewish history through displays of documents, scrolls, and religious objects and offers knowledgeable, enthusiastic guides. (Although visiting hours are Monday through Thursday, from 10 A.M. to 1 P.M., as with all things Italian, the schedules are subject to sudden change. Phone ahead—655-051—to avoid disappointment.)

Before you leave the synagogue, which can be viewed on request, walk around to the back. There you can see the bullet holes from the devastating Arab terrorist attack on the synagogue on Shemini Atzeret, October 1982. The event has left scars on this sensitive community; visitors to the synagogue and museum are given a careful security screening.

Diagonally across from the synagogue is a curious church, with Hebrew and Latin inscriptions above the door lintel. Little remains of the building of the Church of St. Gregory (San Gregorio della Divina Pietà) except its puzzling exterior, but it is infamous in Roman Jewish history as one of the churches where the Jews were subjected to weekly conversion sermons during the Middle Ages and after. The Hebrew inscription is from Isaiah: "I have spread out my hands all the day to a rebellious people which walketh in a way that was not good after their own thoughts."

The ghetto, by the way, is not frequented only by Jews. It is where Romans go to buy wholesale clothing and electrical appliances. And the Italian Jewish delicacies of Limentani Settimio, a bakery at Via Portico d'Ottavia 1, are popular throughout the city.

Beyond the confines of the ghetto, the Jewish presence in Rome crops up in unexpected places. In the Church of San Pietro in Vincoli (Piazza San Pietro in Vincoli) is Michelangelo's statue *Moses*, with the horns. The statue, which is the source of the old misconception that all Jews have horns, is based on Michelangelo's misreading of a description of Moses descending from Mount Sinai in the book of Exodus. The Hebrew text says, "Moses' face sent forth beams," but the word for "beams" can, in other contexts, mean "horns."

Although much of the Judaica collection in the Vatican cannot be seen, the walls of the Sistine Chapel feature frescoes of Hebrew Bible stories. There's also the Arch of Titus, which commemorates the capture of Jerusalem and displays bas-reliefs of Jewish captives carrying the spoils of the Temple—the menorah and the silver trumpets.

Most visitors to Rome wouldn't dream of missing the catacombs. But instead of exploring the Christian catacombs just outside the city gates, consider a trip to the Jewish burial sites located along the Appian Way. Formerly under the jurisdiction of the Vatican, as were all the Christian catacombs, since 1984 all the catacombs have been placed under the authority of the Italian Government which, in turn, has given de facto control of the Jewish burial sights to the Jewish community. The main tunnels of the Via Appia Randanini catacomb have burial crypts, stacked three and four high like railroad berths, along both walls. Off the main corridors are family crypts, rooms in which the more prosperous among Rome's Jews reserved space. Some of the family chambers have elaborate decoration—menorahs, palm trees—along with inscriptions in Greek, the *lingua franca* of early Roman Jewry; they also have a lot of more recent graffiti. (A second Jewish catacomb complex, along the Via Torlonia in the northeast of the city, is sealed, but the community eventually hopes to open it.) Check with the synagogue office about tour arrangements, or call the Jewish community offices at 580-3667.

In the gardens of the Villa Borghese, one of Rome's more tranquil and lovely spots, note the walkway named in honor of a Polish Jewish refugee, David Lubin, a businessman and philanthropist who contributed much to Roman life. Even the Coliseum, one of the more popular and certainly one of the most visible tourist attractions in Rome, has Jewish origins. Scholars and historians believe that it was constructed by Jewish slaves, much as were the Egyptian pyramids.

Two guides who offer tours of Jewish Rome are G. Polombo (telephone, 810-3716) and Ruben Popper (761-0901).

SIDE TRIP: For a special day trip, make time for a visit to Ostia Antica, near Leonardo da Vinci International Airport. This ancient port city is about an hour's drive (or forty-minute ride on the Rome subway) from the city and is the site of the oldest known synagogue, built between the first and third centuries. The ruins mark the presence of what was once a prosperous and thriving Mediterranean merchant community of five hundred Jews in a port city that had one hundred thousand inhabitants at the peak of Rome's power. Identified among the ruins are the synagogue's prayer hall, study hall, mikvah, bet din, and an oven for baking matza. The synagogue remains are in the extreme southern corner of the excavations. The adjacent town, Lido di Ostia, is Rome's beach and also has, in virtually every coffee bar in town, Italy's best cappuccino.

After your excursions, relax in the Piazza Navona, a five-minute stroll from the Pantheon, and enjoy the special ice cream dish, concocted by the Le Tre Scalini café, known as *tartufo*—bittersweet chunks of chocolate nestled inside creamy chocolate ice cream.

CULTURE: For information about cultural events, such as lectures, concerts, or plays, check with the Jewish Cultural Center at Via del Tempio 4; telephone, 655 051. Or read about local happenings in *Shalom,* a monthly newspaper.

RESTAURANTS AND HOTELS: A superb place to dine is Luciano's Restaurant, at Via Portico d'Ottavia 16, on the main street of the former ghetto. It is just behind the main synagogue and attracts non-Jewish Romans as well as American tourists. The menu features Italian food, prepared for kosher consumption (although not certified), as well as unusual dishes that are part of the Italian Jews' own cuisine. Many specialties reflect Sefardic and Middle Eastern influences. Try the sumptuous antipasto which features a garlicky eggplant dish and tasty fish salads or the risotto prepared with artichokes, a specialty of the house. Equally appetizing are Italian-style meat dishes, such as veal scallopini or Luciano's version of stuffed cabbage.

There are a few kosher hotels, such as the Pensione Carmel at Via Gioffredo Mameli 11 (telephone, 580-9921), several kosher butchers, a bakery, and a food store, the Makolet, located at Piazza Armellini 6.

READING: To learn more about Rome and its Jews, an ambitious place to start is the classic *The Jewish War* by Flavius Josephus. For a more condensed, yet still comprehensive, treatment, read *Jewish Rome* by Ruth Liliana Geller, published in Italy by Viella and available at the synagogue museum. *Popes from the Ghetto* by Joachim Prinz (Schocken) tells the story of the popes with Jewish ancestry and is also quite evocative of Rome, Christian and Jewish, in the Middle Ages. Some insight into Italian Jewry can be gained by reading the novels of

Moravia and Bassani. The catch is that Bassani's work, though Jewish, is set outside Rome, mostly in his native Ferrara; Moravia's work, like his *Roman Tales,* is evocative of the Italian capital but not Jewish.

—MERRI ROSENBERG

San Francisco

Congregation Emanu-El *(Congregation Emanu-El)*

San Francisco is the city where everyone leaves his heart, a city whose charm is as much man-made as naturally endowed. And since Jews are like everybody else, only more so, they've been attracted to the Bay City right from the start. In fact, when Commander John Drake Sloat sailed with his marines into El Parage de Yerba Buena (the place of the good grass, the future San Francisco) in 1847 during the Mexican-American War, awaiting him there was one Lewis Adler, a German Jew who had converted to Christianity at age nine, selling whale oil barrels, wooden bathtubs, and buckets.

HISTORY: When gold was discovered in the hills of Northern California, Jews came from Europe and the East Coast, making the arduous journey overland or sailing eighteen thousand miles around Cape Horn, to join the new center of commercial activity. While the Jewish forty-niners included a few prospectors and Pony Express riders, most were merchants who sold food and dry goods to the miners and exerted a stabilizing influence on the rough-and-ready town. The first Jewish services on the West Coast were held in a wood-framed tent on Jackson Street near Kearny for Rosh Hashana 1849. By spring of 1851, the forebears of Congregations Sherith Israel and Emanu-El, then both Orthodox, today both Reform, proved the adage—"one hundred Jews, two synagogues."

Sherith Israel's first rabbi was London-born H. A. Henry, while Emanu-El's was Julius Eckman from Germany. When Eckman ran into conflict with his Reform-leaning congregants, he resigned and began to publish *The Gleaner,* the first Jewish weekly in the West.

In 1860, when there were only 150,000 Jews in all of the United States, 5,000 of them lived in San Francisco, comprising 10 percent of the city's population; in 1877, the 16,000 Jews of San Francisco constituted the second largest community in America. In the open and egalitarian society of the West, Jews faced little anti-Semitism and prospered quickly. The peddlers and tradesmen soon transformed themselves into department store magnates (the founders of Gumps, I. Magnin, and Joseph Magnin were all Jewish), blue-jean empire builders (Levi Strauss, today the Haas family), seal and fur traders, and real estate developers. Make it they did in civic life as well: Elkan and Isaac Cardozo were elected to the first state legislature; Washington Bartlett was an early mayor of San Francisco and governor of California; Adolph Sutro, the engineer and bibliophile, was another mayor; Michael and Charles de Young founded the *San Francisco Chronicle*. Jessica Blanche Peixotto was the first woman professor at the University of California at Berkeley; Florence Prag Kahn, the first Jewish Congresswoman. Alice B. Toklas and Gertrude Stein both had San Francisco roots. More recent Jewish personalities born in or associated with San Francisco include Rube Goldberg, the Pulitzer Prize-winning cartoonist noted for his madcap machines; Irving Stone, the author; and Herb Caen, whose column in the *San Francisco Chronicle* is perhaps the most widely read in the Bay Area.

COMMUNITY: The social acceptance of San Francisco's Jews may explain the absence of an old ethnic Jewish neighborhood comparable to New York's Lower East Side. Though they left their mark on the city with many public monuments, the early Jews didn't cluster in one area. The pattern continues among contemporary San Francisco Jewry: individual prominence combined with a low-key community profile. The city again has a Jewish mayor—Dianne Feinstein—but the Bay Area still doesn't have a strong Jewish fulcrum of shuls, communal agencies, kosher butchers, restaurants, and bookstores.

Subsequent waves of immigration—from Eastern Europe around the turn of the century, from Germany in the 1930s and '40s, most recently from Russia—combined with a continuing influx from the East Coast and the Midwest, have given the Bay Area its present demographic makeup. Many San Francisco Jews today live in the Golden Gate, Richmond, and Sea Cliff districts, but you'll find Jews everywhere in the Bay Area—from the hills of Marin, to the Petaluma chicken farms (founded around the turn of the century by Russian Jewish socialists), to the newer East Bay suburbs of Concord and Lafayette, and the peninsula towns down to San Jose. The San Francisco side of the bay has about eighty thousand Jews, while Alameda and Contra Costa counties across the Bay Bridge account for another thirty-five thousand. San Jose at the tip of the peninsula has an additional eighteen thousand Jews.

"There is no homogeneous Bay Area Jewish community," writes San Francisco historian Irena Narell. "It is a series of communities." Add to the geographical dispersion the California tendency to "do your own thing," and it is easy to see why this area is where many of the "lost generation" came to get lost. But the vaunted California individualism cuts two ways: while many fall between the cracks of the organized Jewish community, new institutions and experiments in creative Jewish living flourish. Berkeley, which probably takes the prize for individualism and experimentation, abounds with small minyans and batim (student houses), ranging from the countercultural Aquarian Minyan to the long-established Habad House near the campus.

SIGHTS: Even the standard tourist circuit will include a number of the cultural legacies that early civic-minded Jews bequeathed to San Francisco. In Golden Gate Park, for instance, there is the M. H. de Young Memorial Museum, the patrician of San Francisco art museums, with a fine collection of Old Masters. Across the park is Steinhart Aquarium, another Jewish legacy, which houses some 14,500 species of reptiles, marine animals, and fish, and includes a hands-on section where kids can pet the starfish. (And when you cross the Golden Gate Bridge, keep in mind that it was built by a Jew, Joseph Baerman Strauss, with help from consultant Leon Solomon Moisseiff.)

Not far from Golden Gate Park, at Arguello and Lake streets, stands a gem of synagogue architecture, the magnificently domed Temple Emanu-El, with its Byzantine-cum-California styling. Completed in 1927 to replace the Sutter Street Temple, which was gutted in the earthquake and fire of 1906, it was designed by architect Arthur Brown, Jr. It combines Byzantine features such as its great red cupola, suggestive of the Hagia Sophia in Constantinople, and antique marble columns, with such California touches as open patios. The centerpiece of the sanctuary is the free-standing Ark with thick bronze doors and jewel-encrusted walls covered with the symbols of the twelve tribes of Israel.

Temple Emanu-El has an illustrious history as well as an ambitious architectural design. Back in the 1920s, when the temple was being built and for a half century thereafter, the congregation was served by Cantor Reuben Rinder, a Jewish musical innovator who not only composed and performed himself, but was the discoverer of Yehudi Menuhin and Isaac Stern. It was Rinder who commissioned Ernst Bloch's *Avodath Hakodesh*, a rendition of the Sabbath service in contemporary music.

Another historic synagogue, much humbler in appearance is Temple Beth Sholom in San Leandro (642 Dolores Avenue), south of Oakland. Here the rough-hewn one-room synagogue which dates back to pioneer days has been preserved on the grounds of the newer temple.

If California Jewish history is your hobby, the place to explore it is the Western Jewish History Center, which is part of the Judah L. Magnes Museum in Berkeley. The center is an archival research library concentrating on the achievements of Jews and Jewish institutions in the West, and includes Anglo-Jewish newspapers going back to 1860, oral histories of western Jewish personalities, and the archives of Zionist leader Judah L. Magnes. The museum's namesake is perhaps Oakland's most famous Jewish son—the first rabbi born west of the Mississippi; a founder of Hebrew University in Jerusalem; and a friend of Henrietta Szold and Hadassah.

The Magnes Museum, founded in 1962, is housed in the lovely wood-shingled Burke mansion at 2911 Russell Street in north Berkeley. It is the oldest and probably the foremost Jewish museum in the western United States. Its permanent collection includes Jewish ceremonial objects, an extensive collection of coins and medals, and Holocaust artifacts. Especially worth seeing is its large collection of Torah binders (wimples) and other textiles and costumes from North African and European Jewish communities. The Magnes also contains a Judaica library of some seventy-five hundred books and periodicals, including the Lowdermilk records of early agricultural efforts in Palestine.

Another Judaica library of note in the Bay Area is the Sutro Collection housed in the Gleason Library at the University of San Francisco. Adolph Sutro was an obsessive book collector, and when he died, he had the largest private library of his day, with approximately a quarter million items, which he willed to the state of California. Among his treasures was an extensive collection of Hebrew and medieval Judeo-Arabic manuscripts. Unfortunately, almost half of his collection was destroyed in the 1906 earthquake and fire, but the remainder still make up the foremost collection of medieval Jewish manuscripts in the West.

In 1984, San Francisco became home to a new Jewish community museum, located in the Jewish Federation building (121 Steuart Street, near Market). Its first exhibit, created by Beit Hatefutsot (the Diaspora Museum) in Tel Aviv and mounted in cooperation with the local Chinese community, was "The Jews of Kaifeng."

A sculpture by George Segal, installed in Lincoln Park in 1984 as a Holocaust memorial, has become both a work of public art and a community rallying spot. *The Holocaust,* a bronze work depicting ten bodies heaped on the ground with a figure standing nearby in prison clothes, peering through a barbed-wire fence, was spray-painted by vandals only four days after it went up. The vandals painted the white figures black and wrote the words "Is this necessary?" The community, infuriated by this act, posted a guard at the memorial at night (an anonymous donor sends fresh flowers daily) and now uses the spot for communal gatherings.

Many tours of the Bay Area include a trip to wine country. If you want to add kosher wineries to your itinerary, you can try the Yayin Corporation, makers of Gan Eden wine, in Sebastopol; HaGefen in Napa; Kedem, which leases facilities from Italian Swiss Colony in Asti; and Winestock in Cloverdale.

Off the beaten path for Jewish sightseers is the Hills of Eternity Jewish Cemetery in Colma, where Wyatt Earp is buried beside his Jewish wife, Josephine Marcus Earp. Colma is just south of San Francisco and the cemetery is between El Camino Real and Hillside Boulevard. You may have difficulty finding the gunslinger's grave, however, because curiosity-seekers keep stealing the grave marker. Incidentally, if tombstones interest you, there are quite a few old Jewish ones in the Sonoma Jewish cemetery north of San Francisco, which dates back to gold-rush days.

CULTURE: One of the perpetual delights of Bay Area life is the ubiquitous artists and craftsmen—displaying their wares in boutique-y shops in Sausalito or Palo Alto, or in the open air on Berkeley's Telegraph Avenue, performing on street corners, creating street theater. So it is natural that the area should be fertile ground, too, for Jewish artists who experiment with a wide variety of media and modes. In an attempt to harness the many independent creative endeavors, a Jewish artists' network, J.A.C.O.B., Jewish Arts Community of the Bay, came into being. J.A.C.O.B. (121 Steuart Street, Suite 402) is the brainchild of J. Picheney, whose first name just happens to be Jacob. Omanim, the visual artists' division of J.A.C.O.B., mounts periodic exhibits of Jewish crafts.

Theatre Pardes, an innovative three-person troupe, is permanently based in San Francisco, where it performs three months out of the year—when it is not traveling around the country. This highly original dramatic group performs new works of its own creation. Company members do not start with a script in the traditional sense, but take a legend or theme from Jewish folklore and spin it out into a performance. Pardes also runs workshops and classes for the public.

The Berkeley Jewish Theater is a repertory company that works out of the Jewish Community Center of Berkeley-Richmond at 1414 Walnut. Berkeley, too, is the home of the Klezmorim, a six-man brass and percussion ensemble, which has been reviving the folk-based klezmer music of Eastern Europe. They have received national attention since a Carnegie Hall performance in 1983 and a Grammy nomination for their album, *Metropolis.*

Deborah Kaufman runs a Jewish film festival which screens movies in theaters around San Francisco and Berkeley. She also has an information bureau on films of Jewish content. For information call (415) 548-0556.

Intellectual life, like artistic creativity, is fertile and free-style in the Bay Area. The Hillel Foundation at the University of California at Berkeley (2736 Bancroft Way) runs a Lehrhaus Judaica program which offers a wide range of courses, some for college credit and some lishma (for their own sake). This successful educational experiment, under the direction of Fred Rosenbaum, has been "exported" to San Francisco State College and Stanford.

Congregation Beth Shalom in San Francisco, at Fourteenth Avenue and Clement Street, has a stimulating endowed lectureship series which brings international as well as local personalities to speak. Temple Emanu-El also offers a popular adult education program. The Bureau of Jewish Education (639 Fourteenth Avenue) presents lectures and films of Jewish content.

For Jewish books there is Bob and Bob's in Palo Alto (151 Forest Avenue) and Liebers bookstore (3240 Geary Boulevard) in San Francisco.

RECOMMENDATIONS: Playing host to some three million tourists a year, San Francisco abounds with good hotel accommodations in every price range. In the luxury class, located in the middle of the stately downtown district, near Union Square and Nob Hill, is the Fairmont Hotel, a citadel of tradition yet thoroughly modern. Its original seven-story structure withstood the 1906 earthquake but was gutted in the resulting fire.

If you prefer a neighborhood atmosphere and a budget price, there is the El Drisco in lovely Pacific Heights. The decor is comfortable Victorian, the ambiance bohemian, and many rooms have wonderful views of the city.

EATING: In downtown San Francisco one can sample Moroccan Sefardic cuisine at the Marrakech Palace restaurant (419 O'Farrell Street, 776-6717). In keeping with the Bay Area's tradition of pluralism, there are two kitchens here—one kosher and one not—as well as a belly dancer.

If you want to sample San Francisco's Chinese cuisine and still stay within the bounds of kashrut, try the Lotus Garden restaurant, in the heart of Chinatown. There are also two vegetarian Chinese restaurants: Shangri-La in San Francisco's Sunset District, and Vegi Food, which has outlets in both San Francisco and Berkeley.

READING: Local Jewish historians have in the past few years produced several carefully researched and lovingly written histories of the Bay Area. Irena Narell in *Our City: The Jews of San Francisco* (Howell-North Books) traces the success stories of the early pioneer families—their interlocking family trees and their remarkable achievements. This book does for San Francisco what *Our Crowd* did for the Eastern aristocracy. Fred Rosenbaum has chronicled the history of Oakland Jewry in *Free to Choose: The Making of a Jewish Community in the American West* and the development of Temple Emanu-El in *Architects of Reform,* published by the Western Jewish History Center of the Magnes Museum in Berkeley. For a fictional look at the way Jewish San Franciscans were, read the Howard Fast trilogy—*The Immigrants, The Second Generation,* and *The Establishment* (Houghton Mifflin). For a portrait of one of San Francisco's most colorful characters, Joshua Norton, see William Drury's *Norton I: Emperor of the United States* (Dodd, Mead).

MISCELLANEOUS: It should not come as a surprise to anyone familiar with San Francisco that the Bay City has a gay synagogue, but now it has two. The original congregation split, proving again the old San Francisco adage: "one hundred Jews, two synagogues."

There has been an attempt in the past few years to consolidate a few community institutions around Menorah Park, located in back of the San Francisco Jewish Community Center at 3200 California Street. A new community mikvah has been built there, and subsidized housing for senior citizens and Russian immigrants is being built nearby.

The mikvahs in the East Bay are at Beth Jacob Congregation in Oakland and another on Waring Street in Berkeley (845-7791).

The San Francisco Bay Area has been in the vanguard of every cultural revolution and Jews have been in the forefront of each new wave in recent decades. In the fifties, when the beat generation poets were gathering in San Francisco, Allen Ginsberg was there writing

Kaddish. In the sixties, when the flower children came to Haight-Ashbury, Rabbi Shlomo Carlebach set up the House of Love and Prayer nearby to attract Jewish spiritual seekers. In the seventies, when political activism was the word of the day, the Berkeley Union of Jewish Students and its newspaper, *The Jewish Radical,* were born. In the eighties, when creative individualism and small community clusterings seem to be on the rise, the Bay Area is full of Jewish art and communal experiments. If you want to know what's happening next in the Jewish world, take a trip into the future by visiting the beautiful Bay Area.

—ROSELYN BELL

São Paulo

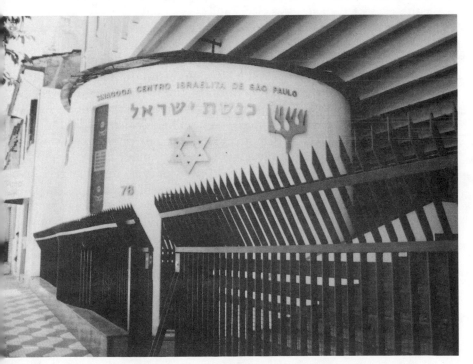

Sinagoga Centro Israelita Paulista *(Phyllis Ellen Funke)*

At the entrance to Ibirapuera Park, São Paulo's great patch of urban greenery, stands a mammoth stone statue depicting a boat being transported over land. Before the bow prance some jaunty riders on horseback; at the stern are men pushing with all their might. The statue honors the *bandeirantes,* the pioneers who created a nation in Brazil's uncharted vastness; the boat represents the ship of state. And, in the eyes of Paulistas—as São Paulo's residents are called—those traveling on horseback are the fun-loving citizens of Rio de Janeiro, while those doing the heavy work are the Paulistas.

Indeed, intercity rivalries notwithstanding, São Paulo *is* the dynamo of Brazil. The largest and richest metropolis in South America, it is the commercial and industrial center of Brazil, not to mention the heart of its cultural life. This sprawling city, with skyscrapers sprouting everywhere, manufactures cars, textiles, steel, rubber, cement, paper, and a host of other products. It also offers Paulistas a myriad of nightclubs, restaurants, theaters, and museums when they play.

São Paulo, in existence since 1554, owes its drive today largely to the immigration of the last one hundred and fifty years. It sought industrial rather than agricultural workers, and it got them—more Italians than in Venice, more Lebanese than in Beirut, and the most Japanese in a community outside Japan. Not for nothing is one of the main highways leading to São Paulo named for these immigrants and, not surprisingly, among the city's staunchest boosters are Paulista Jews.

HISTORY: The first Jew in Brazil arrived with its Portuguese discoverer, Pedro Alvares Cabral, in 1500. He was Gaspar da Gama, a New Christian, or Marrano, and he led the way for the large number of Marranos who followed. According to Anita Novinsky, a specialist on New Christians, at the University of São Paulo, "Brazil was made by Jews." She notes that colonial Brazil was agricultural and that 60 percent of the sugar plantations were owned by Marranos, who brought the sugar cane from Madeira. They were also deeply engaged in the slave trade. Bento Texeiro (Pinta), a New Christian, wrote "Prosopopeia," the first poem composed in Brazil.

Some Marranos moved to São Paulo, in southern Brazil, to get far away from the Inquisition's headquarters in the north. Scholars claim that they assimilated quickly and thoroughly, thus erasing Jewishness from the Brazilian scene until the nineteenth century. But evidence of jungle tribes who light Friday night candles and don't eat pork and the appearance at one São Paulo synagogue alone of at least one Catholic a month searching for Jewish roots seem to belie this.

Novinsky notes that despite claims that Brazil is the largest Catholic country on earth, its Catholicism is weak, in part because of its Marrano heritage. "This was a country of heretics," she says. "Because of the Jewish involvement, it is a peculiar civilization. Brazilians have a different approach to life and religion. They are not Orthodox; they are very liberal—because Judaism left its roots in the mentality."

This, then, was the climate that Jews from Alsace-Lorraine found when they began immigrating to São Paulo in the mid-nineteenth century. At first, only individuals came, but after the Franco-Prussian War of 1870–71, groups started arriving. It wasn't until the century's end, however, that they started organizing as Jews.

Waves of immigrants came to São Paulo in the new century, and Jews joined this flood—not only from Eastern Europe, but also from Syria, Lebanon, and North Africa.

By the 1920s, both the Ashkenazim and Sefardim had established communal organizations. After the Nazis took power in 1933, many Jews came from Germany, Austria, Czechoslovakia, and Italy and, in 1936, the Germans, primarily, founded what was to become São Paulo's most important synagogue, Congregação Israelita Paulista (CIP), in the liberal tradition. Other substantial immigrations followed World War II—those of the Hungarian Revolution and Sinai campaign, both in 1956. Jews from Argentina, Chile, and Uruguay have arrived more recently.

Because of the diversity of Brazilian society and its liberal background, there has been little anti-Semitism in the country. Some developed during the dictatorship of Getúlio Vargas, 1930–45, and restrictions were placed on Jewish immigration. But despite Josef Mengele and other Nazis having been hidden in the environs of São Paulo, the Jews of the city do not feel affected by it and are dumbfounded that their haven could have harbored such evil.

Even under military rule, the Jewish community fared well; indeed, Brazil's newly established democracy may prove a greater problem because it allows room for extremists. However, at this time, the feeling is that the primary threat to Paulista Jewry is the absence of threat.

COMMUNITY: Of Greater São Paulo's thirteen million people, seventy-five thousand are Jewish—more than half of all those in Brazil. Vibrant, outgoing, proud of being Jews and Paulistas, these generally affluent Brazilians can be found in virtually all fields of endeavor. About half are in trade; a quarter are in industry; the rest are in communications, construction, education and health services, politics, and the arts.

Jewish families own Brazil's two biggest publishing companies, the Safra Bank, Brazil's sixth largest, and its two largest jewelry concerns, H. Stern and Amsterdam Sauer. Leon Feffer, one of Brazil's ten wealthiest men, who is responsible for 50 percent of the country's paper production, is a Paulista. So are Jacobo Lerner, the principal owner of the São Paulo Hilton; Marcos Lazaro, a top impresario; Etty Frazer, Brazil's Julia Child; Mario Adler, Latin America's premier toymaker; and Déborah Bloch, the latest sex symbol in Brazil's films. Even Brazilian argot has been affected by Jews, since Petitstyl, the name of a Jewish-owned chain of children's clothing stores, has entered the language as a word of teasing.

São Paulo boasts about twenty synagogues, but only a handful are active. They range from Reform to Lubavitch—which runs young people's programs that attract people from all segments, including, on occasion, those who are habitués of Régine's, the Gallery, and other "in" nightspots in São Paulo. About 60 percent of Jewish Paulistas are Ashkenazim. CIP, with a two-thousand-family membership, is the largest congregation on the continent. The other leading Ashkenazic synagogues are Templo Beth-El (Rua Avanhandava 137-Esquina Rua Martinho Prado 128, telephone, 256-8671) and Sinagoga Centro Israelita (Rua Newton Prado 76, telephone, 220-0185).

The primary Sefardic synagogues are Ohel Yaakov and Beit Yaakov (Rua Bela Cintra 801, telephone, 256-3115). The Sefardi and Ashkenazi groups experience their tensions, but mix socially, professionally, and, according to CIP's Rabbi Henry I. Sobel, even religiously with his congregation, now including Sefardim. (CIP, in its attempt to serve the community at large, has an Orthodox minyan and takes public stands on such issues as human rights and interfaith action.)

São Paulo's Jews support the Hospital Israelita Albert Einstein, considered the best in the country, if not on the continent. Jewish Paulistas send their children to four Orthodox and four secular Jewish schools. (There are three thousand students in the Instituto de Educação Hebraico Brasileiro Renascença, Rua Prates 790.) The social club, A Hebraica, with a membership of over twenty thousand, is one of the largest in the world.

Jewish publications include the Portuguese-language national bi-monthly *Resenha Judaica* and monthly *O Hebreu, Menorah, Shalom,* and *Sefaradi Magazine.*

CULTURE: Every Sunday, at 11 A.M. on São Paulo's Channel 11, there is "Programa Mosaico," featuring community news and interviews with outstanding Jews. While most Jewish cultural activities—such as theater and Israeli dance programs—take place within the synagogues and clubs, there is a Casa da Cultura Judaica (Jewish cultural house), which sponsors debates, folk dancing classes, and other activities.

SIGHTS: Jewish Paulistas give the impression that they are far too busy *doing* things to spend time contemplating them. Ask for sightseeing suggestions for the Jewish traveler and the response is a quizzical, "What could you possibly mean?"

One Jewish institution worth visiting is the club, A Hebraica. Except for the absence of sleeping quarters, it resembles a self-contained resort community, complete with swimming pools, tennis courts, indoor gyms, a theater, dance studio, ballroom, library, synagogue, art gallery, several snack bars and restaurants (including a kosher one), bank, barber shop, and multilevel park areas with tree-lined walkways —all within the confines of the city. Jewish tourists may enter by showing their passports at the entrance; members of other Jewish organizations may, for a fee, use certain facilities. The club is located at Rua Hungria 1000.

On the northern fringe of central São Paulo is Bom Retiro (Good Retreat)—the old Jewish neighborhood. In this well-worn but well-kept area of low buildings and little shops, the Jews began, as one person put it "in the shmatte business." And still today, with Koreans moving in, there is a concentration of clothing and textile stores bearing names like Naomi, Rachel, and Apelbaum.

Here, too, are the offices of *O Hebreu,* on Rua Mamore 570, across the street from a tiny hasidic synagogue, whose rebbetzin appears on the balcony to chase away trespassers. Nearby, at the "V" formed by Rua Correa dos Santos and Rua Da Graça, is a larger, more modern synagogue, Sinagoga Israelita do Bom Retiro, its two main walls coming nearly together, like the Allied Chemical Building's on Times

Square in New York, to present a panel covered with Jewish motifs. The grillwork on its windows also forms Magen Davids.

At Rua Ribeiro de Lima 604 is Weltman's Papeis and Livros Ltda. (stationery and bookstore), with Hebrew-Portuguese dictionaries and titles like *Presença e Integração" (Presence and Integration: The Contribution of the Jews to the Life and Progress of Brazil)* and *Judeus de Bombachas e Chimarrão (Riding Chaps and Brazilian Tea),* about Brazil's Jewish cowboys.

Most of Bom Retiro's Jews have moved on to neighborhoods like Brás, in the north-northeast, and Jardims, in the south-southwest, and many have places at Guarujá, a fashionable coastal resort an hour away, whose buildings were constructed almost entirely by Jews.

The Jews of São Paulo are particularly proud of Albert Einstein Hospital, which opened in 1971. It symbolizes, for them, their integration into the São Paulo community. The hospital is south of São Paulo's business center in the Morumbi area, known for glorious, though well-hidden, private estates. The street on which it is located, Albert Einstein, intersects another street named Fighters of the Ghetto (Rua Combatentes do Gueto). (Other streets in the city are named for the State of Israel, Habad, and Horacio Lafer, a former Jewish finance minister of Brazil.) To visit the hospital, call 240-33-22.

GENERAL SIGHTS: With its bustle, São Paulo offers more atmosphere than specific sights. Some of its special flavor can be enjoyed browsing in those ethnic neighborhoods that retain their traditional character. One is Barrio Oriental, with its colonies of Japanese, Chinese, and Koreans, in the streets adjacent to Rua Galvão Bueno in the Liberdade district; another is Barrio do Bixiga, with its Italian colony, in the streets adjacent to Rua 13 de Maio.

Another good pastime is to window-shop in one of the city's vast, architecturally intriguing shopping centers. Among those worth a look are Shopping Center Eldorado (Avenue Reboucas 3970, Pinheiros), and Shopping Center Ibirapuera (Avenue Ibirapuera 3103, Moema).

Check out the flea market in Praça da Republica on Sundays from 8 A.M. to 1 P.M. or take a stroll in Ibirapuera Park. While there, stop in at the cavernous building that, every other year, houses the city's huge art show, the Bienal; the Museum of Contemporary Art is located in the park as well. The Lasar Segall Museum has a fine art collection, although, despite its name, it has nothing particularly Jewish.

BOOKS: If you want to do your homework and read up on Brazil and its Jews before getting there, try *The Jews in Colonial Brazil* by Arnold Wiznitzer (Columbia University Press) and *Masters and the Slaves: The History of Brazil* by Gilberto Freyre (Knopf). To get the flavor of South American myth and fantasy in a novel on Jewish experience, read *Centaur in the Garden* by Moacyr Scliar (Ballantine).

RECOMMENDATION: The São Paulo Hilton, in the heart of town, is a fine hotel, and will be happy to make arrangements for kosher meals. What is more, its public relations director, Roberto da Veiga, is knowledgeable about the Jewish community and will answer all your questions. Few cities offer as convenient a source for the Jewish traveler.

—PHYLLIS ELLEN FUNKE

Stockholm

General View *(Stockholm Information Service)*

A historic Old City of narrow, twisting cobbled streets lined with churches, shops, and restaurants, sunk in the middle of a strikingly modern city of skyscrapers and superhighways: no, it's not Jerusalem that's being described, but Stockholm. True, Gamla Stan, Stockholm's Old Town, isn't old by Jerusalem's standards; it's only medieval; located on three small islands, it is water, not a wall, that divides it from the new city. But its soft, pastel hues and its seamless blending of historic sites and trendy shops make it one of the most picturesque old/new cities around.

HISTORY: The Jewish presence in Stockholm is relatively modern, too, as diaspora communities go. The first Jew to settle in Stockholm, a gem cutter and seal engraver named Aaron Isaac, arrived in 1774, over a century after the first Dutch Jews arrived in old New Amsterdam. A year later, the Jewish community came into being when the formal right of residence was extended to Isaac, his business partner, and their families. By 1780, the first rabbi, Levin Hirsch Levi, had arrived from Strelitz, in Germany; a few years later, he asked for and received the title of Chief Rabbi of Sweden, a title held by all subsequent rabbis of the Stockholm community.

Emancipation began in 1838, the year Swedish authorities reorganized the Jewish community, granting citizenship in exchange for an end to communal autonomy. Jews became eligible to own property in 1860, to vote in 1866, and to stand for elective office in 1870.

Until the middle of the nineteenth century, most Jews who immigrated to Sweden came from Germany and were bankers, engravers or textile and tobacco merchants. The German Reform movement was strong among them. Assimilation took its toll, and most of Sweden's first Jewish families disappeared through intermarriage or low birth rates.

After 1860, a wave of Eastern European immigrants, more traditional than their predecessors, arrived. As in America, some tensions developed between the two groups, and at the beginning of the twentieth century, the Jewish community of Stockholm tried to persuade the Swedish Government to encourage the East European immigrants to leave Sweden. A similar incident occurred in the thirties, when Stockholm's Jewish community, fearing native anti-Semitism, tried to discourage other Jews from coming to Sweden. This prompted the Swedish Minister of Welfare to state that "the Swedish Government, with regard to letting Jews come into the country, was at least as generous as the Jewish community in Stockhom."

Although at first Swedish student groups and unions opposed loosening immigration quotas, when the Nazi policy of genocide became apparent, both the Jewish community and the Swedish Government rallied behind the rescue movement. By the outbreak of World War II, three thousand Jews had found refuge in Sweden and another thousand had passed through Zionist hakhsharah camps on their way to Palestine. After the German invasion of Norway in 1940, some seven hundred to nine hundred Jews managed to escape over the border. Their presence turned Swedish public opinion decidedly in favor of rescue, and the Swedish Government offered asylum to fleeing Danes —Jews and non-Jews alike. In a dramatic nighttime rescue effort, nicknamed "Little Dunkirk" for its use of small civilian boats under the cover of darkness, some 93 percent of Danish Jewry (about seven thousand people) were ferried across the channel to Sweden. During the war years, Sweden became a center for the dispatch of food packages to concentration camp inmates, under the direction of the World Jewish Congress. Near the end of the war, another thirty-five hundred Jews were rescued directly from concentration camps through the efforts of Count Folke Bernadotte, a Swedish diplomat in Hungary. (It is one of history's bitter ironies that Bernadotte, while trying to mediate the Arab-Israeli conflict in 1948, was assassinated in Jerusalem; the Israeli Government suspected the extremist Sternists, but no one was ever convicted of the murder.)

But the greatest rescuer of them all, and the first non-Jew to receive honorary Israeli citizenship as a righteous gentile, was Raoul Wallenberg. This by-now legendary figure went to Budapest in July 1944 at the behest of several Jewish organizations as an attaché to the Swedish Embassy. There he worked tirelessly and unconventionally to save Jews from deportation to the camps, by issuing Schutzpasse, passports claiming the bearer was under the protection of the Swedish Government, and by setting up "free houses" where Jews could take refuge under the flag of neutral countries. He risked his life to pull Jews off deportation trains and is credited with saving thousands of Jews from certain death. When the Russian Army liberated Budapest,

Wallenberg was taken east and was sighted in the Russian Gulag in the early fifties. Though the Swedish Government inquired about him to the Soviet authorities, it was anxious to preserve its neutral status and did not press the matter; whether Wallenberg is still alive remains unknown.

After the war, most of the Jewish refugees from Norway and Denmark returned home, but the rest stayed on, making Sweden the only European country to double its Jewish population after World War II. (There were six thousand Jews in Sweden in 1933 and fourteen thousand in 1970.) Later waves of Jewish immigration came from Hungary after the 1956 revolution and from Poland after an outbreak of anti-Semitism in 1968.

COMMUNITY: About eight thousand Jews live in Stockholm, of whom about five thousand belong to the organized Jewish community (Judiska Församlingen). Membership in the community requires the payment of a 2.4 percent tax levied bimonthly, and allows one to vote for the twenty-five-member Board of Deputies, elected every three years. Members benefit from social, religious, educational, and cultural programs and are represented by the board to the government and the non-Jewish community.

Jews are scattered throughout the city and well integrated into the general society. Intermarriage is high—estimated at between 40 and 60 percent—a figure typical for all of Scandinavia. But the intermarried are not necessarily lost to the Jewish community. Though not halakhically Jewish, many intermarried Swedish families are active Jewishly or identify as Jewish. Even those whose Jewishness is uncontested do not associate only with other Jews; to do so would be most un-Scandinavian.

The most committed Jews send their children to Israel and may be candidates for aliyah—but their overall aliyah rate is no higher than other affluent Western countries. In fact, there may be a higher aliyah rate among non-Jewish Swedes, who frequently spend six months volunteering on a kibbutz and not infrequently end up marrying sabras. Israel influences Swedish Jewry in other ways, too, supplying it with teachers and emissaries.

Religiously, most Stockholm Jews would be considered Reform or Conservative by American standards, although those designations are not used. The Chief Rabbi, who serves the Great Synagogue, is Rabbi Morton H. Narrowe, a graduate of New York's Jewish Theological Seminary and a native of Philadelphia. At Sabbath services at the

Great Synagogue, men and women sit separately, but there is a mixed choir, and an organ and a Conservative-style prayerbook are used.

SIGHTS: A good place to begin to explore Stockholm is in picturesque Gamla Stan, where the city and nation began. Here King Gustav Vasa, after wresting Swedish independence from the Danes, consolidated his power in the old Stockholm Royal Palace of the Three Crowns, which he used as his treasure-house. In Gamla Stan, too, began the Jewish presence. At 19 Själagårdsgatan is the building that housed Stockholm's first synagogue; today it is a museum and center for Lapp culture.

Another point of interest in Gamla Stan is the Stock Exchange building, the top floor of which belongs to the Swedish Academy, which awards the Nobel Prize in literature. A disproportionate number of Jews have received the prestigious and remunerative Nobel awards—from S. Y. Agnon, Saul Bellow, Elias Canetti, Boris Pasternak, and I. B. Singer in literature to Albert Einstein in physics and Roslyn Yalow in medicine. Though Jews account for less than .5 percent of the world's population, they account for nearly 20 percent of the Nobel Prizes given in all categories since the first awards were made in 1901.

Most of the major Jewish institutions are centrally located, not far from the section of new Stockholm you enter when you cross the bridges from Gamla Stan. The Great Synagogue, at Wahrensdorffsgatan 3 (telephone, 63-95-24), was built in 1870. Its cathedral-ceilinged sanctuary, with a seating capacity of 830, has dark wood paneling on the walls and elaborate wood carving and painting in the tall, gold-capitaled columns, the almost Moorish bimah, and the scallop-domed Ark. The women's gallery above is fronted by intricate grillwork, and stained-glass windows, including a beautiful rose window, let in light at the upper level.

Smaller synagogues, more traditionally Orthodox, are Adas Jisrael at St. Paulsgatan 13 (telephone, 44-19-95) and Adas Jeshurun at Nybrogatan 12 (telephone, 61-82-82).

Judaica House at Nybrogatan 19–20 is the Jewish community center in the best sense of the word. It houses the Hillel kindergarten and day school, the Yiddish association, a gymnasium, a kosher cafeteria which serves meat or fish meals at lunchtime to students, senior citizens, and tourists during the summer, and a library with a Raoul Wallenberg room, in which the Swedish diplomat's picture hangs. In this building, too, are the offices and meeting rooms for most of the major organizations, Zionist and communal—Benei Akiva, Habonim, Keren Kayemet, Maccabi, the Zionist Federation, and the Jewish Students Club. Judaica House publishes a bulletin, *HaChaver.*

The Jewish cemetery at Hagaparken, in the suburb of Solna, is the newest of the city's four Jewish burial grounds and the site of a Holocaust memorial. A T-shaped memorial recalls the victims of Nazism, while the Hebrew inscription is taken from the oldest grave in the Sefardic cemetery at Oederderk-on-the-Amstel in Holland.

GENERAL SIGHTS: A fascinating day can be spent exploring Skansen, Stockholm's open-air museum and amusement park, a kind of cross between Disneyland and Beit Hatefutsot. Built in 1891, to preserve rural Swedish culture as urbanization was beginning to encroach, Skansen includes a collection of 150 old buildings—farmhouses, windmills, churches, and trade shops—brought from all over Sweden; artisans and guides explain the way life was lived long ago. Also of interest in Skansen are the open-air zoo, the aquarium, the largest in Sweden, and live entertainment in the evenings.

Near Skansen on the island of Djurgården is Gröna Lund, Stockholm's answer to Copenhagen's Tivoli, and, close by, an amazing artifact of maritime archaeology, the seventeenth-century warship *Wasa.* This ship was the pride of the Royal Navy until it sank in Stockholm's harbor on its maiden voyage. After three centuries below water, it was raised in 1961 and since then has been undergoing elaborate restoration. It is worth seeing for the elaborate wood sculptures that decorate prow and stern.

Another worthwhile stop is the Town Hall, a magnificent building whose Gold Hall traces the history of Sweden in mosaic murals and whose Blue Hall is used to entertain Nobel Prize winners after they have received their awards.

The Stockholm City Council recently designated a Raoul Wallenberg Square, the first public Wallenberg memorial in Sweden. There is a Raoul Wallenberg Föreningen, a society dedicated to preserving the World War II hero's memory (telephone, 10-26-53).

GETTING AROUND: Stockholm is an easy city to get around in— by boat, subway, and bus—and the Stockholm Card, which you can purchase, gets you on all public conveyances. The subways are an esthete's delight, with many of the stations beautifully decorated. Since Stockholm is built on fourteen islands and surrounded by thousands more, a boat ride around the harbor or out to Drottningholm

Palace, the residence of the Royal Family, or to Vaxholm or to Gripsholm Castle at Mariefred is a pleasurable way to spend a day.

SIDE TRIPS: For a more extensive excursion, visit Göteborg (Gothenburg) on the west coast of Sweden, the country's second largest city and site of its oldest synagogue. The Liberal Synagogue, at Östra Larmgatan 12 (telephone, 13-67-78), faces a scenic canal and is housed in a building dedicated in 1855. The Jewish community center, which contains the community offices, a kosher eating facility, and a chapel for Orthodox minyans, is adjacent.

PERSONALITIES: Though few in number, Jews have made their contribution to Swedish society and culture. In the nineteenth century, Jacob Josephson, a Stockholm-born conductor and composer, established the Uppsala Philharmonic, while meteorologist Robert Rubenson was the director of his country's Central Meteorological Institute. Oscar Levertin was a poet and literary critic for *Svenska Dagbladet,* one of Stockholm's leading daily papers. Martin Lamm, another literary critic, was elected a member of the Swedish Royal Academy. Nelly Sachs, the Nobel Prize–winning poet, lived the last thirty years of her life in Stockholm; the Swedish Royal Family was instrumental in getting her out of Germany in 1940. Sophie Elkan's novels on the Royal Family and other Swedish historical themes won her national acclaim.

Hjalmar Mehr served as mayor of Stockholm in the 1960s. Peter Freudenthal, an abstract painter whose work has been exhibited at the Jewish Museum in New York, and Fritz Hollander, head of the European Council of Jewish Community Services, the European equivalent of the Council of Jewish Federations, are prominent members of the Stockholm community today.

EATING: Other than the lunch canteen at the Jewish community center, there is no kosher restaurant in Stockholm. Kosher supplies can be purchased at the community center and at Kosher Livs, Timmermansgatan 22 (telephone, 41-47-40).

There are, however, several good vegetarian restaurants, among which Gröna Linjen at Mastersamuelsgatan 10 (upstairs, lunch only, telephone, 11-27-90) is particularly pleasant in atmosphere and imaginative in menu. Since the Swedes are the originators of the smörgåsbord, many restaurants feature an extensive salad and herring bar— with more kinds of herring than you ever imagined existed. A very elaborate salad bar, with predominantly vegetarian combinations, is featured at Örtagården on Östermalmstorg (telephone, 62-17-28).

READING: The Jewish newspaper of Stockholm is the *Judisk Kronika,* written in Swedish, of course. For an in-depth, English-language study of the Stockholm community, see *The Jewish Communities of Scandinavia: Sweden, Denmark, Norway and Finland* by Daniel Elazar, Adina Weiss Lieberles, and Simcha Werner, published by the Center for Jewish Community Studies of the Jerusalem Center for Public Action and University Press of America.

In recent years, there has been a spate of books about Raoul Wallenberg. Among the best are *Righteous Gentile* (Viking) by John Bierman, *Wallenberg: The Man in the Iron Web* (Prentice-Hall) by Elenore Lester, and *With Raoul Wallenberg in Budapest* (Holocaust Library) by Per Anger, the man who assisted Wallenberg in Budapest. In addition to chronicling Wallenberg's life, the biographies offer some insights into the nation that produced him.

—ROSELYN BELL

Sydney

Opera House and Skyline *(Australian Tourist Commission)*

"We live in a WASP fairyland," wrote one of Australia's best-known columnists. "[Australia is] the most multicultural country on earth, after Israel—but we don't admit to it."

The best-kept secret about Australia is, in fact, that one out of every five Australians has been born overseas—giving the country an exuberant plethora of nationalities, including about eighty thousand Jews.

HISTORY: When Britain lost the United States as a colony, it turned to the far-off continent of Australia as a destination for its prisoners. In 1788, the First Fleet—fifteen hundred convicts, including at least half a dozen Jews, and their guards—landed in Sydney to start a new colony. And while some Australians used to be ashamed of their ancestors, now it's become fashionable to claim that one's forebears stole a sheep or a loaf of bread and then helped build the country.

The first free Jewish settler was Esther Isaacs, who arrived after her husband, a deported convict, in 1816. Sydney's first congregation was organized in 1832 and its first president was Joseph Barrow Montefiore, a cousin of Sir Moses Montefiore. It wasn't until 1844, however, when there were about nine hundred Jews in the city, that the first synagogue building was constructed.

During the gold rush of the 1850s, more Jews moved to Australia—mainly from England but some from Germany as well. Many who disembarked at Sydney initially set up stores in the smaller towns of New South Wales.

Most of Sydney's Jewish population is the result of two waves of immigration following the world wars, and subsequent smaller waves reflecting the crises that have affected Jews around the world. The 1956 Hungarian Revolution doubled the city's Hungarian Jewish population; Polish anti-Semitism after the Six-Day War brought new Polish immigrants, followed by Russian Jews, and, most recently, Jews from South Africa.

Although Australia's "white policy" in the 1940s and early 1950s limited immigration to the country, more recently, its leaders have let

in a flood of immigrants. Now the government turns to—where else?
—Israel for programs to help arrivals adapt to their new land.

COMMUNITY: While the majority of Melbourne's thirty-two
thousand Jews are of East European, particularly Polish, origin,
Sydney's 27,000-member community is predominantly Hungarian
with a mixture of German, British, and Australian-born Jews. The
stereotype is that Melbourne's Jews are more observant than those in
Sydney but, in reality, the Jews of Sydney are far from assimilated.
Over half of Sydney's Jewish children attend Jewish day schools and,
as Susan Bures, editor of the *Australian Jewish Times* points out, "Sydney is completely Zionist. Since 1967, there has been an increased
identification of Jews as Jews and connected to Israel."

Indeed, Sydney's Jewish leaders are proud of the high rate of aliyah
among their young people, and they're optimistic that Australia's
relatively low intermarriage rate—less than 20 percent—will not increase. "With few exceptions," Rabbi Raymond Apple of Sydney's
Great Synagogue says, "most Australian Jews who achieved high offices retained their Jewish observances." Other Australian authorities
confirmed that there is less pressure for Jews to assimilate in Australia
than in other diaspora countries.

Anti-Semitism, although not widespread, is still felt by the Jewish
community. One observer explains that it consists of traditional anti-
Semitic feeling among those of British origin and of other new immigrants. This, however, has not prevented the success of Jews in professions such as medicine and law, nor the proliferation of shops in
downtown Sydney with names like Cohen's Stamps.

NEIGHBORHOODS AND SIGHTS: The first Jewish convict settlers
were illiterate in both English and Hebrew, and there was no kind of
Jewish organization until a hevra kaddisha was formed in 1817. By
1878, the Great Synagogue, the first permanent synagogue in Sydney,
was established and services are still conducted there every day. The
synagogue is in an impressive, twin-turreted building in Sydney's
bustling center, adjacent to Hyde Park; the interior, with its stained-
glass-filtered light and decorative arches, is in the best tradition of
Victorian style. The building also houses a Jewish museum and library
and sponsors educational and cultural activities (166 Castlereagh
Street, telephone, 267-2477).

Most of Sydney's Jews, however, have settled outside the city in two
suburban areas: Bondi and the North Shore. Bondi has the weathered
look of an old-time seaside resort. Its stores, with their faded awnings,

are on streets with manicured lawns and are perched on a cliff over-looking the ocean. At the Hakoah Club, 61–67 Hall Street, there are legal poker and slot machines, a dining room with a kosher section, and other game facilities, making Bondi seem like a Jewish miniature version of Atlantic City. Also in the area are the Lubavitch Yeshiva College, at 32 Flood Street, the Central Synagogue on Bon Accord Avenue, Jewish bookstores, and kosher butchers and bakeries.

The North Shore suburbs, about a half hour away from Bondi, also boast a coastline of lovely beaches. The suburbs, though, are spread out and, since there is no Jewish shopping area, most North Shore Jewish residents shop in Bondi.

The largest institution, the North Shore Synagogue (15 Treatts Road, Lindfield), which also sponsors two Jewish day schools, is set on several lush and tropical acres. One Sydney Jew observes that their Shabbat kiddush, which is held outdoors, is like a "garden party." Rabbi David Rogut, spiritual leader of the synagogue, says that his facilities in Lindfield, and that of North Shore Temple Emanuel in Chatswood (28 Chatswood Avenue), cater to a growing community of young professional families. The North Shore's suburbs are about a half hour from downtown Sydney and can be reached easily by bus or train.

CULTURE: Sydney has a Jewish theater and a folk center which sponsors Yiddish and other Jewish cultural activities. Check the listings in the weekly *Australian Jewish Times.*

PERSONALITIES: John Harris, one of the Jewish convicts on the first ship to Sydney, must have been rehabilitated; he became Australia's first policeman. Also among the convict settlers was Isaac Solomon, said to be the model for Fagin in *Oliver Twist.* The first Australian governor general—the highest ceremonial officer, who is appointed by the Queen—was Sir Isaac Isaacs, a Melbourne Jew; Sydney got its turn with Zelman Cowan, who held the same post until 1982. Some rising stars on the Australian arts scene include new Jewish immigrants such as Moscow-born Alexander Semetsky, a concert pianist who performs throughout Australia.

EATING: The B'nai B'rith center, near the Great Synagogue but on the opposite side of Hyde Park, has a formal restaurant with unusual kosher dishes, such as honey chicken and beef curry. It's at 22–38 Yurong Street (telephone, 33-6035). Another restaurant with atypical kosher cuisine is Bondi's Wei-Song Vegetarian Chinese Restaurant, at 96 Bronte Road. More traditional fare may be had at Shalom

College, University of New South Wales (telephone, 663-1366), and Lewis's Continental Kitchen at 2 Curlewis Street in Bondi and on Victoria Avenue in Chatswood.

GENERAL SIGHTS: Historic Sydney has been restored at the Rocks, the rocky area near Sydney's harbor where the convicts first settled. Sydney's oldest surviving house as well as the Argyle Center—built with convict labor and now a mall filled with boutiques selling antiques and gems—are found there. Also in the area are restaurants which feature fresh fish, where jazz bands often play.

For a panorama of both old and new Sydney, visitors can ride up to the observation deck of the Centre Point Tower in Sydney or ride around the city in ferries that cruise through Sydney harbor. Both afford interesting perspectives on Sydney's landmark opera house, which was designed to look like sails billowing in the wind. One of the opera house's founders was Sir Asher Joel.

There are lovely parks and gardens in the city, particularly the Royal Botanic Gardens, which feature a palm grove and Australian rainforest trees. Spectacular scenery can also be found two hours from Sydney in the Blue Mountains, where visitors, if they're lucky, might spot a koala bear.

READING: Sydney's Jewish literature is not as rich as Melbourne's, but Judah Waten's book *Alien Son* (Angus and Robertson), about his growing up in Melbourne, sheds some light on the Australian Jewish community. Another Australian Jewish author is Morris Lurie, whose comic short story collections, such as *Inside the Wardrobe* (Outback Press), are available in the United States. For an introduction to a WASP fairyland with a multicultural layer just beneath the surface, Waten and Lurie are good bets.

—DIANA KATCHER BLETTER

Tel Aviv

Old City Hall *(Werner Braun)*

It may not be easy for a visitor to get the keys to the city of Tel Aviv, but if you know the right people, you can get the pirated master key to the Denver boot. The device is called the "Denver sandal" in Israel, and some enterprising illegal parkers had the key reproduced to indicate that no authorities were going to restrict their movements, justice aside.

The sandal story recalls the observation attributed to Haim Nahman Bialik (1873–1934), Israel's national poet, that the Jewish state would be a normal country when it had its thieves as well as its shopkeepers, lawyers, and scientists. Of all the cities of Israel, Tel Aviv is perhaps the most "normal," for better and for worse. Envisioned as the first modern Jewish city, plunked in the dunes north of Jaffa, it has become the center of Israel's only metropolitan area, the Dan Region. It has neither Jerusalem's history of siege and border fighting nor Haifa and Beersheba's distance from the center. Stylish but brash, inviting but impolite, entertaining but unkempt, Tel Aviv embodies the best and worst images of Israel. To its boosters it is the only place to live. To some idealistic kibbutzniks and more spiritually oriented Jerusalemites, it is, according to one observer, "Gomorrah in its worst depravity."

HISTORY: Tel Aviv-Jaffa has been jointly administered since 1949, but Jaffa is the original, ancient port city. In modern times, Jewish settlement in predominantly Arab Jaffa dates from 1820, when Rabbi Yeshaya Adjiman of Constantinople bought a house which became a hostel for the Jewish craftsmen and merchants, mainly from North Africa, who came to settle in the Holy Land. They were followed by Ashkenazi Jews from Europe, and the integrated communities began to settle north of Jaffa after the walls of the city were razed in 1888.

Neve Zedek, today being renovated, was Jaffa's first Jewish quarter, started in 1887 and followed four years later by Neve Shalom to the north. But the founding of Tel Aviv dates from April 11, 1909, when a portion of land bought jointly by the Ahuzat Bayit housing society was parceled out in a lottery among the sixty member families. About a year later, the name of the neighborhood, Ahuzat Bayit (Housing

Property) was changed to Tel Aviv (Hill of Spring), which was a Babylonian city mentioned in the *Book of Ezekiel* and was taken for the Hebrew title of Theodor Herzl's novel *Altneuland*—about his proposed utopian society. Meir Dizengoff, leader of the founders group and Tel Aviv's first mayor, prophesied a city of twenty-five thousand.

Tel Aviv's growth was prompted more by history than geography. Started as a suburb of Jaffa, it grew into Israel's leading city even though its shore was unsuitable for a port and the offshore sandstone ridges bar the sea breezes that make other parts of Israel's coast more comfortable during the hot summer. After World War I, the Third Aliyah and anti-Jewish riots in Jaffa boosted the city's population to 15,000. The Fourth Aliyah in the 1920s brought many middle-class Polish Jews; by 1925 the city had 34,000 people. The Fifth Aliyah, largely from Germany in the 1930s, brought the population to 120,000. Tel Aviv was bombed by Italian and French Vichy planes during the war, but its growth and vitality continued, as thousands of Allied soldiers passed through.

The city gradually grew northward, with the wealthier residents moving into the new neighborhoods, where services were more expensive. In the 1948 war, all but about four thousand of Jaffa's Arab residents fled the city, and Jews, many of them new immigrants, moved into the abandoned homes. The population of Jaffa remains mixed today, but its original Oriental flavor predominates; most of the Jews who live there are of Middle Eastern origin.

COMMUNITY: If Jerusalem is the most Jewish city in Israel, Tel Aviv is the most Israeli. While Tel Aviv contains all of Israel's religious elements, it is more secular than the capital. While it has Israel's full ethnic range—Russian, Polish, Yemenite, Turkish, German, and everything else—you'll hear more Hebrew and less English on the street than in Jerusalem.

Though Jerusalem is Israel's political and spiritual capital, the 1.4 million people of the Tel Aviv area—fifty-six times the number Dizengoff dreamed of—lead the nation in many other ways. Tel Aviv is Israel's cultural and financial center. It hosts the Defense Ministry and the diamond industry. It is also the publishing center; all Israel's major newspapers, except *The Jerusalem Post,* are based in Tel Aviv.

NEIGHBORHOODS AND SIGHTS: When visiting, you may want to combine some of the more obvious guidebook sights with a glimpse of normalcy, Tel Aviv style. Many of the older sections of Tel Aviv-Jaffa are poorly maintained, but one exception is the part of ancient Jaffa just above the old port. It has been renovated and turned into an attractive if commercialized tourist center, with galleries, restaurants, and nightclubs. One of the recently added features is *The Israel Experience,* a multimedia "introduction" to the country presented on one twenty-yard-long curved screen. It's kitsch, but it has some beautiful photography. Jaffa's eastern flavor is most pronounced in the Flea Market, along Olei Zion Street.

The older neighborhoods in south Tel Aviv (just north of Jaffa), including Neve Zedek, Neve Shalom, and Hatikva, tend to be populated by poorer Jews whose families came from Asia and North Africa. Some became nouveau riche in the late seventies and early eighties, but not riche enough or willing enough to leave their extended families. Instead they added rooms or colored windows or lampposts to their balconies, or whatever signaled their improved status.

Neve Zedek, with its narrow streets and crumbling buildings, is now the focus of a public debate over whether it should be preserved or torn down entirely. In addition to some gentrification, the community-oriented Neve Zedek Theater Center (6 Yehieli Street), the Chelouche Gallery (14 Chelouche Street), and a few restaurants are among the attempts to revive the area as an artists' quarter.

The north end of Neve Zedek marks the start of what is now central Tel Aviv. The Shalom Tower, tallest building in the Middle East, stands on the former site of the Herzliya Gymnasium, Palestine's first high school. The thirty-four-story tower has an observation deck with spectacular views of the city, the Mediterranean, and the surrounding countryside.

It is near the center of the city that some of the most interesting residential architecture can be found. Prime examples of the International Style—promoted by the Bauhaus school of the 1930s—can be found on and around Rothschild Boulevard. Among the features of the International Style are balconies with rounded corners and porthole windows aligned over the entrance and up through the stairwell. Unfortunately, even in the better neighborhoods, the buildings are poorly maintained.

Habima Square, at the north end of Rothschild Boulevard, is the nation's cultural heart. It is the site of the Mann Auditorium, home of the Israel Philharmonic Orchestra, under the direction of Zubin Mehta; Habima, Israel's national theater; and the Helena Rubenstein Pavilion, a branch of the Tel Aviv Museum. (One leading national company not on the square is the Israel Ballet, which makes its home at 60 Weizmann Boulevard.)

The guidebooks will tell you about the justly famous Israel Philharmonic, but there is also good chamber music, particularly at the small Tsavta Theater (downstairs in the arcade at 30 Ibn Gvirol Street) on Saturday mornings at 11. For other chamber concerts (and cultural events in general), consult the weekly listings in *The Jerusalem Post*'s Friday magazine section.

Some theater productions are offered with simultaneous translation at Habima and the Cameri, Tel Aviv's municipal theater (Dizengoff and Frishman streets). Earphones don't make for the ultimate in theater art but if you're curious about the experience of theatergoing in Israel, try it. Israeli movies are even more accessible to the non-Hebrew speaking; all have English subtitles.

The principal art collection is at the main building of the Tel Aviv Museum (at 27 Shaul HaMelekh Boulevard), which includes some halls devoted to Israeli works. The Helena Rubinstein Pavilion, about a brisk twenty-minute walk from the main building, has recently been featuring works by young Israeli artists. Many of the city's commercial galleries are on Gordon Street between Dizengoff and the sea, and tend to be less tourist-oriented than those in Old Jaffa.

There's a threesome of small museums farther south, on Bialik Street, which combine historical and artistic interest. The buildings, and some of the others on the street, date from the mid-1920s, when this was still the center of town. One of them, the home of Haim Nahman Bialik (at No. 22), is undergoing restoration and scheduled to reopen soon. The Rubin House at No. 14 is the renovated home of painter Reuven Rubin, whose story is closely interwoven with the development of the country. His studio is preserved upstairs, and a twelve-minute slide show on his life and work is available with English narration (telephone, 658-961). At the northern end of the street is the Museum of the History of Tel Aviv-Jaffa (telephone, 653-534), which was the city hall in the twenties. Its display of photographs of "Little Tel Aviv" is perhaps the best way to understand why the first streetlight and the first cold-drink stand were such sources of pride. Not everything is explained in English, and what English there is is sometimes quaint, but for a glimpse of the people who made "the first Jewish city," it's worth the effort.

There are many other museums worth visiting in Tel Aviv. A selective list includes Independence Hall (16 Rothschild Boulevard), the former home of Meir Dizengoff and the building in which Israeli independence was declared in 1948; the Haganah Museum (23 Rothschild Boulevard), devoted to Jewish defense in Israel from the early part of the century through the Yom Kippur War; the Israel Theater Museum (3 Melchett Street), with its exhibits on Jewish theater; and Ben Gurion House (17 Ben Gurion Boulevard), which houses the library and many personal effects of the father of Israeli independence.

One of the most original museums is Beit Hatefutsot, the Diaspora Museum, on the beautiful grounds of Tel Aviv University in Ramat Aviv, in the far north of the city. Conceived as a teaching museum by poet Abba Kovner, it gives a global view of the development of Jewish culture in different parts of the world. It includes a changing photo exhibit on the ground floor, usually devoted to a particular Jewish community—from the largest in Europe and America to the most obscure in India and China.

Among Beit Hatefutsot's most popular attractions is the computer and video area. The computer has access to descriptions of Jewish communities and to Jewish family-name derivations, but this is often a disappointment, since the data are limited. Try anyway—the printout makes a nice souvenir—but you may want to concentrate on the video tapes. The museum also sponsors lectures and films on topics of Jewish interest.

PEOPLE WATCHING: Café life, like balcony sitting, sprouted in Tel Aviv's soggy climate. Before the era of air conditioning, it was the only way to breathe in the summer. But it has developed into a year-round social and cultural phenomenon. Dizengoff Street is one of the best-known spots for seeing and being seen. The cafés on the west side of the street are favorite gathering places on Friday afternoon, but the big parade—if the weather is good—is on Saturday, late morning and early afternoon. The street is closed to vehicular traffic, aside from skateboards and strollers, from Ben Gurion Boulevard south to Frischmann. The café tables spill out into the street, and people walk their dogs, children, spouses, and sweethearts.

During the week, the city's cafés are distinguished by their clientele. They may be characterized by age range, national origin, profession, or political affiliation. Painters and writers can be found at the Frak (Dizengoff and Gordon) in the morning. Mornings are also the time to find elderly German Jews at Stern (Dizengoff south of Arlosoroff); in the afternoon the clientele switches to writers and editors of literary journals. The Oslo, 192 Ibn Gvirol, has perhaps the most unusual mix of clients: members of the National Religious Party in the morning and assignations in the afternoon.

Another spot for ogling is the new beachfront promenade (officially, the Herbert Samuel Esplanade), attractively paved and furnished with benches and chairs. At the end of Bograshov Street is the new Bograhof café and restaurant, on the beach; facing the beach but on the other side of the street, is a series of cafés. Friday and Saturday are the busiest days, and you can choose your cream cake and then walk it off.

Tel Aviv has its share of early morning beach freaks who knew the advantages of exercise long before the aerobic era. A particularly interesting breed goes to the Tel Aviv Pool, popularly known as the Gordon Pool, borrowing the name of the adjoining beachfront. It's an outdoor, saltwater dunk between the café and restaurant area called Kikar Atarim, at the end of Ben Gurion Boulevard, and the marina. The "serious" swimmers, many of them over sixty, go between opening time (4:30 A.M.) and 8 A.M., all year round. Younger people tend to go later, and whenever you go (it closes at 6 P.M.), you are likely to hear a medley of Eastern European languages, Hebrew, and Arabic. On weekends in summer, some families bring their picnic coolers, card games, and sheshbesh sets.

In addition to swimming, the sea offers sailing. The Tel Aviv Sailing Club, located at the marina in front of Kikar Atarim, rents sailboats by the hour, with or without a skipper. If you want quieter waters, try a boat ride on the Yarkon River, at Tel Aviv's north end. Rentals are available from Tikvah-Dagon (telephone, 412-921) and Irgun Ha-Yarkon (488-422). Gan Ha-Yarkon (Yarkon Park), also offers outdoor concerts during the summer.

PERSONALITIES: Singling out the prominent Jews in a metropolis that is 98.5 percent Jewish is no easy task. From the beginning of the Zionist movement, much of the leadership of Israel, from poets to politicians, has made Tel Aviv its home. Among the poets, Bialik and Natan Alterman are particularly identified with the city. Others in the arts have included the painter Reuven Rubin; the sculptor Menashe Kadishman; humorist Ephraim Kishon; and Naomi Shemer, the composer and lyricist best known for *Jerusalem of Gold.* Two violinists from Tel Aviv are Pinchas Zuckerman, who still lives there, and Yitzhak Perlman, who now lives in New York. Prime Minister Shimon Peres is from Tel Aviv, as are President Chaim Herzog and former Prime Minister Yitzhak Rabin.

RECOMMENDATIONS: There are many ways to experience Tel Aviv beyond traditional sightseeing. Two recommendations, from many possibilities, are to shop in a local department store, like HaMashbir on Allenby Road, and to attend a soccer game. The noisy fans at a typical game exhibit the depth of insult and the height of faith; when an opponent scores a goal, the crowd routinely chants, in Hebrew, "son of a prostitute." When the home team scores, the cheer is, "There *is* a God."

Tel Aviv has no shortage of hotels for every level of luxury. On the beach, the beautiful sand-colored Tel Aviv Sheraton is a good bet, as is its near neighbor the Penta, which is somewhat more intimate and European in style and clientele. Among the less expensive hotels across the street from the beach, the Basel is notable for its comfort and friendly staff.

READING: Yaakov Shabtai's novel *Past Continuous* (Jewish Publication Society) is an "atmospheric" book about the ways in which the sons and daughters of the founding generation in Tel Aviv deal, or don't, with disappointed hopes for the new society.

To balance the challenge of a style some have called Faulknerian, look at a picture book: *Pillar of Fire,* Yigal Lossin's album, published in America by the Anti-Defamation League of B'nai B'rith and based on a TV series done for the Israel Broadcasting Authority on the development of Zionism. It has pictures of early Tel Aviv scattered through it, but the fifth chapter, on the 1920s, might be of particular interest. It's the period of the Fourth Aliyah, whose immigrants, many of them businessmen and craftsmen from Poland, tremendously accelerated the city's growth. One of the photos shows the casino on the beach—not exactly in keeping with the image of Zionist socialism, but terribly normal.

—MARSHA POMERANTZ

Toronto

❧❧

Nathan Phillips Square *(Ontario Ministry of Tourism & Recreation)*

When Toronto's government-backed Harbourfront Corporation missed a deadline in securing zoning permits for its vast lakefront development, the Reichman brothers, builders of the project, had the option of converting the mixed residential-commercial project into a far more profitable commercial-only development. The builders stuck to the original deal, Albert Reichman said, because it was a civic duty.

The Reichmans are known in Canadian and American business circles for their ethical practices, widely attributed to their Talmudic studies. They are also reflective of their milieu on Lake Ontario. "Civilized" is the operative word these days for Toronto. It's a civilized city. Its streets are safe. Its subways are clean. Its people are pleasant. In fact, it has been hailed as the continent's newest metropolitan superstar, a place that urbanologist Jane Jacobs has called "the most hopeful and healthy city in North America."

It has tall, modern buildings, but has also kept its neighborhoods. It has its commerce, but it also has culture. It abounds with good shopping and dining and, in its urban malls, often meshes the two. In short, it exudes the good life.

Once, Toronto was so "good" it was considered stodgy, gray, dull. But that was before Canada began nurturing the multiculturalism of which Toronto has become a leading exponent. In the last fifteen to twenty years, the city has welcomed so many newcomers that it now boasts seventy-five ethnic groups, segments that are not melding together but proudly retaining their identities. Against this influx, the Jews are such old-timers that Toronto is hard-pressed to consider them "ethnics" anymore.

HISTORY: Though Canada's first Jewish settlement was in Montreal, by 1849 there were enough Jews in Toronto for Abraham Nordheimer—of a musical family relocated from Montreal—to obtain burial land for a Toronto Hebrew Congregation. In 1856 the Sons of Israel held Rosh Hashana services, and shortly thereafter the two groups merged into the Holy Blossom Synagogue (so-called because a member's father gave the congregation a silver Torah pointer on which were engraved—probably to encourage the flourishing of this then untamed section of Canada—the words "Pirhei Kodesh," or "Holy Blossoms.")

The congregation, which has since grown into Toronto's largest Reform temple, was at its inception Orthodox, and was made up of English, German, American, and East European Jews.

In 1871, however, there were only 157 Jews in Toronto; Russia's pogroms helped boost the figure to 3,000 in 1901 and 18,000 in 1911. By 1931, there were 45,000. Most were Poles; many had come to Canada after the United States clamped down on immigration in 1924.

Not that Toronto was prejudice-free. While the Jews themselves, despite the prevalence of spiritual leaders for each national segment, began mingling across their own ethnic lines—with affluence, not ancestry, becoming the chief social criterion—Toronto's once straight-laced, Anglo-Saxon society closed many social and economic avenues to Jews. Before World War I, Christian missionaries proselytized so much that the rabbi of Holy Blossom, in 1911, delivered a powerful sermon criticizing the Presbyterian Church for supporting such activities.

Since the missions offered medical and social services, however, and since there were restrictions against Jews in certain areas—including the opportunity for doctors to admit patients to hospitals—the Jews established their own self-help institutions, among them Mount Sinai Hospital and what has become the Baycrest Center for Geriatric Care.

In addition, Toronto's Jews fostered strong ideologists, including radicals and communists who remained loyal to their causes until recent times. (Little wonder that the American anarchist, Emma Goldman, after her deportation to Russia, lived in Toronto until her death above Switzer's Delicatessen on Spadina Avenue.)

Despite Canada's own immigration restrictions preceding and during World War II, German and Austrian Jews made their way to Toronto; later, the Canadian Jewish Congress worked with various needle trade groups—often having to sponsor more non-Jews than Jews —to bring over displaced persons.

After the war Canada began establishing antidiscrimination codes and relaxing its immigration laws. The 1956 Hungarian uprising propelled a new wave of Jews to Toronto—including many Hasidim. In the 1960s, Sefardic Jews began arriving for the first time, from Morocco. Recent years have brought Jews from South Africa, the Soviet Union, the United States, Israel (an estimated ten thousand), and, during its separatist period, Montreal. While the number from Montreal was relatively small, it was part of a historic change in the position of the two cities. When Quebec's separatists came to power in 1976, Montreal was Canada's largest city and had the largest Jewish community. By the time the Liberal Party returned to power in Quebec in 1985, Toronto ranked first in both categories.

Still, with Toronto's ethnic explosion, today's Jewish community of 125,000 seems no more visible than when it was half that size. They are just one minority among many in a metropolitan area of more than three million people.

Recently, the equilibrium of Toronto Jewry has been disturbed by two court cases—one against James Keegstra, a teacher in Alberta accused of inculcating his students with Nazi doctrine; the other, against Ernst Zundel, in Toronto, for calling the Holocaust a fraud.

By and large, though, Toronto Jews today live free of anti-Semitism. And for having, early on, kept their religious and cultural identity, they are sometimes credited with pointing the way to multiculturalism.

COMMUNITY: Despite the (relative) depth of Jewish roots in Toronto, the majority of Jewish Torontonians are only one or, at most, two generations removed from their immigrant background. Perhaps this explains in part why Toronto's Jews tend to be somewhat more traditional than their American counterparts.

About half of Toronto's Jews are affiliated, in some way, with the community and, of these, 40 percent are Orthodox (including some who are ultra-Orthodox); 40 percent are Conservative (often in a stricter manner than Americans); and 20 percent are Reform. Of the fifty-odd synagogues in the city, there are five Reform (of which Holy Blossom is the leader); a dozen Conservative (Beth Tzedec is the largest in Canada); three North African Sefardic; one each Reconstructionist and European Liberal; and the rest Orthodox in various forms, led by Shaarei Shomayim.

Toronto's Jews have established an extensive day school network which, be the education ultra-Orthodox, secular, or socialist, contributes considerably to promoting Jewish identity.

Originally, Toronto's English and German Jews lived in the once-fashionable downtown area east of Yonge Street, while the earliest Eastern European Jews were concentrated in St. John's Ward. Around the time of World War I, they began moving to the Spadina Avenue-Kensington Market area. In the early fifties, they started pushing

north and today live in Don Mills, in the northeastern section of
Toronto, as well as such bedroom communities as Unionville, Mark-
ham, Richmond Hill, Thornhill, and Vaughn, not to mention such
towns to the west as Mississauga and Brampton. But, beginning
roughly where St. Clair Avenue intersects Bathurst Street, with pockets flaring out on either side all along the artery, there are, one after
the other, Jewish-inhabited apartment buildings; Jewish-owned
houses (including those in the wealthy Forest Hill section); synagogues from the shtiebl—or storefront—variety to the grand and
grandiose; Jewish schools; Jewish service organizations; and Jewish
businesses, shops, and restaurants. About 60 percent of the community lives in the vicinity of a five-to-six-mile strip of Bathurst.

The Jews of Toronto have good relations with other ethnic communities, many of whose causes they defend. Blacks and Jews, Italians
and Jews, Chinese and Jews have traditionally worked well together.
But when it comes to living quarters, according to Stephen A. Speisman, director of the Toronto Jewish Congress, "In Toronto, Jews like
to live together."

SIGHTS AND CULTURE: Call it multiculturalism at its best. Or
good-neighborliness. Or hacking par excellence. The fact is that the
black taxi driver—a ninth-generation Canadian—immediately recognized the 4600 Bathurst Street address as the Jewish Community
Center. "And while you're out there," he said, "there's a building a
little farther on that has a lot of old photos of the Toronto Jewish
community you should see."

How right he was. He failed only to mention that there were other
sights in this vicinity as well, in both buildings that occupy the same
tract of land. The Jewish Community Center, or "Y," is at 4588
Bathurst—virtually, but not quite, adjoining 4600, the Jewish Community Services Building officially named for Lipa Greene.

To be sure, on the walls of the Lipa Greene Building hang photos of
the champion Toronto Jewish Softball League Team of the 1920s, the
rhythm band of the Farband Shule, a Jewish farmer from rural Ontario, and the zaftig Ladies Auxiliary of Mount Sinai Hospital. Such
are mere samples, however, from a six-thousand-photo collection
housed in the building. Under Speisman's direction, the archives also
include diaries and cemetery records, oral histories, and artifacts such
as Magen Davids from demolished synagogues and a weatherbeaten
sign that reads, unequivocally, "Gentiles Only."

Also on the walls is a series of original contemporary paintings,

"Jewish Life in Canada," by William Kurelik, a leading Canadian artist from a Ukrainian Catholic background. The paintings belong to the province of Ontario, but are on permanent loan to the Toronto Jewish Congress. Among the subjects covered are a Jewish wedding in Calgary, a Jewish baker, Passover, Yom Kippur, Jewish home life, and Jews in the clothing industry.

In addition, the Lipa Greene Building houses a fifty-thousand-volume Jewish library; the Oskar Asher Schmidt Jewish Museum (which is still in its infancy and beginning to assemble its collection); and a Holocaust Memorial and Education Center. Designed primarily as a place of learning, this memorial features a slide presentation called "Images of the Past"; a photo exhibit of Jewish life before the war; a display on Nazism; and a half-hour documentary narrated by Lorne Greene.

The Jewish Community Center, too, boasts outstanding attractions. One particularly fine facet is its 444-seat Leah Posluns Theater. Built in 1977 and currently under the artistic direction of Reva Stern, the theater specializes in presenting works that deal with issues and concerns of Jewish interest— "plays of Jewish sensibility and significance," Stern explains. Five productions are mounted each season in what is arguably the best Jewish theater facility in North America. Recent offerings have included *Golda, Raisons and Almonds, Are You Now or Have You Ever Been* . . . , and *Fiddler on the Roof.*

The Jewish Center also features art exhibitions—including works with Jewish relevance—in its lobby, and the Koffler Gallery, which mounts separate exhibits. Each fall, the center hosts the Jewish Book Fair. Call the center's box office (636-6752) for information on theater and other events.

The Canadian Jewish News, published weekly in Toronto, is the best place to check for Jewish cultural happenings. There are programs of Jewish interest on CHIN, Toronto's multicultural radio station, and Channel 47, its multicultural television station. A Jewish Information Service (635-5600) offers advice on such questions as kosher restaurants and Jewish neighborhoods.

At 1700 Bathurst, in the Beth Tzedec Synagogue, is the Canadian Branch of the Jewish Museum, under the auspices of the Jewish Theological Seminary of America. The Beth Tzedec congregation owns and houses the Cecil Roth Collection, one of the world's leading aggregations of Judaica, as well as numerous other exceptional items. Among the works displayed are an eighteenth-century gold-illuminated Chinese Megilla from Kaifeng; a 1645 illuminated Venetian marriage contract, decorated with miniatures; a 1767 velvet-covered circumcision chair from Berlin; copies of the Song of Songs and the Book of Ruth inscribed on eggshells; and two century-old Persian rugs from Kashan, portraying the symbols of Judaism, and ordered by a Persian Shah to commemorate the exposure of an assassination plot against his Jewish court physician.

Beth Tzedec itself boasts such noteworthy items as a set of the Chagall lithographs of the twelve tribes (along the lines of the Chagall windows in the Hadassah-Hebrew University Medical Center in Jerusalem); and a floor mosaic of the zodiac which replicates the floor of the sixth-century synagogue excavated at Beit Alfa. The museum is open Monday to Thursday, 2–6 P.M., and Friday and Sunday, 10 A.M. to 3 P.M. Call the curator, Samuel Simchovitch, at 781-3511.

Additional artifacts from Kaifeng, on loan from the Royal Ontario Museum, may be found a block away at Holy Blossom Temple, 1950 Bathurst. Note that Holy Blossom's sleek, cathedral-like facade closely resembles that of Temple Emanu-El in New York.

Apart from its specific sights, the visitor can easily become engulfed in the experience of Jewish Bathurst where, on a Sunday, there is a stream of people going into the Negev Importing Company asking for *Ma'ariv* the way they would ask for *The Times* in New York; and where, if one isn't careful, one can land in the middle of a Talmudic discussion on the relative merits of Gryfe's Bagels versus The Bagel Factory's. (In any case, there are those convinced that Toronto's bagels are better than New York's; surely, its pickles are.)

Indeed, along a three-block section in the vicinity of the Baycrest Center for Geriatric Care, there exist such establishments as The Maven, a kosher MacDonald's-style burger joint; Chocolate Charms, purveying handmade chocolates; The Kosher Gourmet; a kosher pizza place; Isaac's Bakery, specializing in Sefardi and French pastries; a storefront synagogue; two Jewish bookstores; Marrakesh, a Sefardi restaurant; and Malkat Peking, a kosher Chinese restaurant under the proprietorship of Rabbi Asher Turin, who considers his ministry the neighborhood people who just drop in.

For a glimpse of the old neighborhood, walk around the Spadina-Kensington area bounded by Dundas Street West, McCaul Street, College Street, and Bellevue Avenue. Along Spadina Avenue, which is now the heart of Chinatown, stands the Golden Harvest Theater, formerly Toronto's Yiddish Theater; the celebrated United Dairies

Restaurant; and, at the corner of Nassau and Spadina, a red brick building whose wall proclaims, in white letters, Halpern's Drugstore, but whose sign now announces that it's Kwong's Pharmacy.

At 58 Cecil Street, there is a beige brick building with turquoise windowsill trim which is now a community center but was once a synagogue. At the corner of Cecil and Henry streets is a red brick building topped with the crosses of the Russian Orthodox Church; this, too, was once a synagogue.

At 12–14 St. Andrews Street stands the Russian and Romanesque Minsker Synagogue (Anshei Minsk). And at Denison Square and Bellevue Avenue stands the Kiever Synagogue, officially called Rodfei Sholom Anshei Kiev, built in 1926 by Ukrainian Jews. This synagogue is still operating and has been painstakingly restored. Among its exceptional features are its elaborately carved oak, chestnut and walnut Ark; its extensive brasswork; and its wall paintings of the signs of the zodiac, which were executed by an eleven-year-old girl and remain as examples of Canadian primitive art. Stephen Speisman, at 635-2883, can tell visitors how they can visit the synagogue when it is not holding services, as well as how to take a walking tour through the neighborhood—which includes the Kensington Market, now a collection of Portuguese and West Indian outdoor food stalls, but formerly called the Jewish Market.

GENERAL SIGHTS: Toronto boasts a number of institutions that belong to everyone, but which are, in one way or another, the creations of its Jews. Among the most touted are those proper ties of "Honest Ed" Mirvish. Mirvish is a flamboyant retailer who made his fortune with a garishly decorated, loudly hyped discount store at the corner of Bloor and Bathurst streets—where customers still line up outside to be the first in for the day's specials. Bordering the store, however, is "Mirvish Village," a block of restored, pastel-colored Victorian houses, with antique shops, bookstores, and restaurants on the street level and artists' quarters upstairs. Bitten by the restoration bug, Mirvish went on to acquire the Royal Alexandra Theater, Toronto's flagship playhouse, which he redid in grand style (before he acquired London's Old Vic). The theater itself is worth visiting; on the same street stand a cluster of Mirvish restaurants, decorated with antiques, serving everything from steak and ribs to Chinese food.

Among Toronto's—if not the world's—wealthiest Jews are the Reichman brothers, Ralph, Paul, and Albert. (Paul was named 1985's "Businessman of the Year" by Canada's *Financial Post.*) In addition to developing Toronto's waterfront, they put up the seventy-two-story First Canadian Place, otherwise known as the Bank of Montreal building. Designed by Edward Durrell Stone, the bank is Toronto's tallest building and embraces extensive office and shopping space as well as a kosher restaurant. (Indeed, the Reichmans hold minhah and maariv services in their inner sanctum.) The brothers also have substantial real estate holdings and ongoing projects in Manhattan.

And at the base of the CN Tower, advertised as the world's tallest freestanding structure, is the new "Tour of the Universe," a kiddie ride simulating a space trip, which is the brainchild of Moses Znaimer —who also founded Toronto's popular independent television station, City TV, and a cable music network.

Also to be seen are the Toronto Islands, offshore in Lake Ontario; the Casa Loma, a ninety-eight-room, twentieth-century Victorian castle in the center of the city; Eaton Centre, a vast, indoor shopping mall; and Harbourfront, along Toronto's waterfront. From Toronto, Niagara Falls is an easy day trip.

PERSONALITIES: Among the best-known faces to come out of Toronto's Jewish community are performers Lou Jacobi, Lloyd Bochner, Marilyn Lightstone, comedians Johnny Wayne and Frank Shuster, and CBS newsman Morley Safer. One of the leading CBC reporters is Barbara Frum. John Hirsch, formerly the director of the Shakespeare Festival in Stratford, Ontario, is a Torontonian, as is Sorel Etrog, a world-renowned sculptor. Lorne Greene, a native of Ottawa, moved to Toronto to start his professional career, while Bora Laskin left Toronto for Ottawa when he was appointed Chief Justice of Canada's Supreme Court. Toronto's Jews have been involved in politics since the nineteenth century and the city has had two Jewish mayors, Nathan Phillips (1955–62)—for whom the plaza in front of the beautiful city hall is named—and Philip G. Givens (1963–66).

The most famous character to have been produced, or at least half-produced, by Toronto's Jews is the co-creation of Joe Shuster (a cousin of Frank Shuster). In his earliest days, Clark Kent, a.k.a. Superman, worked not for *The Daily Planet* but *The Daily Star*—which was based on the *Toronto Star.* Shuster's collaborator was Jerry Siegel, of Cleveland.

READING: Despite other achievements, Toronto's Jews have produced nothing like the wealth of literature that has come out of Montreal. A general fictional picture of Toronto life, with some Jewish characters, can be found in Marian Engel's *The Year of the Child* (St.

Martin's). *A Good Place to Come From* (St. Martin's) and other works by Morley Torgov are set outside Toronto but deal with experiences common to Canadian Jews. Also worth a look are *The Jews of Toronto—A History to 1937* by Stephen A. Speisman (McClelland and Stewart) and *Spadina Avenue,* a history of the area with photos by Rosemary Donegan (Douglas and McIntyre).

CHOICES: The Windsor Arms Hotel, a small, intimate, antique-furnished and ivy-covered hostelry near Toronto's "Fifth Avenue" is also well-located for trips up Bathurst. Like Toronto itself, it is utterly civilized.

—PHYLLIS ELLEN FUNKE

Venice

Bridge of Sighs *(Leni Sonnenfeld)*

"The most beautiful and magical of cities," writes John Julius Norwich in his recent *A History of Venice,* and only partisans of Jerusalem will dispute his claim. The Italian masterpiece, its towers rising in subdued purples from the sea mists, expresses a people's determination to contrive shelter against the implacable forces of storm and wave.

The miracle of Venice is survival. Despite the fragility imposed by its unending struggle against slow submersion into the Adriatic, La Serenissima ("The Most Serene"), as the city is known, has remained virtually unchanged for over a thousand years, since its first settlers, fleeing the barbarians ravaging the Italian mainland, established themselves on the marshy islets off the coast to build their sanctuary.

Compare an eighteenth-century Canaletto engraving of the Rialto with a contemporary photograph of the storied bridge. Except for the difference in the dress of the pedestrians making the crossing, the scene is unchanged. During the week of Carnevale, when every second Venetian, it would seem, is parading the streets in the periwigs and pantaloons of remote ancestors, time seems to have made a complete stop.

Nowhere is this stasis more apparent than in the ancient Venice Ghetto. Established on April 10, 1516—the second day of Passover—it was the first officially mandated ghetto in Europe.

HISTORY: Jews settled in Venice as early as the tenth century and became an important factor in the economic life of the city whose well-being depended on its commerce with the rest of the Mediterranean and, particularly, with the prosperous cities of the Middle East, where Jewish merchants were already well connected.

In 1516, however, their contributions to the economy of Venice were conveniently overlooked. The city was overcrowded with refugees as Venice was recovering from a disastrous war with the mainland. The Council of Ten, Venice's ruling body, yielded to priestly clamor to "get the Jews out of the way."

Geto is the Italian word for "foundry," and it was to the site of the Ghetto Nuovo, or new foundry—a swampy, malaria-ridden district far removed from the central Piazza San Marco—that the reigning Doge consigned Venice's entire Jewish population. There were at the time more than a thousand men, women, and children involved in the move and the Ghetto community would ultimately grow as large as four thousand.

The Ghetto Nuovo district was cut off from the rest of Venice by a network of canals and enclosed by a high wall of fortress-like dimensions. The existing walls were further strengthened and made higher, as one can see today, and all windows facing outward were bricked over, to circumvent unauthorized entrance or exit. Only two gates breached the walls, one leading west toward the Cannaregio Canal and the other, at the extreme east, facing the Church of San Girolamo. These passageways were guarded by shifts of Christian watchmen—paid for by the Jewish community within.

During their ghettoization, Venice's Jews were forced to wear distinguishing red hats, and they were barred from every livelihood except trading, moneylending, and selling secondhand clothing. They were capriciously and excessively taxed whenever the city ran short of money, and their holy books were incinerated in the Piazza San Marco. As Mary McCarthy writes in *Venice Observed*, "They bled the Jewish community in every conceivable way. Since the law forbade Jews to own land, the Republic forced them to rent the Ghetto in its entirety on a long lease; the day the Jews moved in, rentals were raised one-third."

Nevertheless, the Ghetto community flourished as one of Europe's great centers of Jewish culture. Jewish merchants from every city in Italy, from Germany, Salonika and Constantinople came to do business in the Ghetto. Marranos from Spain and Portugal poured in, finding sanctuary from the Inquisition and expressing their long-buried Jewish identity. Paradoxically, the Venetian government that segregated its Jews also protected them. It needed their commercial skills, their enterprise, and their willingness to lend to the Christian poor at low rates—a risk no others would undertake. While the Ghetto is a stain on Venetian history, its inhabitants escaped the mob violence and pogroms that decimated Jewish communities across Western Europe, from Toledo to Frankfurt, from the Middle Ages to the French Revolution.

The Renaissance was a movement whose stimulating effects could not but infiltrate the Ghetto. By 1475, just two decades after Johannes Gutenberg invented movable type, Venetian Jewish artisans had set up the first Hebrew press and were carving out of wooden blocks as many as six different fonts of Hebrew characters.

Daniel Bomberg, a Christian from Antwerp, had earned the "privilege" from the Venetian Senate to engage in the printing of Hebrew books. Employing Jews to fashion the letters and to run the crude press, he produced his first work, the Torah, in November 1516, seven months after the Ghetto had been created. For the next thirty years, Bomberg and his staff of Jewish craftsmen, editors, and scholars pioneered in turning out such major works as the first Bible with commentaries (the *Mikraot Gedolot*) and the first printed Talmud—an edition whose organization and page arrangement are followed to this day.

In 1553, thirty years after Bomberg's Talmud appeared, Pope Julius II declared the work blasphemous. On the first day of Rosh Hashanah that year, the Talmud was publicly burned in Rome. The Venetian Council of Ten followed suit and the Talmud, along with other Hebrew books, was burned in Venice a month later. Nevertheless, Hebrew printing survived in Venice, setting standards of book production and scholarship for the next 250 years.

The Jews of the Ghetto maintained their own free school, the only one in the city, and illiteracy was unknown. They were no less eager to acquire, or to create, works of art. The five synagogues that remain in the Ghetto today are an expression of this esthetic refinement.

The early seventeenth century was a golden age for the Ghetto. The risky but lucrative trade with the Middle East had become a virtual Jewish monopoly. The Ghetto's shops displayed spices, jewels, bolts of silk. The narrow streets were alive with well-dressed merchants speaking the languages of their travels or Judeo-Venetian—the special, almost secret, dialect Ghetto inhabitants used to discuss confidential matters. Simone Luzzatto was the community's rabbi for fifty years, during which he wrote the first major statement advocating official toleration of the Jews. Among the many *responsa* he prepared was one sanctioning travel by gondola on the Sabbath.

Another figure of the period was Sara Coppio Sullam, a patron of the arts whose Ghetto salon was a meeting place for both Jewish and Christian writers and scholars. She composed sonnets, some of them enunciating her pride in Judaism.

Sullam was a benefactor of one of the most engaging figures in the annals of Venetian Jewry. Leone Modena—rabbi, scholar, poet, playwright, composer, alchemist, marriage arranger, and incurable gambler—was the wunderkind of the Ghetto. At two and a half, he was on the bimah reading the haftarah of the week. At three he was translating Torah passages from Hebrew into Italian and at thirteen he was translating Italian poetry into Hebrew. As a young rabbi in the Italian Synagogue, his sermons became so famous throughout the city that Christians joined Jews in the pews on Shabbat to hear him.

Modena was as profound in his scholarship as he was brilliant in his speaking. His critique of the kabbalistic movement still serves modern scholars, and his refutation of Christian dogma is a classic of Hebrew literature.

The early seventeenth century was a unique period for the Ghetto, never to be repeated. It was followed by new indignities. As the fortunes of the Venetian Republic declined through the eighteenth century, the government demanded ever greater tributes from the Jews.

When French troops opened the Ghetto in 1797, some of the quarter's young men volunteered to join Napoleon's army in its sweep of Italy, afterward enduring the long march to Moscow and the bitter retreat in the frigid Russian winter. There are stories of Hebrew songs being chanted around the French campfires during the disastrous campaign.

The spirit of freedom was renewed forty years later when Jews played a leading role in the revived but short-lived Venetian Republic of 1848–49. Daniele Manin, whose father was Jewish, was the head of the provisional republican government, and two members of his cabinet was Jewish.

The democratic revolution of 1848 had forced even the most reactionary governments of Europe to make concessions to their Jewish populations. In Rome, Pope Pius IX ordered that the walls of the ghettoes in the Papal States be destroyed. When Venice was incorporated into the new kingdom of Italy, Jews were given full equality. That status was interrupted only during the eight years of Mussolini's alliance with Hitler.

The generation of Venetian Jews which grew to maturity after the establishment of a united Italy is best represented by figures like Luigi Luzzatti, Italy's first Jewish prime minister (and a cousin of New York's Mayor Fiorello La Guardia). He had started his political career by organizing a mutual aid society for the gondoliers of Venice, an ill-paid group whose profession had been passed on from father to son since the invention of the gondola in the thirteenth century. Luzzatti went on to serve in the Italian parliament for fifty years, and was elected prime minister in 1910. Until his death in 1927, he was also an active supporter of the Zionist agricultural settlements in Palestine.

Since the unification of Italy, the Jews of Venice have experienced only one interruption in more than a century of freedom. Mussolini treated Jews much as the Council of Ten—a combination of restriction and protection. That changed when German troops occupied Venice. On November 9, 1943, the Nazis began rounding up Venice's Jews. By the following August, 205 had been caught (another 500 had fled or were hidden by Christian friends). Assembled in the Campo di Ghetto Nuovo, Jews were marched down the Ghetto Vecchio, over the bridge spanning the Cannaregio Canal to the railroad station two hundred yards away and thence, by freight car, to their deaths at Auschwitz. Among them was Chief Rabbi Adolfo Ottolenghi, who chose to stay with his flock rather than escape.

COMMUNITY: Government and church pronouncements notwithstanding, the relations of the people of the Ghetto with their fellow Venetians were "constant and intimate," as the historian Cecil Roth put it. "Jews and Christians worked together, played together, and quarreled together." Rabbi Luzzatto described the Venetian people as "more pleasing and kindly with the Jews than any other in the world." If you're lucky enough to be in Venice for the annual Carnevale, you'll delight in the spectacle of thousands of Venetians filling the vast Piazza San Marco, dressed in costumes of the sixteenth and seventeenth centuries—when all the city flocked to the Ghetto to observe the elaborate and imaginative Purim balls. The Council of Ten passed ordinances forbidding Christians to attend them, to no avail.

The Jews of Venice today—no more than 600 in a city of 450,000—are completely assimilated into the life of the city and live all over. There is perhaps no Jewish community in the world more indigenous to its city; most Venetian Jews trace their roots in Italy back many centuries. No more than twenty reside within the confines of the Ghetto, where the community offices are still based.

The Jews are largely in business and the professions—doctors, lawyers, engineers, and civil servants. S. Lattes and Company, publisher of scientific literature, continues a tradition that has been in the family since 1839. The Levi Foundation, on the Grand Canal, supports a variety of artistic enterprises in the tradition of Joshua Ben David Levi, an eighteenth-century Venetian poet who composed his works in Hebrew. The Luzzattos, who came to Venice in the fifteenth century, have produced a line of poets, scholars, rabbis, and public figures who have been outstanding in every generation. Danielle Luzzatto Gardner, the Venetian-born wife of President Carter's ambassador to Italy, has been active on the Save Venice Committee. With the help of that organization, her generation of Luzzattos fulfilled the restoration of the Luzzatto Chapel, in which their ancestors had worshipped four centuries ago, as one of the architectural ornaments of the Ghetto.

SIGHTS: The Jews of Venice are dispersed throughout the city but their roots are still in the Ghetto. The area now teems, as it did before 1516, with working-class Christian families. Their bright-colored and freshly laundered shirts and skirts are strung out on rope lines suspended between the top floors of the buildings facing one another across the narrow waterways. The Fondamenta di Cannaregio (the embankment along one side of the Ghetto) bustles with neighborhood trattorie; fishermen display their catch from boats tied up along the canal; men and women hawk fresh fruits and vegetables barged in from nearby islands. Only a few yards distant is the entrance to the Ghetto, a living museum of Jewish culture and history.

The modern visitor approaches the Ghetto by motor-driven vaporetto instead of the traditional gondola, and no longer passes through the heavy gates which once sealed Jews in the Ghetto from sundown to sunrise. Holes in the worn brick indicate the position of the hinges of the gates. Though the gates have vanished, the Ghetto itself remains as it has been for nearly five centuries. Beyond its entrance on the embankment of the Cannaregio Canal is the long, narrow, tunnel-like alley which leads into its center. The passage is barely ten feet wide and, like a canyon, threads its way between the rows of "skyscrapers"—the drab, seven- and eight-story tenements which were raised to that elevation, of necessity, to house the thousands who were herded into the meager quarter's confines.

To get there, take the Number 2 vaporetto. Disembark at the Ferrovia (railroad station) landing, walk to the right along the Lista di Spagna, cross the little bridge over the Cannaregio Canal, and immediately turn left on the Fondamenta di Cannaregio for about seventy-five yards to Farmacia Zechini. At that point, walk through the old passageway into the narrow alley called Ghetto Vecchio, which leads into the heart of the old Jewish quarter.

The Ghetto's five surviving synagogues are the highlight of any tour, but visitors must seek them out behind the shabby façades and on the upper floors of the crowded tenements in which they were housed, and hidden. Four of the synagogues represent the "nations" that made up the Jewish community: the Levantine, immigrants from the Near East; the Spanish, exiles from Spain and Portugal; the German, composed of Ashkenazim from Central Europe; and the Italian, descendants of Jews who had migrated to Venice from cities on the Italian mainland.

The synagogues were designed by the foremost Venetian architects of the sixteenth century. Master craftsmen—sculptors, really—carved the mahogany bimahs and the oak benches. The curtains before the Ark and the mantles covering the Torah scrolls were embroidered by the most expert needlewomen, from the finest silk imported from China. The city's leading silversmiths were employed to impart a richness and an intricacy of detail to Torah ornaments, candelabras, chandeliers, spice boxes, and Seder plates.

The museum of the German synagogue has a comprehensive display of these artifacts. Guides, mostly students from the University of Venice who are fluent in English, conduct tours of all five synagogues. The Spanish and the Levantine have been substantially restored and are in use, though the Spanish still needs work. The Italian, Canton, and German synagogues are in poor condition, but ask your guide to take you into them anyway. You'll get a hint of their past magnificence, along with the message that financial aid is sorely needed so that the small Jewish community can proceed with restoration.

The tour begins at the Ghetto Vecchio. Follow the alley as it widens into the Campiello delle Scuole (the Little Square of the Synagogues). To the left is the carved wooden door which opens into the Spanish Synagogue. It is the largest of the five and has functioned with only one interruption—the years of the Nazi occupation—since the sixteenth century. Services are held under the guidance of Rafaele Grassini, the young Venetian-born rabbi.

On the opposite side of the square is the ornate building which contains both the Levantine Synagogue and the Luzzatto Chapel. Unique among the five synagogues, the Levantine was not placed inconspicuously in a preexisting structure but built as an edifice unto itself. It was dedicated in 1538.

Beyond the Campiello delle Scuole, the Ghetto Vecchio continues over a bridge and into the much greater expanse of the Campo Ghetto Nuovo, the central plaza and heart of the Jewish quarter, where the other synagogues are located.

The oldest is the German, built in 1528 for the German community, some of whose ancestors had come to Venice as merchants as early as the thirteenth century. In the Ghetto's discreet style, the façade blends into those of adjoining buildings; only the motif of five high windows (three walled up) with arches in white stone distinguishes the synagogue from the dwellings around it.

To the right of the German is the Canton Synagogue, erected in 1531 and the second oldest in the Ghetto. It probably takes its name from the Canton family, German bankers who had it built as a private chapel. Another theory is that the name derives from its location: *Canton* is the Venetian word for "corner" and the synagogue stands at the corner of the great plaza. Often confused with buildings around it, the Canton Synagogue is identifiable by its high wooden dome, in the shape of an umbrella, mounted on what appears to be an octagonal drum.

Next to the Canton, on the south side of the plaza, is the Italian Synagogue. It dates from 1575 and is the "newest" and least elaborate of the five, a reflection of the status of the Italian "nation," the poorest and smallest segment of the community. The Italian Synagogue is also scarcely distinguishable from its neighbors, except for the five high, arched windows (like the German Synagogue's) and a crest above the center window with an inscription, in Italian: "Holy Italian Community in the year 1575."

Sabbath and holiday services are conducted at the Spanish Synagogue during the summer and the Levantine in winter, when crowds are smaller. Details on Sabbath and weekday services are available from the Jewish community office at Ghetto Vecchio 1188 (telephone, 715-012), which is also a social and cultural center of the community.

In addition to the synagogues and community center, visitors to the Ghetto should see the grim, artistic reminder of more recent history—a sculpture by the Lithuanian-born artist Arbit Blatas. Along the western side of the Campo Ghetto Nuovo is a brick wall, its surface chipped and faded after the passage of centuries. Atop the wall there are still strands of barbed wire installed by the Nazis when they used the Ghetto as a gathering place for Jews. It was on this Ghetto wall that Blatas and his wife, opera star Regina Resnik, proposed to mount the seven bronzed tablets of the completed sculpture. The preservation-minded city fathers, who deliberate on the replacement of even a single paving block in the Piazza San Marco, were quick and enthusiastic in granting approval.

RECOMMENDATIONS: Once you reach the Marco Polo airport outside Venice, be sure to take the motor launch across the lagoon to the city rather than the motor bus. The boat affords the classic—and breathtaking—approach by water and you land in the center of everything, at the foot of the Piazza San Marco. A good place to stay is the Londra Palace, a former palazzo with the intimacy and charm one looks for in Europe. All the rooms face the lagoon, and the walk to San Marco is only five minutes along the lagoon's broad embankment.

Venice is a walker's city and simply by virtue of this there is eye contact and communication with other pedestrians on tiny bridges, in the narrow twisting alleys and the unexpected plazas. Mass transport is the best in the world, aboard the various lines of the vaporetti. The fare is cheap (about fifty cents) and there are reduced fares for getting on and off, as one should, to explore.

EATING: There are no kosher restaurants in Venice, but kosher lunches are available at the Casa di Reposo (the home for the aged) at Ghetto Nuovo 2874. Make a reservation well in advance at 716-002. Among the restaurants favored by Venetians themselves are Paradiso Perduto, Cannaregio 2540, a few hundred yards from the Ghetto, and Montin on the Fondamenta di Borgo. More expensive is the Corte Sconta, near the Arsenal, at Calle del Pestrin 3886. The pasta and fish dishes are superb and the meal is concluded with amaretti, the almond-flavored cookies that originated in the bakeries of the Ghetto.

SHOPPING: The Ghetto Vecchio and the Campo (the Ghetto's central plaza) offer good craft shops selling the products of local artisans in brass, silver, and glass. There is a lot of kitsch but also much of good quality. Judaica is available from Mordehai Fusetti at Ghetto Vecchio 1219; glass figures of Jewish interest are blown at Tosi Gianni, Ghetto Nuovo 2884. Elsewhere in the city, try Vogini for leather goods, Paul & Co. or Salvati for glass, Jessurun for laces and linens, and Roberta di Camerino for high fashion. The Jessurun family and Mrs. Di Camerino are Venetian Jews.

READING: There is a vast literature on Venice, from Niccolò Machiavelli to Jan Morris. The definitive guidebook is Lorenzetti's *Venice and Its Lagoon* (Edizioni Lint). Two invaluable paperbacks are *History of the Jews in Venice* by Cecil Roth (Schocken) and *Venice: A Portable Reader* by Toby Cole (Lawrence Hill). A more recent history is *The Ghetto of Venice* by Ricardo Calimani (Dutton). Another useful work is *The Ghetto of Venice, Its Synagogues and Museum* (Carucci Editore) by Giovannina Reinisch Sullam, a descendant of Sara Sullam. It is well worth the trouble of finding—which is something you might say of Venice itself.

—GABRIEL LEVENSON

Vienna

Seitenstettengasse Synagogue *(Austrian National Tourist Office)*

In November 1918, with the end of World War I and the collapse of the thousand-year Austro-Hungarian Empire, Sigmund Freud told Ernst Lothar, a young disciple who was interviewing him: "Like you, I feel an unrestrained affection for Vienna—although, perhaps unlike you, I know her abysses."

Freud would always have this love-hate relationship with the city in which he spent seventy-nine of his eighty-three years, sharing such feelings with the other great Jews of his time—Herzl, Schnitzler, Buber, Schönberg, Mahler, and scores more—who made Vienna, for half a century, one of the major intellectual centers of the world.

A like dualism must affect sensitive visitors to the Austrian capital today. They will find—more readily than its abysses—the apexes: Schönbrunn and the Prater, the Ringstrasse and the Kunsthistorisches Museum, the elegant shops on the Kärntnerstrasse and the *gemütlich* wine cellars of Grinzing. At the same time, beyond the whipped cream and the waltzes, they can uncover the evidence of a rich, often tragic history that cannot but enhance their travel experience.

In the seven decades since Freud spoke with Lothar, Vienna has gone through the great social programs of the 1920s, the crushing attacks on the progressive (and mainly Jewish-led) Social Democratic Party during the early 1930s, the Anschluss with Nazi Germany in 1938, the destruction of a Jewish community of almost two hundred thousand between 1939 and 1945, and the postwar reconstruction of Austria. The Austrian Government belatedly and reluctantly accepted its obligation to reeducate a population whose families have been steeped in anti-Semitism for generations and who themselves still admit—85 percent of them according to a recent survey—to lingering prejudices against their Jewish fellow citizens. Then, in an apparent backward step in 1986, the revelations of Kurt Waldheim's Nazi past seemed to win him more votes in the presidential election than it cost him. Perhaps Freud would not have been surprised.

HISTORY: Jewish history in Vienna follows the same sad pattern as in almost every other city of Western Europe: early settlement in

Roman times; persecution when the indigenous tribes adopted Christianity; intermittent toleration and expulsion during the Middle Ages; capricious cycles of reform and repression in the sixteenth century to the eighteenth; and the beginnings of the genuine acceptance after the French Revolution. Perhaps the most important exception from the European rule came during the Black Death epidemic that wiped out a third of the continent's population in 1348–49; Vienna was one of the few cities where Jews were *not* accused of causing the scourge and the city became a refuge for Jews fleeing other stricken cities.

A turning point came in 1683 when financial support from Imperial Court agents Wertheimer and Oppenheimer helped the Austrian Army to repel Turkish invaders, driving them out of Central Europe for good. Since then, Jews have been active in every sphere of Viennese life.

There were still restrictions, however, and as late as 1777 there were only 520 Jews in the city. By 1793, following the "Toleranzpatent" of Emperor Joseph II (which paved the way for ultimate emancipation in 1867), there was already such growth that the community could set up a Hebrew printing press that soon became the center for Hebrew publishing in Central Europe.

Opportunities expanded for bankers and merchants, for clerks and civil servants, scholars and journalists. Vienna became a center of the Haskalah movement which opened the hitherto closed world of traditional Jewish thought to the influences of secularism.

Vienna's Jewish golden age really began after the revolution of 1848, in which Jews participated. During the succeeding ninety years the Jews would dominate Vienna's cultural and intellectual life. Even before the official emancipation, however, the liberalized atmosphere reached out to previously sheltered Jewish womanhood, and there emerged such figures as Fanny Arnstein, daughter and wife of prominent bankers, whose salon was a meeting place for the personalities of the time, including the emperor himself and Mozart, who was for some time on her payroll.

There was hardly a field in which Jews did not make remarkable contributions to the city and empire. Jews prominent in medicine in Vienna were Sigmund Freud, Alfred Adler, Wilhelm Reich, and Theodor Reik; in politics Theodor Herzl and Max Nordau; in theology Martin Buber; in music Arnold Schönberg, Gustav Mahler, and Emmerich Kálmán; in theater Max Reinhardt, Fritz Kortner, Lily Darvas, and Elisabeth Bergner; in letters Arthur Schnitzler, Franz Kafka, Stefan Zweig, and Felix Salten.

Three of the four Austrians who won the Nobel Prize in medicine were Jews, and by the late nineteenth century more than half Vienna's physicians and dentists, 60 percent of its lawyers, and substantial numbers of university teachers and others in the liberal professions were Jewish. Most of the leaders of the Social Democratic Party also were Jews—men like Viktor Adler, one of its founders, Max Adler, and Otto Bauer.

It was a brilliant period, from the 1880s—when Herzl was writing his feuilletons in the *Neue Freie Presse* and Freud beginning his medical practice—until 1938, when Austria's Anschluss with Germany brought the era to a tragic end.

In the polyglot, multinational Austro-Hungarian Empire, with its heady mixture of races and cultures, there was a kind of aesthetic democracy, in which the Jews were the first among equals. For all of that, Vienna was steeped in anti-Semitism. The traditional animus against the Jews had been essentially religious. The prejudice acquired a new rationale—racism—with the writings of Wilhelm Marr, a German demagogue of the mid nineteenth century who in 1879 coined the phrase "anti-Semitism" to describe the mission of the organization he founded that year, the League of Anti-Semites. Marr's spiritual heir was Vienna-born Georg von Schönerer, who elevated anti-Semitism into a major disruptive force in Austrian political life.

Schönerer's career ended when he was jailed for wrecking the offices of the Jewish-owned *Neues Wiener Tageblatt* and beating up members of what he had described as a "Jewish rag."

But he was soon followed by another anti-Semite, whose influence has persisted to this day. Karl Lueger, who started as a liberal, lacked the total conviction of Schönerer but utilized anti-Semitic slogans with much greater success. A handsome, blond, archetypical Aryan—known as *Der schöne Karl* (the beautiful Charles)—he was idolized by the lower middle class and the artisans of Vienna to whom he cynically appealed as the "victims" of Jewish bankers and businessmen. Though he actually had some Jewish friends, he was repeatedly elected mayor of Vienna on a platform of anti-Semitism. As mayor, he implemented a municipal socialism of sorts—a city-owned gasworks, electric street lighting and electrified trams, improved waterworks. To this day, Lueger is revered as one of the greatest mayors of Vienna. A street and a square are named for him. The consequences of his ideology and the National Socialism it inspired are insufficiently recognized.

Lueger died in 1910, and his funeral evoked one of the greatest outpourings of humanity, up until then, in Vienna's history. Among the mourners was Adolf Hitler, then a struggling young artist who lived in a hostel for men on Mazzesinsel (Matza island), a working class district of the city with a large percentage of Jewish residents. Hitler had just been rejected from the Academy of Fine Arts and was earning a few groschen by selling his sentimental Vienna cityscapes to Jewish frame dealers. The paintings had little intrinsic value but they served as fillers for the picture frames which were being promoted.

Both von Schönerer and Lueger figure in *Mein Kampf*. Lueger's techniques—rallying the alienated mobs—and the slogans of anti-Semitism would reach their apocalypse in Hitler's hands. Just as the mayor's funeral brought out the people of Vienna in 1910, the Anschluss in March 1938 would bring many, many more into the streets. By then, any opposition to union with Germany had been stifled. The Social Democratic Party had been crushed; the thousands of Austrians opposed to Nazi rule would be thrown into concentration camps, most to be executed.

World War I had reduced the vast, multinational empire to an insignificant monolingual country. Its language was German, and the dream of fusion with another nation speaking the same tongue had been shared by almost every element in Austrian society—from the Social Democrats to the most extreme monarchists, from Cardinal Innitzer who welcomed Hitler to the Viennese poor who could suddenly find jobs in the German arms industry. Austria's anti-Semitic tradition didn't hurt its enthusiasm for union with Germany. Kristallnacht, the night of November 9–10, 1938, when Germany's synagogues were burned, was celebrated as much in Vienna as in Berlin.

The dream of many Austrians, however, was an immediate nightmare for the country's 200,000 Jews, 180,000 of whom lived in Vienna. In the first, frenzied days of Anschluss thousands cheered and jeered at the spectacle of the leading Jewish citizens parading the square with "I am Jew" placards around their necks. They were forced to scrub the pavement, on which opponents of the plebiscite had futilely painted election slogans. Among the street cleaners was Chief Rabbi David Israel Taglicht, who declared, "I am cleaning God's earth."

The Austrian Nazis had been assiduous students of the tactics of their German comrades, and they moved much more rapidly to rob, expel, and eventually murder their Jewish fellow citizens. One hundred thousand escaped before war broke out; seventy thousand died; less than a thousand, who had somehow hidden in Vienna until it was liberated by the Red Army, survived to form the nucleus of a new postwar community.

Austrian Nazism had made its own contribution to the extermination of Austrian, and all European, Jewry. Such native sons as Hitler and Eichmann had set an example. The undoing of their deeds is a major and difficult undertaking to which all Austria's postwar governments have addressed themselves, with varying degrees of energy and success.

COMMUNITY: Leon Zelman, director of Jewish Welcome Service, likes to describe Vienna's present-day Jewish community (virtually the entire Jewish population of Austria) as a phoenix risen from the ashes. Indeed, from the ashes it rose, but it is a modest phoenix. The eight hundred who emerged from the ruins of the city were joined by displaced persons from the concentration camps, by refugees from the Hungarian counterrevolution of 1956 and from the Czech and Polish expulsions of 1968–69, by Soviet Jews in the 1970s and by natives who felt impelled to return "home" from Israel and the United States. There are now about seven thousand members of the community, and they enjoy the facilities of a wide range of institutions.

Zelman, a native Austrian, was liberated from Mauthausen, Austria's "own" concentration camp, at seventeen. The Welcome Service he organized in 1980 serves as a resource center to provide local people and visitors with information about Jewish life and history. It is under the city's auspices, with a former Vienna mayor as its honorary president and the World Jewish Congress as its "support system."

Once the center of an empire, Vienna is now a center of neutrality, and the result is often the same. The meeting place for both confrontation and conciliation between Russians and Americans, it has served as the point of entry for more than two million refugees from other lands since 1945, including more than two hundred thousand Jews.

With a constant movement of peoples through Vienna and beyond, to Israel, the United States, and Western Europe, the Jewish community has managed, miraculously, to sustain its structure. An older generation of natives, who returned to collect reparations or to spend final days in a beloved "hometown," is dying out. A middle generation has taken root—children of the returnees and, on a larger scale, Rus-

sian Jews (many coming back to Vienna from Israel) who now constitute a majority. Most of the children of the community—there are half
a dozen bar mitzvahs a week—are Russian.

The editor of *Gemeinde,* the official monthly publication of the community, found that the Russians—so long cut off from mainstream
Judaism—lacked a sense of Jewish roots and frequently avoided regis-
tering with the community. Mainly through the efforts of Habad, the
Lubavitcher movement, Georgian and Bokharan Jews have joined in
increasing numbers and attend services, at their own synagogue.

Their connection with religious life has helped these Jews make
what would otherwise have been a difficult adaptation to the West.
Many run vegetable and grocery stalls, or shoe repair shops on Mex-
icoplatz—in contrast to the longer established European Jews who
work in medicine, law, engineering, the government, and business.

Perhaps 10 percent of the community is actively Orthodox, although all ten of the synagogues and midrashim are fully observant.
There are no Reform, Conservative, or Reconstructionist congregations in Vienna, but the Stadttempel, the 150-year-old synagogue,
ecumenically embraces worshippers along a wide range of commitment—from atheists to adherents of Agudat Israel.

The Gemeinde (community), with offices next to the Stadttempel
on Seitenstettengasse, is the official body of Viennese Jewry, recognized as such by law. Those who register with it pay it a percentage of
their annual income tax. The government partially subsidizes the
agency with an annual allocation besides covering the salaries of the
sixteen top executives (out of a total staff of 150).

Gemeinde funds help support an old-age home, the maintenance of
cemeteries (including one dating from 1571), and Zvi Perez Chajes, a
recently built day school with two hundred students. The Gemeinde
also supports a half dozen Talmud Torahs and kindergartens, a Jewish
student organization, and several Zionist youth groups.

There is a growing trend among young Jews in Vienna to identify
with Judaism—if not religiously, certainly culturally and socially. They
are conscious of the importance of a Jewish presence in the city and
the country which Hitler had pledged to make *judenrein.* Until recently,
this growing consciousness was, by and large, a quiet phenomenon.
The Waldheim campaign and election, which uncovered a layer of
Austrian anti-Semitism, has also prompted Viennese Jewry to be more
outspoken than at any time since the war.

The pantheon of Jewish greats may never reappear in Vienna.

Today's community doesn't have the critical mass to generate a specifically Jewish culture, with writers like Schnitzler or Zweig who gave voice to the Jewish condition of their times, let alone infuse the general culture with Jewish elements. There are no longer Jewish neighborhoods, as in pre-Anschluss days, when there were forty-two synagogues in the city. Most of Vienna's prewar Jewish population lived either in the First District (the heart of the Old City) or in the Second and 20th districts on Mazzesinsel, the island opposite the First, separated from it by the Danube Canal. But there is a Jewish presence, nonetheless, and a Jewish past that is an ineradicable part of the Viennese experience.

PERSONALITIES: There are a few exceptions. Former Chancellor Bruno Kreisky, though ambivalent about his Jewishness and a friend of Yasir Arafat, was instrumental in the campaign to educate Austria about Nazism. Two Viennese Jews who have played major roles in dealing with the Holocaust are Simon Wiesenthal, whose Documentation Center has been a prime clearing house in the worldwide search for war criminals, and Peter Sichrovsky, of the postwar generation, whose book *Strangers in Their Own Land* (Basic Books) addresses the perennial question of how Jews can live in Germany and Austria today. Topsy Kuppers, a Dutch-born Jewish actress, is known for her one-woman shows at the Freie Bühne Theater; one recent performance was *Lola Blau,* a traditional Viennese cabaret production about a Jewish actress before, during, and after Hitler.

Though Vienna's decline began with the breakup of the Austro-Hungarian Empire in 1918, its Jewish intelligentsia helped create an afterglow of greatness until 1938. And to this day, Vienna's Jewish sons and daughters enrich the parts of the world in which they are settled. A highly selective list of the Viennese Jews who have made their marks after emigrating includes the composer Frederick Loewe, Charles Bludhorn of Gulf + Western, Supreme Court Justice Felix Frankfurter, film directors Billy Wilder and Otto Preminger, film star Theodore Bikel, and the mayor of Jerusalem, Teddy Kollek.

SIGHTS: There is much to see in and around Jewish Vienna, and the office of the Welcome Service, in the heart of the city, is the place to pick up brochures, information, and knowledgeable guides. It is at Stephansplatz 10, First District, in the very center of the Old City, where the Romans built their encampment almost two thousand years ago. The Welcome Center (telephone, 63-88-91) can arrange tours of Jewish Vienna and of Jewish sites outside the city as well. Be sure to get a copy of the booklet distributed by the Welcome Service entitled "Heritage and Mission: Jewish Vienna."

For almost a thousand years the broad, cobblestoned expanse of Stephansplatz has been the heart of the city. Dominating the square is Stephansdom, the magnificent fourteenth-century cathedral which was gutted by Allied bombers during World War II and has been meticulously restored to its former grandeur, including the replacement of the original medieval stained-glass windows depicting the Vienna Jews of the period. Building stones from the nearby Rothschild mansion, which had been razed, were used in the repairs. The forty synagogues destroyed by the German and Austrian Nazis were not rebuilt; there was no need to, since there were no longer worshippers to use them.

A short walk from the cathedral is the one synagogue which survived—perhaps because it is inconspicuously blended into a continuous façade with adjoining buildings. Dedicated in 1826 and, hence, the oldest existing Jewish structure in the city, the Stadttempel (City Temple), at Seitenstettengasse 4, conceals an elaborate, elliptical interior. Thanks to the insistence of the government, in 1826, that the synagogue not be erected as a separate structure, it escaped notice when the other synagogues were attacked in 1938. Guided tours can be arranged through the secretary, at 36-16-55. Next door, at Seitenstettengasse 2, is the community office telephone, 63-89-81. (Another community center at Bauernfeldgasse 4 has an exhibit of Jewish religious items in the lobby.)

Around the corner from the Stadttempel and part of the same, large community-owned building is the kosher Noah's Ark Restaurant (telephone, 63-89-82). Also community-owned, it is now run by two experienced restaurateurs from Warsaw. The food is first class; the ambience, elegant and discreet; the cost, very reasonable.

In the area formerly known as Mazzesinsel—now Leopoldstadt in the Second District—is a kosher restaurant, operated by the Lubavitchers. The address is Hollandstrasse 3 (telephone, 33-46-74 or 33-35-65).

Vegetarian food is available in the First District at Siddartha, Fleischmarkt 16. Such restaurants are rare in a city of carnivores. This one is expensive, but very good.

A few blocks distant is Judenplatz, the main square of the Jewish community for five hundred years. The Mizrachi organization maintains a small midrash and school here at Judenplatz 8 (telephone, 66-

41-53) and does a fine job of educating young Iranians in the principles of Judaism. At any given time in recent years, there have been two hundred to three hundred Iranian children sheltered in Vienna, transients who remain in the city only long enough to obtain visas to the United States. The modest school is well worth seeing. Its head is Josef Meir, a Vienna native who emigrated to Israel and has returned for an extended tour of duty. He is delighted to show visitors about— and to take them down five flights of cellar stairs, illuminated only by candlelight, to a subterranean mikvah dating from the fifteenth century.

In the square outside the five-story Mizrachi walk-up is a statue of Gotthold von Lessing, the philo-Semitic author of *Nathan the Wise.* The bronze sculpture was moved from its spot in an obscure part of the city to this site of greater relevance. The monument has helped establish the tone and direction of Vienna's Jews in affirming their enduring presence and of the city's authorities in attempting to secure it.

There are many other locations of special interest in the First District of the city, all within easy walking distance of the Welcome Service on Stephansplatz. Most significant is the Austrian Resistance Museum at Wipplingerstrasse 8 (telephone, 63-07-31). It offers schoolchildren and the public a permanent collection of documents and oral history, a library, traveling exhibits, and other materials relating to the Austrian struggle against Nazism.

There is a statue of Karl Lueger, the mayor who inspired Hitler, but, as a counterbalance, there are now dozens of statues and plaques throughout the city in honor of those who died in the underground fight against Nazism. The monuments and street signs named for prominent Viennese Jews, systematically removed after Anschluss, have been returned to their appropriate places, along with newer memorials. A recent brochure, published by the Social Democratic Party, available at the Welcome Service, lists all these memorials, with a brief description of each. Among the streets and monuments in the brochure are Theodor Herzlhof, a municipal housing project in Leopoldstadt, the heart of the old Jewish quarter; Desider Friedmanhof, at Ferdinandstrasse 23, an apartment house named for the last president of the Jewish community before the Holocaust; Arnsteingasse, a street in the 15th District named for the Baron Nathan von Arnstein and his wife, Fanny; and Viktor Adlerplatz, a square in the 10th District named for the founder of the Social Democratic Party. The many streets named for Jews include Rosa Luxembourggasse, Mahlerstrasse, Spinozagasse, Stefan Zweigplatz, Kafkastrasse, and Werfelstrasse.

Also among the listings in the brochure is the Zvi Perez Chajes day school, named for Vienna's chief rabbi between the World Wars. The handsome new building was constructed on the site of the old school. It became the deportation point at which the city's Jews were gathered by the SS—under the direction of Adolf Eichmann—and shipped to Auschwitz. At the time of the rededication of the school in 1984, Rudolf Kirchschlager, then president of the Austrian Republic, delivered the keynote speech. Visits to the school, at Castellezgasse 35 in the Second District, can be arranged by calling 63-99-73.

Back in the First District is the Max Berger Collection of Judaica, at Schottenring 35 (telephone, 34-53-62). In an enormous apartment in the grand *fin de siècle* style, Max Berger—a retired furniture dealer—has put together a private museum of more than three thousand artifacts and a library of twelve thousand books. Representing the work of almost forty years, Berger's collection is one of the largest in the world. It is open to the public without charge.

At Salztorgasse 6 is the Simon Wiesenthal Documentation Center (officially the Documentation Center of the Union of Jewish Victims of the Nazis), where the famed Nazi hunter maintains an ongoing file on the history and present whereabouts of his "clients." For permission to visit the center, call 63-91-31.

A ten-minute metro-plus-tram ride from Stephansplatz is the Sigmund Freud House at Berggasse 19. The second-floor apartment where Freud lived and worked from 1891 to 1938 (the year of his flight to London, where he died in 1939) has been preserved as it was during that period of his life. The hundreds of items on display were assembled by Freud's daughter, Anna, and by the family housekeeper, Paula Fichtl. The memorabilia include pipe and walking stick, cigar boxes and books, letters and photographs, writing desk and psychoanalytic couch.

It is all laid out in affectionate detail, as if the great man had just walked out of the apartment for coffee and conversation at his favorite café. It was (and is) Café Landtmann, at the corner of Dr. Karl Lueger Ring and Löwelstrasse. Freud would relax over tarok, a four-handed card game he loved passionately—as did that bane of his being, none other than Lueger himself.

SIDE TRIPS: Mauthausen, the former concentration camp two hours west of Vienna, attracts hundreds of thousands of Austrians annually, and is regularly visited by schoolchildren. In recent years, recruits into the Army take an oath of allegiance there. The preserved camp has been the focal point of the government's efforts to educate the nation about the fate of the country's Jews, Austrian collaboration with Hitler and, not least of all, the Austrian resistance.

The Jewish museum of Eisenstadt, thirty-two miles south of Vienna, is located in the mansion of what was once the home of the Wolf family, the most prominent Jews of the area—the province of Burgenland. Financed by the government, the museum collection memorializes the Eisenstadt Jewish community of 446, which was never reconstituted after the war, and presents a detailed picture of Jewish life in the twelve countries which were, at one time, part of the Austro-Hungarian Empire. The museum is on Museumgasse, adjacent to the Unterberggasse, in the city's old Jewish quarter. On the Unterberggasse itself is Wertheimer's Synagogue, built in 1750 and recently restored.

READING: Two important general studies of Austria, and Vienna, are Carl E. Schorske's *Fin-de-Siècle Vienna* (Vintage Press) and William M. Johnston's *The Austrian Mind* (University of California). Evocative portraits of the city include Frederic Morton's *A Nervous Splendor* (Little, Brown), Heimito von Doderer's *The Demons* (Knopf), Robert Musil's *The Man Without Qualities* (Coward-McCann), and the works of Arthur Schnitzler—like *Viennese Novelettes, The Little Comedy,* or *My Youth in Vienna.* The best guidebook for an insider's view of the city is *Viennnawalks* by J. Sydney Jones (Holt, Rinehart & Winston). Marsha L. Rozenblit has written *The Jews of Vienna, 1867–1914: Assimilation and Identity* (SUNY Press), a detailed study of the Community during its golden age.

If you have trouble finding books on Vienna at home, try Shakespeare & Co., an English-language bookstore at Sterngasse 2, just around the corner from the Noah's Ark Restaurant. The combination of good kosher food and good literature is unbeatable. If Vienna had its abysses even as the capital of an empire, it has its apexes even as the capital of a small country.

—GABRIEL LEVENSON

Washington

Signing of Israeli-Egyptian Peace Treaty at White House, 1979
(Alan M. Tigay)

With the Star of David unfurled on their banners, they mass, in the searing heat, on Capitol Hill to protest the sale of sophisticated weapons to an Arab state. Across from the White House, they gather in a sukkat shalom to demand a nuclear freeze. On a wintry afternoon, they demonstrate for Soviet Jews through a daily vigil (which has gone on every day since 1969). They are members of the 160,000-strong, dynamic, activist, and Zionist Jewish community of Washington, D.C., exercising the freedom of expression that few countries permit.

This diverse Jewish community of government officials and workers, professionals, merchants, homemakers, and students is part of the pulsebeat of the national capital, helping to shape the country's laws, culture, and development. Jewish visibility is strengthened by the presence of the national offices of many Jewish organizations which monitor congressional legislation, such as school prayer and aid to Israel.

HISTORY: Isaac Polock, the first Jew to settle in Washington, in 1795, built six townhouses between the White House and Georgetown, the last of which was torn down in 1983. Polock, who arrived five years before the Federal Government was moved to the District of Columbia, later returned to his native Savannah, Georgia; but a member of his household, Raphael Jones, a teacher and possibly a shohet, lived in Washington until his death.

In 1840, Washington's Jewish population numbered only 25 in a total population of 23,340. It grew rapidly, however, with a large influx of Jews, many of whom settled in Georgetown, where they worked as artisans and shop owners. During the Civil War, Jews came to Washington as civil servants or soldiers, afterward making it their home. Poverty-stricken Jews who left the South after the conflict also put down roots in the growing city. Between 1860 and 1910, flourishing jewelry, shoe, furniture, and department stores were established by the Lansburgh, Hecht, Rich, Harris, Hahn, Kann, and Schwartz families.

Between the two world wars, especially during the New Deal, many young Jewish college graduates joined Washington's official ranks. As the Jewish population grew, many moved from "D.C." to the fast-expanding suburbs of northern Virginia and southern Maryland. Beautiful synagogues, community centers, kosher markets, and day schools were built, making these communities vital and self-sustaining.

COMMUNITY: The Washington Jewish community gained cohesiveness with the founding of its first synagogue, Washington Hebrew Congregation, in 1852, under the leadership of Navy Captain Jonas Philips Levy and twenty-one other members. When this congregation joined the Reform movement and installed an organ two decades later, some of its more traditional members built their own synagogue, Adas Israel, at Sixth and G Streets, N.W.; President Ulysses S. Grant and his Cabinet attended the synagogue's dedication in 1876.

With the community's growth, other Orthodox congregations were soon formed—Ohev Shalom, Talmud Torah, Beth Shalom, and Kesher Israel in Georgetown, still in use today at 2801 N Street, N.W. Most of these substantial buildings are now churches, their Jewish symbols still visible.

Social support organizations were gradually organized, and Washington's first Jewish Community Center was founded in 1925; its first day school in the 1940s. The first Embassy of Israel was established in 1948 in an elegant old townhouse on Twenty-second Street, just off Embassy Row. Three major Jewish organizations that maintain their national headquarters in Washington are B'nai B'rith, the Jewish War Veterans, and the American Israel Public Affairs Committee, the Jewish community's foreign-policy lobby.

Between 1943 and the present—while its numbers were escalating from 13,000 to 160,000—the Jewish community's expansion into the suburbs was diffuse rather than concentrated in one neighborhood. In the Silver Spring, Maryland, area, a community of Orthodox Jews centers its activities around the Silver Spring Jewish Community Center on Arcola Avenue and the Chaim Weizmann Yiddish-Hebrew Folk School on Middlegate Road. The Greater Washington Jewish Community Center, at 6125 Montrose Road, in Rockville, Maryland, is centrally located to serve Jews of Rockville, Bethesda, Potomac, Silver Spring, and upper Montgomery County.

A variety of religious and cultural activities has also developed in the northern Virginia suburbs of Fairfax, Falls Church, Alexandria, Arlington, and Reston.

Perhaps because Washington itself is a city with a large transient population, the Jewish community, too, lacks deep roots, in contrast to other large Jewish communities in the East, where families and businesses go back many generations. Curiously, Washington's younger generation, mostly highly trained professionals, have not remained in Washington to carry on family businesses, but have settled all over the United States and overseas, making the native-born Washingtonian hard to find. Some notable exceptions are the late Hyman Goldman, whose son, Aaron, followed in his business and philanthropic footsteps; and the Smith, Rodman, and Kay families— all in the construction business—also known as philanthropists and community leaders.

A Washington cantor's son, Asa Yoelson, gained fame as singer, vaudevillian, and actor Al Jolson, and starred in the first full-length talkie, *The Jazz Singer*. Contemporary Washingtonians making a name for themselves in the arts are Zelda Fischandler, founder and director of the Arena Stage repertory theater; Martin Feinstein, general director of the Washington Opera, and the actress Goldie Hawn. Daniel Boorstin, the Pulitzer Prize–winning historian, is the Librarian of Congress. Many Jews work in the news media including *Washington Post* publisher Donald Graham and Watergate ace Carl Bernstein, now a reporter for ABC News. There are also eight Jewish senators and thirty-four Jewish members in the House of Representatives.

To see the community's activists in action—and perhaps to join them—go north from the White House to the world's longest-standing continuous protest: the Soviet Jewry vigil. Sponsored by Washington-area Jewish groups, it is held daily from 12:30–12:45 P.M., across from the Soviet Embassy on Sixteenth Street, N.W., between L and M streets. Visitors are encouraged to join.

SIGHTS: There's no need to go off the beaten track to see Washington's meaningful Jewish sights. Most can be seen on walking tours around or in the national shrines and museums.

What better way to begin a tour of Washington than with a visit to Capitol Hill, its panoramic vista stretching across the mall to the Lincoln Memorial, where guided tours begin at the main rotunda.

Statues by American Jewish sculptor Jo Davidson of the late Senator Robert La Follette and humorist Will Rogers can be seen on the House side of the Capitol. Davidson's bust of Henry Wallace is in the corridor east of the Senate chamber. While on "The Hill," a visit to your congressman or senator can be arranged by calling the Capitol exchange at 224-3121.

Nearby at the majestic Supreme Court building, First and East Capitol streets, N.E., among the portraits of deceased Supreme Court Justices are exhibited those of Louis Brandeis, Benjamin Cardozo, Felix Frankfurter, and Abe Fortas.

Near the Capitol, the exquisite Italian Renaissance Library of Congress (First and Pennsylvania Avenue, S.E.), has the largest collection of rare Hebrew and Yiddish texts in any governmental collection.

Washington's historic first synagogue, the original Adas Israel, built in 1876, is a short walk from Capitol Hill at Third and G streets, N.W. Today it houses the Lillian and Albert Small Jewish Museum of Washington and the Jewish Historical Society of Greater Washington. Exhibits highlight the history of Washington Jewry and how the synagogue structure was saved from demolition and moved to its present site in 1969. The restored sanctuary, of great simplicity, is on the second floor (open Sunday, 11 A.M. to 4 P.M.).

Portraits of Americans who have made great contributions in a variety of fields are exhibited at the National Museum of American Art (formerly the National Portrait Gallery), Eighth and G streets, N.W. George Gershwin and Albert Einstein are so honored. Golda Meir and Winston Churchill are the only non-Americans included. In the same building, the National Museum of American Art has large collections of works by Jewish artists Chaim Gross and Ben Shahn.

On the Mall, about midway between the Capitol and the Washington Monument, is the intriguing, circular-shaped Hirshhorn Museum and Sculpture Garden, named for the late art collector, Joseph Hirshhorn, who donated his multimillion-dollar art collection to the government. Hirshhorn arrived in the United States a poor Latvian Jewish immigrant and grew up in New York's Williamsburg section. While quite young he made a fortune in the stock market and later in uranium. Works by many leading Jewish artists are shown in the museum's permanent and changing exhibits and in its magnificent sunken sculpture garden.

Just across the Mall at the Natural History Museum, a small collection of Judaica, contributed by Cyrus Adler in 1893, is on display in the Hall of Asiatic Cultures.

The headquarters of B'nai B'rith International, 1649 Rhode Island Avenue, N.W., houses the Klutznick Museum, one of the nation's outstanding Judaica collections. Permanent exhibits portray twenty centuries of Jewish life, ranging from ancient coins to modern ceremonial objects. Special exhibits depict milestones in the Jewish experience.

In 1984 the Jewish War Veterans dedicated their new national headquarters at 1811 R Street, N.W., which houses its National Memorial and Museum, honoring American Jews who served and died in America's wars.

In the Foggy Bottom area, many foreign nations contributed exquisite furnishings to the John F. Kennedy Center for the Performing Arts, 2700 F Street, N.W. One of the loveliest is the Israeli lounge, a reception room near the concert hall, decorated by Israeli artists commissioned by the State of Israel. One wall of carved African walnut by Nehemia Azaz portrays biblical musical instruments. On the other walls, line drawings by kibbutz artist Yehezkiel Kimchi depict the vitality of modern Israel, and forty ceiling panels by Shraga Weil, in vibrant blues, reds, and golds, re-create musical scenes from the Bible. The lounge is open only during tours of the Kennedy Center and during special performances.

The impressive new chancery of the Embassy of Israel, 3514 International Drive, N.W. (off Connecticut Avenue), is designed with graceful Mediterranean arches and decorated with Israeli art and sculpture. While private visits are permitted only by invitation or on official business, special briefings for groups may be arranged by writing to the embassy's speakers bureau several weeks in advance.

OTHER SIGHTS: The Smithsonian and other museums facing the Mall offer as much education and entertainment as one's time—and feet—allow. America's most revered documents, the Declaration of Independence, the Consitution, and the Bill of Rights are displayed at the stately National Archives, Pennsylvania Avenue at Eighth Street, N.W. President Harry Truman's letter acknowledging Israel's statehood is also displayed. The National Archives is a good place to go for geneological research; among other things, it has the passenger manifests of almost every immigrant ship to America since the Mayflower.

Since its opening on July 4, 1976, the Air and Space Museum has become the city's most popular museum. Its fantastic exhibits illustrate every facet of man's exploration of space. In its Spacearium, named for Albert Einstein, you can gaze into the wonders of the solar system.

The Museum of American History, at Constitution and Fourteenth

Street, N.W., has a "Nation of Nations" exhibit, with an overview of the diverse cultures that shaped America. This includes articles the immigrants brought to America, the benches from Ellis Island, and items of popular culture of that era.

CULTURE: Visitors are always welcome to join in the many activities at the Greater Washington Jewish Community Center in Rockville (telephone, 301-881-0100). Its Goldman Fine Arts Gallery mounts excellent exhibits by Jewish and Israeli artists and craftsmen. A typical weekend features a concert by the JCC symphony or choral group, or a show by a world-class performer. Films, book fairs, and Yiddish plays and programs are frequently presented. Visitors are also welcome at the Jewish Community Center of Northern Virginia, 8822 Little River Turnpike, Fairfax, Virginia (telephone, 703-323-0880).

Popular Sunday morning lectures held at many area synagogues and centers are open to the public. The outstanding Sunday Scholar Series, offered free of charge, October through March, at the Washington Hebrew Congregation, McComb Street, N.W., at Massachusetts Avenue, features world-famous writers, theologians, and rabbis. For listings of Sunday breakfast lectures at Temple Sinai, 3100 Military Road, N.W., and Beth Shalom, Thirteenth Street and Eastern Avenue, N.W., check the *Washington Jewish Week,* available on newsstands.

GENERAL CULTURE: Works by top artists are exhibited at the National Gallery of Art, Corcoran Art Gallery, Phillips Collection, and the Freer Gallery. The Kennedy Center presents concerts, operas, and plays with leading performers. From June to September, Wolf Trap Farm in Virginia presents varied musical performances—from bluegrass to Vienna waltzes—in a lovely outdoor setting. The National Theater, Arena Stage, and Folger Shakespeare Theater present the classics, new works, and Broadway hits. Washington newspapers carry current listings.

READING: The Jewish Historical Society of Greater Washington has published two condensed oral histories of Washingtonians, available from the Society, 701 Third Street, N.W., Washington, D.C., 20001, for three dollars each. *Jews in Greater Washington, A Panoramic History of Washington Jewry for the Years 1795–1960* by Hillel Marans is out of print, but may be obtained through the library. *Jews and American Politics* by Stephen D. Isaacs (Doubleday) is available, however. For a general fictional look at Washington life and politics, read *Advise and Consent* by Allen Drury (Doubleday). For an idea of what it might be like to have a Jewish President, read Michael Halberstam's novel *The Wanting of Levine* (Lippincott). The book may be fiction, but its hero is emblematic of the very real participation of Jews in every facet of life in Washington.

—HELEN SILVER

Zurich

Chagall window in the Fraumunster Church. *(Swiss National Tourist Office)*

Israel, according to the dream, was supposed to be the Switzerland of the Middle East—a refuge, an oasis of peace and neutrality, a bastion of stability that would attract investment. It hasn't exactly worked out that way, but it doesn't take many days in Switzerland to realize that there are some striking parallels with the Jewish state. Both are small countries surrounded by large neighbors. Both are democracies which embrace great cultural diversity. In Zurich, Switzerland's largest city as well as its financial and cultural capital, the parallels are particularly visual. The city's symbol, like Jerusalem's, is a lion (the main synagogue is on Löwenstrasse, or "Lion Street") and the streetcars are all painted the color of the canton's crest—blue and white.

But perhaps the strongest parallel is military. Like Israel, Switzerland has universal military service, and Swiss men do several weeks of reserve duty every year until they are in their fifties. This similarity is not lost on the Swiss people who, despite their country's official neutrality, have always been kindly disposed toward Israel. Army connections play a major role in advancement at Switzerland's banks, and the admiration of Switzerland's military leaders for Israel's army has, according to one Jewish community leader in Zurich, had a positive impact on trade between the two countries.

Where do Switzerland's twenty thousand Jews fit into this picture? They are Israel-oriented but fundamentally Swiss, participating in every facet of the country's life, including those for which it is best known. Zurich's major banks include Julius Baer and Co., founded by a Jew whose descendants are Jewish and Christian; one of the main financial institutions in Basel is the Dreyfuss Bank. One of the country's leading chocolate makers is Camille Bloch, a former president of the Jewish community of Berne. There are Jewish watchmakers in the French-speaking part of the country. While there are no prominent Jewish cheese makers, there have been Jewish cattle farmers in the canton of Aargau for more than three hundred years. The country has yet to produce a Jewish Olympic champion, but Zurich does have a Jewish ski club.

HISTORY: Jews may be a minuscule part of the Swiss banking elite today, but they were the prime moneylenders of Zurich after their arrival in 1273. From their base in the Judengasse (Jews' Street) they loaned money to the city, the aristocracy, and borrowers as far away as Frankfurt and Venice. They were allowed to own property and to practice their faith. Though small, the community did produce one Talmudic scholar of note, Moses of Zurich, who wrote the *Semak Zurich.*

It was not all comfort and prosperity, however. Jews were heavily taxed and required to wear distinguishing hats. When the Black Death swept Switzerland in 1348—and with it the rumor that Jews had caused it by poisoning the wells—the municipal council in Zurich initially tried to protect the Jews. Public pressure ultimately forced the council to yield, and Jews were burned at the stake on February 22, 1349. Over the next century the Jews were repeatedly expelled and allowed to return to Zurich. The cycle of expulsion and readmission went on throughout Switzerland until the seventeenth century, when Jews were permanently expelled from the entire country.

But not exactly. Jews continued to live in Aargau—a canton that did not join the Swiss Confederation until 1803—mainly in the towns of Endingen and Lengnau. When the French Revolution and developing industrial economy opened the door for Jews in the larger cities of Switzerland in the nineteenth century, village Jews from Aargau formed the core of the new communities. They were joined by migrants from Alsace, in France, and Germany. Pressure from France, which complained about discrimination against French Jews in Switzerland, and from the United States Senate, which once refused to ratify a commercial treaty with Switzerland because of the absence of civil rights for Jews, was instrumental in achieving emancipation for Swiss Jewry. Equality came in 1866, when a new Swiss constitution granted Jews freedom of residence throughout the country and guaranteed them the same civic status as Christians; Switzerland was the last country in Europe to make such guarantees. The only exception to Jewish religious freedom is a law that, in effect, bans kosher slaughtering. After a campaign by animal rights activists, an 1893 plebescite outlawed slaughtering in which the animal is not stunned first. To this day, Swiss Jews must import kosher meat from France and the Netherlands.

Switzerland was the primary venue for the congresses of the World Zionist Organization. While most were held in Basel, two of particular importance met in Zurich. It was at the 16th Zionist Congress, in

1929, that the expanded Jewish Agency was set up as an independent authority to represent the *yishuv* in Palestine in dealings with world Jewry, the British Mandatory Government, and other countries. The 20th Zionist Congress, held in Zurich in 1937, was the first in which the official record was kept solely in Hebrew.

Despite the hospitality to Zionist Congresses, during World War II official Swiss policy was inhospitable toward Jewish refugees. It was a Swiss suggestion that led to Germany stamping the passports of Jews with the letter "J", so that authorities would be able to identify potential refugees at their borders. Swiss Jews, and some non-Jews, bitterly fought this policy. There are many stories of Swiss residents harboring Jews who managed to enter the country illegally, and toward the end of the war more refugees were admitted. Even those who criticized official policy, however, noted that on a proportional basis, Switzerland's record on admitting refugees was no worse than that of any other neutral nation (it admitted twenty-five thousand during the war). Criticism of the wartime policy played a role in the government's decision to admit Jewish refugees from Hungary and Egypt in 1956 and from Czechoslovakia in 1968.

COMMUNITY: Zurich's Jewish population is about seven thousand, 1 percent of the seven hundred thousand people who live in Zurich and its environs. Nevertheless it is not only the largest Jewish community in Switzerland, but also the largest in the German-speaking world. Many still trace their roots to Endingen and Lengnau, others to France and Germany. Because of the complications of becoming a citizen of Switzerland—where national citizenship is granted only after cantonal citizenship—only about 60 percent of Zurich's Jews have Swiss nationality.

The city actually has four separate "communities." By far the largest is the Israelitische Cultusgemeinde, nominally Orthodox but embracing people whose personal practice varies widely. The Israelitische Religionsgesellschaft and Agudas Achim are Orthodox in name and practice and include larger proportions of East European Jews. Or Chadash is a liberal congregation, with a ritual akin to Conservative Judaism in the United States; because of opposition from the more Orthodox communities, it has not joined the Federation of Swiss Jewish Communities.

Altogether Zurich has four synagogues and an additional sixteen minyans. While Jews can be found all over the city, they tend to cluster near the synagogues, particularly in the Enge section. Enge is also home to the closest thing the community has to a nerve center. The building at Lavaterstrasse 33 houses both the Federation of Swiss Jewish Communities and the headquarters of the Israelitische Cultus-gemeinde. It also has a day school (one of two in the city), a library, a discotheque, a theater and cultural center which hosts lectures and symposiums. Call the Federation, 201-55-83, for information on programs.

Switzerland's cultural mix, in which everyone is a member of one minority or another, makes it an essentially tolerant place. It is 65 percent German-speaking, 18 percent French, and 11 percent Italian; a good number of the German Swiss are Catholic and a majority of the French Swiss are Protestant. Nevertheless, there is some social anti-Semitism, not to mention the sizable portion of the population that is virtually unaware of a Jewish presence. Two things have helped change the picture in recent years. Since 1982, an exhibition on the Jews of Switzerland, mounted by the Federation, has traveled to the main exposition halls of Switzerland, attracting many non-Jews. *The Boat Is Full,* a dramatic film about Swiss refugee policy during the war, has prompted much discussion. The movie, made by Markus Imhoof, who is not Jewish, was the Swiss entry for an Academy Award as best foreign film in 1981.

SIGHTS: It would be difficult to find a city in which the Jewish sights are better integrated into the landscape than Zurich. Virtually all the places of Jewish interest are near the center of town and easily reached by streetcar or on foot.

The oldest Jewish site in the city is the Judengasse. Although it no longer exists, it was more or less on the site of today's Froschaugasse, a narrow alley, less than a hundred yards long, in the heart of the old quarter on the eastern bank of the Limmat River. A medieval street of pink, yellow, and gray buildings, it has antique dealers, bookstores, and boutiques. There are no traces of its Jewish past, although Pinkus Genossenschaft, one of the bookstores, still bears the name of its Jewish former owner, and people on the street are generally aware of the area's Jewish past. In one of the buildings opposite Pinkus's, the remains of a mikvah were found. Period maps of the street indicate that the synagogue stood about at the corner of Froschaugasse and Rindermarkt.

Today, most of Zurich's Jews live on the western bank. The largest congregation has its synagogue near the heart of the city, at Löwen-strasse 10 (telephone, 201-16-59). The brown-and-white Moorish-style building, with its twin domes, was built in 1883. A bit weather-beaten on the outside, it is sparse on the inside. Its high-backed wooden pews, traditional in Europe, look impermanent and its stained-glass windows are of modest design. Next door to the synagogue is Adass, a kosher grocery.

In America, synagogue architecture and upkeep tend to be more utilitarian among the more observant. In Switzerland it is the opposite. Zurich's most attractive and best-kept synagogue is that of the more rigorously Orthodox Religiongesellschaft, at Freigutstrasse 37 (telephone, 201-67-46). The salmon-and-gray building, perched on a small hill, features menorahs and Stars of David around its crown. Inside it has a central bimah, in the Sefardic style, and well-polished, high-backed pews. The stained-glass windows lean toward Art Deco and the ceiling is a series of small arches decorated with Middle Eastern motifs in sand colors.

The most centrally located synagogue, however, is the modest home of Or Chadash, the liberal congregation, at Fortunagasse 13, just steps from the Bahnhofstrasse, Zurich's main shopping street (telephone, 211-11-52).

Bear in mind that most synagogues in Switzerland are open only while services are in progress, although tours can sometimes be arranged by phoning ahead. Daily and Shabbat prayer times for most synagogues are printed in the weekly *Israelitisches Wochenblatt,* published in Zurich, and the *Jüdische Rundschau,* published in Basel with an extensive Zurich edition.

One of the most important sights of Jewish interest in Zurich is a church—the Gothic and Romanesque Fraumünster (located at Münsterhof square). In the church's fifteenth-century chancel is a set of five stained-glass windows by Marc Chagall. It was a Chagall exhibit at the Zurich Kunsthaus, the city's fine arts museum, in 1967, that prompted the Fraumünster's fathers to commission him to do their windows. After they saw his work, Chagall was deemed "better qualified than almost any other contemporary artist to create a cycle of windows with a religious message." What is striking is that the windows are so Jewish. Four of the five are on themes from the Hebrew Bible.

The red window, on the north side of the chancel, depicts the Prophets, most prominently Elisha, Elijah, and Jeremiah. The blue window on the south side represents the Law, with Moses sitting on a throne (at the top) and Isaiah receiving the message of peace (at the bottom). On the east wall of the chancel are the blue "Jacob" window, the only one devoted to a single figure, and the yellow "Zion" window, with its images of biblical and contemporary Jerusalem. They flank the green "Christ" window. Even in the one window devoted to the New Testament, there are signs of the Jewish creator of the images. Joseph, the father of Jesus, appears at the bottom of the window close to the figure of King David in the Zion window, as if to show the link between the Christian messiah and the house of David. The figure of Jesus on the cross is not unusual for Chagall; one of the recurrent themes in his work, from biblical subjects to the Holocaust, is the crucifixion of Jews. In addition to the series in the chancel, Chagall also did the circular "Creation of the World" window on the south transcept, a section of the church that dates to the twelfth century. As striking as the Chagall windows is the way they are regarded. There are other stained-glass windows in the church—beautiful, more classical in design, including one by Augusto Giacometti—that are barely mentioned by tour guides. On the tours, Chagall is always identified as a Jew.

This same emphasis can be found at the Kunsthaus (situated on the Heimplatz). Though the museum has equally large collections of work by Picasso, Miró, and Munch, among others, it is Chagall whose work is housed in its own room, the Saal Marc Chagall. There are only thirteen paintings in the room, but they represent a remarkable cross section of Chagall's career, ranging from 1910 to 1968. Among them are *Passage Through the Red Sea, Above Vitebsk,* and *Lights of Marriage.* Two of the works, *The War* and *The Martyr,* show crucifixions of Jewish figures.

PERSONALITIES: Zurich has been the birthplace or the adopted home of many prominent Jews. David Farbstein, a native of Warsaw, was the first Jew to serve in the Swiss Parliament, where he spoke Yiddish. The Swiss Government's reaction to the Arab oil shock of 1973 was to appoint Michael Kohn, a prominent engineer, president of the nation's energy commission. More recently, Ursula Koch, a Socialist environmentalist, has been elected to the Zurich cantonal government. Zurich natives include Felix Bloch, an American who won the Nobel Prize for physics in 1952 and Paul Guggenheim, a judge in the International Court of Justice. Perhaps the most prominent Jew ever to make Zurich his home was Albert Einstein. Einstein earned his degree at Zurich's Federal Institute of Technology in 1900; during his studies there he also became a Swiss citizen. Denied a teaching post on graduation—for reasons that may have included anti-Semitism—he took a job at the patent office in Berne. After the publication of his "special theory of relativity" in 1905, the University of Zurich began to pursue him. He finally accepted a teaching post in Zurich in 1912. Zurich was also the birthplace of one of the best-known fictional Jews, Leopold Bloom. James Joyce's hero may have been a Dubliner, but he was created during Joyce's Swiss exile.

EATING: The kosher restaurant Schalom, located in the community center building at Lavaterstrasse 33, must have one of the most extensive menus in the world. Its fare ranges from the Swiss (fondue and wienerschnitzel) to the East European (gefilte fish and potato latkes) to the Middle Eastern (humus and lamb kabob).

Some of the dishes for which Switzerland is best known, like fondue and rösti (fried potatoes), can be enjoyed even by those who observe kashrut. While there are many excellent restaurants in Zurich, one particularly good one is Le Dezaley, at Römergasse 7–9.

GENERAL SIGHTS AND SIDE TRIPS: Zurich is a walker's city, from the elegant shops on the Bahnhofstrasse to the quays and gardens that line the banks of the Limmat and Lake Zurich (the Zürichsee). Two things that should not be missed are a boat trip on the Zürichsee and a visit to the Swiss National Museum, with its striking exhibits of every aspect of Swiss life and culture.

No one, however, comes to Switzerland just to see Zurich. There is virtually no area of the country that can't be reached in a day from Zurich. Berne, the Swiss capital, is seventy minutes away by train. The old town, surrounded on three sides by a bend in the Aare River, is a fantasy world of colonnaded seventeenth- and eighteenth-century buildings. Just a few minutes' walk from the old town, at Kapellenstrasse 2, is Berne's synagogue. A small gem, the yellow-and-white stone building is the center for Berne's 600 Jews. The interior features floral-patterned stained-glass windows and the polished-wood pews and floors characteristic of Central European synagogue design. In addition to being an attraction in its own right, Berne is also a good starting point for tours of the Bernese Alps. Aside from ski centers, two of the most popular, and spectacular, lookouts are the Schilthorn and Jungfraujoch.

Fifty minutes south of Zurich is Lucerne, a medieval city and contemporary resort. Closer to the mountains, the city and the excursions on Lake Lucerne offer more spectacular scenery than Zurich. Lucerne's synagogue is at Bruchstrasse 51. In addition to its views and its ambience, Lucerne is noted for the Swiss Transport Museum.

If you want to see the cradle of contemporary Swiss Jewish life, Endingen and Lengnau are less than an hour from Zurich, to the northwest. (Take the train to Baden and, from there, a bus to the two towns, which are seven minutes apart. Don't be confused by Swiss maps. The country has several towns called Lengnau; the one with Jewish connections is the one closest to Zurich, in Aargau Canton.) In Lengnau, ancestral home of the Guggenheim mining family, the oldest synagogue in Switzerland, built in 1847, stands on the town square. In Endingen, once a veritable shtetl, the synagogue, with its belfry, is still the tallest building in town, and the only house of worship. There is still one Jewish family in Endingen, the Blochs, at Buckstrasse 2.

READING: There is a fair amount of literature on the Jews of Zurich and Switzerland, but little of it has been translated into English. Kurt Guggenheim based some of his novels on his Zurich childhood, but they are available only in German. Two informative books published by the national and local communities, and available at the Lavaterstrasse center, are *Juden in Zürich* and *Juden in der Schweiz.*

Jewish characters do appear, usually somewhat marginally, in the books of Switzerland's two leading novelists, Friedrich Dürrenmatt and Max Frisch. Their works are available in English. Look particularly for Dürrenmatt's *The Quarry.*

RECOMMENDATIONS: There are plenty of good hotels in Zurich, though they tend to be expensive. One hostelry noted for both price and location is the Florhof, at Florhofgasse 4, located in what was once a private mansion. It is a three-minute walk from the Kunsthaus and a five-minute walk from both the Froschaugasse and the university.

There are no kosher hotels in Zurich but there are many in the resort areas. Arosa, Crans-sur-Sierre, Grindelwald, Locarno, Lugano, Montreux, and St. Moritz all have kosher hotels. The Swiss National Tourist Office, with branches in New York, San Francisco, and Toronto, has information on all of them.

Switzerland is an easy country to travel in. The rail system is superb, the people are helpful, and the scenery unbeatable. Though some Swiss may be barely cognizant of Jews, the tourist authorities are sensitive to Jewish needs and concerns. The main synagogue in Zurich is pointed out on the tours arranged by the municipal travel office and the Jewish community is described. There is a Jewish chapel in Terminal B of the Zurich airport, which serves not only visitors to the city but also the many transit passengers who go through the O'Hare of Europe. While the differences between Switzerland and Israel are still more numerous than the similarities, you'll find a warm welcome nevertheless.

—ALAN M. TIGAY